PASSAGES

FAMILY JOURNEYS THROUGH SPACE
AND TIME

GAIL E. EVANS

Author: Gail E. Evans

ISBN: 978-1-7774635-0-2 (Softcover)

ISBN: 978 1-7774635-1-9 (Ebook)

Grateful acknowledgment for permission to reproduce photographs is made to the following: field and distant Kingsmans Farm on cover and in Chapter 5 by Alfred J. Padgett, ca. 1920, courtesy of the Essex Record Office, Chelmsford, Essex, England; Mabel's school, Hockley, Chapter 1, courtesy of Hadleigh & Thundersly Community Archive, southeast Essex, England; Upper Falls from Pratt Street Bridge, Rochester, New York, 1892, Chapter 3, (Accession No. rpf00658), courtesy Local History and Genealogy Division, Central Library of Rochester and Monroe County, New York; Canadian Coronation Arch, Chapter 3, Glenbow Western Research Centre at the University of Calgary, Calgary, Alberta, Canada; Grand Trunk Railway map, Chapter 3, courtesy Toronto Railway Historical Association. Many photos taken in England, Africa, and New England are by J. Harvey Evans. Other photographs are in the family collections of Gail Evans, David Evans, and the Harvey and Evans families in the United States and United Kingdom.

Editing by Tatiana Wilde; editing by Leslie Buck; cover design by Anton Pshinka; interior design by Stephanie Candiago; photoshop preparation of photos by Sharon Connaughty; and proofreading by Jo-Ann Gordon and Amanda Bidnall. Experienced guidance and generous support in the final stages of book preparation by Cynthia Stowell.

1. England and Wales 2. Evans and Harvey families. 3. Biography 4. Immigration 5. World Wars I and II 6. New York and New England, USA 7. Passages: Family Journeys Through Space and Time.

The quest to better understand her father and family roots . . . takes Gail Evans on a journey of discovery in space and time, the subtitle of her new book *Passages*. It is a story that is detailed and lovingly revealed through copious archival research, family journals and materials, interviews with relatives and friends in America and the United Kingdom, and lived experiences. . . . Ms. Evans . . . relive[s] her father's extraordinary marathon 300-mile bicycle trips, for him born out of financial necessity. . . . She thoughtfully chronicles 19th and 20th century social and political events to capture lives in the context of local, national, and world happenings. . . . In *Passages* we . . . vicariously appreciate the joy of unearthing one's genealogy and heritage.

— MH, SAUSALITO, CALIFORNIA

This family resonates with the very human lived experience of one couple coming to America at a time of great promise as they encounter the highs and lows of the early twentieth century. Maintenance of parental family bonds and resolve for realizing their hopes for their children made me reflect on my own family's parallel life journey at this time in history.

— SC, VANCOUVER, BC, CANADA

I just think the whole book is amazing. [Gail Evans] deserve[s] to celebrate.

— CG, N. READING, MASSACHUSETTS

I finished your family history last night with tears in my eyes—sad that it finished. What a powerful lesson for enduring friendships and family loyalties. I felt like I really knew your father and his two brothers. You are rightly so proud of your father. What courage, tenacity, endurance, intellectual skills, and social skills he displayed throughout his life. I was so impressed with his biking prowess. I loved the book on so many levels: learning about the war contribution made by the three Evans boys and their cousins, the impressive number of sources, historical research, and numerous letters and emails, and the wealth of pictures.

— CGD, SOUTH LONDON, ENGLAND

Gail Evans, a professional historian and a skilled storyteller recounts the history of Wales, England, and America through the history of her family. The story centers on the life of her father, J. Harvey Evans, who was a respected naval architect during World War II and contributed to the success of American forces around the globe. The book describes the many adventures of Harvey's family members and shows how his close family relation-ships sustained him through rigorous naval archi-tecture training at the University of Liverpool during the Great Depression and his remarkable career after returning to America.

— DG, BELLINGHAM, WASHINGTON

Dedicated to J. Harvey Evans and the many Evans and Harvey family members who contributed to making this book a reality.

"The greater the difficulty, the more glory in surmounting it. Skillful pilots gain their reputation from storms and tempests."

Epictetus

PUBLISHER'S NOTE

This is a work of historical nonfiction. Names, characters, places, and incidents are based on actual people and places that have been extracted from the diaries, letters, photographs, and other reliable material largely dating from the time and event or reconstructed several years after an event in collaboration with family members alive at the time.

CONTENTS

PASSAGES

PROLOGUE

On my twelfth birthday, in May 1960, my father, John Harvey Evans, presented me with a deep-teal, three-speed Raleigh bicycle. He was almost more delighted with the gift than I was. I had no idea then why my father seemed so pleased with his gift to me. Admittedly, this beautiful new bicycle was unique. None of my friends owned a Raleigh. I especially loved the teal color. Immediately I began riding my bike up and down the street at the end of our long driveway and beyond.

Since 1885, Nottingham, England, had been the home of Raleigh Bicycles. By 1913, the company became the largest bicycle manufacturer in the world. I loved my new Raleigh bicycle. For many years I took my Raleigh with me every time I moved, eventually transporting it from Massachusetts to the West Coast of the United States. I kept my special Raleigh bicycle for fifty-five years.

The reason that my father's gift of a Raleigh gave him such enormous pleasure mystified me for years. I discovered the importance of this Raleigh many years later buried in one of twenty boxes that contained his personal papers: the diaries, maps, scrapbooks, letters, and photographs of John Harvey Evans (known as Harvey). In the mid-1980s, all these boxes, along with the contents of my parents' entire house, had to be moved. They were leaving their family home of thirty years in Lexington, Massachusetts, and moving to a smaller house, which would be more manageable in their retirement. I helped them move and eventually became the custodian of the contents of my father's personal history. Time passed. More than fifteen years later, after both my parents had died and my own life had settled down a bit, I had time to examine the contents of my father's boxed archives.

One day, while doing a preliminary survey of Harvey's papers, I stumbled across what I came to believe was the reason he took such delight in giving me a Raleigh bicycle. Buried in the pages of a thick five-year leather-bound diary, along with a large folded Philips' Main Road Map of Great Britain, were details of my father's unique relationship with a bicycle that he had ridden many times across England in the mid-1930s. When I opened the map, I discovered numerous winding routes that he had carefully marked. These dark penciled lines stretched between Liverpool and the small village of Hockley, Essex. Alongside the penciled routes, he had neatly written the dates, direction, and time of his many trips. No two routes were the same, revealing my father's life-long passion for always discovering new places.

At first, I did not know what these penciled routes represented, but the answer soon became apparent when I read my father's diary and looked for the dates marked on the Philips' map. Together, the Philips' map and the leather-bound diary revealed a story of multiple cross-country bicycle treks that my father had made between 1934 and 1937. What a memorable impression the ever-changing sights and smells of cities, villages, and countryside must have made on him. My father and his steadfast steed—his bicycle—made these sometimes-grueling three-day trips across England in all kinds of weather during his four years at the University of Liverpool. His bicycling adventures surely must have inspired him to give me the gift of a British Raleigh bicycle.

I was immediately curious about this discovery. I speculated that there must be a buried backstory that explained the reason for these long bicycle journeys between the University of Liverpool, where he was enrolled, and his Harvey family aunts, uncles, and cousins who often gathered at Kingsmans Farm. I was immediately curious about his 275- to 300-mile cycling excursions between Liverpool and his mother's family home at Kingsmans Farm on the south shore of the River Crouch.

From a young age, my older brother, David, and I had only a vague knowledge of our father's parents. We knew that John Evans, born in Wales, and Mabel Ida Harvey, born in England, had immigrated to the United States in the early 1910s when in their twenties. Although we never met John, since he died around the time of our births, we felt his influence throughout our lives.

Before he died on his birthday in late December 1944, John had asked that his grandchildren use the Welsh words "Taid" and "Nain" for grandfather and grandmother. David and I grew up hearing many stories about where he was born and grew up in Camarthenshire, South Wales. We saw photos of his family home in Pentre-cwrt taken by our father in the 1930s. We still had Taid's weighty pinking shears, the emblematic tool of a tailor. To this day, Taid's three grandchildren (David, me, and Christine Evans Gehret) still refer to our grandparents as Taid and Nain. David and I also tried to learn from our father the pronunciation of the longest Welsh place name: "Llanfairpwllgwyngyllgogerychwyrndrobwllllantysiliogogogoch," which John had taught Harvey.

My brother and I knew our grandmother, who came from a large farming family in Essex, England, well. After Taid died, she lived near us until she died in 1967. Although her British accent softened over many years of living in America, her quaint expressions, and odd British jokes never failed to provoke a chortle from our father and his two younger brothers. Nain returned to England once or twice to visit her family and always returned with children's books whose glue and paper had a distinctive smell that I still recognize and relish.

My father's Philips' map and diary accounts of his travels across England in the mid-1930s motivated me to attempt a similar cycling adventure. Following one of his routes across England between Kingsmans Farm and Liverpool on my bicycle, I believed, might be a fantastic way to experience his own story of living in England in the 1930s and might uncover an intriguing piece of my family history. A cycling adventure would bring me closer to understanding my father's strong life-long tie to England and Wales, as well as my own family history. Combining my cycling with research at a handful of libraries and archives would also inspire me to write my Evans-Harvey family history.

As it happened, the discovery of my father's map and leather-bound diary came at an ideal time. In mid-2015, I had time, the training and experience as a historian, and a great personal interest in reconstructing the details of my father's life and my Evans and Harvey family backgrounds. My father's bicycle adventures captivated me as I reconstructed his family history over the next five years. The outcome is this book.

More than eighty years after my father rode his bicycle across England, in the spring of 2016, I began training for my cycling adventure. Week by week, I gradually increased my daily mileage from 10 to eventually 55 to 60—not the

100 miles my father had done, but, then, I was a few (forty-five) years older than he was when he cycled many times across England. By the end of May, I reached the 55-mile-a-day mark without any weight in my panniers. By mid-August, with my rear panniers fully loaded, I donned my Spandex cycling knickers (nothing like my father's basic cycling attire!) and cycled over 50 miles. Fair enough, I declared to myself.

In late August, my bicycle and I were ready to fly to England. With the bike partially disassembled and packed in a large cardboard box loaded into the airplane's belly, we lifted off from the Vancouver International Airport runway. Several hours later, the aircraft glided down the runway at Gatwick Airport south of London. From there, my bicycle and I made our way north by train to the City of London.

In the dusk of my first day, I walked from my hostel near St. Paul's Cathedral to Marylebone, where my grandparents had worked, lived, and met over one hundred years earlier. Based on the research I had done, I quickly found the five-story red and tan brick building where my grandmother, Mabel Harvey, had lived in the early 1900s while working as a draper for John Lewis & Co. department store. The address of John Evans's residence when he worked as a draper for Marshall & Snelgrove (now Debenhams) department store on busy Oxford Street, however, was nowhere to be found. Instead, earth-moving bulldozers occupied the entire block on which his employee housing had once stood.

The next morning, I made my way out of London with my bicycle and traveled east to Pitsea, southern Essex, the birthplace of my grandmother. Amazingly, I found the farm—Little Chalvedon Hall Farm—where Nain had been born. The building was unoccupied and in a deteriorating condition. I was thrilled to find it! From there I cycled a few miles to Kingsmans Farm, one mile east of Hullbridge and a stone's throw south of the River Crouch. Several years earlier, I had visited Kingsmans with my father and mother, but it was a delight to see it again.

It appeared well maintained. I soon learned that it was listed as a Grade II historic building (with a history and physical integrity of particular interest that warranted its preservation). Long gone was the giant elm tree that had cast an enormous shadow across the house and front yard in the mid-1930s. The cluster of thatch-roofed farm buildings encircling a small waterhole behind the house had long ago been removed. The farm field behind the house still existed. The expansive fields, once part of Kingsmans Farm, had disappeared and were slowly replaced by seasonal dwellings owned by vacationers escaping from London to the nearby countryside.

Kingsmans Farm and Gail's bicycle, 2016.

Leaving my bicycle near a fence alongside the road, I squeezed past a rear gate and quietly headed down a narrow dirt road toward an open field behind the house. Immediately dogs in the rear yard of Kingsmans Farm began barking loudly, alerting a woman relaxing in the rear yard to my presence. Curtly she asked who I was and what I was doing. I explained that my great-grandparents, Stephen and Martha Harvey, had owned and lived at Kingsmans Farm for forty years, and that my grandmother, Mabel Harvey, had grown to adulthood in the house. Her intrigue soon replaced irritation and softened her demeanor. After talking for several minutes, I promised to send her a copy of an early 1900s photo of the entire Harvey family posing in front of the Kingsmans farmhouse. I gratefully thanked her for allowing me to view the back of the house, then climbed onto my bicycle and headed down Kingsmans Farm Road toward Hockley village.

Energized by the experience of meeting the present owner and caretaker of my Harvey ancestors' home, I cycled south a short distance through small farm fields, then up a steep hill to the thirteenth-century Anglican church of St. Peter and St. Paul. Looking north, I could see Kingsmans farmhouse and the outline of the fields against the backdrop of the meandering River Crouch. In the graveyard, I found the headstones of my great-grandparents, Stephen and Martha Harvey, and several other Harvey family members. Gratified by a day that had been full of discovery, I turned my bicycle toward Liverpool, 275 miles to the northwest.

Several days later, I traveled to the tiny village of Pentre-cwrt in the rolling hills of Camarthenshire, South Wales, where a somewhat similar, newer stuccoed home stood on the site of Parke, the Evans family stone home for over one hundred years, just south of the River Teifi. Although I could not cycle to all the places I planned to visit in 2016, I eagerly anticipated the intimate encounters I would have with the English countryside and its people that my father had experienced int he 1930s. Many of my traveling adventures that summer took me to places that my father had visited or passed through on his bicycle eighty years earlier. Retracing some of his bicycle route and following it all in his diary convinced me to write about his time at the University of Liverpool and its influence on so many of his decisions in the UK in the mid-1930s and later in his life. Over time, this short story expanded into a full-length family history extending from the early 1800s to the death of Mabel and John's three sons, Harvey, Evan, and Frank. In the process of researching and writing I soon realized that each son had their own very unique and fascinating story to tell profoundly influenced by overwhelming historical events and personal choices that unfolded during their lifetimes. this history of humble beginnings grew into the tome that is now before you.

1

FROM DIFFERENT WORLDS

1805–1910

Around 1910, it was a chance meeting in London's fashionable Marylebone district that changed their lives forever. Twenty-seven-year-old John Evans, born the son of a tailor in a tiny village in South Wales, and twenty-two-year-old Mabel Ida Harvey, daughter of a landowning farmer living just 40 miles east of London, crossed paths one day near the high-style department store district along Oxford Street.

No one now living knows where and how they met. It may have been at one of the dozens of small shops lining the narrow side streets that crossed Oxford Street. It may have been at church, perhaps the Hinde Street Methodist Church, not far from where they lived and worked. They may even have interacted while they worked as drapers. Sometime in the early 1900s, they each had come to London, like hundreds of others, to work as drapers. A draper's knowledge of woolen, cotton, linen, and silk fabrics, as well as notions—linings, trimmings, thread, and buttons—was highly specialized. Back then, drapers customarily sold these items in small shops and department stores to tailors, dressmakers, and the general public.

John and Mabel's occupations as drapers probably
precipitated their meeting. Their strikingly different backgrounds would make their growing attraction, emerging
romance, and, ultimately, their desire to marry, extremely
challenging for their parents. Although both were from
rural farming country, the Harvey family lived close to
London, reached easily by train. The Evans family lived
many miles from Cardiff, the Welsh capital, and much
further from London. The Evanses' small farm was remote
from markets and served only the family's needs. The
nearby fast-flowing River Teifi provided power for nearby
cloth mills and offered John's father the prospect of
working as a tailor. A most striking difference between
John and Mabel was their religion. Mabel and her family
were Anglican while John's was Congregational. Although
from very different places and backgrounds, their chance
meeting in London sparked a relationship of deep caring
and love . . . and the desire to begin anew their lives
together in America.

John Evans of Rural South West Wales

John Evans's family, which had deep roots in rural
South Wales, descended from Celtic tribes comprised of
Indo-European peoples that flourished around 1200 BC
and that shared a similar language, religion, extended
family structure, and oral traditions. These Celtic tribes
had gradually infiltrated the British Isles between 500 and
100 BCE. The Romans, who followed, pushed further
north and west from the Mediterranean region to invade
Celtic territory. Rugged rolling terrain, however, kept
outlying lands to the far west from becoming fully Roman-
ized. In the fifth century CE, marauding Germanic Anglo-
Saxon tribes displaced the Roman Empire's disintegrating
kingdom. They pushed the Celts even further back to the

northern and western fringes of the British Isles. Celtic myths and spiritual practices, as well as the Welsh language, survived the Norman invasion that followed five centuries later.

The Welsh rebelled against these Norman overlords and re-established their former principalities in the decades after 1070. Welsh culture continued under the subsequent ruling Tudor and Stuart families (1485–1714), even though the English Crown's political and legal administration brought Welsh territory more fully under its control. Welsh inhabitants' long resistance to marauders advancing from the east played a large role in these outliers' ability to perpetuate their distinctive language and cultural identity for generations. Centuries earlier, the mountains of central Wales provided a remote, protected haven for Celtic inhabitants. The Welsh language helped centuries-old oral traditions of epic poems, stories, and music survive in the Welsh people's daily lives.[1]

John Evans's recent Welsh ancestors lived in the rolling, grassy hills cleaved by the seventy-three-mile-long River Teifi, whose tumbling waters emptied into Cardigan Bay on the southwest coast of Wales. The river originated in the Teifi Pools, a series of connected lakes atop an expansive plateau of rolling moorland ridges.

Unlike his tailor father, David Evans, the grandfather of John Evans, worked for other farmers as an agricultural laborer for nearly forty years. He and his family also pursued small-scale subsistence farming. Tracing the Evans family back before the early 1800s is exceedingly difficult since David Evans is such a common Welsh name, and we know only that he was born around 1805. His ancestors probably raised livestock and cultivated grains, like oats and barley, and vegetables for family consumption. David Evans's subsistence farming endeavors probably produced a little excess food that could be sold in the nearby market town of Llandysul, three miles to the east on the sloping hillsides north of the Teifi. In the 1800s, most land in Wales was occupied by tenant farmers living on smallholdings of 100 acres or less.

David and his wife, Hannah Jones Evans, were tenants occupying and farming land they did not own. He and the farmers for whom he worked most likely used methods that dated back to medieval times. Oxen pulling a wooden plow that barely scratched the ground's surface, and manure and lime scattered to improve the soil, were probably the only tools and fertilizers used. Welsh subsistence farmers like David Evans infrequently practiced crop rotation and other modern farming methods. Often farmers favored sheep and cattle grazing over tilling the soil.[2] In addition to farming, the townspeople knew David Evans for his athletic prowess. According to one grandson, Tom Evans, David "was a most remarkable swimmer, runner and all-around athlete—short, broad and strong, and a wonderful craftsman."[3]

Both David and his wife Hannah were born and grew to adulthood near the River Teifi, which then formed the boundary between Carmarthenshire to the south and Cardiganshire (now Ceredigion) on the north. When they married in 1828, they most likely made their home at Pentre-cwrt, a small village just a stone's throw south of the river. By 1838, they and their young family occupied a two-story stone house known as "Parke," situated alongside a narrow lane sloping gently to the north toward the River Teifi. This narrow lane left a main east-west road, connecting Llangeler and Llandysul, between a public house known as Plasparke and a nearby dwelling named Cross Hands. The 1840s tithe map of Pentre-cwrt (meaning "village courtyard") in Llangeler parish clearly shows a simply sketched small rectangular structure, presumably the Evans home, just north of the road connecting Llangeler and Llandysul.

According to Tom Evans, John Evans's older brother, the Evans family had lived at Parke since around 1838. The 1841 census confirmed that David and Hannah, both thirty-five years old, and their four oldest children, lived at Parke. They remained at Parke until they died thirty years later. During their lives, the Evanses probably built one-story wood-frame additions on both sides of their house. These additions sheltered a few animals and chickens, farm tools, and animal feed that sustained the family through the year.[4]

During David Evans's lifetime of sixty-nine years, the subsistence farming dramatically declined. Instead, mining in southern and northeastern Wales offered the Welsh people a lucrative alternative to old labour-intensive farming practices. Lead, silver, coal, copper, and iron mined in Wales, and innovative technological developments such as coal-powered steam engines used for processing metal, fueled the Welsh economy into the 1800s.

The discovery of abundant coal deposits in the Rhondda and Cynon valleys in southeast Wales in the early 1800s further stimulated the Welsh economy. Coal was transported from these valleys to ports on the south coast, first by packhorses, then by canals, and eventually by railroad. By 1830, the southeastern Welsh counties of Monmouthshire and Glamorganshire produced half the iron exported by Great Britain. In addition to metals mining and processing, the woolen industry, spurred by the adoption of water and steam power and the division of labor to increase production, further fueled industrial development in Wales.

The Industrial Revolution in Wales transformed the country. Mining denuded certain regions of forested hillsides and lush green valleys and profoundly influenced the culture. Immigrants flooded to mining regions in Wales and hastened the demise of the Welsh language, culture, and customs. Local farming communities grew smaller as the promise of higher wages from mining jobs attracted the children of subsistence farmers like David Evans. In 1851, when Wales became the world's second-leading industrial nation after England, two-thirds of Welsh families earned their income from non-agricultural work. Explosive population growth accompanied the country's sweeping economic transformation. Between 1830 and 1850, when David and Hannah Evans's children were born, the population of Wales increased by nearly 50 percent. In the southeast region of Wales, the Merthyr Tydfil population grew from 7,707 residents in 1801 to 46,378 by 1851.[5] David and Hannah Evans became the last generation of Evanses to pursue farming as an occupation.

The spectacular growth and change that accompanied mining totally undermined farm work, life, and culture in nineteenth-century Wales. The growing uncertainty that characterized mining communities began to permeate all of Welsh society. In good times, miners earned a salary several times more than that of farmworkers. In bad times, however, the wages of miners, colliers, furnace-men, puddlers (men who converted pig iron to wrought iron), and other mine workers were seldom stable. Long hours of grueling work, combined with unsanitary conditions, the uncertainty of steady work, the prospect of continual debt, and sometimes injury or death in the mines, cast a veil of despair over the Welsh mining regions.

The pervasive uncertainty arising from industrialization became a distinctive feature of Welsh society and culture in the 1800s and greatly influenced the lives of David and Hannah Evans and their family. Nonconforming Protestant denominations, including Congregationalists (also known as Independents), Presbyterians, Baptists, Methodists, and Quakers, rejected the established Anglican Church, which was considered the church of the landed gentry in Great Britain. Nonconformity emboldened the Welsh people's strong resistance to the established Church of England and the British Crown. The 1851 "Census Sunday" reported that 76 percent of church attendees in Wales were Nonconformist. Nonconformism, which extended to the roots of Welsh society, proved much more able to adapt to and embrace the democratic nature of the Welsh working classes. As such, Nonconforming chapels had broad appeal across industrial Wales in the early 1800s. By the mid-1850s, nearly 90 percent of the inhabitants of the industrial valleys of Wales were Nonconformist.[6] One eminent Nonconformist minister asserted that "the Welsh are now emphatically a nation of Nonconformists."[7]

David and Hannah Evans were among the many Welsh who were emphatically Nonconformist. They attended the Nonconforming Congregational Saron Chapel, just south of Pentre-cwrt village, which had been rebuilt in 1825 to replace an earlier 1792 chapel. Saron Chapel became the Evans family's church for the next three generations. Several Evans family members are buried in the Saron Chapel cemetery, serving as a testament to the central role that Nonconformism played in the spiritual and cultural life of the Evanses.

Nonconformist Sunday schools encouraged independent thought. Nonconformism also became a dynamic force in perpetuating the Welsh language and encouraging passionate hymn singing. Nonconformism created a distinctly radical political force in trade unionism and the Labour Party in Great Britain throughout both the rural and industrial regions of Wales. Outside Wales, many were critical of Nonconformism, claiming that its theology and rejection of the English language made the Welsh people backward. All of the children and grandchildren of David and Hannah Evans, including their youngest child, John Evans, spoke Welsh at the Saron Chapel, at home, and in the community. Only when the Evans children began attending compulsory public school, around the age of five, did they learn English. John Evans remained bilingual throughout his life, even after he left Wales.[8]

Despite the enormous changes and social upheaval occurring in Welsh society in the 1800s, the Industrial Revolution also offered opportunities for some people, including the Evans family. It created ideal conditions for the production of textiles in some regions. In the first half of the 1800s, some farming families engaged in market-oriented craft production at home, such as wool-carding, spinning, dyeing, and weaving. The mechanization of spinning and weaving tremendously increased textile production in Wales, and moved these activities out of the home into factories powered by coal or water.

The abundance of swift-flowing rivers descending from steep-sided hills and mountains throughout many parts of Wales, turned spinning machines that produced thread and yarn, and powered looms that wove woolen fabric. The Industrial Revolution of the 1800s in the Teifi Valley employed thousands of weavers, spinners, knitters, tailors, and drapers. Hundreds of millworkers clustered around Dre-fach Felindre, Henllan, Llandysul, and Pentre-cwrt on the River Teifi, including the home and family of David and Hannah Evans.

Pentre-cwrt and nearby Llandysul became the home of large milling operations at the Alltcafan and Derw factories. In the heyday of milling, many two- to four-story gray stone factories stood firmly embedded in the rocky banks of the River Teifi. In the late nineteenth and early twentieth centuries, these factories produced high-quality woolen blankets, shawls, shirts, and underwear in great demand by the sons of rural Welsh farmers and miners working in South East Wales.

The extension of the Teifi Valley rail line along the River Teifi from Llandysul in the east to Newcastle Emlyn in 1895, and the opening of a halt (unstaffed railway platform) at Pentre-cwrt in 1912, facilitated the distribution of woolen goods produced at the Allt-y-cafan woolen mill and further strengthened the link between textile communities along the River Teifi in rural West Wales and the industrial mining valleys of South East Wales.

The Evans family, advantageously living at Pentre-cwrt close to this concentration of several mills, found themselves ideally situated to pursue one of several textile trades: spinning, weaving, tailoring, or working as drapers. Industrialization, combined with the Evans's proximity to the mills on the River Teifi, profoundly influenced all of David and Hannah Evans's children born between 1830 and 1850. Each of their sons left subsistence farming and pursued other occupations, either in mining or in textiles.

The oldest son, John Owen Evans, became a coal miner in Merthyr Tydfil before immigrating to the United States in 1868, where he died in a mine explosion in Illinois in 1896. Another son, Thomas D. Evans, apprenticed as a draper and worked in the South Wales Pontypool mining district before immigrating to Pennsylvania around 1869. A third son, David Evans, apprenticed as a tailor at Parke in Pentre-cwrt, before moving to the Pontypool mining district, where he worked with his younger brother, Owen David Evans. Owen also moved to Pontypool in the 1870s after first apprenticing with his father as a tailor at Parke. The non-agricultural occupational choices made by David and Hannah's four sons reflected both the opportunities and the uncertainties created by the Industrial Revolution in Wales.

Only Hannah and David's second-oldest son, Evan Evans, remained at Parke his entire life. Evan became the first child in the family to apprentice as a tailor. Born in 1836 in rural Bangor Teifi in Cardiganshire, Evan Evans attended school for five or six years before beginning a tailoring apprenticeship in the 1850s. In 1861, then in his mid-twenties, Evan worked as a tailor at Parke. By age thirty-five, he had become a master tailor, suggesting that he had achieved superior skill in his trade and had reached the highest proficiency level. Before sewing machines became widely available, Evan Evans would have sewn a single three-piece suit, comprised of trousers, waistcoat, and jacket, completely by hand.

In 1865, Evan Evans married Frances Thomas. By the end of the 1882 all six of their children had been born at Parke. Evan and Frances Evans lived at Parke for their entire lives. Although Evan's mother, Hannah, died one year after Evan and Frances married, David Evans's father continued to live at Parke with Evan and Frances and their family until his death in 1873.[9]

The shift away from full-time subsistence farming for Evan and Frances Evans is evident in a small but significant alteration made to Parke, most likely in response to master tailor Evan Evans's need for abundant light and space for his tailoring. Clearly visible in an 1889 photograph is a one-story, wood-frame addition projecting from the main facade to the left of the main entrance, probably built to provide space and adequate light for Evan's tailoring. This addition may have been made sometime in the late 1850s or 1860s. In 1861, not only Evan occupied this workspace but also two of his younger brothers, sixteen-year-old David and fourteen-year-old Owen David, who were both apprenticing to become tailors.[10]

Parke from road (J. Harvey Evans photo, ca. 1934).

Aside from the wooden addition on the front of the house, Parke probably remained little changed over the years. The elongated, flat stones in the walls, quarried locally from the bank of the nearby River Teifi, were a favored material for buildings along and near the Teifi River. With two large chimneys at each end of the house and a slate roof, Parke presented a handsome appearance of substantial permanence.

The interior of Parke also probably changed little over the years. Hetty Evans Rowland, born in 1909 and the granddaughter of Evan and Frances Evans, described the inside of the house as she remembered it from her visits as a child to see her grandmother, Frances Evans, before her death in 1916. When I visited Hetty in 2005, she described Parke to me in great detail in her distinctive Welsh accent.

> You went in a passageway and, on the right was a kind of
> . . . I suppose a little sitting room, which we never sat in.
> . . . And then to the left was the living room. Beyond the
> living room was a kind of kitchen, where they kept the
> corn for the chickens [in a back kitchen], you know, and
> all those kinds of things. . . . Upstairs they had three

bedrooms. . . . The one-bedroom—they had low ceilings
—but they were quite big, really. The right-hand side
bedroom was a double room and a double bed. That's
where my grandmother and grandfather used to sleep.
The middle room was where Esther and her sister [Han-
nah] slept. And the other room—because they only had
three rooms and they had four boys . . . had a huge bed . .
. [with] two [boys] at the top and two at the bottom,
[sleeping] toe to toe.[11]

Although industrialization in Wales, both in mining
and milling, stimulated tremendous growth in some areas
of the country, the rural Carmarthenshire population
dropped precipitously from 77 percent to less than half
that in the mid- to late 1800s, no doubt due to the departure of people to the mines in South East Wales. The
Evans family members who remained at Parke were among
the diminishing number living in South Wales who
pursued subsistence farming along with tailoring.
According to Hetty Evans Rowland, the Evans family
relied on the food they raised at Parke.

They didn't have a lot of money, [but] they lived well
because they had a pig [which lived behind the house].
They had a goat. They kept chickens. They had a huge
garden. So, there was not very much they wanted. . . .
They had a lot, you see. . . . There was always a side of
bacon up in the kitchen. And every morning you just
sliced the pieces off to fry, you see.[12]

The wooden outbuildings projecting from both sides
of Parke provided shelter for farm feed, tools, and animals.
These extensions were partially visible in photos of the
house taken in the mid-1930s by John Harvey Evans,
grandson of Evan Evans.[13]

Parke, ca. 1934 (J. Harvey Evans photo).

Evan Evans's decision to become a tailor may have been made of necessity. Evan may have had no choice but to find an alternative to the hard labor that farming or mining required. Either a congenital defect or possibly an injury had deformed his spine and right leg.[14] When photographed around age seventy standing in Parke's doorway in a three-piece suit, the foot on his shorter right leg rested on two thick bricks. Perhaps a little self-consciously, he stood in the shadow of the doorway. His upper body was twisted slightly and leaning toward his good left leg; his right leg, bent slightly at the knee, appears about four inches shorter than the left. None of Evan's children seemed to know what had shortened his right leg and caused his crooked posture. It had "just always been so," according to family stories passed down from one generation to the next. His family later recalled that Evan often sat cross-legged while sewing in his small well-lit wood-frame workshop, with his shorter leg draped over his left.

Evan's photo, standing in Parke's brick doorway, shows his right hand resting atop a thin, straight cane made of black wood with dozens of closely spaced knots from which thorny shoots once projected. This walking stick may have been a *shillelagh*—a stout knotty blackthorn or oak stick with a large knob at the top, associated with Ireland and Irish folklore. For centuries, the weight, heft, strength, and knottiness of blackthorn made it the wood of choice for clubs, cudgels, and walking sticks. Known as *"draenen ddu"* in Welsh, Evan Evans's sturdy blackthorn walking stick would have given him many years of stability and mobility despite his physical challenges. By all accounts, Evan Evans in later years was a "gentle, amiable, countryman" with a long, thin face and intense but kind eyes which turned downward at the corners; he had big ears, a broad nose, thick white hair, and a full white beard.

Evan Evans in Parke doorway, ca. 1904.

Evan's wife, Frances, grew up before the era of compulsory education and could not speak, read, or write English. Hetty believed that her grandmother, although she spoke Welsh fluently, could not read or write in her native tongue. Nevertheless, Frances not only raised her children but was the business person in the family. She managed her husband's tailoring business with a "ready reckoner"—a small handbook of tables used by people without math skills to calculate costs. She also had a reputation as a competent midwife.

One often-told story about Frances conveyed her charming innocence and naiveté about travel and the broader world beyond Pentre-cwrt. Examples of this niaveté never failed to arouse a ripple of chuckles among family members. On a rare train journey she took to visit two of her sons in the mining country of South East Wales, she ordered a cup of tea. When finished, she tucked the cup and saucer into her purse, assuming she had paid for them along with the tea. On another occasion, Frances felt so grateful to the Welsh-born Chancellor of the Exchequer of Great Britain, David Lloyd George, for introducing an old-age pension in the United Kingdom, that she sent him a live chicken as a token of thanks and appreciation.[15]

Frances and Evan (from left to right), ca. 1905.

Evan and Frances Evans epitomized the simple lives and less worldly views of the people living in the rural countryside and villages in Wales in the late 1800s and early 1900s. Pentre-cwrt's remoteness reflected its isolation. This small village was not reached directly by train until 1912, two years after Evan Evans died and four years before Frances passed away. Only then did the Great Western Railroad extend a line from Llandysul to the Pentre-cwrt Halt, and then west to Newcastle Emlyn a few miles downstream. Evan's and Frances's son John, eighteen years old when Frances and Evan were in their sixties, must have realized how far removed their rustic Welsh world views were from those in the cities of Cardiff, the Welsh capital, and London.[16]

John Evans, born in late 1882, was the youngest of six children born to Evan and Frances. Their first- and second-born children, David and Ben, were followed by Hannah, the eldest daughter, known for her gentle, kind disposition and thorough knowledge and strict fundamental interpretation of the Bible. After leaving home, she worked as a servant. Esther, the fourth child, managed the Parke household and looked after her aging parents. Tom, the fifth child, was just two years older than John and a companion at home, in school, and across the countryside in pursuit of adventures. They probably shared chores at home, like feeding and watering the family pig, chickens, and other farmyard animals. John may have joined Tom, an avid fisherman all his life, on trips to the nearby River Teifi. Until they were young teenagers, John and Tom probably walked together to school, which was located a stone's throw from the Saron Chapel that the family attended on Sundays. John was well aware of his father's occupation as a master tailor, since his father worked at home and John, perhaps, assisted him on occasion.

Saron Chapel and school behind.

John completed his compulsory schooling at around age thirteen. By the age of eighteen, he may have worked on a farm near Llangeler, not far from Pentre-cwrt, to help support his aging parents. As a general farm servant, he would have performed a wide array of tasks: plowing, sowing cereal grains, harvesting hay and corn, tending sheep or cattle, mending fences, maintaining hedges that enclosed fields, and doing chores around the house. John's farming experience did not continue for long, however. An adventuresome young man filled with dreams and ambitions of improving his life and experiencing the wider world beyond Pentre-cwrt, John must have considered occupations related to textiles just like those pursued by his father and his oldest brother, David.[17]

In 1902, when John Evans was nineteen, his much-beloved sister Hannah died from pneumonia and a pulmonary embolism at just twenty-nine years old. This undoubtedly caused John great grief and perhaps prompted him to reflect on his family's fragile existence during a time of unsettling social and economic changes. He may have seen the need to take chances and consider life pursuits that might take him far from his rural home and offer him a broader and more fulfilling life. At this distressing time, John's oldest brother, David, working in Cardiff as a draper, might have encouraged him to pursue the same trade.[18]

Mabel Ida Harvey, Born in Agricultural Essex

Mabel Ida Harvey's background contrasted sharply with John's. Five years younger than John, Mabel was the sixth of eight children born to a friendly and gregarious family with deep roots in the low-lying, fertile, coastal farming country of southeast Essex, in England. The Celtic Trinovantes tribes of pre-Roman Britain arrived on the north side of the Thames Estuary before the Roman invasion of 54 BC. Few remnants of the Celts remained, however, after the subsequent invasions by the Romans, who brought the first continental influence to Essex. Historical records suggest that the Romans dug a network of narrow drainage ditches in low-lying areas of the southeast Essex coastline where the rivers Crouch and Roach join. The Romans also engineered some early sea-wall barriers to reclaim areas of low-lying Essex, including land near the mouth of the River Crouch where the Harvey family eventually farmed. Abundant evidence of Roman occupation exists in southeast Essex, such as settlement and road sites, salt-making red hills, and unearthed coins, bricks, and pottery.[19]

Around 400 CE, the Anglo-Saxons arrived in this area from northern Europe. In small boats loaded with tools and farm animals, they crossed the North Sea searching for suitable land to farm, which they found in Essex's flat coastal region and relatively mild climate. Here, the Saxons lived in dispersed settlements and farmed small open fields. They developed the foundations of the English language and culture before the Normans invaded France in 1066. For six hundred years, numerous small farmers and large landholders from London managed sizeable estates overlooking the River Thames and its estuary. They raised cattle, sheep, and pigs and grew wheat for bread, as well as barley, rye, and oats in fields in southeast Essex. It was here that the Harvey family for generations farmed land near waterways in southeast Essex.[20]

By the 1700s, the Harvey family had become respected farmers. They lived and worked near Hadleigh Castle, which stood on high ground above an overflow channel of the River Thames. According to historical records, Mabel's great-grandfather, William Harvey (1782–1854), farmed near Hadleigh Castle at Bramble Hall in the hamlet of Daws Heath.

The Hadleigh Castle farm reputedly became associated with Henry VIII, a Tudor family member, in the 1500s. Its construction began around 1215 when landowning barons rose against the English king. Then, extensively fortified by Edward III during the hundred-year war with France, Hadleigh Castle became a favorite residence of the aging Edward III until the mid-1450s. The king also appreciated the strategic location of the castle for defending the Thames estuary against French raiders. Edward's successor took little interest in the castle. After being sold off for building materials, it was leased to successive tenants until 1551. Farming continued in the vicinity of the Hadleigh Castle remains for centuries.[21]

Other Harvey family members farmed at Hadleigh and nearby Thundersley, Benfleet, Eastwood, and Raleigh, north of the River Thames's mouth. Often, a young Harvey man would move into farming by working first as an agricultural laborer and then as a bailiff or farm manager. A few Harveys became landowners.

By the mid-1850s, the Harveys were part of an extensive and well-respected Essex farming family. The Harveys' success as farmers may have been due to their experience and knowledge and the favorable farm conditions in southeast Essex. In the mid-1800s, Essex was one of the leading farming counties in England according to White's 1848 Directory of Essex:

> The county is on the whole fertile, and possesses some particularly fine land. The greater part is well enclosed, and rendered highly productive by the skillful management of the agriculturists. The farmers of Essex are reckoned among the best in the kingdom. . . . The variety and

goodness of the agricultural products of Essex are not
exceeded by those of any other county.[22]

Additionally, Essex farms' proximity to London and its
expanding urban market gave farmers the great economic
advantage of lower transport costs and a large city market
not far from produce.

During the 1850s and 1860s, in the so-called "golden
age of English agriculture," the high price that wheat
fetched in London gave Essex farmers substantial
economic rewards. Essex farmers, like the Harveys,
continued to benefit from the stimulus of the expanding
London market, where wheat, an essential Essex farm
product in the 1870s, was transported upstream on River
Thames sailing barges and sold in the city. Simultaneously,
manure from carriage horses in the city was loaded on
barges and brought downstream to enrich Essex farm
fields. During this period, hay, grown in abundance by
Harvey farmers and transported up the River Thames to
London to feed the thousands of horses used to pull street
vehicles, was also a great money maker.[23]

All this began to dramatically change by the 1870s,
however, when a deep depression with devastating consequences settled over England. An abundance of cheap
wheat and flour imported from American prairie farms,
and the reduced cost and increased carrying capacity of
steamships crossing the Atlantic Ocean, undercut English
wheat farmers. Essex was among the hardest hit English
counties. Wheat prices collapsed by half over twenty
years; prices fell to their lowest level in 150 years by the
mid-1890s. Meanwhile, Britain's dependence on imported
wheat more than doubled between the 1860s and the
1880s. Beleaguered farming conditions, especially in Essex,
caused a great exodus from the countryside of farm
laborers searching for alternative work in the cities.

Mabel's father, Stephen Harvey—a grandson of William Harvey of Bramble Hall Farm—was working as a farm laborer and then a bailiff when Essex plummeted into this deep depression.[24]

Many Essex farmers, perhaps including those in the Harvey family who managed farms as bailiffs, sought to make adjustments in the crops grown and animals raised to compensate for the changing conditions. Farmers reduced acres previously devoted to cereals. More land became allocated to hay and permanent grass; livestock; and market gardening vegetables such as potatoes, cabbage, carrots, and peas sold in nearby Southend-on-Sea and other towns.

Essex farmers increased by 50 percent the acreage devoted to hay, to feed their farm animals and London's horses. These farmers seemed to respond positively to the depression by considering the particular conditions of their local soil and nearby market opportunities. Some farmers resorted to low (less intensive) farming and rough grazing to economize. Farmers like Stephen Harvey, Mabel's father, who managed farms, were mostly responsible for determining land re-allocation between crops and livestock during the depression. Yet, despite multiple efforts to adjust to the depressed conditions, farmers sometimes left hundreds of acres uncultivated, neglected, or abandoned.[25]

It may have been challenges associated with England's twenty year-long agricultural depression extending from 1873 to 1896 that encouraged Stephen and Martha to leave Little Chalvedon Hall Farm near Bowers Gifford and immigrate to Canada. Four of their children (Ethel, Bertha, Mabel, and Maud) were all born between 1884 and 1892 in the Bowers Gifford Ecclesiastical Parish of the Billericay registration district. Maud, who arrived in April 1892, was the last Harvey child born in Bowers Gifford. It

is unclear where exactly she was born, however, since
Maud's birth registration does not note the location of the
Harvey's home. Maud may have been born before the
family left the Little Chalvedon Hall Farm or after they
moved into the black boarded cottage at the bottom of
the Bread and Cheese Hill, London Road, Benfleet. We do
know that Martha's pregnancy with Maud was challenging,
prompting her doctor to advise the family against making
the strenuous journey to Canada. By early 1895, Stephen
and Martha Harvey had purchased and moved to Kingsmans Farm on the River Crouch north of Hockley.
Martha's last child, Reginald, was born at Kingsmans in
May 1895.[26]

Black boarded cottage, Bread and Cheese Hill, ca.
1912 (courtesy Hadleigh & Thundersley
Community Archive, Hadley, Benfleet, Essex).

Encompassing around 150 acres, the Harvey farm was
bounded on the north by a strip of salt marsh, known as
saltings, extending from the south side of the River
Crouch bordered by a sea wall which kept the river from
flooding the farm during heavy rains. South of this sea wall
were several small, hedged fields planted in grass for
grazing livestock or growing wheat, barley, oats, hay, and a
few root crops like mangels (a beet-like fodder for horses).
The largest concentration of farm buildings existed on

both the 1873 and 1896 ordinance survey maps. Depicted on these maps was a T-shaped, two-story timber farmhouse with a one-story, tile-roofed rear addition. Historical records indicate that the farmhouse, dating from the 1600s, had been modified in the 1800s. A short distance north of the farmhouse were attached thatched barns, stables, and sheds encircling a water hole for the animals. East of the Harvey farm buildings stood Cope's Farm (according to an 1896 ordinance survey map).[27]

When Stephen and Martha Harvey purchased the farm, they named it Kingsmans Farm, perhaps after King George III's volunteer Essex regiments, which had constructed many defenses to repel a possible French invasion during the Napoleonic Wars (1793–1805). Some of these soldiers were periodically stationed along the banks of the River Crouch, where remnants of minor fortifications remained into the twentieth century. For the next fifty years, the Harvey family farmed Kingsmans and created a warm and welcoming gathering place for the large Harvey family and their friends.[28]

Harvey family at Kingsmans Farm, ca. 1907.

Mabel's school, Hockley, Essex.

Farmers in the area viewed landowning Stephen Harvey as a proper English yeoman, a devoted Anglican, and a staunch British patriot. Stephen was a highly respected farmer and was considered a natural leader in the community's social, political, and religious life. Landed families such as the Harveys were natural choices for appointments to Parliament, civil service positions, the army, and the church. While living at Kingsmans Farm, Stephen Harvey served twenty-eight years as the elected chairman of the Hockley Parish Council. He also sat on the Rochford District Council for many years. [29] Mabel Ida Harvey was around six years old when the family moved to Kingsmans Farm. Born in 1888 in Bowers Gifford near Pitsea, Essex, Mabel grew up in a family of amiable and exuberant siblings.

2

BECOMING DRAPERS

EARLY 1900S

John's and Mabel's independent decisions to become drapers in London provided for their chance meeting in London in the early 1900s. Both of them aspired to create different lives than those their parents had pursued. John deliberately decided not to practice subsistence farming in rural South Wales, and Mabel chose not to become a farmer's wife. The industrialized world that they entered at the opening of the twentieth century offered them more choices. A few of their family members provided examples of alternative, available life choices that they might pursue. Training to become drapers seemed like a logical path to follow for them both.

The drapers' profession originated in medieval times. The expansion of the English woolen cloth trade gave rise to a constellation of occupations that dealt with wool, linen, silk cloth, and related items such as thread, needles, and decorative ribbons, flowers, and fringes. The wholesale draper bought expensive imported fabric from cloth weavers, then sold it to retailers primarily for making men's shirts and suits. A draper often arranged or draped samples of their most attractive fabrics across their shop's doorway to attract customers' attention. In this fragmented world of cloth producers and consumers, drapers, tailors, and dressmakers played the vital role of distributing textiles.

By the late 1800s, around 750,000 retail drapers worked in England. One or more dry goods stores existed in every village, town, and city throughout the United Kingdom. Eventually, drapers' shops evolved into large "department stores," where shoppers could purchase every item related to textiles. In the early 1900s, Paris's Bon Marché and London's Whiteleys had become the two largest department stores in the world. Whiteleys employed about 6,000 workers and sold a wide range of goods. Drapers, who founded these department stores, understood well the tastes of emerging middle-class female consumers.[1]

John Evans Becomes a Draper

A few years before Mabel and John met, John had decided to follow his father's and oldest brother's occupations working with textiles. His father, gentle-dispositioned Evan, a tailor, provided John with an appealing example to emulate. In addition to his father, some of John's uncles (Thomas D., David, and Owen) had also chosen careers in textiles, but they had either immigrated to the United States or died before John was born. John may have visited a third uncle, Owen David Evans, a master tailor in Pontypool, Wales, coal-mining country.[2]

In John's own family, his older brother, Benjamin, was employed at a local woolen mill near Pentre-cwrt before becoming a weaver. When this job abruptly ended, however, he moved to South East Wales to work in a coal mine.[3] John's oldest brother, David, who had apprenticed as a draper, may have offered John the greatest influence and encouragement to become a draper. In 1891, twenty-three-year-old David worked as an assistant for well-known master draper David Morgan in the Welsh capital of Cardiff. Morgan had opened his first two draper's shops in the South Wales coal country of Rhymney and Pontlottyn, Glamorganshire. Twenty years later, in 1879, he opened a small draper's shop on The Hays, a bustling shopping avenue in central Cardiff. This small shop gradually expanded into a six-story department store consisting of three adjoining buildings separated by several glass-covered shopping arcades.[4]

The 1891 census reported that David Evans was among eighty men and women, ranging in age from sixteen to thirty, who worked as either assistant or apprentice drapers. By 1901, thirty-three-year-old David Evans lived near central Cardiff and worked as an auditor clerk, presumably for David Morgan. Ten years later, he had become a "clothiers clerk & secretary of L. Co." He and his wife and adopted daughter lived a mile from central Cardiff in a stone townhouse on Llantwit Street (still standing in 2018).[5]

David Evans encouraged John to become a draper, according to John Evans's son, John Harvey Evans. David Evans "played the major part in providing for my father's training through apprenticeship," John Harvey Evans wrote in the 1980s. Other evidence of John's apprenticeship as a draper is hard to find more than one hundred years after his training. Eighteen years old in 1901, John Evans was not among those working at David Morgan with his older brother, David. John's apprenticeship, wherever it occurred, may have lasted about three years. Probably sometime between 1903 and 1910, John looked for and found employment as a draper in London.[6]

By 1910, John had moved to London and was working

as a draper's assistant at the Marshall & Snelgrove department store on Oxford Street. James Marshall had founded a draper's store many years earlier in 1837 in a small shop on Vere Street, just off Oxford Street. With its alternating streets and narrow alleys lined with small houses, Marylebone became a garment district where tailors, dressmakers, and drapers founded shops on Oxford Street. In the mid-1800s, Vere Street attracted a small assemblage of cloth trade businesses like Marshall & Snelgrove.

When Marshall & Snelgrove flourished and expanded, the business moved into a palatial five-story building on Oxford Street's north side near Vere Street. Marshall & Snelgrove was one of the dozens of "continuous drapers' shop[s]" on Oxford Street by the early 1900s. Joining Marshall & Snelgrove were John Lewis & Co., Peter Robinson, Bourne & Hollingsworth, Selfridge's, and other department stores that occupied elaborately decorated Victorian buildings with glass windows displaying artfully arranged goods for passersbys to admire.[7]

In the early 1900s, the greatly enlarged Marshall & Snelgrove store sold textiles, ready-to-wear clothing, and a wide array of carpets and soft furnishings (curtains, cushions, rugs, and hangings). On-site designers made and sold custom-made clothing, which invariably gave the store an air of exclusivity. Marshall & Snelgrove employed an army of drapers with widely ranging areas of expertise who purchased fabric for dresses, suits, and other clothing. There were "silk mercers [cloth sellers], mourning warehousemen [tailors who traveled to provide mourning clothing when a death occurred], dress, costume & mantle makers, lacemen, haberdashers, hosiers, gloves, outfitters, milliners, furriers, carpet, rug & linen factors [a person who acts for another, notably a mercantile and/or colonial agent], whole[sale] & retail warehousemen."[8]

London's Marshall & Snelgrove department store

expanded with new stores in major cities such as Birmingham, Manchester, and York, where up-and-coming middle-class customers purchased luxury goods. The Marshall & Snelgrove label enjoyed an esteemed reputation for high-end fashionable and well-made clothing. Even after the store faltered during the First World War and Debenham's department store purchased it in 1919, the prestige

John Evans, ca. 1907.

associated with the Marshall & Snelgrove label continued for decades.[9]

John Evans secured a job as a draper at Marshall & Snelgrove sometime before 1910. A 1910 London street directory noted that Marshall & Snelgrove "silk mercers" occupied the building at 2 through 24 Marylebone Lane on the east side of the lane. The 1911 London census indicated that John was a live-in employee, residing with over a hundred other drapers' assistants, drapers' merchants, and drapers' clerks at 16 Marylebone Lane, just around the corner from the main entrance to Marshall & Snelgrove on Oxford Street. Roughly two-thirds of all drapers in the early 1900s lived in modest accommodations near their workplace.[10]

Mabel Trains as a Draper

Like John, Mabel Harvey may have also been influenced by family members when considering the work she'd like to pursue. Two of Mabel's father's sisters were dressmakers. Her Aunt Rachel, born around 1861, worked as a dressmaker at the turn of the 1900s. Her Aunt Jennie, born in 1855, also pursued dressmaking. Jennie visited and sometimes stayed with Stephen Harvey's family at Kingsmans Farm for extended periods. As dressmakers, both Rachel Harvey Ellis and Jennie Harvey would have purchased cloth, as well as pins, thread, and other dry goods, from a draper's shop in a nearby village or from London department stores about a one-hour train ride from Hockley. Aunts Rachel and Jennie may have opened the eyes of the curious and observant Mabel to the possibility of becoming a draper.[11]

Mabel also had an older sister, Beatrice ("Bea") Marian Harvey, who worked for many years in the millinery department of a London department store, probably Derry & Toms. Draper Joseph Toms opened this store in 1853 on fashionable Kensington High Street, southwest of Marylebone. The hat-making trade that Beatrice pursued required a variety of dry goods. Milliner Beatrice naturally obtained her materials, such as feathers, bias trim, cloth flowers, ribbon, and various fabrics, from drapers. Although not a dressmaker or draper, Mabel's older sister Ethel Millicent Harvey, a nurse, also worked in Marylebone. Her presence at the St. Marylebone Infirmary in nearby North Kensington may have further encouraged Mabel to seek employment in Marylebone.[12]

Mabel probably moved to London in 1909 or 1910, when she was around twenty-one, to work as a draper. A London city street directory of the time noted that 42 Weymouth Street was the residence of drapers working at the John Lewis & Co. department store, where Mabel became employed. John Lewis opened a small drapery shop on Oxford Street in the 1860s, and then gradually expanded. By the 1880s, Lewis decided to rebuild and transform his department store into an elegant four-story establishment. Mabel became part of the store's large coterie of drapers. Department stores offered many women some of their first jobs outside the home; they also energized the women's rights movement, culminating in a

1918 act giving women over the age of thirty the right to vote.

John Lewis drapers housing, Marylebone, London, (G. Evans photo, 2018).

In 1911, Mabel was one of eighty-five people, mostly women, living at Draper House at 42 Weymouth Street (still standing in 2016). That year, Mabel held a clerk's position, the second-highest of six classes of business labor described in Mary Higgs's 1910 book, *Where Shall She Live: The Homelessness of the Woman Worker*. "Clerkships are sought by girls and boys alike who want to 'rise' into their ranks of business, as distinguished from manual labor," this book claimed.[13] Working as a draper near London's heart, Mabel's life contrasted sharply with life on rural Kingsmans Farm 40 miles from London. Department store employment offered Mabel, her older sister, Beatrice, and other young women interesting new pursuits away from farms and rural villages.[14]

With the rise of industrialization and cities' growth in the early and mid-1800s, department stores and the drapers who founded them contributed to the emergence of a middle class. Mabel's and John's occupations—Mabel as a draper's clerk who worked with letters and figures, and John as an assistant draper who handled fabrics and sold

women's clothing from behind a counter—made them part
of an emerging middle class.

Contemporary fashions also played a role in this.
When John and Mabel first joined the drapers' world in
the early 1900s, many fabric layers were needed to create
fashionable dresses, suits, and coats. When not at work,
Mabel probably wore the traditional corset with a
pronounced S-bend, which thrust the hips back and the
chest forward to replicate an ornamental Pouter pigeon in
profile. Overlaying this would have been frilly, draping
blouses with lacy collars, and a narrow-fitted skirt, fluted
toward the hem, which fell to the top of the boot. Hats
with broad brims and low crowns, adorned with flowers,
feathers, and ribbons, would have been fastened to center-
parted, long hair wrapped around wide pads at the sides.
Even farmers usually wore three-piece suits with small,
high lapels and cloth caps or bowlers. The many layers of
clothing worn by fashionable middle- and upper-class
women and men contributed to the rise of eager middle-
class consumers, who became part of the emerging early-
twentieth-century consumer culture. Department stores
making and selling high-fashion clothing became modern,
middle-class temples of consumerism.[15]

When John and Mabel worked in Marylebone in the
early 1900s, they not only served the emerging middle
class but undoubtedly aspired to be part of it. This new
middle class defined itself by non-manual work and fashion, attitude, and ambition. They saw themselves as
pioneers and agents of change, part of a society rewarded
on personal merit and not on status at birth. This class
challenged the privilege that customarily accompanied
land ownership. The ambitions of the rising middle-class
were more far-reaching than those of their parents and
grandparents.

Many years later, Mabel's son, John Harvey Evans,

observed that she was the third in a series of four "up-and-coming Harvey daughters"[16] who envisioned becoming something other than farmers' wives. Mabel and her three sisters (Ethel, Bertha, and Maud) had an outlook that embraced more middle-class values. Mabel and her sisters wanted greater freedom of movement and expression. For them, fashionable Marylebone, with its high style and high-class fashion, must have been stimulating. This emerging middle class, which included John and Mabel, had a strong desire to succeed in their pursuits and improve their lives.[17] According to British social and cultural historian Donna Loftus in her book *Rise of the Victorian Middle Class*,

> The Victorian middle-class is largely associated with the growth of cities and the expansion of the economy. Giving voice to urbanisation and industrialization this emerging middle-class emphasized competition, thrift, prudence, self-reliance, and personal achievement. . . . Being middle class was defined by taking responsibility for one's self, one's family, and the community.[18]

Blossoming Romance in London

At a different time, John and Mabel would never have met. Yet profound social, political, and economic changes in the early twentieth century, their middle-class aspirations, and their decision to become drapers happened to place them in the same city and neighborhood at the same time. The proximity of their residences—John on Marylebone Lane and Mabel about six blocks north on Weymouth Street—created an opportunity for the two to cross paths and gradually get to know each other. One can only speculate about where, when, and how their romance developed.

Wherever their paths crossed, a spark of interest, curiosity, and desire must have been ignited. Undoubtedly, John and Mabel became attracted to each other's inherent good looks and personal demeanor. Both were slim and small in stature. John, five feet eight inches tall, weighed about 133 pounds, and Mabel, around five feet three inches tall, probably weighed around 110 pounds.

Mabel had a rectangular face with chiseled cheekbones much like her mother's, inquisitive, deep-set, grey-blue eyes, and brown hair parted in the middle and swept back to the sides in a modest version of the early twentieth-century Gibson Girl style— the epitome of female beauty at the time. According to her son, John Harvey Evans, Mabel had a reputation among her sisters and brothers for being high-spirited. She was evidently "a bundle of pranks and giggles." She would never speak out in a crowd and was sedate in her singing in church. Her infectious laugh, although not loud, usually carried others along with her. Her light-hearted spirit and deep-throated chortle, which continued throughout her life, probably endeared Mabel to John immediately.[19]

Mabel Harvey, ca. 1907.

John had a long face framed by thick, wavy brown hair, a sculpted, clean-shaven chin, broad smile, and almond-shaped gray eyes that peered intently from behind wire-rimmed spectacles. Large ears protruded above a long neck, and, as he aged, the fine elliptical lines on either side of his mouth deepened when he smiled. John's demeanor was one of thoughtful, quiet consideration, and he had a passion for music, particularly Welsh hymns. Long after his death, the Evans family unearthed several Welsh hymnals that had belonged to him, clearly suggesting the importance of music in his life. John often sang solos in a clear tenor voice at the church the family attended and, later, sang duets with his sons—Harvey, a tenor, and Evan, a baritone. Family recollections and prayers and letters written by John present a clear image of him as a gentle, humble, and sensitive man with a deep, abiding faith.[20]

Many years after John and Mabel married, their oldest son, John Harvey Evans, recalled that

> Dad and Mother were a decidedly unusual combination; he from deep southwest Wales and she from deep southeast England. Her county, Essex, is certainly one of the most Saxon, and Harvey, her maiden name, just seems to fit properly. While Dad was from a thoroughly Welsh and Welsh-speaking part of the island, he did not match the stereotype of [Welsh] people[:] swarthy, dark-haired, and squat. Instead, he was of light frame, moderately tall for his time at 5'8" and never weighed more than about 135 pounds. Unlike Mother's countryside of rich, productive farmland, Dad's was remote, sparsely populated, with rolling swells of green mostly given over to sheep. The area had a few small woolen mills on the Teifi River and his father, being a tailor, some affinity for textiles might possibly have seemed to come naturally. An apprenticeship served somewhere lost in time took the place of any broad higher education.[21]

Despite their different backgrounds, both John and Mabel undoubtedly found each other appealing for a constellation of reasons: their occupations as drapers, their burgeoning middle-class outlook and aspirations, their shared values related to the kind treatment they felt others deserved, and their physical attraction to each other. Their mutual interest soon led to an upwelling of warmth and affection that grew between them. It was not long before Mabel "broke an engagement [with someone else] to become engaged to him [John]," Mabel's son, Harvey, recalled many years later. John and Mabel's blossoming romance inevitably changed their lives forever.[22]

Lives Forever Changed

Despite the upwelling of their intense feelings for each other, Mabel and John confronted enormous challenges beginning a new life together. One perplexing problem was the gnawing dissatisfaction that both John and Mabel experienced in their jobs. John's position as an assistant draper had some distinctly objectionable aspects. Male assistant drapers were often portrayed in the press as elegant young men wearing fine clothes, displaying effeminate behavior, and putting on social pretensions.

Furthermore, drapers were constrained in their jobs. The English writer H. G. Wells, who served as a draper's assistant in the late 1800s, described this period of his life as a time of incarceration. According to Wells, drapers became prisoners in small sleeping apartments with bare walls, and were condemned to celibacy behind a counter for the rest of their lives. William Paines' 1912 book *Shop, Slavery, and Emancipation* told of myriad injustices experienced by drapers' assistants.

John lodged in a live-in housing system at Marshall & Snelgrove that made store owners surrogate parents and indeed must have humiliated John, twenty-seven years old in 1910. The customary imposition of fines for any infringement of rules, such as lateness or untidiness, must have further irritated him. Drapers' assistants typically worked long hours on their feet, moved heavy bolts of fabric from the storeroom to counters, and earned meager wages. John must have seriously wondered if a physical escape might restore his independent identity and possibly open the door to a new life with Mabel.[23]

Mabel also had concerns about her life as a draper's clerk, such as the constraints and limitations of work and her accommodation in John Lewis & Co. housing in London. Department stores notoriously exploited female drapers as well as male drapers; young women worked long hours on their feet and received low wages. Their accommodations in the live-in system were often demanding and difficult to bear, with water sometimes trickling down walls in the cold and crowded sleeping quarters. In 1894, the drapery union characterized women's working conditions as "The Slavery of the Counter."[24] Probably little changed in the intervening years. Authoritarian management (notorious at the John Lewis & Co. department store) probably made Mabel unhappy in her job.

Skepticism and concern about their intensifying relationship, most likely expressed by Mabel's parents, must also have concerned the couple. Stephen and Martha Harvey may have felt that the humble origins of John Evans made him an unsuitable match for their daughter, Mabel. According to Wayne Gardner, a grandson of one of Mabel's sisters (Maud Elsie Harvey Gardner), Stephen and Martha viewed Mabel's beau as just a "humble Welsh man." If Mabel married John Evans, her family may have thought she would be reaching beneath her landowning family's minor-gentry pedigree.[25]

Additionally, Mabel and John's different religious upbringings must have worried Mabel's parents. John's Nonconformist Congregational chapel background contrasted sharply with the doctrines and practices of the Church of England. Nonconformists from Wales were considered rebels, outsiders. They arose from the non-landowning working classes rather than the land-owning gentry or those aspiring to emulate that class.

As far back as 1662, the British monarchy had attempted to root out Congregationalism from English life by exiling two thousand Protestant ministers from England. Half a century later, religious dissenters could not qualify for public office in England and Wales and were subsequently barred from universities as well. Restrictions against these dissenters were eventually removed, yet Congregational chapels in the countryside remained crucibles of Welsh culture and language as well as independent, democratic thought. The Welsh zeal for self-improvement and a richer, fuller life carried forward into the last half of the 1800s when John Evans was born and grew to adulthood. John and Mabel's different origins, religious and cultural backgrounds, and farming background undoubtedly perplexed and disturbed their parents.

Many years later, John and Mabel's oldest son, John Harvey Evans, speculated about the couple's developing relationship.

> It was a country girl from East Anglia with a boy from the 'outback' of west South Wales. Having come in later years to recognize the antipathy between [the] Welsh and English, which must have been stronger then, [their early and growing attraction to each other] was probably not a happy thing in either family.[26]

A generation earlier, John Evans and Mabel Harvey would never have crossed paths, never have courted, and would never have seriously contemplated immigrating and making a life together.

Nothing is known about John's parents' opinions of their son's deepening relationship with Mabel. John Evans's father, Evan Evans, died in October 1910; he may never have met Mabel. John might have hesitated to bring Mabel to his modest home, deep in the rural backcountry of West Wales, and introduce her to his mother since Frances spoke little English and had limited experience outside villages in South Wales. John might even have felt a tinge of embarrassment about his rural roots at Parke in Pentre-cwrt. As John and Mabel's relationship grew more intimate, they must have wondered how they could live together and raise a family in England with such different family backgrounds.

Leaving England and Wales, immigrating to North America, and starting a new life, although filled with uncertainties, increasingly seemed not only possible but a promising and potentially satisfying prospect. They could leave behind their constricting occupations as drapers and their families' objections to their marriage. They could begin a new life in a new country.

John and Mabel would not be the first in their families to leave their homes in Great Britain. Other family members had set a precedent of immigrating to the United States or Canada during the previous fifty years. John Evans's father, Evan, had two brothers (John Owen and Thomas D.) who had immigrated to southern Illinois and eastern Pennsylvania, respectively, in the late 1860s. John's mother, Frances, had a brother (Thomas Thomas) who immigrated with his wife, Ellen, to Ohio in the 1870s, as well as two sisters (Mary and Margaret) who reportedly "ran away from home" as young women and boarded a ship in Liverpool bound for the United States.

Mabel's father, Stephen Harvey, also had an older brother, John Harvey, who had immigrated to Canada in the 1880s. He first went to Maple Creek, Saskatchewan, where he raised horses and accumulated considerable wealth. Around 1907, John moved to Victoria, British Columbia, where he became active in city government and a church warden at Christ Church Cathedral. Mabel's parents also considered immigrating to Canada until the problematic 1892 birth of Maud, their seventh child, when Martha's doctor advised her against making the strenuous journey.[27]

Most of these Harvey and Evans family members left England and Wales and other parts of Europe when the stream of immigrants to North America reached tidal wave proportions. Between 1870 and 1921, twenty-five million Europeans entered the United States to escape upheaval in their own countries or find better-paying jobs and more opportunities for a better life. Between the 1860s and the 1880s, a flood of Welsh immigrants with mining and manufacturing skills, took their valuable experience with them to North America to seek more lucrative jobs. By the early twentieth century, roughly 14 percent of all U.S. residents were foreign-born.[28]

However, in the late 1800s and early 1900s, far fewer migrants arrived in North America from the United Kingdom and Western Europe. The opening of many steamship companies at that time from Mediterranean ports, which operated larger ships at less cost, encouraged more emigration from the Austro-Hungarian Empire, Italy, and Russia than from the United Kingdom, Germany, and Scandinavia. By 1896, eastern European emigrants exceeded those leaving Great Britain, Germany and Scandinavia combined.[29]

Additionally, John Evans possessed somewhat unique skills as a draper, not as a laborer in mining or textile milling operations in Wales. John may have speculated that North America, where the number of department stores was growing, might offer him more opportunities and better working conditions than those that existed in London.

In other ways, John and Mabel's motivation to immigrate to North America indeed mirrored those who had come before them. John and Mabel, influenced by early-twentieth-century values and ambitions, must have believed that America would offer them greater freedom to make their own decisions and give their children and grandchildren better prospects for a good education and a chance to pursue their life goals. America seemed to them, as it did for so many immigrants, a land of great promise and endless possibilities. America was a place to begin a new life.

3

IMMIGRATING TO A NEW WORLD

1911–1916

In the early afternoon of October 3, 1911, gray clouds threatened to drop a few sprinkles of rain on the Port of Southampton, about 80 miles southwest of central London along Southampton Water, a tidal estuary where the rivers Test and Itchen converged. An icy breeze blew from the west and rippled the estuary waters. In the 1830s, the dredging of mudflats between these two rivers created the city's Eastern Docks, where Cunard ships, like the SS *Ascania,* arrived and departed. On this day in early October, Mabel and her sister Ethel probably accompanied John as he boarded a London and Southwestern Railway train at London's Waterloo Station and headed south to Southampton.[1]

As early as 1840, the London and Southampton Railway connected London to Southampton, where coal, agricultural goods, and imported produce arrived by ship at the docks. Between the late nineteenth and early twentieth centuries, the Southwestern Railway's acquisition and gradual expansion of the Southampton docks, and the subsequent construction of a deep-water port, attracted the attention of a growing number of trans-Atlantic travelers, including those arriving to board the *Ascania*.

On the afternoon of October 3, John, Mabel, and Ethel would have arrived at the Southampton train station located near the remains of the city's old medieval wall, which enclosed a portion of the city center where three- and four-story stone and brick commercial buildings lined narrow streets.[2]

John, dressed in trousers, waistcoat, and jacket, was ready to make the voyage; he carried a single suitcase as he neared the ship. Mabel and Ethel, who came to see John off, and probably dressed according to the fashion of the day—a skirt, blouse, and light coat—made their way to the docks where the Cunard line's *Ascania* had begun boarding passengers bound for Canada.

Eager to begin a new life with Mabel after securing a job in America, John boarded the *Ascania* with high hopes for his new future and a life with Mabel. As he walked up the gangway and onto the *Ascania* along with hundreds of other passengers, John waved Mabel and Ethel goodbye. On this particular Atlantic crossing, the *Ascania* carried 200 first-class passengers and 1,500 steerage passengers, including John Evans. As the captain signaled to remove the ship's gangway and position the mooring and tug lines to ensure a smooth departure from the dock, Mabel stood back from the pier, waving to John, who returned her wave from the lower steerage deck.

As the ship made its way south into the Southampton Water, then moved into The Solent (the narrow strait in the English Channel separating the mainland from the Isle of Wight), John and Mabel must have felt a constellation of emotions—excitement, anticipation, hope, and sadness. John's immigration to North America promised the possibility of a new life and future for them both. Yet there would be many unknown passages to navigate in his journey ahead. His solo immigration would require great determination, stamina, and resolve as he moved from place to place, searching for the right job in a foreign country. There were no guarantees that he would quickly find a job or a welcoming place to settle. For both John and Mabel, the immediate future held many uncertainties. And neither of them knew when and where they would see each other again.[3]

Launching a New Beginning

Regardless of the possibilities that John and Mabel could imagine, Mabel's parents had insisted that she not make the trip until John had first found a job that promised a secure future for them both. John had learned what he could in England about employment possibilities in the United States and contacted some Evans family members who had immigrated to central and northeastern Ohio several years earlier.

Together, Mabel and John must have considered the many challenges and uncertainties that lay ahead, decided on the best immigration route, and speculated about John's most likely prospects of finding a job as a draper. Both must have felt uneasy about being separated for an unknown period.

In the summer of 1911, John booked passage on the *Ascania,* built earlier that year by Swan, Hunter and Wigham Richardson Ltd., shipbuilders in Newcastle. The Cunard Line purchased the *Ascania* shortly before its launch. Samuel Cunard, a native of Halifax, Nova Scotia, started the British and North American Royal Mail Steam Packet Company in 1840 with four paddle-wheel sailing ships equipped with coal steam engines. Transatlantic passenger service began that year.

Over the next several decades, the Cunard Line,

carrying British mail and passengers and cargo on its North American ships, significantly expanded its fleet. Although the first generation of Cunard ships attracted wealthy cabin-class passengers, eventually, Cunard also served a clientele with more modest means. Cunard was one of the first transatlantic companies to create a network of passenger agents that addressed emigrants' transport from Scandinavian countries and, later, from Great Britain. In the late 1800s and early 1900s, Cunard kept adding larger, more powerful ships to its fleet. The giant express steamers—the RMS *Lusitania,* RMS *Mauretania,* and the RMS *Aquitania*—launched in 1906, earned the reputation of being the fastest vessels that naval architects had designed. The speed, size, and frequency of departures from England made the Cunard Steamship Company Limited the favored choice of many emigrants traveling from Europe to North America in the early 1900s.[4]

After John and Mabel decided to begin their life together in North America, they probably chose Canada as their port of entry for several reasons. Starting in the 1880s, the United States imposed more stringent immigration rules at its ports of entry; emigrants increasingly chose to arrive in Canada before entering the United States to avoid delays and problems that might arise at ports in the United States.[5]

In the early 1900s, thousands of Britons immigrated to Canada. In May 1902, at the end of the Boer War between Great Britain and the two Boer (Afrikaner) republics, severe depression and crippling unemployment settled over Great Britain. This coincided with a corresponding sharp rise in the Canadian economy, followed soon afterward by surging emigration. In 1903, a British emigration office opened in Trafalgar Square in London, enticing many more British residents to immigrate to Canada. Simultaneously, Canada's Minister of the Interior, Clifford

Sifton, launched a vigorous campaign to market Canada to potential British immigrants. Extensive publicity appeared in all the major British newspapers.

Additionally, a conspicuous and elaborately decorated Canadian Arch was erected near Trafalgar Square on the ceremonial route from Buckingham Palace to Westminster Abbey for King Edward VII's coronation in July 1902. Fifty-six feet high and capped with a decorative circular, crown-shaped roof, the arch featured bright electric lights on both sides that exuberantly proclaimed, "Canada. Free Homes for Millions" and "Canada. Britain's Granary." This ostentatious feature inspired great enthusiasm among many Brits to immigrate to Canada and undoubtedly contributed to the most significant trans-Atlantic migration from Great Britain in history.[6]

Canadian coronation arch, London, 1902.

Between 1902 and 1903, when the Canadian government established an emigration office in Trafalgar House, the number of Britons immigrating to Canada jumped from 17,275 to 42,198 and peaked in 1912 with 147,619. Clifford Sifton, Canada's Minister of the Interior under Prime Minister Wilfrid Laurier, initially organized vigorous promotional efforts taken up by immigration agents in

London. Both Laurier and Sifton encouraged settlement and farming in the sparsely populated Prairie Provinces. Although this was not John and Mabel's intention, both the Canadian and British incentives to immigrate to Canada probably persuaded the couple to travel there first before crossing the border into the United States, where John hoped to receive support and encouragement from his Evans relatives in Ohio.[7]

Geography and budget may have also played a role in John and Mabel's decision to immigrate to Canada before heading south to the United States. Information about Canadian immigration was readily available around Marylebone, where John and Mabel worked and lived. Not only did the Canadian emigration office stand near Trafalgar Square, but several steamship companies, including Cunard, White Star, Royal Mail, and the Peninsular and Oriental Steam Navigation Company, also had offices on Cockspur Street just south of Trafalgar Square. Additionally, the Grand Trunk Railway, which John planned to take west from the Port of Quebec to the U.S.-Canadian border, had an office on Warwick House Street just south of Trafalgar Square. Finally, steamship companies advertised passage through Canada as an easier, faster, and generally more desirable route into the United States. John had always intended to immigrate to the United States, but there existed multiple incentives to enter Canada first.[8]

By the middle of 1911, John and Mabel had confirmed their plan to immigrate and taken steps to implement it. As Mabel's parents had insisted, John would make the trip first; Mabel would follow once he had found a definite job and begun to settle into a community. John Evans booked passage on the *Ascania* in the least costly, least desirable third-class or steerage accommodations. John boarded the

466-foot-long, 9,111-ton *Ascania*[9] with great anticipation . . . along with concerns.

John's experience aboard the *Ascania* must have mirrored those of thousands of other emigrants who had traveled before him in unpleasant steerage accommodations. In the 1800s and even early 1900s, steerage was notorious for its deplorable conditions. Many family members would often crowd onto one bunk, packed together like "herring in a barrel." The overpoweringly repugnant smell of this accommodation often stayed with passengers long after they had disembarked. According to one steerage passenger, the distinctive odor "originated in the galley; a heavy, warm, sour odor of contaminated food. It fused with the smell of acid vomit. It gathered overtones from the exhalations of sour stomachs and of dirty sweat-drenched peasant flesh. Then it blew into our nostrils in thick pulsating blasts."[10] Steerage passengers had only minimal access to fresh ocean air on the open steerage deck and were therefore compelled to spend most of their time on the stuffy lower steerage deck.

When John crossed the Atlantic in 1911, steerage conditions had improved somewhat from previous decades. The U.S. Immigration Commission reported to Congress that both "good and deplorable [steerage] conditions may exist in immigrant quarters on the same ship." The commission found that bad steerage conditions treated immigrants like so much freight. Immigrant ships provided sleeping quarters in large compartments with 300 or more passengers, and passengers slept on iron berths two feet wide and six feet long arranged in two tiers separated by two-and-one-half feet. Each bed had a mattress and pillow filled with straw or seaweed, plus a single blanket. The only place for baggage was on each passenger's berth or the floor under the bed.[11]

The slightly more comfortable conditions that John

may have encountered replicated conditions in second-class cabins, but on a more modest scale. The beds were small, but the blankets were sufficiently warm. On a 1911 Cunard vessel traveling from Norway to America, steerage accommodations consisted of a six-by-eight-foot room with two bunk beds separated by a very narrow aisle. If all four passengers occupied the space at one time, one person would have to lie in an upper bunk to allow passage of the other occupants. Even in these less crowded conditions, passengers could only tolerate the foul air by taking frequent walks on the open steerage deck.[12]

Arriving in Canada

Regardless of the type of steerage John experienced on the *Ascania,* he must have been eager to disembark from the ship as soon as it arrived in Quebec City on October 12, 1911. John undoubtedly felt a range of emotions—excitement, uncertainty, and myriad questions—as he walked down the gangway and into the busy port. Would he find work that made use of his skills as a draper? How long might it take him to find a good job and become financially secure enough to invite Mabel to join him? Would he find a welcoming and comfortable place for Mabel and him to live? Finding a suitable job motivated John to move forward as quickly as possible.[13]

All these thoughts passed through his mind as he disembarked from the *Ascania* and absorbed the sights, sounds, and smells of a new city and country. Slowly he made his way into the port area with its tight cluster of wooden buildings. Beginning in the 1880s, the Port of Quebec began to modernize and significantly improve its facilities by building a new pier and enlarging existing ones. Dredging and deepening port channels and dredging the Saint Charles River estuary (alongside the port) followed, to accommodate larger ships carrying immigrants and to encourage trade.

The most innovative improvement project involved constructing the Princess Louise Pier and two basins separated by a lock that protected the inner Louise Basin from the huge tidal differential between high and low tides. New port facilities included an immense two-story, wood-frame immigrant hall constructed in 1888 on the Louise Pier, complete with a dining room, dormitories, currency exchange office, and new telephone and telegraph equipment. The immigrant hall served as a center for processing immigrants and accommodated as many as 4,000 immigrants at one time. Since Quebec City had been an immigrant destination for decades, this port had immigration agents with a long history and excellent knowledge of managing new arrivals.[14]

After the SS *Ascania* arrived, John joined the new arrivals being questioned and physically examined by immigration officials. As a new arrival from Great Britain, John probably went through the immigration procedures without difficulty, unlike black immigrants who experienced growing discrimination in the early 1900s. Since John planned to cross the border into the United States, entry officials asked him to complete a passenger manifest form entitled "List or Manifest of Alien Passengers Applying for Admission to the United States."

In 1894, the U.S. Immigration Service required all Canadian steamship and railroad companies to comply with these laws, which specified that all passengers destined for the United States must complete this form. Passengers submitted the form at entry points in Quebec or Montreal (during summer months) and St. John, New Brunswick, or Halifax, Nova Scotia (during the winter).[15] John noted on this form that his occupation was "clerk," his family home was "Parke, Pentre-cwrt, Llandyssul,"

South Wales, and his destination was "West Millgrove, Ohio" (about 40 miles south of Toledo, Ohio).[16]

Soon after going through immigration, John boarded a Grand Trunk Railway train in front of the enormous immigrant hall in Quebec City. Here, those bound for the west transferred easily from water to land transport. Incorporated in 1852, the British-owned Grand Trunk Railway Company of Canada completed its first stretch of track in 1852 between Montreal and Toronto, and then west to Sarnia, Ontario. In 1911, John booked passage for a main line double tracking route along the north shores of the St. Lawrence River and Lake Ontario to Toronto. He then continued west to Sarnia, Ontario, where the St. Clair River formed the Canada–United States border at Sarnia and Port Huron, Michigan.

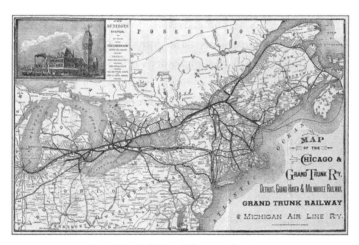

Grand Trunk Railroad Route, early 1900s.

At the international border, John continued on the Grand Trunk Railway through the 6,026-foot-long tunnel under the St. Clair River separating petroleum-rich Sarnia, Ontario, and Port Huron, Michigan. Opened to freight traffic in 1891 and passenger trains a year later, the St. Clair

River Tunnel was the first international underwater railway tunnel in North America and an engineering marvel of its day. John must have been impressed by this gateway into the United States. On October 14, 1911, he entered the United States at Port Huron.[17]

John then headed 160 miles south to West Millgrove to meet Evans family members who had immigrated to the United States several years earlier. Whatever his reason for spending additional money and time to go this far west, then south, John may have been disappointed not to find the people, employment, or circumstances that had persuaded him to travel such a great distance west. He stayed in West Millgrove only briefly before moving east.

From central Ohio, John traveled east across the state to Youngstown in northeast Ohio near the Pennsylvania border. In January 1912, the Youngstown City Directory listed John Evans as a resident there. A coal-mining community since the mid-1880s, Youngstown had attracted many Welsh immigrants from the coalfields of South East Wales. In 1912, John was living with the family of his Aunt Ella (also known as Eleanor or Ellen), the wife of Thomas Thomas, John's mother's older brother.

When John arrived in late 1911, his Uncle Thomas had already died, and his elderly aunt, Ella Thomas, lived at 518 Duquesne Street with one son, Benjamin, his wife, Hannah, and some of their younger children who had all been born in the United States between 1890 and 1903. At that time, Benjamin Thomas worked as an ironworker at the Republic Iron and Steel Company. Founded in Youngstown in 1899, Republic Iron and Steel rose to prominence in the early 1900s, eventually becoming the third-largest steel producer in America.[18]

John, anxious to affirm his intention to make the United States his home, completed a citizen declaration form in mid-January 1912. On this form, twenty-eight-year-

old John renounced "forever all allegiance and fidelity to
any prince, potentate, state, or sovereignty and particularly
George V, King of Great Britain and Ireland." This renun-
ciation probably did not trouble John, since as an independent, democratic-minded Welsh Nonconformist, he may
have felt little allegiance to the British Crown and the
royal family. John also pledged on this form that he was
neither an anarchist nor a polygamist, and that he
intended to become a permanent resident in the United
States. John reported that he stood five feet, eight inches
tall, weighed 133 pounds, and had brown hair and gray
eyes.[19]

In Youngstown, newcomer John took another step
toward making the United States his home; he applied for
employment and began working as a draper. According to
the 1912 Youngstown City Directory, John worked as a
clerk at Strouss-Hirshberg Company department store.
Founded in 1875 and located in the heart of Youngstown's
commercial district, the six-story Strouss-Hirshberg
Company store carried a wide variety of goods ranging
from shoes and gloves to clothing, food, and fabric.
Youngstown's once-booming steel industries in the late
1800s and early 1900s kept Strouss-Hirshberg Company
busy and buoyant for many years.[20]

Eager to connect with his Welsh heritage in his new
home, John soon joined the Welsh Congregational Church
in downtown Youngstown. This wood-frame, clapboard,
richly decorated, 1861 Queen Anne–style church had
become the cultural and spiritual center of Welsh life,
language, and culture in Youngstown. In the mid-1800s,
more Welsh immigrants lived in Youngstown than any
other European immigrant groups. Between 1850 and
1890, the number of Welsh immigrants in industrial
Youngstown jumped from 30,000 to over 100,000. After
1880, immigrants from central and southeastern Europe

came to Youngstown in increasing numbers, creating a city of prodigious ethnic diversity. John arrived in Youngstown just as the city's steel production accelerated; by the 1920s, the town had become the second-largest steel producer in the United States after Pittsburgh. The emerging automobile industry in the 1910s and 1920s contributed enormously to the steel boom in Youngstown and Pittsburgh.[21]

Despite the robust economic conditions and familiar Welsh cultural climate in Youngstown, John Evans's job as a clerk at Strouss-Hirshberg Company must not have been satisfying, or he may have learned of another more attractive job opportunity elsewhere. By early 1913, John had left Youngstown. Evans family folklore suggests that John accepted a job not far to the northeast in Erie, Pennsylvania, at a Sibley, Lindsay & Curr department store branch. His prospects for success there, however, apparently fell short of his expectations. His time at the Erie branch of Sibley, Lindsay & Curr was also brief.[22]

John worked hard to find the right job, one that offered solid prospects for a secure future and advancement and one that would convince Mabel's parents to let her join him in the United States. John may have expressed some disappointment in his letters to Mabel about his initial job search, yet he undoubtedly remained hopeful about finding the right job soon. Sharing their news from another country 3000 miles away and being unable to communicate and support each other spontaneously must have been difficult and discouraging at times. Mabel may have begun to wonder if their plan to immigrate to the United States and build a new life together would ever happen. Whatever doubts they had, however, they probably kept to themselves. This was a time to remain positive and hopeful, to be resilient and resolute in the face of disappointment, and to be supportive of each other's efforts to make their shared dream of beginning a life together become a reality.

Drawn to Rochester, New York

John Evans must have left the Erie store of Sibley, Lindsay & Curr for a good reason. He may have learned that satisfying work that would make use of his training as a draper might be available at the large flagship Sibley, Lindsay & Curr store in Rochester in upstate New York.

Occupied originally by the Seneca people, the earliest European settlers arrived in Rochester in the late 1700s. In the summer and late fall of 1789, an enterprising individual, Ebenezer Allan, erected a substantial timber grist mill at the base of the thundering Genesee River falls, near the future commercial center of Rochester. From its earliest days, the Genesee River waterfalls' power turned water-wheels that spawned several small industries and the birth of a town that eventually grew into a robust industrial city. Known at first as the "Young Lion of the West," by the 1830s, Rochester had harnessed even more power at the Genesee River falls for milling, doubled its population in ten years, and become America's first industrial boomtown.

Developments in transportation contributed enor-mously to its growth. Rochester's small community grew exponentially after the completion of the Erie Canal in 1825, extending 524 miles across New York State from Buffalo on Lake Erie in the west, through Rochester and onto Albany on the Hudson River in the east. On the eve of railroad developments, the canal provided an essential avenue of transportation and commerce through Rochester, across the state. Soon, a railroad was constructed across New York State, paralleling the Erie Canal. Both the canal and the railroad further stimulated industry and the enormous population growth of Rochester. In twenty years, between 1840 and 1860, Rochester's population jumped from 20,000 to 48,000.[23]

The post-Civil War period, after 1865, witnessed the birth of large manufacturing firms in Rochester, including the Eastman Kodak Company, Bausch & Lomb, and Western Union, along with the manufacturing of shoes and precision machine tools and the distillation of liquor. This robust industrial expansion contributed to Rochester's growing reputation as a city with tremendous entrepreneurial spirit. Between 1870 and 1900, Rochester's population grew from 62,386 to 162,800. The city's booming economy continued into the early 1900s when the city emerged as a center of the garment industry. Between 1905 and 1918, the construction of the new, broader, and deeper New York State Barge Canal, which could accommodate much larger boats, replaced the one-hundred-year-old Erie Canal and competed for business with the railroad crossing upstate New York.[24] When John arrived in Rochester in 1912, the city's robust growth, optimism, and dynamism were evident everywhere in its built environment.

Upper Falls of the Genesee River, Rochester, 1892.

Along Main Street and its cross streets east of the Genesee River, many substantial brick buildings dating from the 1870s rose skyward, six or more stories high. Many were granite or marble-faced commercial buildings. By the 1890s, metal-skeleton construction enabled the construction of even taller commercial buildings. Noted western New York architects Andrew Jackson Warner and his son, John Foster Warner, designed many of Rochester's commercial and government buildings, along with schools, churches, and homes, during this period of robust growth. For almost ninety years, these two men dominated the architectural scene in Rochester and other western New York cities, as well as in Toronto and Montreal. They created a cityscape of great variety that remains today and contributes to Rochester's historic character.[25]

In John's new position at Sibley, Lindsay & Curr (known as just Sibley's), he worked as a clerk in the yard goods department, where he applied his experience as a draper. Rufus Sibley, Alexander Lindsay, and John Curr—all previously employees at the Hogg, Brown & Taylor dry goods store in Boston, known as North America's first modern department store—joined to open Sibley's department store in Rochester. Both Lindsay and Curr had emigrated from Scotland, then considered the most well-developed center of textiles in the world. Alexander Lindsay, forty years older than John, had apprenticed as a draper in the mid-1800s. He later worked for a draper in Glasgow, Scotland. At that time, Scottish and English drapers were considered first-class members of their trade.[26]

The Sibley, Lindsay & Curr store in Rochester, often called "the Boston Store" after the department store where all three men previously worked, opened on March 30, 1868. This flagship store occupied a five-story building with a twenty-five-foot-wide frontage facing East Main

Street, located just a couple of blocks east of the Genesee River. The "Boston Store's" first newspaper advertisement announced its stock of "cloths, silks, dress goods, velvets, shawls, laces, embroideries, notions, trimmings, hosiery, gloves, handkerchiefs, and underclothing."[27] Between 1880 and 1890, when the American economy was growing at a breathless pace, department stores like Sibley's offered the emerging middle class an array of enticing consumer products—dry goods, trimmings, laces, china, and furniture.[28]

The growth of Rochester's Sibley, Lindsay & Curr store reflected the city's buoyant economy. By the early twentieth century, Rochester became known nationally as a bustling city of industry and commerce. At the 1893 grand opening of the elegant new twelve-story, semi-classical-style "Granite Building" of steel-frame construction (still standing at East Main Street and St. Paul Street), Sibley, Lindsay & Curr sold an incredible array and quantity of merchandise. The fashionable interior decor combined with the British background, accents, and personalities of Lindsay and his two junior partners contributed to the store's air of old-world panache. Once completed, a newspaper advertisement boasted that the Rochester Sibley's Granite Building was the "biggest department house between New York and Chicago."[29]

In early 1904, the store owners' plans to expand the Granite Building were dramatically halted. In the predawn darkness of a frigid day in late February, a city policeman noticed smoke and flames rising from the roof of a store near the Granite Building, and immediately set off loud, clanging fire alarms. Firefighters from far and wide rushed to the scene with steam pump engines on horse-drawn wagons. Despite their best efforts, the flames' intense heat and fury engulfed the entire middle of the block, where the East Main Street Sibley's building stood. The fire soon consumed Sibley's Granite Building. Decades later, residents referred to this catastrophic 1903 fire as a watershed moment in Rochester's history. Events occurred either "before the Sibley fire" or "after the Sibley fire."[30]

Amazingly, like the mythological phoenix emerging from flames and ashes of destruction, the Sibley, Lindsay & Curr department store rose from the ashes of the devastating fire. In 1904, Sibley's owners commissioned Rochester architect John Foster Warner to design a new Sibley's building. This building featured a distinctive soaring clock, which soon became a familiar landmark in downtown Rochester. In early 1905, the Sibley, Lindsay & Curr store moved into its new five-story, Chicago-style building faced with smooth, orange-brown bricks and granite trim interspersed with expansive grids of large, plate-glass windows.

In 1911, one year before John arrived in Rochester, Sibley's building received another significant addition—a six-story so-called Mercantile Building. This addition expanded the original building further to the east, to the corner of East Main and Franklin streets. This enlarged Sibley's store now contained thirteen acres of floor space and employed 2,400 people during the Christmas season of 1912. When John arrived in Rochester, the new and enlarged department store was Rochester's largest commercial building. Sibley, Lindsay & Curr had by then become a commercial and cultural institution that contributed to Rochester's early-twentieth-century aura of sublime well-being.[31]

Settling in Rochester

The expansive Sibley's building and the company's substantial history surely must have impressed John and raised his hopes that he might have a promising future there. Even though John arrived in Rochester during the waning years of active management by the original owners, Rufus Sibley and Alexander Lindsay, these men tended to hire English and Scottish store employees who continued to "give the store a British atmosphere and an air of Old World professionalism."[32] John's Welsh-English accent (evident by long, stretched vowels and a melodic cadence) undoubtedly contributed to the store's British ambiance.

John's training and decades-long experience working as a draper in Great Britain made him perfectly qualified to pursue similar work at Sibley's. Additionally, John's work ethic and commitment to courtesy, attentive service, and customer loyalty seemed perfectly aligned with Sibley, Lindsay & Curr business ethics and store culture. Lastly, as a newly arrived immigrant to the United States, John joined many other recent immigrants who had been hired by Sibley's owners. The owners and managers made an effort to give immigrants and minority groups in Rochester "a start toward the fulfillment of American life" and an opportunity to achieve a middle-class living.[33]

Soon after John arrived in Rochester, Sibley's managers offered him a job as a clerk. This invitation raised John's hopes that he might be able to advance at Sibley's, known as a Rochester institution—"a fixture in countless lives, [with] the circle of its impact on people constantly widening."[34] As John settled into his position as a clerk, he must have appreciated being with the right people, at the right place, at the right time. Sibley's seemed the perfect place for John to become fully immersed in American life.[35]

Just as Sibley's provided a perfect place for John to become acclimated to American life in Rochester, so too did a church that he discovered shortly after arriving in the city. Located just twelve blocks south of Sibley's, the red-brick South Congregational Church stood at the corner of Alexander and Pearl streets. John soon began attending this church with its monolithic, square bell

tower reaching skyward. The South Congregational
Church quickly became his spiritual home and remained
so for the rest of his life. Organized originally as a Presbyterian mission in 1885, in September 1886, eighty-nine
charter members organized the South Congregational
Church. Two years later, the membership purchased property at Alexander and Pearl Streets. In June 1889, church
members laid the cornerstone of the future imposing red-
brick edifice with round Romanesque arched windows and
entrance.[36]

Similar to the church John
had joined in Youngstown,
Rochester's South Congregational Church proved to be
another acclimating institution
—a welcoming place with practices that mirrored those of his
own Saron Congregational
Chapel near Pentre-cwrt,
Wales. John soon became
acquainted with the church
minister, the Reverend Noyes
O. Bartholomew, who
welcomed him warmly. A graduate of Washburn College in
Topeka, Kansas, Reverend

South Congregational
Church, Rochester, early
1900s.

Bartholomew had come from Wichita, Kansas, to
Rochester about one year earlier. In his early forties,
Bartholomew had recently married his second wife, Opal
Cherry Lapsley, and had young children.[37]

In October 1912, John officially moved his membership
from the Welsh Congregational Church in Youngstown to
Rochester's South Congregational Church. The Reverend
Bartholomew may have offered John a room at the
Bartholomew parsonage at 523 Meigs Street,[38] about three

blocks south of the church, until John found his own accommodation. Meigs Street was a tree-shaded residential street with closely spaced two-story wood-frame houses constructed at the turn of the twentieth century. A stone's throw west of Bartholomew's home ran a narrow section of the old Erie Canal. With John's job at Sibley's secure, welcoming associations developing at the South Congregational Church, and comfortable housing, John felt ready to invite Mabel to join him. After one and a half years apart, Mabel was eager to join John.[39]

4

MABEL AND JOHN REUNITE
1913

Despite John's favorable situation in Rochester, troubling events both in Wales and Rochester caused him great concern in the winter and spring of 1913. In early January, John received news from home that his oldest brother, David—who had guided him in his training as a draper—had died of heart failure at his home on Llantwit Street in Cardiff. He was just forty-five. David left his wife, Elizabeth, and a brother-in-law, John Williams, and a niece-in-law, Ardydfil Mona Williams. John must have felt tremendous shock and grief to learn of his brother's death. Now, two of his siblings and his father had died within the last decade. John must have mourned his inability to be with his family at this sad time.[1]

Another troubling event unfolded just two months after John's brother, David, died and six weeks before Mabel's scheduled arrival in May 1913. In late March, a violent storm system swept across the upper Midwest, then moved menacingly eastward over the eastern Great Lakes region. The storm unleashed its full fury in tornadoes and torrential rain as it moved across upstate New York. Numerous rivers overflowed their banks and set new records for high water and discharge rates. When six feet of water flowed over the Genesee River banks, a large section of downtown Rochester flooded. Contemporary photos captured the raging Genesee River lapping the underside of Genesee River bridges and, in some cases, cascading over them onto downtown city streets.

The Genesee River's gushing waters completely submerged the old Erie Canal aqueduct (at the present Broad Street Bridge), not far from Sibley's department store on East Main Street. The Rochester *Democrat and Chronicle* newspaper exclaimed that the "Heart of the City [was] threatened by record floods" as a "tremendous onrush of the river [flowed] through [the] center of the Flower City . . . breaking all records for high water— exceeding in volume even the famous flood of '65."[2] On March 29, the newspaper reported,

> Building after building is being vacated as the river moves on. Hundreds of people are out of work temporarily, owing to the necessity of building fires in some business houses, which . . . were without heat, power, and light. . . . Most of the downtown business houses made arrangements last night [March 28] to remove perishable goods to places of safety.[3]

Some businesses—especially along Front and Graves streets paralleling the Genesee River's west bank—were closed for days. Many people living close to the river became trapped on the upper floors of their homes. John indeed must have worried about Rochester's condition when Mabel was due to arrive in six weeks.[4]

Crossing the Atlantic on the RMS *Virginian*

In early May 1913, a few weeks before the devastating

March storm swept over upstate New York, Mabel, her twenty-eight-year-old nurse sister, Ethel, and her fifty-five-year-old dressmaker Aunt Jennie, booked passage on a ship to Canada. Probably sometime in 1912 or early 1913, John rented a small apartment at 85 Charlotte Street, a residential street lined with closely spaced two-story, wood-frame, and brick houses standing on long, narrow lots not far from the Sibley, Lindsay & Curr store. East of the store stood the original University of Rochester campus (before its relocation in 1927 to the River Campus on the Genesee River). John's apartment was ideally situated within walking distance of both Sibley's and the South Congregational Church.[5]

Ethel, 1912 (courtesy Nick Hards).

On May 9, 1913, a little more than a month after downtown Rochester flooded, twenty-four-year-old Mabel, her sister Ethel, and Aunt Jennie boarded a train in London bound for Liverpool. After eating lunch along the way, they arrived at Liverpool's Lime Street Station in the late afternoon. The three Harvey women made their way to the River Mersey, where city docks stretched for miles along the river. Here, they boarded a 538-foot-long, 6,826-ton Allan Line steamship. The *Virginian* passenger list recorded the three women's boarding and occupations: "Miss M. I. Harvey, clerk," "Miss E. M. Harvey, nurse," and "Miss J. Harvey, dressmaker." The passenger list also gave the three women's destinations. Mabel and Ethel reported that their travels would end in the United States; Jennie gave her destination as Canada.

All three women planned to disembark at Montreal, Quebec, on the St. Lawrence River.[6]

As dusk slowly darkened Liverpool's evening sky, the *Virginian* carefully maneuvered into the River Mersey's main channel and steamed northward toward the Irish Sea. From the *Virginian* deck, Mabel, Ethel, and Aunt Jennie probably gazed back at Liverpool's Pier Head, where dozens of freight and passenger ships were moored along the River Mersey's east bank. Two new, monolithic buildings standing on the Pier Head dominated the skyline behind the docks. The ornately decorated, Edwardian Baroque-style Mersey Docks, and the Harbour Board Offices Building (later renamed the Port of Liverpool Building) topped with a large central dome, had been constructed between 1904 and 1907. A few hundred yards to the north stood the Royal Liver Building, completed in 1911. Mounted on top of two clock towers projecting 155 feet into the sky were mythical 18-foot-tall liver birds, one watching over the city and the other over the river and sea. According to an ancient local legend, if they mated and flew away, Liverpool would cease to exist. These two buildings and a third one completed in 1917—the Cunard Building—stood at the waterfront as bold physical manifestations of the international prestige Liverpool had achieved in the early 1900s as a great port city. Every day, cargo from British colonies around the world and migrants from Europe and Africa arrived at Liverpool's docks.

Mabel could hardly have imagined that twenty years later, in 1933, one of her sons, John Harvey Evans, would look up at the Pier Head, just as she was doing in 1913, as he eagerly approached Liverpool on a ship from the United States. More than once, Harvey would spot the *Virginian* docked at the edge of the River Mersey and be reminded of his mother's immigration to the United States in 1913.

The steel-hulled *Virginian* featured three decks and accommodation for over 1,700 passengers. Mabel, Ethel, and Jennie were among the 286 passengers traveling in the spacious and well-appointed second-class. A thousand *Virginian* passengers made the voyage in steerage class, just as John had traveled from Southampton, England, to Canada in October 1911. Although second-class passengers did not have access to all parts of the ship, a 1910 *Virginian* travel brochure noted that "staterooms in the second-class cabin are irreproachably clean and are equipped with everything needed for comfort; there are electric lights, electric bells, ample facilities for washing, and the stewards are attentive."[7]

The Allan Line, inaugurated in the 1820s, was the first and oldest Atlantic steamship company offering service between England and Canada. A red triangular pennant atop vertical bands of red, white, and blue identified all Allan Line ships. Launched in late 1904, the *Virginian* and its sister ship, the RMS *Victorian*, boasted the first twin-screw steam turbines for passenger liners. These steam turbines propelled the *Virginian* at a speed of 18 knots, created an economy of space, had diminished vibration, utilized every pound of steam power available from the boilers, and reduced the chance of breakdowns. The general comfort and short trans-Atlantic route and travel time of the *Virginian* bound for Canada combined to make Allan Line's "Canadian Ferry one of the most popular Atlantic lines."[8]

Despite the generous size, modern engineering features, and comfort of the *Virginian,* voyages across the Atlantic Ocean and the St. Lawrence River were not without peril. Just a year earlier, on April 15, 1912, the *Virginian* gained notoriety by becoming one of the first to learn about one of the most tragic ship disasters in maritime history. On April 10, the British White Star

Line's RMS *Titanic* lifted its anchor at Southampton and moved slowly south into the Southampton Water tidal estuary and out into The Solent. On its maiden voyage to New York City, the *Titanic*, with its luxurious first-class accommodations and some of North America and Britain's wealthiest citizens, captured the world's attention.

No one could have imagined the events that would unfold five days later, on April 15. About 375 miles south of Newfoundland and 1,200 miles east of New York City, one of the ship's lookout crew suddenly began frantically ringing a bell signaling that a colossal object lay directly ahead in the path of the vessel. Around 11:40 p.m. ship's time, the *Titanic* swerved to avoid hitting an iceberg. Still, a submerged portion of the berg gouged the *Titanic*'s hull plates on the starboard (right) side, causing them to buckle and open five of the sixteen watertight compartments to the engulfing sea. Only four water-tight compartments on the *Titanic* could flood before it sank.

The *Titanic*'s crew sent flares aloft to attract any ships in the area but to no avail. As the grim reality of the *Titanic*'s condition aroused great panic, the crew and male passengers rushed women, children, and some crew members into the twenty available lifeboats and lowered them onto the water below, even as the ship's structure became increasingly compromised. In a heroic effort to maintain calm on board, a band of eight musicians sat on the frigid deck and played uplifting music to boost passengers' morale, who, panic-stricken, dashed across the deck in confusion. At about 2:20 a.m. on April 15, the RMS *Titanic* broke in two and slowly sank with over 1,000 people still on board.

The *Virginian* had been among the first to pick up and respond to a Marconi wireless message emitting from Cape Race at the southern tip of Newfoundland. The *Titanic*'s senior wireless operator, Jack Phillips, sent the message around 12:40 a.m.; he reported that the ship had struck an iceberg, was in distress, and needed immediate assistance. John Taylor Gambell, the fifty-four-year-old captain of the *Virginian*, located about 178 miles north of the *Titanic,* altered his course and accelerated to full-steam speed. Gambell immediately notified the *Titanic's* captain that the *Virginian* should reach the distressed ship by about 10:00 a.m. that morning.

As the *Virginian* continued to race to the scene, Captain Gambell swung his lifeboats out from the ship into a position ready to be lowered into the chilly water below. Despite Gambell's efforts to assist with the *Titanic's* rescue, the *Carpathia* arrived on the scene first and rescued over 700 terrified passengers from drifting *Titanic* lifeboats, just two hours after the *Titanic* went down.

Roughly 1,500 *Titanic* passengers, mostly men, went down with the ship. Among them were Captain Edward Smith and two-thirds of the crew. Additionally, several wealthy and well-known passengers lost their lives, including John Jacob Astor IV, Benjamin Guggenheim, White Star Line managing director Alfred Vanderbilt, Grand Trunk Railway president Charles Melville Hays, Major Archibald Butt, military aide to President Taft, co-founder of Macy's department store Isidor Straus, and his wife Ida.[9]

In disbelief, John Evans poured over the front page of the April 15 *Youngstown Vindicator* newspaper and slowly read the horrifying news of the *Titanic*. Thirteen months later, Mabel, Ethel, Jennie, and the many other May 1913 *Virginian* passengers heading across the Atlantic Ocean must have silently recalled the critical role that their vessel had played in the effort to rescue passengers on the doomed *Titanic*.[10]

The *Virginian's* attractive décor and enticing menu may have helped distract Mabel, Ethel, and Jennie and other

passengers from recalling the *Titanic* disaster. After leaving
Liverpool, the *Virginian* steamed across the Irish Sea,
before making its first stop in Londonderry. On the way,
the dining crew offered Mabel, Ethel, and Jennie late afternoon tea, which consisted of hot grilled Yarmouth bloaters
(smoked herring), Welsh rarebit, ragout of venison, broiled
Cambridge sausage, mashed potatoes, and "an assortment
of cold selections." From Londonderry, the voyage across
the open Atlantic to the Gulf of St. Lawrence was only
1,650 miles traversed in five days.[11]

Five days later, on May 15, the *Virginian* arrived at the
Port of Montreal on the north shore of the St. Lawrence
River, around 1000 miles inland from the Atlantic Ocean.
Strangely, none of the Harvey women are on the passenger
list of those arriving in Montreal. Only by closely
inspecting the handwritten ship purser's list of passengers
can the very faint names of Mabel and Ethel Harvey,
destined for Rochester, be discerned. Although Jennie
Harvey's name is absent from the passenger list, her name
might be so faint that it could not be deciphered. Despite
remaining uncertainties about Jennie's entrance into the
United States, a 1942 letter from Betty Harvey, a niece of
Ethel Harvey, to John Harvey Evans notes Jennie's remem-
brance of her visit to both Canada and the United States
in 1913 (even though her "Country of Intended Future
Residence" form listed "Canada" and not the "United
States").[12]

The travel method and the exact route traveled by
Mabel and Ethel from Montreal to Rochester, New York,
can only be speculated since the trip was not recorded.
The Harvey women probably boarded the Grand Trunk
Railway in Montreal, not far from the old Port of Montreal, and crossed over the St. Lawrence River upstream
from the city. They then probably continued about 85
miles southwest to the United States border, several miles

north of Malone, New York.[13] Eager to see Mabel after a year and eight months of separation, John may have met the women in Malone, 250 miles east of Rochester.

It is more likely, however, that the Harvey women took the Mohawk and Malone Railroad south into the Adirondack Mountains. Leased from the New York Central Railroad since 1893, the Mohawk and Malone Railroad offered passenger and freight service between Montreal, Malone, and many small tourist destinations in the forested, newly created Adirondack State Park. Established in 1892 to help maintain the flow of abundant water from the Adirondacks into the Erie Canal and Hudson River and to conserve the timber and wildlife threatened by logging, the 6 million-acre Adirondack State Park was one of the first public parks in the United States. The Harvey women must have been awed by the splendid mountain scenery they saw as the train passed through conifer forests dominated by balsam fir and red spruce, along with scattered stretches of white pine and paper birch.[14] "No pleasanter trip than that from Malone to Saranac or Tupper Lake can be imagined," boasted the June 22, 1892 issue of *Malone Gazette*.[15]

John and Mabel Begin a New Life and Family

On May 18, John warmly welcomed Mabel, Ethel, and perhaps Jennie to Rochester. After such a long separation, John and Mabel must have felt tremendous anticipation and excitement as they greeted each other. They undoubtedly had written frequent letters while separated (none of which have survived) and had ample time to express their great affection for each other during their time apart. However, the time had finally arrived to act on their deep love and commitment to become husband and wife.

On May 19, 1913, one day after Mabel arrived in

Rochester, Reverend Noyes Bartholomew united thirty-year-old John Evans and twenty-four-year-old Mabel Ida Harvey in marriage at the South Congregational Church parsonage at 523 Meigs Street. Ethel Harvey and N.O. Bartholomew served as witnesses. A short announcement of the event appeared in the local newspaper.[16]

> Miss Mabel Harvey of Hockley, Essex, England, and Mr. John Evans [...] of this city were married at the parsonage of the South Congregational Church on Monday afternoon [May 19] at 3 o'clock. Rev. Noyes O. Bartholomew officiating. After the ceremony, Mr. and Mrs. Evans left for a journey to Toledo and other Western cities.[17]

John and Mabel likely traveled to the Toledo area, perhaps to West Millgrove just 32 miles south of Toledo, to visit John's relatives that he'd stopped to see after arriving in the United States in the fall of 1911. The newlyweds may have also visited John's Aunt Ella Thomas and her son and grandchildren in Youngstown.

Mabel and John (left to right), ca. 1913.

Their honeymoon rendezvous must have seemed far too brief before John had to return to his job at Sibley, Lindsay & Curr. Sometime after their return to Rochester, John and Mabel rented and moved to an apartment on Goebel Place, a narrow street with closely spaced, two-story, wood-frame houses near the Bartholomews' home on Meigs Street. Mabel and Ethel immediately began creating a home at 28 Goebel Place. The South Congregational Church stood ten blocks away from

Goebel Place. The Sibley, Lindsay & Curr department store was twenty blocks north.[18]

Little is known about Mabel's and John's first year together in Rochester. Undoubtedly, John kept busy with his job at Sibley's and helping Mabel settle into their home. John and Mabel soon created close friendships with several South Congregational Church members. Auley and Egbert Cain immediately became welcoming loyal friends. They and their two children, Howard, born in 1905, and Doris, born in 1911, lived at 50 Mulberry Street, a few blocks south of the Evans's apartment. The Cain and Evans families soon began going on short outings and longer vacations together. Both the Cains and the Bartholomews became anchors and kind and generous friends to newly arrived immigrants John and Mabel.[19]

Slightly less than a year after Mabel arrived in Rochester, on May 1, 1914, she gave birth to a boy, John Harvey Evans, at 28 Goebel Place. Dr. Roland C. Harris attended to the delivery, and Ethel Harvey, a trained nurse, reportedly assisted. John Harvey's name was a creative merging of both the Evans and Harvey family names and suggested something about the thoughtful sharing that Mabel and John practiced in their marriage. Their first son's name also indicated both John's and Mabel's desire to transplant some of their Welsh and English heritage to their new home in America.[20]

John Harvey Evans (known as "Harvey") arrived on a sunny day in Rochester with slightly higher than average temperatures hovering around 58 degrees Fahrenheit. Light variable winds blew from the southwest.[21] On that day, Rochester suffragists joined those in sixty other New York towns and cities in their Suffrage Day celebration. Rochester's new eleven-story Seneca Hotel, opened six years earlier on Clinton Avenue just one-half block south of the Sibley, Lindsay & Curr department store, featured a fundraising dance for suffrage under yellow banners proclaiming "Votes for Women."

Meanwhile, fashionably dressed men and women strolled along Rochester's main downtown streets, perhaps wearing the popular lightweight, loose-fitting, tweed balmacaan coats with angular raglan sleeves, which were then in fashion and on sale at Sibley's. Like many men, John still wore high, stiff detachable collars, popular during the Edwardian era from the late 1890s to around 1914. Women wore long Paris gloves and cotton lisle (a strong fine cotton thread originally made in Lisle, France) or silk hose in black, white, or tan.[22]

Soon after Harvey's birth, the Evans family moved from Goebel Place to one floor in a two-story, wood-frame house at 515 Meigs Street. Their house stood just two houses from the home of Reverend Noyes Bartholomew. Two of the Bartholomews' children, young Noyes (or Lloyd) and Clara, were slightly older than Harvey, but eventually became playmates. The Evanses' house featured a porch across the house façade. Five steps led up to the door into the first-floor apartment from the end of a narrow path from the sidewalk. Behind the house was a small fenced yard. In their new home on Meigs Street, John and Mabel were closer to the South Congregational Church and Sibley's department store. For the next several years, 515 Meigs Street was the Evans family home.[23]

Harvey and Mabel, 515 Meigs Street, ca. 1915.

Soon after John and Mabel married, these two immigrants began realizing their dream of beginning a new life in North America unencumbered by parental expectations, employment challenges, and class distinctions. They had settled into a modest first-floor apartment on Meigs Street in a lively, bustling, prosperous city. They had begun to develop a network of supportive friends in their neighborhood and at the South Congregational Church, and had become familiar with the streets and shops that supported their new life. While Mabel kept busy caring for tiny Harvey, John worked hard at his job as a clerk in the fabric department at Sibley, Lindsay & Curr, keeping shelves stocked, floors swept and customers treated with the utmost personal attention. Although John's clerk's salary was undoubtedly modest, his position allowed him to establish rapport and lasting relationships with regular customers, gaining their trust, loyalty, and confidence in his ability to satisfy their shopping needs. John had high hopes of advancing his position in Sibley's textile department.[24]

Mabel and John must have felt enormously pleased with what they had been able to accomplish together in their first short years in America, especially their success in sowing the seeds of a new family with the birth of their first son. The name "John Harvey" served as a meaningful link to John's and Mabel's families in Wales and England. It also embodied Mabel and John's fervent hope of carrying some of their family histories forward into their new lives in their adopted country—the United States.

5

TROUBLED TIMES

1914–1920

The young Evans family soon settled into a comfortable life at 515 Meigs Street in Rochester. John was adapting to his job, and he and Mabel began to develop friendships with their neighbors and parishioners at the South Congregational Church. Troubling events on the other side of the Atlantic Ocean, however, soon engulfed them.

Less than a year after Mabel and John's joyful reunion and marriage in Rochester, unfolding global events consumed their families in England and Wales and began impacting the Evans family as well. In June 1914, one month after Mabel gave birth to John Harvey Evans, a single act of terrorism—the assassination of Franz Ferdinand, Archduke of Austria-Este—set into motion distressing events in Europe. On August 4, 1914, Great Britain became embroiled in a rapidly developing European conflict. Soon, two entangling military alliances —the Triple Entente (the Russian Empire, the French Third Republic, and the United Kingdom) and the Triple Alliance (including Germany, Austria-Hungary, and Italy, at first)—faced off against each other in what became known as the Great War.

Although the United States remained mostly uninvolved in Europe's escalating turbulence, Mabel and John became fully connected to events in England when they communicated with family members caught up in escalating military preparedness. Eventually, Mabel and John, and all those in the United States, were confronted with a plethora of domestic restrictions. Additionally, the real possibility that thirty-four-year-old John might be required to enlist in the U.S. military deeply troubled the couple. Just as the Evans family strived to plant their feet firmly on the ground of their new home, dark clouds of war threatened to unsettle everything they had achieved and desired for their future in America.[1]

Dark Clouds of War

The outbreak of war in Europe in the summer of 1914 seemed distant to most Rochester residents. The assassination of Franz Ferdinand appeared to be far removed from their lives in Rochester. Many people, especially in rural, small-town America, wanted to remain isolated.

The United States pushed back from engagement in the European war, despite the vast numbers of newly arrived immigrants in America. Hundreds of thousands of recent immigrants in North America, like John and Mabel Evans, had come from countries in Europe that became engulfed in the war. Some foreign-born British, French, and Belgian immigrants in Rochester left to fight as reservists in their native countries. Others, who had immigrated from Germany, Austria-Hungary, or Italy—now part of the Central Powers alliance—decided to fight for the United States instead of their native country.[2]

The rising cost of certain household goods—flour and

sugar—and the growing scarcity of other items (dried fruit, calfskin for shoes, linen, dolls, luxuries of all kinds) were frequent reminders to Rochester residents of the overseas conflict. For Mabel and John, Europe's war seemed much closer and more real than it did for most Rochester residents. The shortage of food throughout Great Britain was one of Mabel's many concerns about the Harvey family. When Great Britain entered the war in early August 1914, the country was only 40 percent food self-sufficient. Britain imported 60 percent of its food from other countries, including Germany and Austria-Hungary.[3]

In 1916, severe weather across England resulted in a poor harvest, making the food shortage even more dire for most British families, including the Harvey family. In 1917, the newly elected British Prime Minister, David Lloyd George, a native Welshman, introduced the Corn Production Act, which guaranteed minimum prices for oats and wheat. This act proved problematic, however, since a third of male farmworkers and many farm workhorses were serving in the war. The British Army had enlisted around 170,000 male farm laborers and taken possession of 500,000 farm workhorses to transport supplies and munitions and provide transport for lancer regiments.

To address food shortages, women organized the Women's Land Army (providing 98,000 new farm workers), which eventually helped reduce agricultural deficits. This women's army somewhat relieved the reliance on workhorses and encouraged the shift to new steam engines and mechanized farm machinery. Stephen and Martha Harvey at Kingsmans Farm experienced conflicting demands to produce food in abundance and encourage some of their children to participate in the war.[4]

Living so far from her family and receiving only sporadic information about its welfare undoubtedly caused Mabel great angst. Most worrying was the enlistment of men who, by birth or marriage, were part of the Harvey family. Ethel Millicent Harvey, who had accompanied Mabel to the United States in 1913, married Maurice Olden Langridge on March 15, 1915. Maurice Langridge had joined the army only seven months before his marriage to Ethel.[5]

Born in 1889, the son of a metal merchant, Maurice apprenticed for two years, beginning in 1908, as a motor engineer in London before working as a motor repairman (1910–1912), then a motor insurance official from 1912 to 1914. Ethel probably met Maurice sometime in 1914, possibly in London, soon after returning to England from the United States. Both Ethel and Maurice worked in London in 1914—Ethel as a nurse at St. Marylebone Infirmary in North Kensington and Maurice as a motor assurance agent in Islington. At the time of their marriage at the St. Marylebone Parish Church in March 1915, both Ethel and Maurice lived at 40 Deancheap Street, St. Marylebone.[6]

Maurice volunteered to enlist in the army on September 3, 1914 and enlisted as a Royal Fusilier, a line infantry regiment raised in 1674. By February 1915, he had moved as a private to the Motor Transport division of the Army Service Corps (ASC), was stationed in London, and worked as a motor driver and engineer. The ASC (sometimes considered the unsung heroes of the Great War) used horses, railroads, waterways, and motor vehicles to transport food, equipment, and ammunition to British regiments. Although horses provided most of the transport for the ASC at that time, motorized vehicles played an increasingly important strategic role in enabling the British Army to move supplies effectively over rugged terrain. At its peak, the Army Service Corps had 10,546 officers and 315,334 soldiers.[7]

Maurice Langridge.

Early in his service, Maurice applied for training as an officer cadet.[8] Ethel continued working in London while Maurice trained not far away. In June 1917, she gave birth to her first child, Raymond Harvey Langridge, in London, just one year after Mabel had given birth to her second child, Evan Reginald Evans, in Rochester.[9]

Mabel's youngest brother, twenty-year-old Reginald John Harvey, also volunteered to serve in the British Army. On November 3, 1915, on the eve of mandatory British conscription in January 1916, Private Harvey swore allegiance to "George V, King of the United Kingdom and the British Dominions and Emperor of India, against all enemies for the duration of the war." His December 1915 medical history reported that this "ploughman and horseman" working on Kingsmans Farm in Hockley, Essex, was five feet seven and a half inches tall, weighed 136 pounds, had blue eyes and dark hair, had a fully expanded chest of 38 inches, and was in "fit" condition. Reginald's attestation reported that he wished to serve in the 17th Lancers—lightly armed and armored troops on horseback, primarily responsible   for   reconnaissance,   raids,   and communications.

In late March 1915, 17th Lancer Private Reginald Harvey was posted at Waterford's cavalry barracks on Ireland's southeastern coast. A year later, Reginald moved from the 17th Lancers to the Eighth Cavalry Reserve Regiment. Reserve cavalry regiments trained men to serve in units that went to the front lines of combat. In late March 1916, Reginald moved to the British army base in Ireland: Curragh Camp, County Kildare, near Dublin.[10]

Reginald Harvey, Fifth Lancers, ca. 1917.

On April 24, 1916, Easter Monday, just one month after Reginald arrived in County Kildare, shock swept through Curragh Camp with news of an Irish insurrection in Dublin. About 1,200 armed Irish republicans staged a rebellion to end British rule in Ireland. Sixteen hundred men, including Reginald Harvey's Eighth Cavalry Reserve Regiment, arrived in Dublin from Curragh on the evening of Easter Monday to try and quell what became known as the Easter Uprising. Over the next few days, thousands of British reinforcements, along with artillery and a gunboat, arrived in the midst of fierce street fighting in Dublin. When, on April 29, the Irish rebels finally surrendered, 485 people lay dead.[11] When Mabel learned about Reginald's involvement in the Irish Uprising, she must have been greatly worried about her younger brother.[12]

Reginald Harvey continued training with the Eighth Cavalry Reserve Regiment at Curragh Camp for the next several months. He then gained admittance to a cadet unit at Curragh and began training to become a commissioned officer. Six months later, in late January 1917, Private Harvey received a temporary commission as a second lieutenant. Maurice Langridge, after several months in cadet training in 1917, advanced to the rank of sergeant. Then, in early 1918, he also received a promotion to "temporary" second lieutenant.[13]

John's family in Wales experienced the Great War very differently. All of John's siblings were several years older than Mabel's. One brother, David, had even died before the war began. Another brother, Ben, aged forty-five in 1914, was four years past the mandatory conscription range of eighteen to forty-one. Two other siblings of John's were women (Hannah and Esther) and could not serve in the military. Tom Evans, John's closest sibling, was thirty-four years old in 1914, and not among the first group of men called to serve. In late 1915 or early 1916, Tom took a medical examination, which revealed that he was flat-footed; this condition prevented him from walking long distances over rough terrain.[14] Tom, therefore, became ineligible for military service.[15]

Even though immediate Evans family members did not participate in the military, the war profoundly affected the broader Welsh economy, culture, politics, and people. Coal production in Wales, a quintessentially critical resource in the Industrial Revolution and the engine driving the Welsh economy for more than a century, peaked in 1913 when Wales became the largest coal exporter globally. The country's high coal production continued through the Great War, only to experience a momentous collapse in the early 1920s. Thousands of migrants who had flocked to Wales during the mining boom fled from the South Wales industrial valleys to London and the West Midlands of England, causing a transformative depression and massive dislocation of the Welsh people and economy at the end of the Great War. A quarter-century of faltering heavy industry followed.[16]

Additionally, the full engagement of the United Kingdom in fighting the Central Powers blurred English and Welsh national identities. This created among Welsh people a "society anxious over its prospects, and uncertain about which of its national characteristics (language, religiosity, and social cohesion) would be sufficiently resilient to retain validity in a world in flux."[17]

These and other grave uncertainties created fertile ground for the upsurge of socialism across Wales. Radical Welsh patriots ardently advocated reducing the wealth disparity between social classes and argued vehemently for economic policies that fostered an equal distribution of wealth. By 1922 half of the Welsh ministers in Parliament were socialists, who strongly advocated equality among all classes. The unsettling impacts of the war on the Welsh people and economy undoubtedly became known to John in Rochester, through his brother Tom.

War in Europe Extends to America

As news of the war in Europe reached John and Mabel, they did their best to digest unfolding events, accept their outcomes, and accommodate as best they could to wartime conditions in Rochester. Amidst great uncertainty, John and Mabel attempted to create an atmosphere of normalcy at home, at work, and in the South Congregational Church. At Sibley, Lindsay, & Curr, John continued to perform his duties as a clerk in the textile department. He kept shelves fully stocked, swept floors, gave his undivided attention to regular clientele, and developed trust and rapport with new customers. At the South Congregational Church, John continued to sing in the choir. He became even more engaged in other church functions.

John became a church deacon—a lay official who welcomed visitors and visited the sick and elderly. As a deacon, he also shared in the ministry and sometimes the governance of the congregation. John also served on the South Congregational Church Committee and helped the minister develop the church's spiritual life and fellowship.[18]

Mabel continued to care for her young son, Harvey, at 515 Meigs Street. Additionally, she learned about substitute foods and products in Rochester that could help reduce shortages and higher prices created by the war.

In the fall of 1915, when Mabel learned that she was pregnant with her second child, the war in Europe and her family's welfare became a constant distraction, particularly at the end of her pregnancy. On July 1, 1916, the British Army suffered the worst single-day death toll in its history, on the first day of the Battle of the Somme in northern France, when the Germans killed 18,800 British soldiers.

Two weeks later, on July 16, 1916, Evan Reginald Evans was born at 515 Meigs Street. The middle name that Mabel chose for her second son had a special significance. His name (Evan Reginald) combined the first names of Evans and Harvey family members. Just three months earlier, Reginald John Harvey, her youngest brother, had been very near the unexpected violence and killing that took place during Dublin's Easter Uprising.[19]

Evan (seated) and Harvey, ca. 1916.

As the Great War's intense fighting escalated in Europe, the United States hesitantly inched away from its adherence to neutrality. Germany's relentless attacks on United States passenger and merchant ships weakened the American people's and President Woodrow Wilson's resolve to remain neutral. On May 7, 1915, a German U-boat sank the RMS *Lusitania,* a British ocean liner traveling from New York to Liverpool, killing 124 Americans. The act enraged President Woodrow Wilson and the American public and hastened the U.S. entrance into the Great War.

In March 1916, Germany sank an unarmed French passenger steamer, the SS *Sussex,* in the English Channel, resulting in eighty casualties and two wounded Americans.

Wilson seriously considered breaking diplomatic relations with Germany once again. When Germany resumed its unrestricted submarine warfare policy in early 1917, President Wilson ended diplomatic ties with the country. A few days later, Congress passed a $250-million arms appropriation bill intended to prepare the United States for war against the Triple Alliance: Germany, Austria-Hungary, the Ottoman Empire, and Bulgaria.[20]

While the United States turned its back on the world, xenophobia heightened across the country. In February 1917, Congress passed the Asiatic Barred Act, a law that restricted the immigration of "undesirables," including "idiots, imbeciles, epileptics, alcoholics, poor, criminals, beggars, any person suffering attacks of insanity, those with tuberculosis, and those with dangerous contagious diseases . . . polygamists, and anarchists . . ." This act applied to all countries adjacent to Asia, south and west of a certain latitude and longitude, including China, British India, Afghanistan, Saudi Arabia, Burma, Siam (Thailand), the Malay States, the Dutch East Indies, and part of the Russian Empire.

This sweeping, all-inclusive immigration legislation starkly revealed the heightened fear that Americans harbored for foreign-born residents and newcomers during the Great War. If John met a Welsh-speaking person on the street or in Sibley's at the time, he probably hesitated to exchange a greeting in Welsh.[21]

John and Mabel responded to these developments with mixed feelings; they wished they could learn more about their families' well-being and support them. They also hoped that the United States would not become involved in this horrific war. As German submarines continued to torpedo U.S. ships, businesspeople and elected government officials in Rochester joined the growing national clamor for the United States to enter the war. Many began advocating for a system of compulsory universal military service. Only twenty-three of 273 Rochester Chamber of Commerce members voted against a draft. The Rochester Chamber of Commerce further attempted to persuade their industry members to encourage workers to enlist and, then, to pay enlisted workers a salary while they served.[22]

By early 1917, multiple acts of German aggression swayed national public opinion to support U.S. entry in the Great War. On April 2, 1917, President Woodrow Wilson went before a joint session of Congress and requested a declaration of war against Germany. "The world must be made safe for democracy," Wilson pronounced. On April 4, the Senate voted to support a declaration of war; two days later, the House of Representatives followed suit. American's decision to enter the Great War brought the country's isolationist policy to an abrupt end.[23]

The distant war in Europe had now arrived in Rochester. American flags flew patriotically from nearly all public buildings as well as homes and businesses. On April 3, the usual matinée at the grand 1907 Romanesque-style Temple Theatre broke for "a brief period of patriotism," when the orchestra played the Star-Spangled Banner. Rochester made preparations for drafting men before Congress passed a selective service act.[24]

President Wilson's war declaration did not immediately supply the Allies with much-needed troops. After the United States entered the war, only about 100,000 American men voluntarily enlisted. President Wilson immediately instituted conscription. On May 18, 1917, Congress passed the Selective Draft Act authorizing the federal government to raise a national army for men's compulsory enlistmentto fight the Central Powers. June 5 was declared National Draft Registration Day. Nearly 27,800 young

Rochester men between the ages of twenty-one and thirty-one registered to serve. Eventually, 50 percent of Rochester men volunteered. The first American troops arrived in France in late June 1917.[25]

In 1917, John Evans was thirty-four and, therefore, exempt from the initial compulsory draft. He decided, however, to make his loyalty abundantly clear. He wasted no time applying for U.S. citizenship at the end of the required five-year waiting period, after he had declared his intention to become a citizen in Youngstown, Ohio, in 1912. In August 1917, John petitioned for citizenship; Reverend Noyes Bartholomew and Judge D. C. Hebbard served as John's witnesses. In November, John was granted citizenship. Mabel's marriage to John automatically entitled her to citizenship as well.[26]

Around this time, Rochester's American Red Cross began to play a significant role in supporting American and British troops. First launched in 1881, Rochester organized the nation's second Red Cross chapter in the country in 1906. Rochester's American Red Cross made a significant contribution to supporting military men at home and abroad. The Red Cross also raised funds and organized a U.S. army base hospital to provide soldiers with surgical dressings and garments. It collected fruit stones and shells to use for gas masks. The Red Cross organized a volunteer nursing service during the emerging influenza crisis. By April 1917, 5000 women actively worked for the American Red Cross, making surgical dressings and knitted garments for American and other Allied service members.[27]

Mabel Evans, known for her proficient sewing, knitting, crocheting, and darning, very likely supported both American and British soldiers by contributing her handiwork to the American Red Cross. She also adapted to the expanded food restrictions and shortages by cooking meatless, wheatless, eggless, butterless, and sugarless meals. Mabel probably stood with other women in long lines outside Sibley's, patiently waiting to purchase expensive, much-coveted, one-pound bags of sugar. She would also have routinely clipped recipes for sugarless dishes published in local newspapers and magazines. All the while, she cared for her two infant sons at home—Harvey, age three, and Evan, age one.[28]

Despite the hardships created by multiple shortages in Rochester, the city enjoyed a period of economic prosperity during the Great War. Eastman Kodak Company and Bausch & Lomb sent Britain valuable optical glass for use in aerial cameras. Other Rochester industries supplied Great Britain with dried fruit and nut stones for gas masks, telephone and radio equipment, and munitions. Roughly ninety Rochester industries produced munitions, clothing, food, and equipment for army camps and navy ships.[29]

The 1918 Spanish Flu Pandemic

Meanwhile, on battlefields on both the Western and Eastern Fronts, Allied forces from Great Britain, France, Italy, Russia, and Japan suffered horrific losses throughout 1917 and again from mid-March through July 1918, during a series of strategic German offensives in France. By the end of May 1918, Allied reinforcements, including Americans, poured onto the Western Front just as the German army approached Paris. By late May, 650,000 American troops were already in France, with an additional 10,000 men arriving each day.

In early 1918, Reginald Harvey, having completed his training in the First Reserve Regiment of Lancers at Camp Curragh, joined the Fifth Lancers. This regiment had fearlessly fought for over three centuries in many significant battles in India, Egypt, and South Africa. It had already distinguished itself on the Western Front in the Great War at Mons, Le Cateau, Marne, Aisne, Ypres, Bellewaarde, Arras, Scarpe, Cambrai, and the Somme.

On May 17, 1918, Reginald Harvey arrived in France with a contingent of Fifth Lancers. Here, he began additional intensive training in the village of Tubersent on the northern coast of France. Tubersent was only 4.7 miles east of Estaples, where German airplanes intensely bombed the British base camp and the Canadian hospital between May 18 and 21 and May 31 and June 1. These horrific air raids, during which bombs rained down not far from Reginald and his Fifth Lancer companions, caused enormous loss of life and tremendous physical damage to the camp, hospital, and town.[30]

Added to this dangerous, frightening wartime environment was a health issue that had plagued Reginald Harvey for several months and had now become intolerable. Beginning in December 1916, he had noticed a loss of hearing after becoming severely ill with influenza. His hearing loss gradually worsened. He soon began discharging a bloody mucous from his nose, had pressure in his nasal cavities, and suffered from throbbing headaches. An ear specialist diagnosed the problem as chronic middle-ear deafness, otosclerosis, which tends to run in families. Often it is caused by a previous measles infection, stress fractures to the bony tissue surrounding the inner ear, or immune disorders.

Increasingly, Reginald found it difficult to perform his duties as a second lieutenant. Consequently, on June 4, 1918, he left Calais on the northern coast of France, traveled to Dover, England, and, two days later, underwent ear surgery at the Prince of Wales Hospital in London. After a hospital stay of a month and sick leave for two and a half months, Reginald returned to the Fifth Lancers at Camp Curragh in late August.[31]

Despite the surgery, however, his ear problems continued. After entering the military hospital in Curragh in the fall of 1918, Reginald Harvey was deemed "unfit for any further military service" and left Ireland for Kingsmans Farm. Foiled in his desire to contribute to England's war effort in the way that he had hoped, Reginald Harvey returned to farming in Essex with a hearing loss that he endured for the rest of his life.[32]

Maurice Langridge also served on the Western Front in France and, like Reginald, also contracted a severe case of influenza late in the war. In February 1918, on the eve of Germany's Spring Offensive launched by General Erich Ludendorff, commander of the German armed forces on the Western Front, Maurice Langridge went to France where he continued carrying out his motor transport duties in the Army Service Corps. After the Allies suffered heavy losses during the German "hurricane bombardment" (which used prodigious amounts of poison gas), they launched a major attack on the German army in July 1918, at the Second Battle of the Marne, where German soldiers suffered heavy losses and were driven back. Two days after the battle ended in early August 1918, the Allies initiated their most successful operations of the war—the Battle of Amiens and the Battle of Noyon-Montdidier. These battles marked the beginning of the Allies' "Hundred Days Offensive" and the war's final three months. Maurice Langridge's exact location on the Western Front in France during the Great War's final phase is not disclosed in his military service record.[33]

In October 1918, after nine months on the Western Front, Maurice was on home leave when he suddenly became ill and succumbed to severe influenza and a pneumonia attack. Maurice and Reginald were among the millions of soldiers and civilians who contracted this deadly virus, the so-called Spanish flu, which killed an estimated 50 million people during the Great War—considerably more than the 40 million soldiers and civilians who died as a result of the war itself. In October 1918, Maurice was admitted to a hospital in Cambridge. Eight months later, in June 1919, he left military service and was demobilized a short time later. In the summer of 1919, Maurice and Ethel moved from Kingsmans Farm, where Ethel had lived after the birth of her first son, Raymond, to Folly Lane in Hockley. Like Reginald and so many other soldiers in the Great War, Maurice had suffered from the effects of influenza more than from military combat.[34]

Preparing for Military Service; Celebrating Peace

Back in Rochester, on September 12, 1918, the full ramifications of U.S. participation in the Great War were being realized at the home of the Evans family at 515 Meigs Street. A third mandatory registration period now required men between the ages of eighteen and forty-six to register for military service. On that rainy fall day, thirty-five-year-old John Evans walked to the local Draft Board No. 6 office and waited in a long line to complete his registration form.[35]

John certainly must have felt anxious that day, wondering if he might soon be fighting on the dreaded Western Front in France—just seven years after immigrating to the United States. On the one hand, he undoubtedly wanted to demonstrate his loyalty to his newly-adopted country and contribute to the war effort. Yet he must also have feared what might happen to his young family if he were called to serve and subsequently killed. Rochester and the United States now seemed engulfed in threats caused by both war and disease.[36]

Just as John worried about his future in the fall of 1918, the influential Right Reverend Charles Gore, the Bishop of Oxford and one of the best-known Nonconformist church leaders in England, arrived in the United States. Reverend Gore spent seven weeks on a speaking tour intended to "quicken the spirit of America in support of the President's policies in prosecuting the war for democracy."[37]

6

GOING HOME TO ENGLAND

John and Mabel did not have long to wait to discover if John would be called to serve in the United States Army. Just two months after he registered, on November 11, 1918, the war ended when Germany agreed to the terms of the armistice on the eleventh hour of the eleventh day of the eleventh month. Rochester residents, like those in towns and cities across America and throughout Great Britain and the other Allied countries, celebrated the armistice with unbridled patriotic fervor. Residents crowded onto East Main Street in front of the Sibley, Lindsay, & Curr store with its distinctive clock tower. On Armistice Day, John, Mabel, and their two young sons, Harvey and Evan, might have also joined the wildly cheering crowd in front of the store.

In this euphoric post-war climate of great relief and pride, the Rochester Chamber of Commerce expressed unabashed patriotism in *The Book of Industrial Rochester*, published for the Allied Trade Commissions of Great Britain, France, Italy, and Belgium. "The story of Rochester's growth . . . is a story of enterprise and thrift, coupled with an intense desire for advancement in educa-

tion and the things which make life more worth while
[*sic*],"[1] the booklet proudly asserted with great hyperbole.
According to the booklet's author, Rochester was a typical
city with a remarkable spirit of service, cooperation, fair
play, and a concern for the health and happiness of
workers and all people, young and old.[2]

Following the armistice, the United States pulled back
from its wartime European commitments to other countries. Despite President Woodrow Wilson's efforts at the
Paris Peace Conference in 1920 to persuade the Allies to
fashion a just, long-lasting peace agreement, Great
Britain's David Lloyd George, France's Georges
Clemenceau, and Italy's Vittorio Orlando strongly favored
the retribution embodied in the Treaty of Versailles.
When President Wilson presented this treaty to the
Senate for ratification, the Senate firmly rejected it. One
article in the treaty—the formation of a League of Nations
—proved especially contentious for some senators, who
believed that it would limit the power of the U.S. government to act independently from other nations and might
entangle the United States in future dangerous alliances
with Europe. The Senate also rejected the Treaty of
Versailles and its Article X, which created the League of
Nations. The United States once again embraced isolationism.

The United States now turned away from Europe and
focused all its attention on domestic affairs. Escalating
xenophobic fear continued to sweep across America and
influence congressional legislation. Four years after the
1917 Asiatic Barred Zone Act, Congress passed a law
restricting immigration of "undesirables" in 1921. This act
established a system that invoked a numerical quota to
determine the number of immigrants that could enter the
United States, based on that country's number of U.S. residents recorded in the 1910 census. Only 3 percent of U.S.

residents born outside the United States were allowed to enter the country each year. Many felt this act was not restrictive enough. In 1924, an additional immigration act revised the original legislation by reducing eligible immigrants' quota. This more restrictive 1924 act sought to create barriers against the immigration of Poles, Italians, Slavs, and eastern European Jews. John and Mabel felt relieved to have immigrated to the United States from western Europe before U.S. xenophobic prejudices swept across the country.[3]

Mabel and John, Evan and Harvey, ca. 1919.

Like millions of Americans, Mabel and John Evans jubilantly returned to their lives of pre-war "normalcy."

Mabel resumed her everyday routines of caring for her children and home, now with a less restrictive food selection. In May 1919, Harvey and Evan were five and almost three years old.

John continued his job at Sibley's, with a much lighter spring in his step. In the fall of 1918, he advanced from clerk to "silk salesman." In this new position, John certainly put his training as a draper and his silk knowledge to good use. He could competently talk with his customers about the variety of silk fabrics sold at Sibley's —satin, crêpe, taffeta, moiré, pongee, and charmeuse— along with silk thread, ribbon, and trim. He also acquired expertise displaying and arranging silk in an appealing, attractive display on large tables where customers could feel and assess the fabric's texture and quality. In his new role, John could effectively mingle more confidently with customers. As a silk seller at Sibley's, John would have also kept abreast of all the latest women's silk fashions, such as the "Oriental" and "Old French" styles that were popular in the 1910s and 1920s.[4]

Going Home

After years of worrying about family members in England and Wales, the end of the war and John's new promotion and salary increase made 1920 seem like an ideal time to return to England and Wales, introduce John Harvey and Evan Reginald to their grandparents, aunts, and uncles, and spend time with family members in Essex, England, as well as in South Wales. Mabel had not seen her family since she had left England in 1913. Harvey and Evan were the first-born grandchildren of Stephen and Martha Harvey and the proud product of Mabel and John's decision to immigrate, marry, and start a new life in America.

John decided he could not make the trip: he needed to continue working and earning an income for his family.

On March 11, 1920, Mabel, age thirty, applied for and was issued a passport, suggesting her intention to travel outside the United States. Soon afterward, John Evans purchased tickets for Mabel, Harvey, and Evan to cross the Atlantic to England on the British White Star's RMS *Adriatic*. In 1920, the heightened wariness and suspicion of immigrants became embodied in a series of restrictive immigration policies passed by Congress in 1917, 1921, and 1924. It was also evident in the diminishing number of third-class steerage passengers on trans-Atlantic ships arriving in the United States.

Mabel's passport photo, 1920.

At this time of growing anti-immigrant sentiment, European shipping lines offered economical cabin class, or tourist class, rates to the rising number of middle-class Americans. A 1920s White Star brochure highlighted the amenities of the new tourist cabin accommodations.[5] It promised to "bring back a new self," "a different person— fresh, vivid, eager." Despite the shipping company appeals to middle-class Americans, travel to Europe for a "grand tour" remained relatively uncommon for most people, including the Evans family. For Mabel, however, the trip was not a holiday to explore exotic places or historical sights. Her purpose was to visit her family after being away for seven years and introduce them to Harvey and Evan.[6]

In late May 1920, the Evans family made their way from Rochester to New York City's Chelsea Piers, which extended from Manhattan's west side shoreline into the Hudson River. Opened in 1910 after eight years of construction, the impressive miles-long row of piers, entered through a magnificent row of grand Beaux-Arts style buildings embellished with pink granite facades, were pronounced "the most remarkable urban design achievement of the day" by the *New York Times*.[7] As many as twenty ship stacks projected skyward from ocean liners preparing to depart from the piers on incoming evening tides. The Chelsea Piers welcomed some of the world's great ocean liners and became the New York City home of the White Star Line, rival of the Cunard Line. In the 1910s and 1920s, Cunard's great luxury liners, like the RMS *Lusitania* and the RMS *Mauretania,* routinely docked at Pier 54 at Chelsea Piers. Hundreds of ships, crowded with soldiers dispatched to the Western Front during the Great War, also arrived and departed from these piers.[8]

Mabel, Harvey, and Evan could barely contain their excitement when they arrived at the Chelsea Piers and made their way to the *Adriatic.* Launched in 1906, the *Adriatic* was the fourth and the fastest of four ocean liners owned by the British White Star Line cargo and passenger company. Appealing to tourist-class travelers, the *Adriatic* boasted that it was the first ocean liner to have both an indoor swimming pool and a Turkish bath. The *Adriatic* inaugurated the White Star Line's service from Southampton's newly constructed 1912 dock that accommodated the world's largest ocean-going vessels. On August 14, 1919, less than a year before the Evans family trio boarded the *Adriatic*, it became the first White Star ship to resume full civilian passenger service after the Great War.[9]

When the Evans family arrived at the Chelsea Piers on May 20 for the *Adriatic's* afternoon departure, Mabel, Harvey, and Evan were bundled up in warm coats and hats since frigid winter temperatures persisted across New York State. On the deck of the *Adriatic* just before its departure, Mabel appeared relaxed and smiling with her

head characteristically tilted to the right, wearing a fashionable long coat with a high collar and wide waistband
and a beret pulled down snugly over her stylish bobbed
hair. At her waist stood her two young sons, one clutching
her hand. As the ship pushed away from the dock, John
captured them in a photo with Mabel holding her sons
from behind while they perched on the ship railing and
gazed excitedly at their father standing on the dock.
Slowly the ship eased into the chilly breeze and the Upper
Bay's rippling water and steamed past the Statue of
Liberty into the open Atlantic Ocean. The Evanses had
begun a memorable travel adventure home. [10]

The *Adriatic*, Chelsea Piers. Harvey, Mabel, and Evan
on left side of deck railing, 1920.

Spending a week traveling as second-class passengers
on the *Adriatic* must have been relaxing for Mabel and a
memorable adventure for Harvey and Evan. Although
second-class passengers could not venture into first-class
or third-class quarters, Mabel and the boys had a deck
where they could rent chairs and steamer rugs to warm
their laps and legs. They also had access to the library and
three sittings a day for meals. After about six days, the
Adriatic dropped anchor at Cherbourg on the French

Normandy coast. Here, a few passengers disembarked before the ship continued north across the English Channel to the much improved and expanded docks at Southampton, where John had waved goodbye to Mabel nine years earlier.

On June 8, a chilly day with a biting northerly wind, the captain of the *Adriatic* slowly maneuvered the ship into place alongside the new Southampton dock. From Southampton, Mabel, her boys, and probably one or two Harvey family members who had come to greet them went by train northeast to London. They then traveled east to Hockley station, where they were met and taken to Kingsmans Farm. Mabel's parents, Stephen and Martha, and other family members eagerly awaited their arrival.

The Harvey family's reunion with Mabel and two new members of the Harvey-Evans family proved immensely heart-warming. For the next four months, Kingsmans Farm became Mabel's home once again, and a new home for Harvey and Evan to explore with dozens of adoring and generous family members. For twenty-five years, Kingsmans Farm had been the warm and welcoming home of the Harvey family, where most of the Harvey children had grown to adulthood. Farm buildings and fields occupied gently rolling and low-lying fields reclaimed from tidal flats alongside sea wall embankments several feet high. Periodically, waters rolling off the North Sea during occasional storms breached the sea wall along the River Crouch. A ridge of low hills visible from the Kingsmans Farm fields rose gradually from the broad Crouch valley.

Kingsmans Farm, ca. 1925. (Alfred Padgett, photographer.)

Around 1925, a local photographer, Alfred John Padgett, who owned a photographic postcard business in nearby Leigh-on-Sea, captured the pastoral scene of Kingsmans Farm in an atmospheric image. The photographer, looking east towards a cluster of thatch-roofed buildings in the distance, captured the Kingsmans Farm buildings and their pastoral setting. Barely visible beneath a towering elm tree stood the two-story Harvey family home.[11]

In the summer of 1920, Harvey and Evan became part of the large and bustling household at Kingsmans Farm, one full of the comings and goings of aunts and uncles, some of whom lived at the farm. Others lived nearby with their spouses. Three of the unmarried Harvey children (Frank, Bertha, and Maud) all lived at Kingsmans Farm in 1920. Stephen and Martha Harvey remained the heads of the household.

Frank Harvey.

Many years later, Harvey Evans recorded his memories of the Harvey family at Kingsmans Farm in the summer of 1920. Stephen Harvey, in his mid-sixties, and Martha, in her early seventies, made a definite impression on six-year-old Harvey. He clearly recalled that Stephen Harvey was something of a country squire who, with his light, short pointed beard and hair parted down the middle, took full advantage of his likeness to King George V.

> He has come down to me as a most benign figure, who his children referred to as 'Dad-ah.' When, as a child of six, Evan, Mother and I spent the summer of 1920 back at her old home, he was less physically active and he seemed to enjoy his first grandchildren [Harvey and Evan] greatly. He went into the fields with us during haying ('hay making' they called it), made me a pitch fork from a small branch and chuckled happily as he tried to console Evan when we all slid off a load of loose hay once on the way to the farm yard. He was evidently a highly respected friend and neighbor who more than carried his weight in the community and

local [Anglican] Church in the nearby town of Hockley, Essex.[12]

Active in community affairs, Stephen served as chairman of the Hockley Parish Council for twenty-eight years and was on the Rochford District Council. He also had chaired the Hockley School Board in the early 1900s. At the end of his life, one man who knew him well at St. Peter and St. Paul's Church in Hockley captured the essence of Stephen's nature.[13]

> He loved Essex; he was proud to be a farmer; he seemed part of the banks of the Crouch; he had affectionate regard for fellow farmers. His deep knowledge was always at their service . . . He was transparently honest, he was clear as crystal and clean as a rill of spring water. He could be firm, I daresay he could be angry . . . I would rather have faced the blazing anger of any ruffian I have ever met, than face the quiet moist anger of the deep blue eyes of Stephen Harvey . . . He has the truest judgement and insight of any man I have ever met. . . . His sympathies and outlook were not limited. He sought no honours. He had an imperial outlook. He was a British Patriot and a fine type of English Yeoman.[14]

Harvey Evans's recollection of his grandmother Martha in 1920, although sketchy, still conveyed her demeanor.

> Grandmother Martha has left less of an impression, the only one being when she straightened me out for some misdemeanor I had committed. She was a very pretty woman, seven years older than my grandfather, who passed along to my mother [Mabel] her high cheekbones. As a girl, she had sung in the choir of a most remarkable small church in Greensted (a part of Chipping Ongar)

where she came from in Essex. [The Greensted church]
is the only surviving Saxon church (dating from 1013)
with a nave wall built of logs. They are split and set
upright in an oak sill.[15]

Harvey later recalled, of his Aunts Bertha and Maud,
that:

> Aunt Bertha was the 'lady' of the family, in demeanor,
> looks, and speech. There was evident gentility in my
> English grandparents, so perhaps her cultivated dignity
> and grace were not so surprising as that Uncle Frank and
> Auntie Maud . . . had so much less.[16]

Maud Elsie, twenty-eight in
1920, was an entirely different
character. Harvey recalled that
Maud "was the least self-
assured of the family" and had a
mournful face.

Another Harvey family
member who may have lived
periodically at Kingsmans Farm
in 1920 was Stephen Harvey's
sister, "Aunt Jennie" to the
family and a great-aunt to
Harvey and Evan. She never
married; she pursued dressmaking as an occupation.
Throughout her long life, she

Bertha Harvey, 1920
(courtesy Nick Hards).

seemed to be present at many Harvey family gatherings
and celebrations. Although she had a home of her own,
she often stayed for a few days or weeks with various
family members, thus becoming an extended family
member of several Harvey family branches.[17]

During their 1920 visit, Mabel, Harvey, and Evan undoubtedly spent time with other Harvey family members who did not live at Kingsmans Farm but were not far away. Beatrice Marian Harvey, tall, thin and substantial in stature, worked for many years in a millinery department store (possibly Derry & Toms, known to have supplied goods to the upper class of Kensington) in London. Forty-year-old "Auntie Bea" would undoubtedly have come to Kingsmans Farm most weekends. Mabel and the boys may have made occasional trips to London and visited her there.

Two other Harvey children—Reginald, who married Winnie Coe, and Ethel, who married Maurice Langridge— lived nearby and often visited Mabel and her two sons. Thirty-five-year-old Ethel Millicent, a subdued and dutiful wife, and her husband Maurice Langridge, who only a year earlier had returned in 1919 from the war, lived on Folly Lane in Hockley with their three-year-old son Raymond and three-month-old son Desmond. Twenty-five-year-old Reginald Harvey, the youngest child of Stephen and Martha, in 1919 married the spirited Winifred (Winnie) Coe, daughter of a Hockley farmer living near Kingsmans Farm. In 1920, Reginald and Winnie had an infant son, Vernon Sylvester. Recently back from the war and his ear operation, Reginald was establishing himself as a farm manager, just as his father had done earlier.[18]

Although Mabel, Harvey, and Evan spent most of their time at Kingsmans Farm, Mabel, at John's request, planned a trip to South Wales to visit the few remaining Evans family members. Harvey stubbornly refused to make the trip since he had developed a great affection for one of the farm horses, which he refused to leave. Although both of John Evans's parents and two of his siblings had died, Mabel, Evan, and one of Mabel's sisters (possibly Bea) traveled to South Wales to visit Tom Evans, his wife Liza, and their eleven-year-old daughter Hetty. The family lived in the South Wales coal-ming town of Aberaman on Bryn-heulog Terrace, situated on a steep hillside overlooking the Afon Cynon (River Cynon). They probably made the trip in July despite the dull wet weather in the summer of 1920. Mabel, Evan, and Beatrice may have continued west to Pentre-cwrt, where Esther, John's sister, lived at the Evans's family home, Parke. Harvey and his family could never have imagined that he would return to England—to Kingsmans Farm and Parke—just thirteen years later.[19]

Leaving Home to Go Back Home

The summer spent at Kingsmans Farm, visiting family members in Essex and London, celebrating birthdays, and making a trip to Wales, passed all too quickly. During the summer, Mabel turned thirty-two, and Evan celebrated his fourth birthday. After nearly four months with family and friends in Britain, it was time to return to Rochester and John. Mabel, Harvey, and Evan must have been filled with mixed feelings of regret about leaving their extensive and amiable Harvey family and of great anticipation about returning to the United States and John. Sadly, they would never see Stephen and Martha Harvey alive again. Both died in the early 1930s, less than a year apart.

The Harveys booked passage to New York City on the Cunard Line's RMS *Mauretania*, sister ship of the ill-fated RMS *Lusitania*, sunk by a German U-boat in 1915. Built on the River Tyne at Wallsend in northeast England, the *Mauretania* was launched in 1907 to the tumultuous cacophony of shrieking ship sirens and thousands of applauding spectators. The impressive and infamous *Mauretania* was the most massive moving structure then traveling on the open ocean.

The *Mauretania* on its way to New York City.

The *Mauretania* and *Lusitania*, powering their way through "heaving water with their dark hulls, gleaming white superstructures, and towering raked funnels, were compelling images of human achievement and astonishing luxury."[20] Both ships held the Atlantic speed record of 26 knots (30 miles per hour) for twenty years. Coal stokers in the engine room shoveled 850 to 1,000 tons of coal a day in blistering heat to keep the four-stacked *Mauretania* moving at top speed. In 1924, the *Mauretania* crossed the Atlantic in a record five days, one hour, and forty-nine minutes. Designed to carry 560 passengers in first class, 475 in second, and 1,300 in third, as well as 812 crew members, the 30,000-ton *Mauretania* steamed her way between Liverpool, her home port, and New York City.[21]

Known by the moniker "Grand Old Lady of the Atlantic," the *Mauretania* was impressive not only for her speed but also for her comfort and elegance. In the fashionable ocean-liner style of the day, English architect and landscape designer Harold A. Peto had created the ship's most elaborate interior spaces in a mixture of French and Italian Renaissance styles. The eighty-foot-long lounge, complete with columns that supported a cream and gold-painted dome, featured design elements used during the

Louis XVI era. There was a special children's room with paintings of scenes from the nursery rhyme "Sing a Song of Sixpence" and a rocking horse that must have delighted Evan. The music lounge may have also thrilled Evan, who had shown a great aptitude for music at a young age, and Harvey, who also appreciated music in his youth.

Although the first-class accommodations were the most luxurious, the more modestly-priced second-class section of the ship featured an attractive children's room, drawing room, music lounge, and second-class stateroom. The open deck, available to second-class passengers, would have been a place of great intrigue and excitement for Harvey and Evan.

Whatever experiences they might have enjoyed, Harvey's adventures on the *Adriatic* and particularly on the impressive *Mauretania* made a lasting impression on him. Many years later, at age seventy-five, Harvey recounted that his voyage on the *Mauretania* sparked his romance with the sea and a fascination with ships, which later blossomed into his pursuit of naval architecture as a career. Not long after returning to Rochester and all through high school, Harvey remained fascinated with ships of all ages, sizes, and designs. This love of ships took tangible form at a young age when he began assembling from scratch intricate model ships of wide-ranging ages and designs. He continued model shipbuilding through high school, university, and his early years as a naval architect.[22]

The *Mauretania's* September passenger list for the sailing to New York reported that Mabel was age thirty-two, Harvey was six, and Evan four. The ship's manifest noted that Mabel was foreign-born, and her sons were born in the United States.

Seven days after leaving Southampton, the *Mauretania* arrived at Chelsea Pier 54 in New York City on September 25, where John Evans eagerly awaited their arrival. After nearly four months of separation, this family reunion must have been especially joyful. John Evans expressed tremendous delight to have Mabel, Harvey, and Evan back with him in their home at 515 Meigs Street. As a welcome-home gift for Evan, who had already demonstrated a natural talent for music, John had purchased a piano.[23]

Many years later, Harvey recalled that four-year-old Evan sat down at the new piano and immediately played several tunes by ear without knowing how to read sheet music. John's gift of a piano to Evan suggested his strong desire to encourage his children to pursue their talents and interests and follow whatever life path they chose. Although John and Mabel must have missed family members and the familiar places back "home" in Great Britain, they still felt strongly that America represented a place with limitless possibilities for themselves and their children. The return of Mabel, Harvey, and Evan to the United States in the fall of 1920 marked the beginning of a new chapter in the lives of the Evans family.

7

AT HOME ON MEIGS STREET

1920–1931

After 4 million Americans who served in the Great War returned home and experienced the euphoria of victory parades held in Rochester and cities across the country, a new reality settled over the United States. Despite President Woodrow Wilson's postwar vision of American internationalism embodied in his League of Nations, and his diplomacy aimed at creating a new world order in the wake of World War I, America swiftly returned to the presumed security of its prewar isolationism. As the nation turned inward, the new highly skilled workforce and industrial developments during the war materially contributed to improving the lives of Americans. During the Calvin Coolidge administration (1923–1929), technological innovation and increased industrial production invigorated an emerging mass-consumer economy. Residents of Rochester, including the Evans family, experienced an environment of expanding personal improvements.

The 1920s also witnessed spectacular growth in merchandising fueled by a significant proliferation of chain stores and department stores like Sibley, Lindsay &

Curr, which became temples for aspiring middle-class consumers. At the end of the 1920s, almost half of all Americans owned automobiles, radios, and durable appliances like vacuum cleaners, washing machines, and stoves. Although installment plans made such purchases possible, ordinary people all too often became mired in onerous, unremitting debt. John and Mabel Evans, eager to continue building their middle-class life in America, began to plan for a future of consuming beyond their means during the 1920s.[1]

The consumerism of the 1920s and John's job in Sibley's department store reinforced John and Mabel's conviction that their immigration to America offered them and their growing family excellent prospects for prosperity and the attainment of a comfortable middle-class life. Domestic consumerism surrounded them at Sibley's and in some of the new products developed by Rochester industries like the Eastman Kodak Company, Bausch & Lomb, and Xerox. Artist Norman Rockwell captured the abundant satisfying life of the times in reassuring images featured on the front covers of the *Saturday Evening Post.*

Overproduction, false prosperity, and uncontrolled spending, however, ultimately represented a different reality. For the Evans family, unexpected challenges arose in the mid-1920s. John witnessed a gradual but irrefutable downturn in his world of silk, accompanied by cutbacks among the long-time "old help" who worked with him in Sibley's fabric department. Mabel also confronted a challenge—a mid-life depression at age thirty-seven following the birth of her third son, Frank, in early 1926. Finally, the stock market crash in late 1929 cast a long, foreboding shadow over the Evans family on Meigs Street, as they prepared to make the largest purchase of their lives in 1931.

John's World of Silk at Sibley, Lindsay & Curr

John and Mabel Evans's lives in the 1920s reflected the lives of their contemporaries who strived to make material advances at a time of conspicuous middle-class consumerism. After a promotion John received around 1920, from clerk to a silk salesman at Sibley's,[2] John became intent on further developing his knowledge of new silks and merchandising silk, and on advancing his stature and pay. For his efforts, John Evans, the draper from the backcountry of Wales, received a promotion to silk buyer by 1923 and an accompanying pay raise; an achievement for which he remained forever proud.[3]

John became a silk buyer at a fortuitous time. The silk industry reached an apex of production and popularity during the 1920s. Many converging factors had created fertile ground for the birth of the silk industry in the United States a century earlier. Silk, one of the strongest, most durable natural fibers, became a favored material, used to make thread, hosiery, gloves, underwear, fabric for dresses and suits, ribbons and other millinery items, ties, lace upholstery, nets, parachutes, and more.

In the late 1830s, Cheney Brothers, headquartered in Manchester, Connecticut, emerged as one of the first successful silk manufacturers in the country.[4] Following the Civil War, "American silk manufacturing expanded rapidly, and brought voluminous quantities of silk goods within reach of more middle-class, moderate-income consumers."[5]

Between 1882 and 1922, the value of the United States' annual silk production jumped from $16 million to $700 million. *The American Silk Journal* in 1914 proudly reported that the past twenty-five years had witnessed "marvelous growth" and "unprecedented expansion" in silk production.[6] Silk manufacturing became concentrated in New

York, New Jersey, Pennsylvania, Rhode Island, Massachusetts, Connecticut, and Maine. While John Evans
worked as a silk buyer at Sibley's, "a vast army of [silk]
firms, over 1,000 strong, camped in the New York
market."[7]

John became a silk buyer when the public considered
silk the queen of fabrics. To satisfy his loyal silk customers
at Sibley's, John kept abreast of all the new silk weaves,
colors, finishes, patterns, and prices, as well as silk fashion
trends. He learned his customers' silk preferences and the
right price, place, and time for purchasing and showcasing
the various silks sold at Sibley's. John aimed to buy silk for
well-informed middle-class women with common sense,
good taste, and average middle-class means.[8]

Around the beginning of each year, and sometimes in
the summer, John attended silk markets in New York City.
In the 1920s, silk manufacturing companies moved to the
neighborhood near Madison Avenue and 34th Street. By
1924, several silk companies displayed their products in
showrooms occupying the lower floors of modern, new
skyscrapers in Manhattan's Silk District. Before traveling
to these showrooms, John would write ahead to individual
salespeople, arrange meeting times, and ask them to set
aside goods that he might inspect and possibly purchase
for Sibley's. In addition to the New York silk market, John
also probably made occasional trips to fashion shows and
fairs to keep up-to-date on the latest silk fabrics and
fashion trends.[9]

John's pair of hefty, ten-inch long Samuel Briskman
pinking shears, purchased in the 1920s, the most indispensable and emblematic tool of his trade, served as
tangible evidence of his ascension to the position of silk
buyer at Sibley's. Samuel Briskman, who had emigrated in
the 1880s from Kyiv (part of the Soviet Union in the 1920s)
to New York City as a silk merchant, began milling the

John Evans's Briskman pinking shears (G. Evans photo).

serrated teeth of pinking shears in the 1920s. Soon, he opened the American Pinking Shears Corporation on Greene Street in New York City, not far from its silk district. Briskman patented his pinking shears in the early 1930s. John Evans may have bought his pinking shears while on a silk buying trip to New York. Pinking shears, indispensable for making a clean cut in fabric without frayed edges, were the single most crucial tool of John's trade. (His well-worn pinking shears remain in the Evans family, in 2022 ninety years after John worked as a silk buyer at Sibley, Lindsay & Curr.)[10]

After his promotion to silk buyer, John Evans became more engaged and visibly more present in Sibley's employee affairs and social events. In the mid- and late 1920s, he served on the Entertainment Committee of the Employees Mutual Benefit Association, which aimed to provide its members with protection against financial losses in times of sickness. As a member of the Entertainment Committee, John helped arrange company dinners, dances, and picnics. For several years in the late 1920s and early 1930s, John, an enthusiastic Welsh tenor, presided over Sibley's department store chorus. In mid-July 1930, he served on a committee of employees that organized an afternoon of picnicking and sporting events at Seabreeze Amusement Park at Irondequoit Bay on the south shore of Lake Ontario, attended by 4,000 Sibley, Lindsay & Curr employees and their families. [11]

Sibley, Lindsay & Curr experienced remarkable growth and optimism in the 1920s. In 1926, the Sibley company constructed a six-story addition on top of its 1911 Mercantile Building. The prominent new Sibley Tower, which housed the well-regarded Tower Restaurant, dominated Rochester's downtown commercial district. The store then boasted a total of 1.1 million square feet of floor space.[12]

Welsh Culture and the Congregational Church

As John Evans became established in his job as a silk buyer at Sibley's, he blended his new life with meaningful cultural and spiritual aspects of his Welsh culture. In the 1920s and early 1930s, he became fully immersed in the newly formed Cambrian Welsh Society in Rochester. Although Welsh immigrants had settled in Utica, New York, as early as the late 1700s, only a small handful lived in Rochester when John arrived in 1912.

A decade later, however, many Welsh immigrants had moved to the city looking for employment after the devastating industrial decline in South Wales during World War I. An increase in the number of Welsh immigrants in Rochester encouraged the Cambrian Welsh Society's formation in February 1922. Early on, John—a native Welsh speaker and enthusiastic Welsh hymn singer—joined the Cambrian Welsh Society and remained actively involved throughout his life.[13]

The Rochester *Democrat and Chronicle* newspaper often reported the activities of the Cambrian Welsh Society and its members, including John. In 1925, both John and Mabel were members of the Cambrian Society Reception Committee. In 1926, John served as president of the society; members elected John as the vice-president in 1933 and, again, in 1942. He also served on the nominating committee of the society in 1928 and was chairman of that committee in 1930. In 1926, John served as chairman of the committee that sold tickets to the annual St. David's Day banquet, held every March 1 to celebrate Welsh patron St. David's feast day. On one occasion, John may have facilitated the society's St. David's Day banquet in Sibley's Tower Restaurant. St. David's Day was the largest event organized by the society each year. In the 1920s, John may have facilitated Cambrian Welsh Society meetings in Sibley's tea room.[14]

By the late 1930s, Rochester's Cambrian Welsh Society swelled to 400 members. Many were born in Wales and had immigrated to Utica, New York, before moving to Rochester. Some were the sons of coal miners in Wales. Others were businessmen or held administrative positions at businesses such as the Rochester Cold Storage and Packing Company, the Tire Merchant Association, and the Egbert F. Ashley Insurance Company. One society member worked as a sugar broker. Another owned and operated a grocery business. D. Clyde Jones, another member, was a well-known patent attorney who practiced at the U.S. Court of Customs and Patent Appeals.[15]

Regardless of their origins and employment, all Cambrian Welsh Society members shared a great appreciation and love of the Welsh language and culture. Some were the sons of Welsh coal miners. Other society members were distinguished soloists or musicians who sang professionally, directed choirs, played instruments, or acted. Many had a strong association with Rochester's emerging Eastman School of Music and the Rochester Philharmonic Orchestra. At a St. David's Day banquet, the Reverend David Jones Evans, professor at Colgate-Rochester Divinity School, captured the great fondness that Welsh native sons had for Welsh music and language. "Wherever [the Welsh] have gone," Reverend Evans observed, "they have carried characteristic Welsh qualities [embodied in the Welsh language]. . . . The Welshman's contribution is also in an attitude, an emotion . . . it is the Welsh emotion, which gives wings to all men's thoughts."[16]

John's passion for Welsh culture and his commitment

to the Cambrian Welsh Society equaled his intense devotion to the South Congregational Church. Immediately
after arriving in Rochester in 1912, John received a warm
welcome and tremendous support from Reverend Noyes
Bartholomew, pastor of the South Congregational Church,
and his wife, Opal, who lived just two doors away from the
Evans's home. Early on, John served as a deacon and eventually chaired the Board of Deacons. John also
contributed to church maintenance and played a role in
nearly all church activities, including acting in church
plays along with his two sons. John's life-long friend,
Egbert Cain, served with John as a church deacon for
many years.

John also became involved in other church activities:
singing in the choir, organizing and participating in music
programs, ushering at services, teaching Sunday school,
and, sometimes, serving as Sunday school superintendent,
secretary, and treasurer. Over many years, he became
chairman of the Board of Trustees, led the Senior Christian Endeavor Society, captained church visitation teams,
served as the vice-president of the men's Bible Club, led
fundraising campaigns, acted in church plays, and helped
decorate the church for special events. As a deacon and
active church member, John became known for his
integrity and his knowledge of the Bible, and he was well
respected by church members for his faithful devotion to
the church.[17]

John's immersion in the life of the South Congregational Church took many forms. On March 2, 1930, the
day after St. David's Day, John encouraged the South
Congregational Church to host a Cambrian Welsh Society
event featuring evening worship with hymns and solos
sung in Welsh. The sermon that evening focused on "The
Great Preachers and Hymn Writers of Wales."[18] Just as in
Wales at the Saron Chapel in Pentre-cwrt, the Noncon-

formist South Congregational Church became the center of John's life and identity.

Church play, John in a dress, Evan to left, Harvey in rear.

In the 1920s, John's two sons Harvey and Evan participated with John in numerous activities—choir, singing solos, theatrical plays, and fundraising bazaars. Mabel attended church services, supported her family's activities, and attended women's events such as church bazaars. She developed some of her closest friendships with women in the South Congregational Church. The church was at the center of the Evans family's spiritual, social, and cultural life.[19]

Mabel and Expanding Women's Rights

Mabel's arrival in Rochester in 1913 coincided with a period of strong pro-suffrage sentiment and public advocacy in both England and the United States. In 1918, five years after Mabel immigrated to the United States, British women over the age of thirty won the right to vote and serve as Members of Parliament.

New York State had been at the epicenter of the

suffrage movement since the 1848 suffrage convention in Seneca Falls, southeast of Rochester. For decades, influential suffrage leader Susan B. Anthony lived in Rochester, attracted suffrage leaders to her home, and devoted much of her life and energy to achieving equality for women of pay, the passage of divorce laws, and voting rights. Although she died seven years before Mabel arrived in Rochester, Anthony laid the groundwork for women's suffrage awareness in the city and region. Around the time Mabel immigrated to the United States, suffragettes were marching in Washington, D.C., and elsewhere, advocating greater rights and freedoms. In early June 1919, six months after the National Women's Party lit a "Watch Fire for Freedom" in front of the White House, the U.S. Senate passed the Nineteenth Amendment to the United States Constitution, granting all women the right to vote.[20]

In her marriage to John, Mabel, although not a woman to wave banners about her independence and personal beliefs, became an equal partner in decision-making, conferring with John about significant decisions and large purchases such as buying automobiles and, ultimately, a home. When her children were young, Mabel was the primary caregiver. She trained and expected her sons to carry out certain household chores like washing the evening dishes and cleaning.

Mabel and John together shared the responsibility of welcoming friends and strangers into their home. If others ever criticized family members, she never hesitated to speak out and strenuously defend them. Mabel had many women friends in the South Congregational Church, whom she often joined on outings. Auley Cain, the wife of Egbert Cain, a church deacon and close friend of John's, became Mabel's closest friend. Mabel played the role of family communicator, writing letters to family and friends.[21]

Much of Mabel's household work was unexpectedly interrupted when, at age thirty-six, she became pregnant with her third child. On January 24, 1926, Mabel gave birth to Frank Harold Evans, named after her gentle, sweet-dispositioned older brother, Frank Harold Harvey, who farmed at Kingsmans Farm nearly his entire life. At the time of Frank's birth, Harvey was age eleven and Evan age nine. The postpartum depression Mabel experienced after Frank's birth seemed to have continued for quite some time.[22]

Mabel with women friends and Frank, ca. 1930.

Later that same year, with the addition of a fifth family member and the apparent stability and higher income of John's job as a Sibley's silk buyer, the Evans family moved to 516 Meigs Street, where they occupied the entire two-story house. Like their ground-floor home across the street at 515 Meigs Street, 516 Meigs Street was owned by Louis and Clara Jacobs, who lived at 519 Meigs Street.[23]

Life on Meigs Street

Harvey and his younger brother Evan grew up on Meigs Street in an idyllic residential neighborhood in

Rochester located about one mile southeast of East Main Street where John worked at Sibley's. With the advent of the City Beautiful Movement in the early twentieth century, Rochester planted numerous young trees, creating shady tree-lined avenues. North of Meigs Street, East Main Street boasted older, more substantial homes owned by some of Rochester's wealthier citizens. Just a stone's throw to the west of Meigs Street and the Evans's house, the narrow Erie Canal still meandered through its original 1820s channel. Within walking distance of the Evans's home stood the South Congregational Church, No. 15 Grade School, and Monroe Junior-Senior High School, all clustered around the busy Alexander and Pearl streets intersection. Myriad attractions and the possibility of endless adventures in the Meigs Street neighborhood kept Harvey and Evan entertained as they grew up.

Playmates abounded in the Meigs Street neighborhood. Two doors away from the Evans's home lived Lloyd and Clara,[24] the children of Reverend Noyes Bartholomew and his wife Opal. Harvey also developed a close friendship with Charles Harris, who was one and a half years younger than Harvey and the son of Dr. Roland C. Harris, who had delivered Harvey in 1914. The Harris family lived just two blocks away on Monroe Avenue. Harvey and Charlie roamed the neighborhood on foot and bicycle, and swam in the nearby Erie Canal until it was re-routed south of Rochester in 1918.[25] The two of them also explored their neighborhood from streetcars. In the winter, they sledded on the canal's sloping, snowy banks near the Meigs Street Bridge. Charlie Harris later recalled that "one of Harvey's earliest memories was of a team of horses falling partway into the [Erie] canal, [and being] impaled by the tongue of the wagon [that the team was pulling]. Harvey was four at the time." [26] Harvey carried this horrific memory with him for many years.

At Halloween, Harvey and Charlie delighted in playing pranks on neighbors. Much later in life, Harvey and Charlie vividly recounted their adventures playing a Halloween prank on a grumpy neighbor by leaning a dead rabbit, skewered on the end of a stick, up against his front door. After positioning the rabbit carefully against the door, the boys rang the front doorbell and quickly scampered away—tittering all the while—as the disgruntled neighbor opened his door and watched the dead rabbit fall onto his feet. Charlie also remembered riding his tricycle through Rochester, following fire trucks.[27] Harvey may have first learned to ride on Charlie's bicycle before purchasing his own much later. Harvey and Charlie remained friends throughout their lives, despite the distance that later separated them.[28]

In the first half of the 1920s, Harvey attended No. 15 Grade School on Alexander Street, across from the South Congregational Church. Since 1842, a grade school had occupied this site. After a fire destroyed the existing school building in 1881, a new school building replaced it; Harvey and Evan attended this school before it was abandoned and torn down in 1923. That year, the combined Monroe Junior-Senior High School, a three-story, buff-colored brick building with Corinthian columns framing the front entrance, faced Alexander Street near the old No. 15 Grade School.[29]

The South Congregational Church stood diagonally across the intersection of Alexander and Pearl streets from Monroe Junior-Senior High School. Both the church and the school became the social and cultural center of the young lives of Harvey, Evan, and Charlie as they grew up. Harvey acted in several church plays performed by "The Mummers" acting group with his father, Evan, and Charlie.[30] As he matured, Harvey also sang tenor parts in the church choir and special concerts. Evan began singing

in the Junior Choir in the mid-1920s, and in the 1930s, he
sang baritone solos.[31] In the 1930 "Old Folks' Concert" at
the church, John, Harvey, Evan, even four-year-old Frank,
and Charlie Harris and his family, all participated. In 1932,
both Harvey and Charlie had roles in the "The White
Elephant,"[32] a three-act comedy performed at the church.
In December 1932, Harvey accepted the job of stage
manager, with Charlie assisting. In 1933, Harvey and
Charlie acted in "The Old Plantation Minstrels."
Reflecting many years later on his acting experiences,
Harvey recalled that around age fourteen, when participating in a recitation competition, he forgot his lines while
on stage. Embarrassed and unnerved, young Harvey
slapped his face and walked off the stage, to gales of
laughter from the audience.[33]

In 1926, twelve-year-old Harvey began attending the
combined Monroe Junior-Senior High School on
Alexander Street; Charlie Harris began classes there a year
later. Evan entered Monroe High School in 1928. William
E. Hawley served as principal until 1932, the year Harvey
graduated. During his six years at Monroe Junior-Senior
High School, Harvey pursued many activities, expanded
his circle of friends, and seemed to become conscious of
the fascinating trajectory his young life was taking. His
"genuine cowhide"-bound scrapbook, embossed with gold
letters forming his name, became the repository of several
thoughtfully-selected reminders of memorable events and
accomplishments at Monroe High School and the South
Congregational Church. Harvey also collected mementos
from family travel adventures, each one carefully glued to
the thick black paper in the scrapbook.[34]

One of Harvey's early scrapbook mementos was a
Rochester Standard Bearers Association membership card.
In 1926, twelve-year-old Harvey accepted an invitation to
join the Standard Bearers Association, formed in

Rochester in 1889 by the Grand Army of the Republic (GAR), originally a branch of the Republican Party. Each February, the Rochester GAR gathered at the city arsenal and marched to the city hall, where standard-bearers presented new flags to all of the Rochester schools. Harvey was selected to be standard-bearer because of his "excellence in scholarship and 'deportment,'. . . school citizenship involving much more than good conduct, [but also] qualities [of] leadership, service to the school, and good character and personality."[35]

Harvey's scrapbook also divulges the numerous classes he took in junior and high school, including English, French, history, civics, chemistry, algebra, geometry, drafting, shop, and typing. He usually received higher grades in geometry, physics, algebra, chemistry, and drawing and always got lower marks in French.[36] In high school, Harvey took part in numerous social activities, such as the Sigma Delta fraternity, the Monroe Senior Chorus, and dances featuring bands like the "Dixie Ginger Snaps" and "Bus' Blum and His New Commanders." He also joined the high school track and field team, the "Spikemen."[37]

Harvey also pursued several hobbies. He collected stamps, inspired by those that arrived at the house on England and Wales letters. He joined an airplane model league around 1928. Harvey also assembled, from scratch, twelve model ships, including a sixth-century BC Roman galley, a seventh-century pirate ship, the *Viking Galley* dating from 900, America's Cup *Enterprise* yacht, the fishing schooner *Bluenose,* and a British motor lifeboat. Proudly, he photographed all of his ship models and pasted images of them in his scrapbook. His most serious hobby, however, became not only building model ships but also pasting newspaper photos of British and American vessels in his "Composition Books." Over the next several years, he filled two volumes of these books with newspaper photographs of ships. Smitten with ships throughout his teenage years, Harvey wrote a high school essay entitled "The Evolution of the Hull and Sail." His teacher gave him an A-minus.[38]

Harvey's early interest in ships and boats may have been inspired by family vacations taken on nearby lakes, like enormous Lake Ontario and the many Finger Lakes not far from Rochester. Harvey, Evan, Mabel, and John often enjoyed part of their two-week summer vacations in and around water with members of the South Congregational church, including their dear friends Auley and Egbert Cain and the Cains' daughter, Doris. When Harvey grew older, he visited the Harris family on Lake Ontario, where they owned a small barn they had converted into a two-story summer "cottage."

In the mid-1920s, the Evans family often went with Auley and Egbert Cain to the small village of Sodus, 44 miles northeast of Rochester on the south shore of Lake Ontario. Once occupied by Seneca Native Americans, sheltered Sodus Bay became a settlement built up around lumber mills, fisheries, and, later, a port for shipping coal to Canada. Eventually, the refreshing, marine landscape spawned the development of Sodus and its bay as a summer resort. The families stayed at a camp with a short pier jutting into the Great Sodus Bay. Swimming, rowing, and fishing for pickerel, black bass, and lake perch were the main attractions. In 1928, the two families also vacationed in the Thousand Islands, a group of over 1,800 picturesque islands at the northeast end of Lake Ontario, about 100 miles from Sodus Bay. [39]

In the early 1930s, the Evans family, now including young Frank, sometimes vacationed on Sixth Lake, part of the Fulton Chain Lakes in the Adirondack Mountains. The 6 million-acre Adirondack State Park, established in 1894 to preserve the outstanding scenic, recreational, and ecological features of the Adirondacks, encompassed the small town of Old Forge along with hundreds of lakes. The creation of this park became a hallmark in the conservation history of the United States. Hiking adventures in the Adirondacks may have sparked in Harvey an early love of hiking in nature.[40]

Occasionally, Harvey went with friends on a ferry across Lake Ontario from Charlotte, a major coal port a few miles north of Rochester on Lake Ontario's southern shore. The five-hour ferry ride ended in Cobourg, Ontario, northeast of Toronto. This ferry, operating between 1907 and 1950, was the only water-borne railcar vessel on Lake Ontario. Along with passengers and automobiles, the *Ontario I* ferry transported as many as thirty railroad cars filled with Pennsylvania coal destined for Canadian railroad engines waiting in Cobourg. The 5,146-ton, 317-foot-long *Ontario I* traveled year-round in sometimes freezing temperatures. The ship rode up on lake ice during frigid winters and crushed it, like a modern-day icebreaker, thus allowing the vessel to move forward.[41]

A 1928 photograph captures fourteen-year-old Harvey posing with a group of seven friends from the South Congregational Church, all leaning against a lifeboat on the deck of the *Ontario I*, with twin funnels puffing wispy, wind-blown columns of smoke into the air.[42] The group had probably taken the "boat train" from downtown Rochester to the Genesee docks in Charlotte, where they boarded the *Ontario 1*. This ferry was unique since it had the only railcar-passenger train that traveled on a car ferry across Lake Ontario. After riding on two ships across the Atlantic Ocean in 1920, this trip must have been another fascinating nautical adventure for Harvey.[43]

The late 1920s may have been when Evan realized that his sexual orientation was a little different from Harvey's and that of most of his friends. As a young teenager, Evan began wearing some of Mabel's dresses at home, according to family friend Charlie Harris. The family never talked about this openly. John and Mabel simply appreciated Evan's musical talent and his love of theatre and ballet. They accepted Evan as the talented, sensitive, and kind young man that he was.

Evan experienced this sexual awakening in the late 1920s and early 1930s—twenty years after gay activities blossomed in New York City theatres, restaurants, and bars. Gay, lesbian, and transgender men and women became an integral part of many neighborhoods in the city. Gay writers, actors, and musicians created a distinctive literature and performance style. During the 1920s, gay impresarios organized drag balls that attracted thousands of gay dancers and straight spectators. The gay community established a notable presence in Harlem and the bohemian mecca of Greenwich Village. This cultural awakening became so famous by the late 1920s that gay performers moved from New York society's margins to Broadway. With a population of over 325,000 in the 1920s, and known for its many music and theatre venues, Rochester probably felt the influence of the so-called "Pansy Craze." This craze, however, did not last long. By the mid-1930s, the Pansy Craze's flourishing cultural experimentation experienced a fierce backlash with the Great Depression's arrival in the early 1930s and the end of Prohibition in 1933. Evan indeed became aware of these shifting attitudes towards gays and would have experienced them on Rochester streets.[44]

Memorable adventures in the Meigs Street neighborhood and around the waterways and lakes in Rochester contributed to what seemed to Harvey, in retrospect, as an ideal childhood. Aside from fighting over who would wash dishes after dinner, Harvey and his brothers enjoyed their young lives in a relaxed, warm, and loving family home.

Evan's piano music often filled the Evans home at all times of the day and night.[45] Charlie Harris recalled decades later that the Evans family "often stayed up until midnight playing games or visiting with friends who dropped by."[46]

"The doors were always open at our house," Harvey later recalled, "even well into the night, to friends and waifs and strangers of all ages and conditions."[47] Looking back, Harvey described his father and mother "as genuinely warm, generous and open-hearted people with not a strain of maliciousness, ill-will, or malice—at least not for more than a flashing moment. And they were thoroughly decent and upright." According to Charlie Harris, the Evans family was "a happy family—musical, and delightful actors in South [Congregational] Church plays."[48] Harvey later conceded that for "those of my generation, the Norman Rockwell view of life [was] not everyone's but it was definitely mine. . . . Things are often as much what they seem to be as what they really are. I recognize that attitude in my mother, too."[49]

The decade of the 1920s proved to be a time of well-being for the Evans family. Throughout the 1920s, when John and Mabel rented their home near downtown Rochester, the city thrived. In 1920, with a population of 290,720, it ranked as the 23rd largest city in the United States. Ten years later, its population swelled to 328,132. A surging stock market, an atmosphere of confidence, a sense of endless possibilities, and high expectations for the future—all characteristic features of 1920s America—would not last, however.[50]

A New Reality at Sibley, Lindsay & Curr

In the late 1920s, it seemed that the Evans family's happy and financially stable life would continue forever and that John and Mabel had achieved their aspirations for a middle-class life in America. The reality, however, proved to be somewhat different. As the 1920s came to an end, a barely perceptible shift in the silk industry slowly arose. Gradually the appeal of silk waned. Fashions in clothing started to change. The 1920s witnessed the introduction of new synthetic, less expensive fabrics such as rayon and nylon. A lack of capital to upgrade and modernize looms, reorganize the evolving textile industry, and meet the growing garment industry's intensifying demands compounded this trend.

Additionally, textiles, including silk, had historically been sold at department stores to customers who made their own clothes. In the late 1920s, however, customers increasingly chose to buy ready-to-wear clothing. As home sewing declined, retail fabric departments steadily lost customers, and the "cutting-up" (garment-making) sector took over: "By the 1920s, mass production and mass merchandising became fully integrated into the ready-to-wear industry."[51] John saw this shift in his specialty—silk —and worried about what it might portend.

An even more troubling national and international event occurred in 1929. In late October, the New York stock market crash signaled the arrival of a dizzying national and global economic downturn. Harvey and Evan were probably too preoccupied with their teenage activities and friends to be more than slightly aware of the crash. They couldn't imagine what it might mean for their family, for themselves, and, indeed, for the world around them. Frank, age three in 1929, had no awareness of the immediate or prolonged effects of the Great Depression, or of the decisions made by his parents that he poignantly felt a decade later as a teenager.

Rochester's *Democrat and Chronicle* newspaper reported news of the crash in hyperbolic prose, in a front-page dispatch from New York:

An incredible Stock Market tumbled toward chaos today despite heroic measures adopted by the nation's greatest bankers. Wall Street throbbed with excitement all day and tonight the men who guide its destiny are wondering whether they have won a hard fought victory in their back-to-the-wall battle to stem the unprecedented and frenzied liquidation pouring in from the four corners of the country.[52]

In Rochester and across the country, thousands of banks closed as people frantically rushed to withdraw their money, which only caused additional panic. Two weeks later, the Rochester Gas and Electric Corporation president, who lost more than $1.2 million when the market crashed, took his life.[53]

That same issue of the *Democrat and Chronicle* also reported the impact of the crash in London. "Scenes which amazed old-timers here witnessed during the final hour of business in the London Stock Exchange. Few could hear the chimes of the big clock above the uproar as the clock struck four, the closing hour [of the exchange]."[54] Over the next two years, Britain witnessed the value of its exports cut in half, unemployment reach 20 percent, public spending cut drastically, and taxes increase astronomically. In some areas, notably the London suburbs, the economy thrived due to the building boom then underway, but this failed to reach as far east as Kingsmans Farm. In Wales, post-war unemployment began to extend into large, previously unblighted areas of the country in the 1930s.[55]

In the United States, those employed in industrial cities like Rochester often suffered the most. By 1933, unemployment reached 50 percent in Cleveland and 80 percent in Toledo. Industrial Youngstown, Ohio—a steel industry center and the home of several of John Evans's relatives—suffered tremendously. Unemployment there rose to three times the national average. The purchasing power of the working and middle classes dropped precipitously, thus deepening the economic crisis.

In the United States, the severity and longevity of the Great Depression had many long-term consequences for hundreds of thousands of people, including the Evans family with their idyllic life on Meigs Street.

Inadvertently, the Great Depression had an enormous impact on John's work at Sibley's. The depression accelerated the popularity of cheaper ready-to-wear clothing and prompted a downturn in the silk market. The combined effect of introducing synthetic fabrics like rayon and the widespread popularization of ready-to-wear clothing significantly impaired the health of silk manufacturers in the 1930s. In the early 1930s, silk became viewed as a luxury fabric too expensive for most middle-class Americans. Displays of silk and related dry goods slowly moved from Sibley's street-level display windows to the store's less well-trafficked upper floors. John Evans observed this migration of silk with tremendous unease and worry. [56]

In addition to the silk market's downturn, Sibley, Lindsay & Curr experienced a gradual evolution in management and management protocols. The company headed into the depression not long after losing its founders and long-time management leaders, including Rufus Sibley, Alexander Lindsay, and the store's two younger, long-time partners. In the early 1930s, John Sibley, Rufus's son, introduced modern management methods in the store. Buyers, like John, were now required to report to division managers trained in modern merchandising methods. Additionally, the new management leaders enthusiastically embraced the store's focus on the expanding ready-to-wear clothing market. This approach further eroded the high regard John had enjoyed as a Sibley's silk buyer. John and several other merchandise buyers managed to hold on to their jobs for a while, but many long-time employees began to leave Sibley's in the mid-1930s. The depression, combined with the growing popularity of ready-to-wear clothing, new management, and modern methods and markets, ultimately took its toll on many of John's co-workers, and on John.[57]

8

REALIZING A DREAM

1931–1933

Around 1930, despite significant changes that raised great uncertainties, John and Mabel felt they should take a giant step toward realizing a middle-class dream for their family. Known for their general optimism about life and the future, John and Mabel must have believed that they were secure enough in John's job and confident in the economy's resilience to buy both a car and a home. Unable to imagine the 1929 crash's possible long-term consequences, John and Mabel decided to move the family from their modest rental home on Meigs Street to historic, picturesque Pittsford, 7 miles southeast of Rochester.

A quiet farming community in the 1800s, Pittsford became a busy shipping port when the Erie Canal arrived in the farming village in 1825. Forty years later, when Rochester expanded outward, Pittsford became a stop on the Rochester & Eastern Rapid Railway between Rochester and Geneva, New York. In 1902, when passenger railroad service arrived in Pittsford, the town had gained a reputation as "a beautiful suburban village with fine shade trees and many handsome residences."[1] Many residents commuted to Rochester on the train before automobiles became available in the 1910s and affordable in the 1920s. Around 1930, Pittsford was a pastoral community of around 7,500 upper-middle-class residents occupying sizeable homes on spacious lots.[2]

On September 22, 1930, eleven months after the stock market crash, John and Mabel purchased a gracious 2,300 square-foot, two-story, three-bedroom, two-bath, hip-roof, 1913 Craftsman-style house with broad overhanging eaves set back from the road on a three-quarter-acre corner lot. Substantial, classical round columns supported a hip-roof porch above a wide, welcoming front door. Cedar shingles clad the exterior walls, and decorative glass adorned the upper sash of both the ground- and second-floor windows. A one-story screened-in porch projected from the rear of the house several feet from the hip-roof garage that housed the Evans's automobile used to transport family members to Sibley's and to friends in Rochester. This Pittsford house purchase tangibly represented the culmination of all John and Mabel's hard work and planning, and their arrival in the middle class.[3]

The purchase of a lovely suburban home in Pittsford committed John and Mabel to a $4,000 mortgage payment, plus 5 percent interest held by the previous owners, Rhoda and David Renshaw. John and Mabel Evans also borrowed $7,000 in a second mortgage from Rhoda Renshaw and a partner, at about 8 percent interest. Thus, they were compelled to pay interest on $11,000 in loans with monthly payments of $65 to $80. A balloon payment on both the $4,000 and the $7,000 loans would be due when the loan period ended.

Despite this burdensome debt, John and Mabel remained excited and optimistic about their new purchase. Never having owned a home and managed such a huge debt, and optimistically believing that the economy would soon improve, John and Mabel took a chance on the largest purchase of their lives.[4] This purchase was a life-time dream realized.

Evans home, 179 East Brook Road, Pittsford.

Moving In and Stepping Forward

In the summer of 1931, the Evans family moved into their new home in Pittsford. Harvey was seventeen and finishing his last year of high school at Monroe Junior-Senior High School, Evan was fifteen, and five-year-old Frank would begin grade school in Pittsford that fall. During the summer, the Evans family settled in and began adjusting to their new home and suburban living, dependent on their car to commute to Rochester for work, going to church, and visiting friends. [5]

In addition to their house, John and Mabel purchased one and possibly two new cars between 1928 and 1933. In 1928, they bought a new Ford Model A, one year after its introduction, thus making the Evanses one of a million American Model A owners. Owning a car was essential for the family. After Harvey had obtained his driver's license in 1931 or 1932, he transported his father to work at

Sibley's, Evan to Monroe Junior-Senior High School, and Frank to Pittsford Elementary School.

Around this time, John and Mabel may have purchased a second automobile. Charlie Harris, Harvey's close friend, recalled that Mabel had an accident while learning to drive and damaged their first car. The purchase of both a house and possibly two automobiles between 1929 and 1933 as the Great Depression deepened, sent a clear message to their Rochester friends that the Evans family had become solidly middle class.[6]

In 1931, forty-seven-year-old John seemed to briefly step back from his intense involvement in social activities at Sibley's and the Cambrian Welsh Society, perhaps because of the move to Pittsford. In February 1931, his name did not appear in the *Democrat and Chronicle* as an organizer of any Sibley's benefit dinners. John Evans was also not mentioned as one of the company's annual summer picnic organizers in July 1931, or the Washington party held at Sibley's in February 1932. That year, however, John re-engaged with the Cambrian Welsh Society; in February 1932, the local newspaper reported that John Evans was selling tickets at Sibley, Lindsay & Curr to the society's annual St. David's Day banquet in early March. The next year, in late February and early March 1933, John was elected vice-president of the society.[7]

As the Evans family became absorbed in moving and adjusting to suburban life in Pittsford, distressing news arrived at their home from England. On September 16, 1931, Mabel's father, seventy-four-year-old Stephen Harvey, died at the Victoria Hospital in Southend-on-Sea of myocardial degeneration caused by prostate surgery. Just eight months later, on May 30, 1932, eighty-one-year-old Martha Harvey died of acute bronchitis and myocardial degeneration at Kingsmans Farm. Their daughter, Bertha Longman, was present at both Stephen's and Martha's deaths. It had been more than a decade since Mabel had last seen her parents, and she indeed must have grieved over their deaths. She must also have been saddened by not being able to introduce her parents to their third grandchild, Frank Reginald. It is possible that Mabel, who had struggled with depression around the time of Frank's birth, entered another period of depression as she mourned the death of both her parents during a short eight-month period.[8]

Meanwhile, having John, two teenage boys, and young Frank kept Mabel's life at the new home active and alive with comings and goings to work, school, church, and with the visits of good Rochester friends. Harvey decided to finish his 1931-32 senior year at Monroe Junior-Senior High School. Evan also continued at Monroe High School for the next two and a half years, graduating in January 1935.[9]

During his senior year, Harvey received grades ranging from 75-93 in English, advanced algebra, trigonometry, solid geometry, mechanical drawing and shop, and vocal classes. At the end of 1932, he was one of thirty-six high school graduates who received a "credit diploma" given to students who had no mark below 75 percent on their Regent Examinations, taken for entry into college. In addition to coursework, Harvey participated in many other activities: Senior Mixed Chorus, Assembly Programs, and Hi-Y (associated with the YMCA). He was also an understudy for the Monroe High School senior play, *Tons of Money*, a farcical English play.[10]

Harvey, whose intense interest in ships had convinced him to pursue a career in naval architecture, applied to the Massachusetts Institute of Technology (MIT) in Cambridge. As his senior year at Monroe Junior-Senior High School wound down and preparations for the annual concert of the Monroe Senior Mixed Chorus and commencement exercises approached in mid-June 1932,

Harvey and his parents eagerly awaited word from the admissions office at MIT. In July, the news arrived. Harvey had been accepted but had only been given credit toward admission for the required subjects of algebra, chemistry, geometry, physics, history, and science. MIT insisted, however, that he take entrance exams in three units of

language. Harvey had not done well in French in high school and had never taken German. He did not, therefore, have the requirements to enter MIT in the fall of 1932. This was a huge disappointment, and it posed a severe problem.[11]

After Harvey considered his options and talked them over with family and good friends, he decided to take one year of post-graduate studies at Pitts-

Harvey's graduation photo, Monroe Junior-Senior High School, 1932.

ford High School to improve his French and take history and business courses. He also decided to play football (in the halfback position) at Pittsford High School and basketball (in left field) for the Long Meadow Club. At the end of the 1932–1933 school year, he had scored well on his two French class exams (90 and 85) but had just missed the total score on his French Regents Exams needed for acceptance to MIT.[12]

Once again, tremendous disappointment about another closed door prompted Harvey and his family, perhaps on the advice of respected teachers and friends at the Monroe Junior-Senior High School, to immediately pursue an alternative course. One teacher—perhaps Rena Dumas, a long-time family friend who directed the choir at the South Congregational Church and headed the

Modern Language Department at Monroe High School—advised Harvey about improving his foreign language skills.

In mid-September 1933, perhaps at the urging of Rena Dumas, Monroe High School principal W. E. Hawley signed a "Certificate of Recommendation" for Harvey's admission without examination to the top-ranking School of Engineering at the University of Liverpool in England. Hawley's recommendation confirmed that Harvey had completed all the required units for graduation from Monroe Junior-Senior High School. Notably, his grades, combined with the results of his New York State Regents' exams, placed him solidly in the upper third of his 1932 graduating class at Monroe High School. Harvey applied to the University of Liverpool, and with great relief and delight, soon learned that the engineering department accepted him for the fall term of 1933.[13]

The remaining weeks in the summer of 1933 must have been full of dizzying preparations for Harvey's upcoming departure to England, a trip he had last made in 1920 when he was six years old. Mabel, who was thrilled to have Harvey going to England, immediately wrote to her family members to prepare them for his arrival. John also contacted his older brother, Tom, who lived with his wife and daughter in Aberaman, a mining community in South Wales. With great excitement, Harvey purchased tickets for his passage to Liverpool, assembled travel documents, clothing, and other essential items, and made housing arrangements for his first term at the University of Liverpool. Before leaving, Harvey also spent much time visiting Charlie Harris and his family, friends at the South Congregational Church, and his new Pittsford friends, including girlfriend Helen Hegendorfer (nicknamed "Hod") and her friends, Helen Hatch and Alice Johnston.[14]

In late August 1933, just a month before his departure,

Harvey and his family drove Rena Dumas and her mother to Old Forge in the Adirondack Mountains for a summer holiday. Once in the Adirondacks, the group may have stayed at the Topp's Cabin resort on First Lake. In Harvey's scrapbook, photos and mementos suggest that they traveled east from Old Forge to Blue Mountain and made a stop at the historic log Blue Mountain House, an early and well-known 1876 Adirondack resort hotel. The next day, traveling further east, they crossed a narrow section of Lake Champlain separating New York from Vermont. They then headed a short 18 miles to Middlebury, Vermont, where they probably stayed at the old New England Middlebury Inn and attended the Congregational Church in Middlebury on Sunday morning. Two days later, they continued to Burlington, then went back to Old Forge before returning to Pittsford on September 3.[15]

Evans and Dumas families in Adirondacks, 1933.

A week later, Harvey and his family visited friends on Canandaigua Lake, one of several Finger Lakes south of Rochester. On September 9, Harvey went with Charlie Harris and his brothers to Lake Ontario. He stayed overnight at the Harris cottage on a knoll overlooking the lake. All of these visits became heartwarming send-offs for Harvey, who would soon leave for England and not be back in Rochester for many months, perhaps years.[16]

At the end of the third week in September, John and Mabel helped Harvey make final preparations for his trip to England and his immersion into a world that would be much larger and more complex than his life in Pittsford, Rochester, and upstate New York. Among the essential items Harvey packed was a small book—*All About Going Abroad with Maps and a Handy Travel Diary*. Multiple short chapters described what baggage to take, hints on passing customs, the use of telegrams and telephones, and distances between London, Paris, Berlin, Rome, and other cities in Europe.

On Wednesday, September 20, after several days of visiting friends and buying additional clothing, Harvey finished packing. Before sunrise, the next day, Harvey, Evan, John, and their good friend, Egbert Cain, drove southeast to Binghamton, where they stayed overnight. They continued to New York City the following day and made their way to Chelsea Piers in the mid-afternoon. The beleaguered years of the Great Depression greatly reduced the number of ships at Chelsea Piers, which now appeared aged, tired, and in need of repair. Additionally, the 1930s had witnessed the launching of new, much larger vessels like the 10,000-foot-long RMS *Queen Mary* and the SS *Normandie*, which required much longer piers in an area known as "Luxury Liner Row," built along the shoreline between West 44th and 52nd streets.[17]

Harvey's passport photo, 1933.

Late Friday afternoon on September 22, with great excitement and eager anticipation, Harvey boarded the RMS *Carinthia*. From the ship's deck, Harvey spotted the RMS *Mauretania* in the dock, which he, Evan, and Mabel had traveled on from England to the United States thirteen years earlier. The *Carinthia,* launched in 1925 and operated by Cunard's White Star Line, routinely crossed the Atlantic on the Liverpool-Boston-

New York route. Harvey was fascinated to learn about the *Carinthia*'s recent voyages. Earlier in 1933, it had completed a four-month round-the-world cruise, stopping at several ports in the United States, the Caribbean, the Panama Canal, the Pacific Islands, Asia, Australia, British Ceylon (now Sri Lanka), and the Suez Canal.[18]

At 5:00 p.m. on Friday, September 22, the *Carinthia*, with a crew of 450 and 240 first-class, 460 second-class, and 950 third-class passengers, slowly moved away from the dock and into the North River (the Hudson River's navigation name south of 30th Street). Leaning against the deck rail, Harvey waved farewell to his father, Evan, and Egbert Cain, who stood on the dock waving back. Slowly, the *Carinthia* moved into the Upper New York Bay, where the Statue of Liberty stood visible against the setting sun. The *Carinthia* passed through the Narrows into the Lower Bay, then "dropped pilot," traveling now without guidance from a pilot boat. As the *Carinthia* continued, Harvey eagerly observed and noted in his diary the presence of several older ships, such as a three-mast and a four-mast barkentine and an impressive five-mast schooner with multiple sails fluttering in the breeze. Once through the Lower Bay, the *Carinthia* veered southeast past the Ambrose Lightship and into the Ambrose Channel, a 1,000-foot-wide and forty-foot-deep engineering marvel dating from the 1880s.[19]

As the sun sank lower in the western sky, Harvey descended to the third-class passenger level. The accommodations included a dining room with small tables, a smoking room, a small library, and a shop for the ship's passengers. The RMS *Carinthia* boasted a small swimming pool, sports area, gymnasium, racket courts, and passenger massage rooms. Such accommodations far exceeded what Harvey's father, John Evans, had experienced when he immigrated to Canada in 1911. Awaiting Harvey on board were fourteen letters and cards from his many Rochester friends and family he would not see for many months.[20]

Soon, Harvey would begin his education—not in the history of sailing vessels but in the design and construction of modern ships. Before he went to sleep late that night, he wrote his first diary entry at the back of his *Going Abroad* book: "Boat drill at 12. Sighted airplane at 2:30. At noon [on September 23] 270 miles, fresh breeze, rough seas."[21]

He would soon fill the blank pages at the back of this book and the pages of his small five-year leather-bound diary. These became the place where Harvey recorded the details of his daily life, thoughts, and feelings about people he met, and descriptions of hundreds of new places he visited. His diary became the place where he revealed his growing fascination with a larger world far beyond the comfortable and secure environment of Rochester and Pittsford—a world of rich cultural diversity, human complexity, and visual color. Harvey's diary also became the place where he recorded perplexing and difficult challenges that he would confront in England in the coming years—challenges he never expected.

9

BRITAIN BECOMES HOME

1933–1935

In the 1930s, bustling Liverpool exhibited a fascinating history evident in the sights, smells, and sounds of its unique built environment, which Harvey grew to appreciate over the next four years. The remarkable emergence of Liverpool as a flourishing global center of trade and commerce could never have happened without the brilliantly engineered docks along the River Mersey where dozens of ships docked every day. Immediately, Harvey grew fond of all the naval history and associations that Liverpool embodied.

For centuries, a mile-long tidal inlet flowed in a muddy curve along the River Mersey's eastern shore and served as a place to load and unload cargo from ships arriving from around the world. The name "Liverpool" originated from the merger of the old English word "Liefer," meaning thick or muddy, and "pool." In the early 1700s, the Mersey's high tides, rising thirty-three feet about every eleven and a half hours, along with the swift currents, strong winds, and shallow, silty river bottom, convinced residents to construct an enclosed commercial wet dock—the first in the world. In 1715, engineer Thomas Steers designed an enclosed pool with a brick wall against the shore and wooden gates opening into the River Mersey that, when shut, contained river water at a constant level.[1]

This first dock prompted the construction of many more enclosed docks along the River Mersey's east bank. These docks also encouraged the construction of nearby warehouses, shops, and a row of small adjoining houses standing back from the shore. Within one hundred years of the first dock's completion, thirty more enclosed docks were constructed, extending 7 miles up and down Liverpool's waterfront. In the early 1800s, the city's waterfront and trade development spurred a great surge in population from 5,000 to 77,000 residents.

Liverpool's population exploded in the 1830s and 1840s, stimulated by Britons' migration from the rural countryside, especially from Wales and Ireland. Roughly 10 percent of Liverpool's inhabitants were Welsh, and most spoke little English. They contributed to the dispersal of Welsh culture—Welsh language, singing events, and Nonconformist churches—throughout the city. Collectively, the Welsh, Irish, and other immigrant groups who settled in Liverpool profoundly contributed to the city's distinctive character, making it a place of rich linguistic and cultural diversity, sometimes accompanied by intolerant religious sectarianism and racial strife. By 1860, many more interconnected docks had been built, creating a great complex of gated docks for miles up and down the River Mersey. This inventive system of water containment in multiple docks eventually created docking space for a hundred ships.[2]

In the late 1800s, a significantly transformed Liverpool became one of the world's most important trading ports and Britain's wealthiest city. An 1886 issue of the *Illustrated London News* described Liverpool as "a wonder of the world . . . the New York of Europe, a world-city rather than merely a provincial British town."[3] The docks provided work for thousands of people. "Dockers" loaded and unloaded ships and moved goods to long, narrow warehouses that lined nearby streets. Ethnically diverse communities emerged, occupied by seafarers from the far corners of the globe—Europe, West Africa, China, the Philippines, as well as the British Colonies—spread inland from the docks.

When Harvey arrived in the mid-1930s, 20,000 dockworkers of all national and ethnic backgrounds busily pushed and pulled goods in hand trucks and wagons along the docks. The bustling activity; the intense smell of horses, produce, and human sweat; the sound of hooves and steel wheel rims on stone and brick; and the cacophony of different languages captivated Harvey. He found the history, sights and smells, the docks' clamor, and the Welsh element of Liverpool society extremely intriguing. Soon after he arrived, Harvey began attending a Welsh church and later joined a Welsh choir.

Adding to the many engineered docks was the sixteen-foot-high Liverpool Overhead Railway, which had opened in 1893 and was reputedly the first elevated electric railway in the world. Known as the "Dockers' Umbrella," since it protected dock workers from Liverpool's chilly, winter rains, it was extended twice to the north and south beyond its original seven-mile length. The Liverpool Overhead Railway, which operated until 1956, was one of the notable engineered features (along with its inter-city railway, underground railway, and network of electric trams) that defined Liverpool as a modern city.[4]

Liverpool Overhead Railway along River Mersey docks.

Fifty years later, Harvey recalled, "Several times [I] rode my bike along the dockside road from Bootle [on the north] to Dingle [on the south] sensing the many sights, sounds, and smells (domestic and foreign, sacred and profane, mundane and exotic), which amply confirmed the appeal of ships" and his choice of naval architecture as a career.[5] Over the next four years, Harvey spent much time around the docks for inspiration and a reprieve from studying.

Making Britain Home

By noon on September 23, 1933, the RMS *Carinthia* had navigated 279 miles from New York's Chelsea Piers eastward into "fresh breeze and rough seas."[6] The high seas, often with thirty-five foot swells, continued during much of the week-long Atlantic crossing. Harvey found much to do on the ship despite the occasionally rough seas. On Sunday, he went to church, tried his hand at shuffleboard, watched wooden horses race on the deck, went to dances, attended concerts, and sang with others in the evenings.

He wrote many letters to family and friends back in Rochester. On Saturday, September 30, the *Carinthia* approached the Isles of Scilly, an archipelago off the tip of Cornwall in southwest England. Soaring gulls circled overhead, signaling the proximity of land. Ships now passed the *Carinthia* with increasing frequency. Harvey, curious to see more of the *Carinthia* before disembarking, descended into the ship's bowels and toured the kitchen and the engine room. He marveled at the 120-foot-long propeller shaft, and was amazed to learn that "more men [were] down there to keep things clean than to keep them running."[7]

As the RMS *Carinthia* approached Plymouth on England's southwest coast, the ship passed the famous Eddystone Lighthouse, completed in 1882 on the windswept, sea-battered Eddystone Rocks south of Plymouth. The Eddystone Lighthouse was the most recent of three previous lighthouses. The first one, dating back to 1699, had been destroyed by powerful waves and fire. Ten minutes after the Eddystone Lighthouse came into view on the horizon, Harvey spotted a pod of porpoises, suggesting that the ship was now in shallower coastal waters. Soon afterward, the *Carinthia* dropped anchor in Plymouth, where Harvey picked up a telegram from his uncle, Reginald Harvey, his mother's youngest brother. "Meet you platform Liverpool Street Station [in London] Monday morning," Reg's abbreviated message read.[8]

A day later, after crossing the English Channel, the ship moored briefly at Le Havre in the Normandy region of northwestern France, before again crossing the English Channel and heading toward the 151-foot-tall Old Dungeness Lighthouse on the English Channel. The ship then navigated through the Strait of Dover near the pure white, 300-foot-high cliffs of Dover—a one-million-year-old chalk formation created when the ice sheet covering northern Europe gouged a channel between present-day England and France.

Finally, the *Carinthia* sailed past the Kent coastline's vast sandy beaches, then westward into the mouth and up the River Thames. After slowly navigating up the River Thames in the fading light of early evening, the *Carinthia* arrived at the gates of King George V dock at Woolwich in the afternoon of October 2. Slowly, the hefty gates closed behind the ship, and, twenty minutes later, the *Carinthia* docked in an adjacent basin.[9]

Much had changed in the thirteen years since six-year-old Harvey had first visited England with his mother and Evan in 1920. He hadn't known enough then to appreciate the enormous economic and social consequences of the Great War. The British government had accumulated an immense debt, creating worrisome economic instability by the end of the war, and in 1920–1921 the country had plunged into the deepest recession it had ever experienced. Through much of the 1920s, Britain struggled to pay off its enormous debts and regain economic stability.

The Welsh economy had suffered even more. In the mid-1920s, unemployment among coal miners mushroomed from 2 percent in the spring of 1924 to 29 percent in August 1925, primarily due to plummeting foreign demand for coal and increased coal production elsewhere. At the end of 1929, the United States stock market crash dealt the British economy another blow by halving the value of Britain's industrial exports, thus impoverishing industrial areas in central and northern Britain and causing staggering unemployment. When unemployment in Wales reached 43 percent in 1932, it ranked among the world's most depressed countries. The apparent collapse of capitalism heightened industrial unrest and encouraged broad public support of socialism in Wales. Additionally, industrial Wales's impoverishment undermined Nonconformist chapel culture and, with it, the Welsh language.[10]

Harvey came to England just as the country experienced a slow economic recovery and gradual increase in its gross domestic product, unlike the United States, which, in 1933, descended into the Great Depression's deepest trough. In Liverpool, when unemployment peaked at around 30 percent in the early 1930s, massive public works projects helped mitigate some of the worst effects of the "hungry thirties" and gradually lifted the city out of depression.

For the four years after Harvey arrived in Liverpool in 1933, slow economic recovery spawned a modest economic boom.[11] The increase in the value of British sterling encouraged public spending and stimulated housing construction in the countryside outside London, where direct rail lines linked central London to towns like Hockley and Hullbridge near the Harvey family's Kingsmans Farm. The outward building expansion from London into agricultural areas like Hockley, which had begun in the late 1910s, accelerated in the 1930s.[12]

After a brief nap and a hurried breakfast on the RMS *Carinthia*, Harvey took a train to London, where his fifty-year-old Auntie Bea, a milliner, met him. (Apparently, his uncle Reginald was unable to meet Harvey.) On the night of October 1, Harvey stayed with Auntie Bea in London before they both traveled by train to Hockley, about 3 miles south of Kingsmans Farm. They then went to the nearby home of Harvey's Auntie Ethel and Uncle Maurice for lunch. Ethel, who had assisted with Harvey's birth in Rochester, had not seen him since 1920 when Mabel and her two children visited England for four months. Ethel and Bea then took Harvey to Kingsmans Farm, where Harvey stayed the night.

Harvey's grandparents, Stephen and Martha, had died

in 1931 and 1932, and it was now Frank, their oldest child, who managed the farm with help from family members who lived nearby, and one or two hired hands at busy times of the year. In the mid-1930s, the Kingsmans Farmhouse had changed little since 1920, when Harvey had seen it as a boy. The house's two-story section with exterior red-brick chimney stacks, dating from the 1800s, was entered through a center door. A one-story section with an attic and dormer windows projecting from the roof, dating from the 1600s, extended to the rear.[13] The front door led into a hall with a dining room on one side, a drawing/sitting room on the other, and a small morning room (or buttery) tucked between the drawing-room and the large brick-floored kitchen and cool dairy room at the rear of the house. On the second floor, accessed by front stairs and a secondary rear stairway, there were five bedrooms: two large ones and a small one between them in the front and two small bedrooms in the rear over the kitchen.

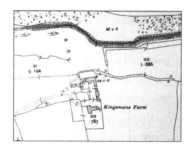

Ordinance Survey Map, Kingsmans Farm, 1935.

Behind the farmhouse stood a coal house, an orchard, and a sizeable garden, as well as a series of connected buildings—a large barn with a lean-to roof, a chaff house (used to store fodder, corn husks, and cut hay), and a cart lodge, cow house, calf pens, horse stables, henhouse, piggery, and open shed—all encircling a barnyard pond. At the rear of the property stood a small timber lath-and-plaster cottage known as Tapps Cottage. The saltings, or marsh pastures (coastal river estuaries often covered by tides), extended from Tapps to the River Crouch. In the mid-1930s, Kingsmans Farm occupied about 150 acres of "easy working" arable plowed land and green meadows, "hedged into small 'corn' fields sloping gently down to the 'sea wall,' a barricade of timber pilings and damp soil" extending alongside the River Crouch.[14]

Harvey immediately became enamored with Kingsmans Farm and its proximity to the River Crouch, which emptied into the ocean just a few miles downstream. "Even in the nineteen-thirties," Harvey observed, there were "a few shallow draft spritsail barges with towering red sails, so heavily loaded with grain that water came up to their gunwales. Placidly these barges made their way three miles up the river to the grist mill at Battlesbridge."[15] Kingsmans Farm's location on the River Crouch, Harvey recalled many years later, rendered it "memorably heavy with dampness: grey, handsome, and muddy in winter, and idyllic in spring and summer." Since the early 1890s, it had been the Harvey family home and "was a place that built itself into all of [those] who became acquainted with it, no matter what [their] age."[16]

Over the next four years, Kingsmans Farm acquired a special meaning for Harvey; it became a place that embodied the Harvey family's long, deeply rooted farming heritage extending back for generations in Essex. It was also a place where Harvey Evans received welcome support and kindness from the Harvey family during his four years in England.

The next day Harvey spent time working with his Uncle Frank, plowing and harrowing fields after recently harvesting wheat, barley, oats, hay, and mangles (a drought-tolerant, nutritious root crop with high sugar content fed to the cattle). Uncle Frank would soon be planting winter grains that he planned to harvest the following summer. On Harvey's last day at Kingsmans Farm, he visited his Auntie Bertha Longman and her young daughter, Patrina, who lived nearby. Harvey ended each day by recording the day's events by candlelight.[17]

On October 5, Harvey bid Uncle Frank and Auntie Bea goodbye and took the train from Hockley to London. At London's Euston Station, not far from Marleybone where his parents had met twenty-five years earlier, he began the 240-mile train ride northwest across the rolling industrial Midlands of England to Liverpool. Harvey arrived at central Liverpool's Lime Street station on a Thursday afternoon.[18]

Liverpool: Port City on the Mersey

From Liverpool Lime Street station, Harvey made his way several blocks southeast to his University of Liverpool housing at an all-male "hostel" known as Rankin Hall. Rankin Hall and nearby Rathbone Hall stood slightly back from an imposing high brick wall along Ullet Road, about a mile from the university campus. The university had acquired these buildings in the early 1920s to help ease the dire shortage of student housing. Rankin Hall, at 44 Ullet Road, and other university residences on Ullet Road housed around 200 students. Most students boarding at these hostels lived outside Liverpool in nearby Lancashire and Cheshire counties. Harvey was one of the few students that had come to the university from abroad.[19]

For the next two years, Harvey made Rankin Hall his home during the school year. Built around 1874, Rankin Hall was an imposing red-brick structure three stories high and referred to as "the Towers"; Scottish architect George Ashdown Audley had designed this substantial building for an American who once lived in Liverpool.

Harvey's "digs" were on the third floor at the rear of Rankin Hall, where a projecting balcony overlooked a lush sloping lawn.[20]

When Harvey arrived in Liverpool, the university's urban campus consisted of a cluster of substantial red-brick buildings, each with dozens of lecture theatres, teaching class-rooms and laboratories, state-of-the-art research facilities, and some administrative offices, all grouped atop the brow of Brownlow Hill rising from the center of Liverpool and the River Mersey. In 1933, the university had about 1,500

Harvey at Rankin Hall, ca. 1934.

full-time degree students. Harvey was among around 160 engineering students. The day after his arrival, Harvey walked to the university campus and soon found the red-brick engineering building where he would attend lectures and spend endless hours studying during the next four years.[21]

The University of Liverpool had deep roots extending back to the early 1800s when northern England and the Midlands experienced unprecedented industrial growth. Alongside Birmingham and Manchester, Liverpool's indus-tries—clock-making, glass, pottery, shipbuilding, and its trade in slaves from Africa to the Americas—contributed to Liverpool's rapid growth and prosperity. During the first seventy years of the nineteenth century, many converging factors propelled Liverpool to the forefront of international trade and commerce: its strategic location on the western seaboard near West Midlands manufacturing cities; the integration of railways and inland waterways that carried raw materials between factories and Liverpool; the opening of new markets in North America and British colonies around the world; and the completion of the Suez Canal in 1869.

All these factors fueled Liverpool's robust growth and emergence as a vibrant center of commerce and industry. The metamorphosis of shipbuilding materials and engineering developments, specifically the gradual replacement of wind with steam to propel ships and the move from wooden ships to iron hulls in the 1860s and 1870s, further contributed to making Liverpool a prosperous seaport by the early 1900s. Liverpool became known as "the second city of the British Empire" during the nineteenth century. From Liverpool, great steamship lines—Cunard, White Star, Leland, Blue Funnel, and others—transported goods and passengers to every corner of the world. Liverpool's nautical and shipping history contributed to Harvey's growing fascination with ships and shipbuilding.[22]

The University of Liverpool had its genesis during the city's emergence as a center of industry, trade, and wealth accumulation. It was then that a handful of enterprising individuals conceived of founding a college. In 1834, a few physicians and surgeons at the Royal Infirmary in Liverpool organized a medical school, which became the nucleus of the future university. After the former university college received a charter of incorporation in October 1881, the infant university witnessed the construction of several well-equipped buildings: a spacious chemical laboratory, a large engineering laboratory, laboratories of physiology and pathology, a handsome botanical laboratory, the monolithic clock tower, and the iconic red-brick 1892 Victoria building. The University of Liverpool became one of six so-called "red brick universities" constructed of pressed red bricks with decorative terracotta details. Early red brick colleges received official university status just before the First World War.[23]

The creation of non-traditional fields of study at the University of Liverpool, such as public health and tropical medicine, architecture and allied arts, and commerce, gave the new university a distinctive character. Naval architecture, first taught in 1910, was one of the university's early departments. That year Sir Westcott Stile Abell filled the department's endowed chair. In 1914, Abell's younger brother, Thomas Bertrand Abell, replaced him as chair. T. B. Abell had previously attended the Royal Corps of Naval Constructors in the British Royal Navy and Admiralty, where he received practical engineering training. He worked as a senior instructor at the Royal Naval College in Greenwich when he accepted the Naval Architecture Department position at the University of Liverpool. In 1933, the highly esteemed Professor Abell chaired the small but vibrant naval engineering department and served as the vice president of England's Royal Institution of Naval Architects.[24]

Harvey and his classmates viewed Professor Abell as a distinguished naval architect and an imposing gray-haired man with a twinkle in his eye and perfect self-control. Professor Abell would play a significant role in Harvey's education and, later, helping him secure a job as a naval architect in the United States.

After Harvey had explored the university campus, he headed down Brownlow Hill to the convergence of several streets in the city center dating from the eleventh century. He then walked down to the docks along the River Mersey.[25] Immediately, Harvey's attention was drawn to three elegant, imposing buildings—the Royal Liver Building (with mythical liver birds perched atop its two domes), the Cunard Building, and the Port of Liverpool Building—all constructed between 1903 and 1916. The

"Three Graces," located at the Pier Head, stood as a testament to the great wealth of Liverpool during the late nineteenth and early twentieth centuries and of the city's remarkable rise to world prominence as a center of international trade and commerce.[26]

Three Graces at the Pier Head. (J. Harvey Evans
photo, 1935).

With its monolithic Three Graces and miles of River Mersey-side docks, the Pier Head immediately became a magnet for Harvey. In front of Three Graces, he would meet friends, reflect on his chosen ship design profession, and wrestle with perplexing problems he confronted during his four years in England. Occasionally spotting ships that he or his parents had traveled on tied up near the Three Graces prompted Harvey to reflect on his parents' immigrant heritage, his nautical travels beginning at age six, and his great fascination with ship travel. The docks were a place of past departures and arrivals for Harvey, and a place that inspired travel adventures.

Life as a Student

On the evening of his arrival, Harvey settled into his room in Rankin Hall with his two roommates, W. A.

Major ("Maj") and Geoff Holborn, then visited some of the hostel's fellows. "Had a real good time," Harvey wrote in his diary that evening.[27] During his first few days in Liverpool, Harvey attended a few dances, went to the "pictures" (movies), watched the Liverpool hockey, rugby, and soccer teams practice, and went into town to buy a warm coat. On October 8, he attended services at both the Welsh church and the monolithic Liverpool Cathedral, then in a state of partial completion. Harvey soon joined a student choir that sang periodically at church services in the Liverpool Cathedral. He also began singing with the Blue Pigeons, a men's chorus at his hostel.[28]

Harvey began his classes on October 10. His four courses included pure mathematics, applied mathematics, physics, and chemistry—all held in the Harrison Hughes Hall engineering building, a three-story, red-brick building erected in 1912. Constructed around a U-shaped courtyard, it stood slightly behind the substantial, iconic, red-brick Victoria Building. Once classes began, Harvey routinely took an electric tram or walked the 2 miles from Rankin Hall to Harrison Hughes Hall for his lectures. Long hours of study followed for Harvey at the "varsity" (university).[29]

Harrison Hughes Hall engineering building. (G. Evans photo, 2016).

As Harvey settled into life and a routine at the university, he eagerly looked forward to the arrival of mail from home. Often, he listened to U.S. radio broadcasts. In his diary, Harvey recorded all the letters he received from his family and friends. On one day, November 15, Harvey received eleven letters from the United States, plus a magazine from his dad. "What a day!" he exclaimed in his diary; he then sat down and immediately responded to all his letters. Harvey's frequent letters and his diary accounts of mail he received from family and friends in the United States suggest homesickness that he felt, especially during his early months in Liverpool.[30]

As Christmas approached, Harvey prepared for examinations and spent time sending Christmas gifts to his family in the United States. He also packed in preparation for visits to his Harvey and Evans's families in Essex and South Wales. Finally, after his last exhausting exams on December 19, Harvey walked down Brownlow Hill to the city center and then to the docks. Here he strolled along the Pier Head in buffeting winds blowing off the river, reveling in the sights of many ships and the bustling human activity along the River Mersey docks.[31]

On December 20, two and a half months after arriving in Liverpool, Harvey left the city and headed south to be with his many aunts, uncles, and cousins at Kingsmans Farm during the Christmas holidays. Leaving the Liverpool docks at 9:00 a.m., he took the ferry from the Pier Head west across the River Mersey to Birkenhead, where he caught a long-distance bus. Soon, Harvey arrived in Chester, with its narrow main street lined with half-timber buildings and overhanging arcades. Heading south to Wolverhampton, Harvey described in his diary the lush green moss covering the hedges and fences enclosing churchyards. In the mid-afternoon, he arrived in Stratford-on-Avon, the birthplace of William Shakespeare. Still further south, the small town of Long Compton, with its buildings of honey-colored local Cotswold stone and steeply pitched thatched roofs, struck Harvey as quaint and picturesque.

Arriving in London after sundown, Harvey made his way to the Alexa Hotel, where he stayed for two nights with his Auntie Bertha and her husband, Martin Longman, a well-established London florist. Over the next two days, Harvey visited London's many tourist attractions—the British Museum, Natural History Museum, Science Museum, Westminster Abbey, the Palace of Westminster, Trafalgar Square, Piccadilly, and Buckingham Palace. On his final day in London, Harvey arose early on a chilly, damp, dark morning and went with his Uncle Martin Longman to the bustling Covent Garden Market. As the merchants exchanged goods, money, and news amidst their lively banter, Martin selected some prime foreign and domestic flowers for his Longman's Florist shop, near St. Paul's Cathedral on Ludgate Hill.[32]

On the evening of December 22, Harvey took a train 40 miles east to Hockley. He spent the next two weeks at Kingsmans Farm helping Uncle Frank with chores around the farm and visiting his many Harvey relatives—Great Aunt Jennie, Uncle Reg and Aunt Winnie and their children, and Auntie Ethel and Uncle Maurice and their children. Most nights, Harvey stayed at Kingsmans and slept with his cousin Vernon in one of the five bedrooms.

On Christmas Eve, Harvey visited the graves of his "Gramps" and grandmother in the cemetery surrounding the 600-year-old St. Peter and St. Paul Church, which was set on a hilltop above Hockley. From the church, Harvey had a panoramic view of the pastoral fields around Kingsmans Farm and the River Crouch just beyond. On Christmas day and afterward, Harvey visited the families of several aunts, uncles, and cousins, played games, went to the cinema, read, listened to the radio, and wrote letters home.[33]

In early January 1934, Harvey went by train from Hockley to London. He again stayed the night with Auntie Bertha and Uncle Martin in the Alexa Hotel before going by bus to Cardiff. Harvey then continued northwest to Aberaman to meet and visit his Uncle Tom—his father's brother—and Liza, Tom's wife. Only two years apart in age, Tom and Harvey's father, John, had been close as boys. They often explored the countryside together, rode on donkeys, and fished in the River Teifi near Parke in Pentre-cwrt, South West Wales.

As a young boy, Tom ran errands for a local doctor and, after completing school, apprenticed with a carpenter in his home village of Pentre-cwrt. Since there were many more jobs in the South Wales coal-mining valleys than around Pentre-cwrt, Tom (along with some of his older brothers) moved there as a young man to find employment. Early on, Tom worked as a joiner and made coffins for an undertaker in Glencoch near Pontypridd. Later, Tom moved further up the River Cynon valley to Aberaman, where he met and married Liza. In 1909 Liza gave birth to their only child, Hetty May. After taking evening classes and receiving certification as a teacher, Tom began teaching metal and woodworking classes in a local school.[34]

When Harvey visited Tom and Lisa, they lived in a brick house on a terraced hillside overlooking a landscape of coal mines and slag heaps above the rushing Afon Cynon (River Cynon). In early 1934, Tom was a skilled craftsman and taught cabinet-making classes. He also fashioned furniture, bookends, toys, walking sticks, and decorative items, sometimes with beautifully inlaid or contrasting laminated woods. Tom, a good-natured, cheerful soul, was the shortest member of the Evans family

Liza, Hetty, and Tom Evans.

and had a pointed chin and a substantial thatch of unruly white hair. Like his younger brother John, Tom was active in a local church. He served as a deacon, taught Sunday school, and, with the other deacons, led the congregation in singing. Harvey's early January 1934 visit with Tom and Liza was the first of several trips he made to see them.[35]

Tom Evans, upper right, with fellow deacons.

Harvey's visit with Tom and Liza in early 1934 had a serious purpose beyond visiting with them. He also wanted to talk with his Uncle Tom about worrisome money matters. Harvey's finances were dwindling fast, and his father had not sent him the money that he had been expecting and that John had promised. Eager to help, Tom introduced Harvey to banker Griffith, who Uncle Tom knew at the Lloyds Bank in nearby Ferndale. Griffith arranged for a loan of more than £50.[36]

Harvey spent the next four days with Uncle Tom,

going to church twice on Sunday, touring Tom's workshop at school, visiting Cardiff and the nearby town of Merthyr Tydfil, and writing letters to his family in Pittsford. On his last day, Tom took Harvey to the village of Pentre-cwrt and the Evans's family home, Parke, where Tom introduced Harvey to his Aunts Esther and Mary (the wife of Tom's deceased brother, Benjamin). Recalling this first visit many years later, Harvey described Esther as "still buried deep in the Welsh countryside; she was small, had broad cheekbones and clattered about on the tile floors [of Parke] in clogs. She spoke no English [only Welsh], so Uncle Tom was required for our brief dialogs. But she smiled warmly and often nodded in my direction so I knew I had been adopted as a legitimate member of the family."[37] On January 10, Harvey left Aberaman and took a bus from nearby Aberdare north to Liverpool.[38]

Finally, on January 13, 1934, Harvey received long-awaited money from his father and letters from family and friends. The next day, feeling much relieved, Harvey happily spent the entire day writing letters to family and friends back home. The long wait to receive money from John became an often-repeated occurrence during Harvey's time in Liverpool, causing him great anxiety.[39]

As the new winter term got underway, Harvey quickly became immersed again in a routine of attending lectures, studying, socializing with his classmates, and practicing with the student choir at Liverpool Cathedral. The imposing cathedral stood without a nave and tower until it was completed in the late 1970s when it became the largest cathedral in Britain and the fifth largest in the world.

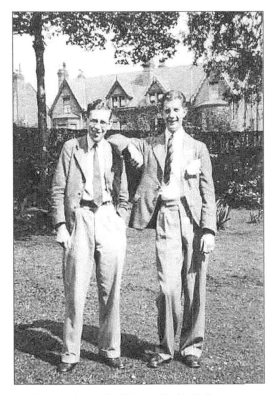

Frank Graham and Bob Lynn at Rankin Hall, ca. 1934.

Soon, Harvey became friendly with two engineering classmates—Frank Graham and Bob Lynn. Frank, Bob, and Harvey shared not only an interest in engineering but also in singing, hiking, and "the pictures" in an era of revolutionary sound techniques and full-color movies. Frank and Bob became fast friends over the next four years, supporting Harvey in numerous ways when he confronted challenges. Along with engineering student Tristram ("Trist"), these classmates remained Harvey's friends throughout his years at the University of Liverpool and long afterward.

10

CYCLING ACROSS ENGLAND

1934–1935

T he year 1934 proved to be incredibly challenging for Harvey. His desire to hear from family and friends at home suggests that he continued to experience great pangs of homesickness. In mid-February 1934, Harvey received news from his parents explaining that they could not pay for his ship passage home that summer. His diary entries revealed great disappointment and difficulty focusing on his studies. "I seem to be going stale and can't work," Harvey wrote in his diary.[1] He very likely struggled with occasional depression, particularly in the wet, chilly winter months of February and March. Harvey spent considerable time alone in the evenings either studying or writing letters home, when his roommates, Maj and Geoff, were out.[2]

In February, however, one particular event seemed to push back his angst, raise his spirits, and improve his outlook. On February 21, he borrowed a bicycle and a camera from a classmate and rode along the River Mersey docks for 6 miles. Anchored at one dock was the *Adriatic,* the ship that he, Evan, and Mabel had traveled on to Great

Britain in 1920. This was a "great day," Harvey exclaimed in his diary when he spotted this ship.

Another reprieve from Harvey's thoughts of family and friends at home, concerns about money, and long hours of studying for winter term exams in March 1934, when he booked a train from Liverpool to Aberaman, Wales. For one month, Harvey again stayed with his Uncle Tom and Aunt Liza. In his new car, Tom again drove Harvey to the Evans's family home at Pentre-cwrt to visit Aunt Esther. Tom also took Harvey to the nearby River Teifi to fish and visit an old stone woolen mill on the Teifi bank.

During this visit, Tom and Harvey stopped to see Mr. Griffith at Lloyds Bank in Ferndale to discuss money matters. Refreshed and reassured, Harvey returned to Liverpool on April 24 to begin the first day of the third and last term of his 1933–1934 classes. Perhaps as a diversion from money worries, Harvey decided to resume his model shipbuilding hobby, which he had first taken up soon after his 1920 voyage to England. This time he worked on the USS *Indianapolis*, a heavy cruiser commissioned in November 1932.[3]

Despite these pleasant distractions, money remained a persistent worry. While in Wales, Uncle Tom had loaned him more money. Harvey, however, had not yet paid the last term's hostel fees. "Things don't look so bright," Harvey wrote in his diary. Finally, on May 19, a letter from home arrived with money in it. "What a day!" Harvey exclaimed.[4]

In late May and continuing into June, Harvey studied for upcoming third-term exams, only breaking to write letters home and, one morning, to take a ride to the Pier Head along the River Mersey on a borrowed motorbike belonging to a fellow engineering student (R. T. Simpson). In mid-June, Harvey studied for and took his last examinations of the year. The Pure Mathematics exam posed the most significant challenge. "Was it tough!" Harvey exclaimed in his diary.[5] "Halfway through, I seriously wondered why I hadn't taken up street cleaning. It is easy to see why people crack up," he lamented.[6]

With examinations over by June 20, 1934, the engineering students began to relax and go on adventures in the countryside. Harvey must have been inspired by the expedition of his two roommates, Geoff and Maj, who had cycled 240 miles to North Wales and back in three days. Soon afterward, Harvey again borrowed a friend's bicycle and did some short-distance cycling. At the end of June, he again borrowed a bicycle and rode alongside the River Mersey docks, where he spotted the *Adriatic*.

On the last day of June, when his dire shortage of money required concentrated thought, Harvey cycled with a friend to the new Liverpool Airport that had opened in 1930 about 17 miles southeast of the city. Built to respond to the growing demand for fast Irish Sea crossings, this airport was Britain's first provincial airport. The next day, Harvey cycled with his roommate, Geoff Holborn. Harvey had begun to develop a fondness for cycling. He also realized that bicycling gave him pleasure and, importantly, provided him with an inexpensive way of traveling to his mother's family in Britain.[7]

If Harvey felt somewhat down about his lack of money, homesickness, and anxiety over exams, he soon received even more troubling news. On July 4, 1934, Harvey found he had "pipped" (British slang for falling short) of his final year-end examinations. "Tried all day to see the Dean," Harvey anxiously wrote in his diary. "Can't see how I failed," he agonized. The next day, Harvey wandered around town, contemplating his predicament and trying to imagine a remedy. Finally, he met with the stern Naval Architecture Department Professor Abell, who told him that he probably could pass his exams if he retook them in

September and improved his grade. "What to do," Harvey pondered.[8]

In early July, Harvey wandered along the River Mersey docks as he continued to consider his options. He knew he must retake the exams in September, but he had limited funds and could not pay for housing at the university during the summer. Harvey was already in debt to Mr. Griffith at the Lloyds Bank and Uncle Tom; he felt he could not ask for more money. Sadly, his parents could not pay for his ship passage home that summer, where he could have studied, had free housing, and been with his family and friends. Neither could Harvey afford the bus or train fares to travel to his family in Essex.

As Harvey walked along the docks, he pondered his troubling money problems. Finally, after weighing all his options, Harvey decided to buy a cheap one-speed bicycle. A bicycle, he determined, would be the only way to reduce his travel costs, allowing him to stay at Kingsmans Farm for the summer and to enjoy the support and friendly company of his Harvey family. Having made this decision, Harvey decisively walked to a cycle shop in Liverpool that very afternoon and bought a one-speed bicycle. "Hope I have not done wrong," he wrote in his diary.

Bicycling Across Britain

On July 8, Harvey spent most of the day packing. The next day he picked up his new bicycle and attached a few possessions behind the seat. Heading out of Liverpool, he cycled east through Warrington then southwest across the Cheshire Plain's lowland dairy farms on the Peak District's fringe. Approaching Buxton, the gateway to the Peak District, he cycled up the winding "Cat and Fiddle Road," where he had a "Hell of a climb" on a steep road with continuous and sometimes blind hairpin turns. Up he pedaled to nearly 1,700 feet. Stray livestock sometimes wandered onto the road from adjoining fields with little warning. After cycling for 50 miles, he found a place to sleep under the bright starlit sky, just west of Buxton—the highest market town in the East Midlands.[9]

Harvey and his bicycle in front of Kingsmans.

The next day, Harvey rode his bicycle from Buxton through intermittent patches of green forest, open hilly meadows, and wild open moors that eventually rose to the craggy heights of the Peak District. He then continued through Chesterfield and Mansfield. After a quick detour to see Robin Hood's Sherwood Forest, Harvey headed south to Nottingham and Derby. That day, he had cycled 86 miles and was happy to be able to spend the night in comfort at a university friend's home.

The next day Harvey continued, cycling 113 miles through Loughborough and Leicester to Market Harborough and on to the old seventh-century wool and silk town of Kettering. The next day, it was on to Huntingdon and the university town of Cambridge, where Harvey found a large number of "antiquated" buildings in and around the city "extremely absorbing." Also fascinating were the "picturesque" church steeples seen from miles away, rising above farm fields and treetops on the low, rolling East Anglian hills. "There is something about the rural atmosphere . . . which is very pleasing. I can't see how people can stay away," Harvey mused.[10]

After cycling a few more miles south from Cambridge, Harvey arrived at 9:30 p.m. at Uncle Reg and Aunt Winnie's home, Paynes Farm in the village of Radwinter, where he spent the night. Reginald Harvey had managed and maintained estate farms for others and collected rent from tenants for most of his farming life. "Uncle Reg had things go right for him," Harvey recalled fifty years later, "and being a 'people person' too, he lived a nice life. He must have been modeled on his father—a gentleman farmer, perhaps even a minor country squire."[11] Eventually, Reginald and Winnie bought Rectory Farm in Great Chishill, south of Cambridge, and farmed there until Reginald retired. Harvey recalled that Uncle Reg used modern and costly equipment, like combine harvesters.[12]

The next afternoon, after leaving Paynes Farm, Harvey cycled 45 miles southeast to Kingsmans Farm, becoming drenched in a downpour during the last 15 miles. I looked like "a traveling sponge," Harvey wrote in his diary. On this, his first cycle trip across England from Liverpool to Kingsmans Farm, Harvey cycled over 250 miles in three and a half days. The day after he arrived at Kingsmans Farm, Harvey described the details of his epic bicycling adventure in a letter to his family.[13]

Desmond Langridge on hayrack, ca. 1935.

At Kingsmans Farm, Harvey began a disciplined daily routine of studying for his September examinations. Often, visits from Harvey family aunts, uncles, and cousins, who all lived quite close to Kingsmans Farm, interrupted his studying when they stopped by for tea, dinner, or a friendly chat. Some days, every one of Uncle Reg's and Aunt Winnie's four children, and Auntie Ethel and Uncle Maurice and their two sons, Raymond and Desmond, as well as Auntie Bertha Longman, who lived at Mill Hill in Hockley during the summer, all came at once. When he took a break from studying, Harvey helped Uncle Frank with chores on the farm. He fed the cows, horses, and other farm animals, dipped sheep in an insecticide to ward away parasites, and helped with plowing, haying, stacking, and loading wheat and barley onto wagons. Cousins Raymond and Desmond stopped by often to give Frank a hand with the farm chores and have a chat.

Haying, Kingsmans Farm, 1930s (courtesy David
Langridge).

Near the end of July, Harvey cycled to Southend-on-
Sea 10 miles away and bought a camera. Fascinated by all
his new experiences, Harvey started photographing his
English family and their homes and his cycling adventures
across Britain. He continued to write about his experiences in his diary and in letters to family and friends in
Pittsford and Rochester.[14]

On August 15, Harvey set out on his bicycle with his
camera, heading west through London and then northwest
to Wheatley, near Oxford, where he slept his first night
under a bridge. The next morning, he pedaled through
Oxford to the gently rolling hills and distinctive honey-
colored stone buildings of the Cotswold region, then on to
Worcester and Kidderminster's towns. After cycling 90
miles that day, Harvey slept in a trave (a wooden cage
formed by stout crossbeams) of wheat sheaves.

On his fourth day, after cycling 350 miles, Harvey
continued north from Liverpool and Preston to Kendal,
the rugged, mountainous Lake District and the home of
his good friend and classmate Frank Graham. From Frank's
home in Kendal, Harvey and Frank rode on a motorbike
through some of the Lake District's most scenic areas and
to lakes Windermere and Coniston. Once back in Kendal,
Harvey wrote a long letter home, expressing his worry
"about his studies, money . . . ."[15]

On August 21, Harvey left Frank and joined Trist, a fellow Liverpool engineering student, and two other university friends. For five days, they hiked in the Lake District. They climbed to the top of 3,054-foot-high Skiddaw peak, where they enjoyed panoramic views of the surrounding mountains and lakes. After another night with the Grahams, Harvey headed south toward Kingsmans Farm in late August.

At Kingsmans, a rare letter from Harvey's father awaited him. John reported that the family was on vacation in Canada and the Adirondacks in upstate New York. "I sent you a card from Ottawa so you probably know we are on vacation . . . the most beautiful city I have ever been in. . . . We left early last Friday for Wales, Ontario. . . . Sunday morning we started for Old Forge, a long-time tourist gateway into the Adirondack Park."[16] Soon afterward, a letter from Mabel arrived from Old Forge. Stories of twelve-year-old Frank took up most of the letter.

> Frank has sure made a hit with six girls from Utica who are staying at the upper camp. He spends most of his time there. . . . You would laugh, too, for he pals around with everybody. Yesterday we saw him sailing up the lake in one of those passenger boats looking so pleased with himself sitting up beside the man running the boat. . . . Altogether he is having the time of his life. I think you will see a big change in him.[17]

At Kingsmans Farm, Harvey again settled into a routine of six-hour days studying for his upcoming repeat exams, interrupted only when Uncle Frank needed a hand on the farm. His money worries were never far from his mind. During his days at Kingsmans Farm, Harvey's relationship with his Uncle Frank became closer. Reflecting on his uncle many years later, Harvey reminisced:

Dear old Uncle Frank [was] a true rustic yeoman—sweet, simple, innocent soul with a great good heart. Of all the Harvey family, he alone never left the farm, and as a dutiful elder son cared for his parents and carried on as best he could. . . . He had a heavy East Anglian manner of speech, and loved to recall old times and odd characters with anyone who could share his visions.[18]

Intrigued by his East Anglian accent, Harvey later recalled a few of the local East Anglian words and their pronunciations undoubtedly used by Frank. "Hogg" meant yearling sheep, "gostsbrad" meant a corn mower, "raabin" meant robin, and "undernean" meant underneath. Although Harvey at first puzzled over some of Frank's words and pronunciations, he soon realized that his uncle's distinct dialect distinguished local East Anglians.

Harvey and Frank hay-racking ca. 1934.

In 1934, Essex folklorist Hugh Crammer-Byng also captured the peculiarities of Essex speech when he wrote,

We have in our dialects a quality of tone, phrase, and idiom which reveal the innate, underlying genius of the country folk. . . . In Essex the intimate sense of humour, and, to a lesser extent, a sense of guardedness in the attitude to strangers. These two qualities combine to give you the main characteristics of the Essex countryfolk."[19]

In mid-September, Harvey left Kingsmans Farm on his bicycle once again, loaded with thirty-five pounds of books and clothes for another cross-country trip back to Liverpool. This time he passed through Chelmsford, Aylesbury, Bicester, and Banbury in the Cotswolds. Harvey stopped only seven times during nine hours of cycling, spent not a penny, and slept that night in a group of trees under some brush beside a canal. Over the next two days, he passed through Warwick, Coventry, Birmingham, Wolverhampton, and then through Whitchurch, Chester, and Birkenhead and, finally, through the new Mersey Tunnel to Liverpool.

Unfortunately, Harvey paid the penalty for pushing so hard to complete 252 miles in three days. After studying for the second round of examinations the next day, he felt sick to his stomach and soon had a "midnight mess to clean up."[20] Although plagued by a stiff neck and a chest that ached with every deep breath, Harvey again took all of his first-year exams: pure mathematics, applied mathematics, physics, and chemistry. Very discouraged afterward, he wrote: "By only a miracle can I have made 33 percent" (the passing score).[21]

In late September and early October 1934, Harvey made two more bicycle trips between Liverpool and Kingsmans Farm. On September 25, on a wet, dreary day with ominous skies and strong winds, he headed southeast from Liverpool by another new route—this time through Shrewsbury to Hereford then Monmouth. After crossing the River Severn by ferry two days later, Harvey cycled on through Bristol, Bath, Reading, and Slough to London. Here, he took a "new road" east to Southend. After traveling 325 miles in three and a half days, Harvey arrived at

Kingsmans Farm that evening, sick with a sore throat and a terrible cold. Great Aunt Jennie, grandfather Stephen Harvey's sister, and letters from home awaited him. Little more than a week later, on October 5, Harvey mounted his bicycle again and headed northwest toward Liverpool, reaching the city on October 8, after cycling 280 miles.[22]

In early October, recognizing that his cycling had toughened him physically and mentally, Harvey penned a few lines of Sir Walter Scott's famous 1808 epic poem, *Marmion*, in his diary. He then made his last cycle trip of the year from Kingsmans Farm to Liverpool.

> *O young Lochinvar is come out of the west,*
> *Through all the wide Border his steed was the*
> *best;*
> *And save his good broadsword he weapons had*
> *none,*
> *He rode all unarm'd, and he rode all alone.*
> *So faithful in love, and so dauntless in war,*
> *There never was a knight like the young*
> *Lochinvar.*[23]

Harvey's multiple bicycle marathons across England in three months proved to be memorable. Between July and October, he had cycled over 1,800 miles, traversing terrain ranging from the steep and winding Cat and Fiddle Road in the Peak District to the low, rolling hills of southeast Essex. On some days, Harvey cycled nearly 120 miles. Even when exhausted, feeling down, soaking wet, or suffering from a stiff neck, sore throat, numbness in an arm, or a wildly pumping heart, he pushed on. The commitment, courage, endurance, and resilience required to complete these epic cycling adventures served as a kind of rite of passage from adolescence into manhood during a time of unsettling worries.[24]

Harvey's cycling not only tested his endurance and transported him to his families; it also opened his eyes to a larger world of new places and people across Great Britain. Although he could have chosen one familiar cycling route between Liverpool and Kingsmans Farm for all of his trips, he decided to follow different routes so that he could experience new places. Harvey seems to have understood that, despite his concerns about money and grades, his heavy workload, and his longing for family and friends, his cycling trips across Britain tested his will and showed him so much more of his parents' and ancestors' homes. He carefully memorialized all the details of his travels on a map and in his diary.

Confronting Financial and Academic Challenges

Harvey's return to Liverpool at the end of the summer was well rewarded. He learned that he had passed his first-year repeat exams, taken in mid-September. In celebration of this accomplishment, classmates Frank Graham and Bob Lynn took him to the pictures to see *My Song for You*.[25]

Harvey began his second year at Liverpool on October 8, 1934. After settling into his room in Rankin Hall with new roommates, Corlett and Watterson, he registered for five classes: Strength of Materials, Heat Engines, Naval Architecture, Pure and Applied Mathematics, and Descriptive & Drawing. He also talked with the university accountant and wistfully wrote in his diary, "maybe things will be alright." Harvey's second year began much the same as his first. He attended lectures, spent long hours at "varsity" (university) studying, sang in the student choir at the Liverpool Cathedral and the Welsh church choirs, visited classmates, frequently went to the pictures and "rugger" games, and regularly wrote letters home.[26]

As in the first year, a shortage of money continued to plague Harvey that fall. In mid-November, he wrote to both Uncle Tom and banker Griffith in Ferndale on the same day, asking to borrow more money. On December 1, Harvey candidly expressed gloomy thoughts in his diary after a troubling day of studying. "I am terribly fed up, tired & at present in a dangerous destroying mood," he confessed.[27] In mid-December, Harvey stayed up many nights until 1 or 2 a.m., studying for his first-quarter, second-year exams.[28]

On December 20, 1934, Harvey headed again to Kingsmans Farm, but this time he traveled by coach (bus) to London, then by train to Hockley station and, finally, walked 3.5 miles from there to Kingsmans Farm, where his Uncle Frank greeted him warmly. On Christmas Day, just as in 1933, most of Harvey's aunts, uncles, and cousins—Maud and Charles, Reg and Winnie and their children, along with Great Aunt Jennie—gathered at Auntie Ethel's and Uncle Maurice's Hutton House for a "great feed," singing, and listening to the radio.

Cards and letters arrived for Harvey from his mother, Uncle Tom in Wales, his classmate Frank Graham, and Mr. and Mrs. Griffith in Rochester. On December 31, Harvey and his Uncle Frank welcomed in the New Year at Kingsmans Farm as they listened to celebrations on the radio. Before heading back to Liverpool in early January, Harvey rode Uncle Frank's "archaic bike" to visit several aunts and uncles.[29]

Weighed Down by Studies and Indebtedness

On January 9, 1935, Harvey rode from London to Liverpool on a Crosville Motor Services' bus. Arriving back in Liverpool, Harvey was delighted to learn that he had passed all of his fall term exams. This heartening news coincided with annual Panto Day celebrations, highlighted by a rowdy entourage of university students dressed in comic costumes, who paraded down Brownlow Hill to the city center and collected money for Liverpool hospitals.[30]

During the winter term of 1935, Harvey's course load proved incredibly daunting. Many times, between February and late March, he wrote in his diary of his tremendous doubt, angst, and discouragement over his workload. "How can anyone be expected to know all this stuff," he wrote on February 1. "We are simply buried alive with it! Lord help us!" . . . "Work is piled on at such a rate that it is a job to keep from getting discouraged." In mid- and late February, he exclaimed, "The old brain definitely decided to go on its annual strike. One could hardly blame it. . . . How much longer can this crazy whirl keep on? . . . Worked all day until 12:15. What does it all matter? I wonder. . . . This discouraging pile of work is enough to drive one to drink if not worse."[31] The heavy load continued up until mid-March, when Harvey took his winter term exams. He was relieved and astonished to learn on March 26 that he had passed them all.[32]

Harvey and Frank Graham studying.

Intent on finally turning his mind away from the last two months of mounting stress, Harvey prepared for his first cycle trip of 1935. After his last examination, he and fellow naval architecture student Reg Jones set off for North Wales, cycling west from Liverpool through some extraordinarily rugged and picturesque country. From Chester, they cycled west into Wales, then through Mold, Betws-y-coed, Bethesda, Bangor, Conway, and, finally, on to Llanrwst. Despite the wet weather and rugged terrain, they managed to cycle 230 miles in four days.

Harvey was then off to South Wales to again visit his Uncle Tom. Harvey continued from there by train to London, then to Hockley and Kingsmans Farm, where Harvey and cousin Vernon helped Uncle Frank set potatoes and drill an acre of mangolds (mangels). Harvey returned to Liverpool on April 24.[33]

Harvey's severe shortage of money caused him great angst. Since January 1935, his finances had been meager. Even when his father promised to send money to the university to pay his hostel and class fees, often he didn't. In late January, Harvey was "unpleasantly and suddenly shocked" to find out that his hostel fees were overdue; he promptly wrote his father a short note. Two days later, Harvey visited the registrar. Harvey waited through February and into early March, but "still no mail nor money" arrived. "I wish I knew how this would all end," Harvey lamented in his diary.

In early March, Harvey again visited the registrar, who reported that John Evans had promised to send money, yet had not. In mid-March, £30 came, and, four days later, a letter with five dollars enclosed arrived from Evan, who had just graduated from high school and was now working. Despite these encouraging letters, Harvey's money problems continued through April and May. Once again, the registrar sent Harvey a letter informing him that his father's money had not arrived. By May 15, there had been no mail or word of any kind from John and Mabel for three weeks. Then, on May 17, a letter from John arrived, along with $8. Twelve days later, a letter from Mabel came with one dollar enclosed.[34]

Finally, in early June, almost miraculously, $100 arrived in the mail from Mabel for Harvey's ship passage home that summer. Harvey immediately purchased a ticket for the Cunard ocean liner RMS *Scythia*, scheduled to leave Liverpool on June 22. Another $20 arrived from Mabel on June 13. Now, all that stood between Harvey's return to his family in Pittsford after two years away were his second-year examinations. Between June 11 and 18, Harvey took seven exams. [35]

The day after his last two examinations, Harvey mounted his bicycle and took a ride along the full length of the River Mersey docks, spotting some ships he'd seen before, plus the *Scythia*, which he would soon board. After two days of running errands, taking photos, packing, and carrying items to the Cunard building for shipping, Harvey locked up the "digs" that he, Frank Graham, and Bob Harwood would share in the fall. Harvey then, with an entourage of his friends (Bob Lynn, Frank Graham, "Watty," Carter, Bob Harwood, and one other), made his way to the *Scythia* near the Pier Head on the afternoon of June 22. That afternoon, as the *Scythia* moved slowly away from the dock into the main channel of the River Mersey, Harvey took a photo of his university friends, who had supported and encouraged him for the past two years, as they stood waving from the dock in front of the Pier Head.[36]

Harvey gets a sendoff from friends at the Pier
Head, July 1935.

During the next week, the *Scythia* sailed first in blue
waters off the coast of Ireland before encountering heavy
swells. Days of damp, cold, and cloudy weather followed.
Harvey met some Americans on board, played shuffleboard, read, slept, listened to the orchestra, and watched
horse "races" with miniature wooden horses. The last day
before the ship stopped in Boston, Harvey was delighted
to tour the engine room and look over the steering
machinery. On July 1, the *Scythia* arrived at Chelsea Piers
in New York City. As the ship moved slowly alongside the
dock, John, Evan, Mabel, and young Frank stood waiting
expectantly on the pier below. After two years of separation, the Evans family celebrated their reunion by taking
in some of the sights in New York City (Radio City
Theatre and the movie *Love Me Forever*). The next day
Harvey drove the family home to Pittsford.[37]

*The Evans family greets Harvey at Chelsea Piers, New York
City, 1935.*

11

AT HOME IN THE U.S. AND BRITAIN

1935–1936

After being away from home for two years, Harvey's summer with his family in 1935 was memorable. Although Frank had grown taller and matured, little else had changed at home. Two days after arriving in Long Meadow, Harvey's many friends descended on the Evans home. "What a day of handshaking, kissing, and talking," he gushed in his diary on July 4, as the nation celebrated Independence Day.

For the next three months, Harvey visited his many Rochester and Pittsford friends and completed chores around the house (mowing the lawn, painting the windows, replacing shingles on the roof, washing the car, and more). He also returned to his model shipbuilding and completed both the *Texas* and the *Indianapolis.* Harvey's three months at home sped by quickly. All too soon, it was time to return to his good friends and his classes at the University of Liverpool. He was also very eager to return to his family at Kingsmans Farm and in Aberaman, Wales. A chilling rain fell all day on September 26, when Harvey packed and bid farewell to his family and many friends in Pittsford and Rochester.[1]

John, Mabel, Evan, Frank at home, (Harvey Evans
photo).

A chilling rain fell all day on September 27 when his
family and friends saw him off from Rochester on a train
bound for New York City. After boarding the German
ocean liner SS *Europa* later that day, the ship pulled anchor
in the late afternoon, maneuvered from its mooring at
Chelsea Piers, and moved down the Hudson River before
making its way through the Upper and Lower New York
Bays and out into the open ocean.[2]

For the next six days, the *Europa's* helmsman determined the bearing and set Southampton's course. Harvey
kept himself occupied by reading, writing letters to friends
in Rochester and Pittsford, playing bridge, sleeping, and
watching the German movie *Heil Hitler*. Harvey noted in
his diary that this was the greeting used by all the German
ship's crew.

By the third day, Harvey's curiosity about the ship's
operation and equipment lured him down to the engine
room to examine the propeller shaft. Two days later, he
visited the elevated ship's bridge, where the captain navigated the ship. On the fourth day, Harvey wrote about bad
weather that caused the vessel to roll uncontrollably from
side to side. The weather had calmed by his final day on
board when he stayed up all night—filled with anticipation

—before the ship stopped briefly at Cherbourg on France's north coast. The *Europa* then continued due north across the English Channel to Southampton. After disembarking, Harvey made his way to London, where he boarded a train to Hockley. He finally arrived at Kingsmans Farm late that evening, where his Uncle Frank greeted him warmly.[3]

Going Home to Britain

Harvey had relished being back with his family and high school and neighborhood friends in Pittsford and Rochester. However, now he looked forward to going home to his Harvey and Evans families in Essex and Aberaman, and to reuniting with his Liverpool classmates. After spending two years in Britain, Mabel's and John's families had very much become Harvey's family as well.

Immediately after arriving at Kingsmans Farm, Harvey noticed that some changes had been made. Harvey soon learned that the Harvey family no longer owned the farm; signs of this were everywhere apparent. In late April 1935, Kingsmans Farm, consisting of the farmhouse and farm buildings, along with 141 acres of working arable fields and grassland on the River Crouch, had been sold at an auction. The auction details noted that the property could make an inviting summer resort, be developed as a building estate, or be converted to a golf course. For some time, the farm's location along the River Crouch had attracted vacationers. During previous summers, Uncle Frank had received revenue from visiting motorists, picnickers, and bathers eager to relax on the River Crouch near the edge of Kingsmans Farm. The auction agreement specified that Frank could remain a tenant on the property for a rental fee of £123 a year. The new owner's landlord would take responsibility for making reasonable repairs. When Harvey arrived in early October, he immediately noticed a difference in the state of the previously worn farm buildings: "the new landlord certainly has done wonders," he reported in his diary.[4]

Kingsmans haying, early 1930s (courtesy David Langridge).

For the next two days, many Harvey family members gathered at Kingsmans Farm to welcome Harvey and pitch in to help Uncle Frank with fall plowing and other farm chores. Auntie Bertha, Uncle Martin, and their daughter Patrina Longman; Uncle Reg, Aunt Winnie, and their four children (Vernon, Betty, Audry, and Stephen); and Auntie Ethel, Uncle Maurice Langridge, and their four children (Raymond, Desmond, Joan, and Stephen) all gathered at Kingsmans Farm.

Connecting Across the Atlantic

On October 7, Harvey left Hockley station on a London-bound train then continued to Liverpool. From Liverpool's Lime Street station, Harvey walked about two miles to his new digs at 54A Croxteth Road, where he would soon share his lodging with engineering classmates Frank Graham and Bob Harwood. The three men rented rooms in a late-nineteenth-century, three-story, red-brick Victorian house. Nearby was the pastoral Sefton Park, opened in 1872, known as "Hyde Park of the North." The monumental Liverpool Cathedral, where Harvey sang in the student choir, could be seen on the crest of a hill to the northwest. Although not completed, the lower portion of the cathedral's massive bell tower made an imposing sight as the sun lowered in the west.

54A Croxteth, Liverpool (G. Evans photo, 2016).

Harvey quickly settled into his third year at the University of Liverpool. After registering for naval architecture courses—theory of machines, heat engines, pure and applied math classes—he began a familiar routine of studying. Harvey also went to the hostel on Ullet Street, where he had roomed during his first two years, visited some of the lads he knew there, and collected the bicycle and other belongings he'd stored there. Harvey soon began singing again with the Liverpool Cathedral student choir and some choral groups on campus.[5] He eagerly resumed his practice of letter-writing to family and friends in Pittsford and Rochester.

Harvey soon received word that life for the Evans family on East Brook Road in Long Meadow had been anything but uneventful after he had left for Liverpool. After graduating from high school in January 1935, Evan started taking piano lessons at the Eastman School of Music in Rochester in the fall. George Eastman, an industrialist, philanthropist, and founder of the Eastman Kodak

Company, established the Eastman School of Music in 1921. "People need to have an interest outside their occupations," Eastman firmly believed. He felt the broad education of young musicians within a university would contribute to "the musical enrichment and education of the greater community." Eastman convinced the University of Rochester president that the university should found a professional music school. The president agreed.

After Eastman purchased land in downtown Rochester just three blocks east of Sibley's department store on East Main Street, bulldozers broke ground in early 1920. The initial building, completed in September 1921, was intended to house not only a school with classrooms and instrument practice rooms but an auditorium for students to give performances for the Rochester community. Over the next ten years, the Eastman Theatre, a five-floor annex, and, later, a ten-story addition with classrooms and practice rooms were added to the building. In 1922, the faculty had increased to thirty-two instructors.[6]

By the time Evan began taking piano lessons in 1935, the faculty had doubled in size. It included some of the best-educated and notable American musicians with specialties in a wide array of subjects and instruments. Evan, mostly self-taught on the piano that his father had bought for him in 1920, began taking lessons at the Eastman School of Music just as Harvey started his third year of classes at the University of Liverpool. Evan took courses in the so-called "Preparatory Department" at the Eastman School of Music, which required no previous formal music training to enter, led to graduation with a diploma, and aimed to serve the Rochester community. Piano teacher and performer Raymond Wilson, who had studied at the Peabody Conservatory and taught at Skidmore College in Saratoga Springs, New York, arrived at the Eastman School of Music right after it opened in 1921. In addition to teaching piano, Wilson supervised the preparatory piano studies. In 1924, he was the assistant director of the Preparatory Department.[7]

In October 1935, Evan made an appointment to see Raymond Wilson, who "fired questions at me then asked me to play something." He then had Evan take a "theory test." Wilson soon determined that Evan should work with Eastman piano teacher Jerome Diamond and music theory teacher Gladys Leventon. Evan was exuberant. "They're both great, and I like it all very much," Evan exclaimed in a letter to Harvey.[8] Diamond had graduated with the first Eastman School of Music class and then studied at the Paris Conservatory. Gladys Metcalf Leventon received a bachelor of music degree from the Eastman School of Music in 1929.[9]

Over the next several months, Evan continued to express great enthusiasm for his music lessons and teachers at the Eastman School of Music. "The old piano and the lessons are coming right along," Evan cheerfully explained in a letter to Harvey. "I have to play for Ray Wilson before Christmas. Cusses." In January 1936, Evan reported, "I'm prepping for a music test with Mr. Wilson. Pray for me. I'm a little jittery, although Mr. Diamond seems to be very pleased with what I've accomplished so far."

Soon Evan received more good news about his progress at the Eastman School of Music. In late January, he did so well on a piano test given by Ray Wilson that he advanced a whole grade. In early February, Evan reported that he got 96 percent on Mrs. Leventon's theory class test and was the only one to receive an "A" grade in the class. "Do I sound awfully snooty or 'uff-uppy'? I hope not," Evan told Harvey in a letter. Mabel also told Harvey that Evan was "very happy indeed. He really does seem to be in his glory now and is so faithful about practicing. I think he is going to go places and do things," she exclaimed with great pride. Evan now set his sights on studying music in England and began saving money for continuing his education there.[10]

Evan at the piano,
Pittsford, NY, ca. 1936.

Evan worked hard not only at his music but also at Sibley's department store during the holiday season. In October 1935, the general superintendent at Sibley's, pleased with Evan's work, promised he would fit Evan into the work schedule wherever he could. Evan first began working at a basement grocery sale (which Evan detested, explaining that it made him "crabby"). A month before Christmas, he was working as a full-fledged salesman, selling bedspreads and similar items. Evan liked this very much. By the end of December, he had managed to put $26 in the bank. In May 1936, Evan was still working part-time at Sibley's. "You can be sure this is helping us over some tough sledding," Mabel admitted to Harvey in a letter.[11] The family struggled to make their payments for their house, Harvey's education, and Evan's music lessons.

While Evan managed to work part-time at Sibley, Lindsay & Curr, many long-time employees fared less well. In the fall of 1935, Mabel reported to Harvey that Mr. Egglestore had been demoted to a floorwalker (an employee who supervises salespeople). He soon decided to resign. Other employees were also let go or decided to retire. One buyer, who could not make a go of his department, had it taken from him. Soon, four other employees left the store. Evan reported to Harvey that Sibley's "now has an efficiency expert" who taught a five-week course on

"The Psychology of Selling" for all salespeople and floor-walkers. The company dismissed all those who did not receive a final exam grade of 80 percent or higher. All these changes to the store management, as the Great Depression continued, made everyone at Sibley's feel extremely uneasy, including John.[12]

Fortunately, John managed to keep his job as a fabric buyer during this period of troubling upheaval at Sibley's— at least for the time being. He continued to buy silk and began purchasing other specialty fabrics for those employees who had been laid off. In addition to his work at the store, John remained completely engaged in multiple activities at the South Congregational Church. In the 1930s, he served as chairman of the Board of Deacons. He often wrote and recited words for church hymns and prayers. In early 1936, John also became president of the Long Meadow Club in Pittsford. Everyone energetically clapped and cheered when he initially took this position. The following year, he was re-elected.[13]

Mounting Money Concerns

Within weeks after Harvey returned to Liverpool, he became preoccupied with something more than attending classes and preparing for examinations. Money, or rather the lack of it, became an increasingly distressing and distracting concern. More and more, Harvey struggled to make ends meet due to the shortage of money that arrived from home. It is unclear what initial arrangement John, Mabel, and Harvey had made about how much financial support he would receive from his parents for his university education and housing. There may have been only an informal agreement that John and Mabel would pay for Harvey's university classes and accommodation. Harvey certainly had this understanding. However, what money he received fluctuated unpredictably and stopped altogether when John and Mabel became overwhelmed by regular payments owed and those that arose. No one had anticipated that the depression would continue.

Additionally, John and Mabel had never owned property before purchasing their lovely Pittsford home. They had never experienced a financial depression and never wanted to abandon their life-long aspiration to live a comfortable middle-class life. Paying for the education of two sons at once and practicing restraint in spending were not easily reconciled with John and Mabel's middle-class ambitions. Along with millions of others, they were unprepared to handle the overwhelming financial demands confronting them in the mid-1930s. They customarily approached bill-paying by identifying those most pressing bills, then precariously juggled the money John received each month between multiple payees. It was naturally more manageable for John to take care of his family's immediate needs in Pittsford first than to attend to Harvey's financial needs in distant England, no matter how much he wanted to.

A hint of these thorny money issues arose soon after Harvey arrived back in Liverpool in the fall of 1935. Mabel soon reported to Harvey that the University of Liverpool accountant, Mr. Lewis, had sent a letter asking for two large payments for a debt owed from the previous year. Since they could not make the entire payment at once, Mabel and John proposed paying it in three installments. When Harvey visited the university accountant in October 1935, he learned that an arrangement had been made between the accountant and his parents to pay for past overdue university fees and those fees for the 1935 fall term. "Maybe things will be alright," Harvey wistfully speculated in his diary.[14]

This, however, was wishful thinking; money matters

soon got worse. As Harvey pondered the accountant's demand for money, his landlady, Mrs. Heilbron, insisted that he pay the £3 he owed for his portion of his digs at 54A Croxteth Road. "What fun!" Harvey penciled in his diary. Increasingly this became his usual expression when things were *not* much fun at all.

Finally, on November 7, 1935, a letter from home arrived, but without any green bills or promise from his father that he would send them. Four days later, on American Armistice Day, with great relief, Harvey opened a letter with $20 enclosed, sent by some of his Rochester friends—"dear old" Hod Hegendorfer, Olive, and Johnny Jones—plus letters from his parents. Another five dollars arrived near the end of November. Despite additional money that periodically came, Harvey's debt to Mrs. Heilbron continued to swell, reaching £6-7/8 (6 pounds, 7 shillings, 8 pence) by December 11.[15]

With each passing month, Harvey's accumulated debt to his landlady and the university registrar continued to grow. Very little money had arrived from his father to cover this debt or his small daily expenses. Harvey had little money to pay for necessities. That winter, Harvey's shoes provided only thin protection from the wet, cold weather. "When a fellow resorts to wearing blotting paper in his shoes," Harvey wrote in his diary, "it seems time for the Lord to step in and send some money."[16] Nothing arrived from home, however.

In mid-December, Harvey tried hard to push money concerns from his mind as he prepared for his term-end exams. He had a brief reprieve from financial worries after his roommate, Frank Graham, saw him off on the train to London and Hockley to spend the Christmas holidays at Kingsmans Farm. Upon his arrival, Harvey began helping his Uncle Frank with farm chores—repairing fences and the cowshed and digging ditches to drain the farm ponds after heavy rains. He then spent time with his abundantly congenial and supportive aunts, uncles, and cousins on Christmas and Boxing Day.[17]

When Harvey returned to Liverpool in early 1936, he soon heard from Mr. Griffith at Lloyds Bank in Ferndale, Wales. In early January, Harvey received a statement from Griffith itemizing the money he had borrowed and now owed Lloyds Bank. Harvey immediately wrote to banker Griffith, reassuring him that he was expecting the arrival of money from home. Money from Pittsford, however, never came.[18]

As Liverpool experienced an exceptionally frigid winter in early 1936, Harvey became increasingly worried about his continued shortage of funds and mounting debts. The infrequent news he received from his parents about when to expect any money heightened his concerns. By late January, Harvey owed his landlady £6-7/11½ (6 pounds, 7 shillings, 11.5 pence). One month later, this debt had risen to £13-3/5½. Against the backdrop of national events—the death of King George V on January 20, followed by the abdication of Edward VIII (intent on marrying American divorcee Wallis Simpson)—and Harvey's participation in Panto Revere, fundraising activities, and singing with the student choir at the Liverpool Cathedral, Harvey became increasingly distressed about the absence of money from home. "Where is the money I was going to receive?" he ruefully wrote in his diary and to his parents in both February and March 1936.[19]

When only a few dollars arrived from John and Mabel late that winter, Evan wrote to Harvey explaining that John's money must have gone astray in the mail. "He [John] isn't sure that he put 'England' on the envelope (containing the money order), and he also isn't sure that he included the return address. So your money is somewhere between Rochester and Liverpool," Evan conjectured. "Pa is a little hard-pressed for cash at the present time," Evan explained. "We're all squeezing like h--- for you." Evan then promised his brother that he would take money out of his Rochester Savings account the next day and send it to him, an extraordinarily generous gesture, since Evan was paying for his music lessons.[20]

A letter to Henry that followed from Mabel elaborated on the family's financial woes. John had borrowed $500 to pay some of Harvey's accumulated fees in 1934–1935 and made monthly repayments on that debt. In February 1936, the family scraped money together for bills "that absolutely had to be paid. You have certainly been fine about it all, Harvey. It has been anything but easy for us," Mabel wrote a week later. In a very hopeful, optimistic postscript, Mabel concluded that "it won't be so long before we shall be coming over for your graduation" [in the summer of 1937]. In March 1936, yet a third letter with money from John and Mabel mysteriously went astray in the mail. Harvey, like his father, now resorted to borrowing money to get by.[21]

Despite the mysterious loss of money sent from his parents, Harvey soon became preoccupied with taking his March end-of-term exams in naval architecture, heat engines, metallurgy, and pure and applied math. Immediately after finishing his exams, he went by bus from Liverpool to Hockley, then walked to Kingsmans Farm, arriving late in the evening of March 20. During his month-long holiday at the farm, he helped Uncle Frank with the farming chores. He plowed, helped plant peas and potatoes, loaded hay onto a lorry, harrowed wheat, cut wood, spread manure, cut more wood, and rolled the tennis court. Throughout the month-long Easter holiday, Harvey also spent much time with his aunts, uncles, and cousins. He received two letters from his Uncle Tom in Wales, in which he likely may have asked if John had sent

money yet to pay Mr. Griffith at the Lloyd's Bank in
Ferndale.

Langridge family, 1935 (courtesy Nick Hards).

Around the same time, Harvey also received an
"unwanted letter" from his landlady, Mrs. Heilbron, in
Liverpool. On more than one occasion, Harvey noted in
his diary that he had "chats" with a couple of his more
financially well-set relatives—Auntie Bertha's husband,
Uncle Martin, and Auntie Ethel's husband, Uncle Maurice
—hoping they might loan him some money. On April 22,
1936, Harvey very reluctantly borrowed 15 shillings from
Uncle Frank to pay his coach fare from Hockley back to
Liverpool.[22]

Harvey's indebtedness remained at the forefront of
both John's and Mabel's minds that spring. In early April,
Mabel assured Harvey that both she and John had written
to Uncle Tom and promised to send some money to Mr.
Griffith at Lloyds Bank as soon as John received his
monthly pay the very next day. Twenty-five dollars that
John had reportedly sent Mr. Griffith the previous
October had never been received. It was allegedly sent
again in May 1936.

In mid-May, Mabel reported that $125 had been mailed to the university to cover unpaid registration fees. John "expects to send the rest June 1," Mabel wrote to Harvey.[23] By late spring, however, Mrs. Heilbron had not received any money for Harvey's rent. Soon, Mrs. Heilbron moved Harvey and Frank Graham to other digs at 54 Croxteth Road. In mid-May and early June, Mabel reported to Harvey that John had sent more money to him; once again, it mysteriously had "gone astray."

While confusion continued about money and Harvey's concern about the pounds owed Mrs. Heilbron mounted, he may have barely noticed a remarkable historic naval event: the RMS *Queen Mary*'s maiden voyage from Southampton to New York City. After the Great Depression halted construction of the *Queen Mary* in December 1930, the British government eventually gave the newly merged Cunard and White Star lines a hefty loan to complete it, which the company did in three and a half years. The 81,000-ton, 1,020-foot-long *Queen Mary* boasted the world's most massive power train (the combined ship's engines, generators, steering gear, boilers, and water plant), which enabled her to attain unprecedented speeds. On her maiden voyage to New York City, the *Queen Mary* reached the Lightship Ambrose in lower New York Harbor in a record-setting time of fewer than four days. In August 1936, the *Queen Mary* captured the so-called "Blue Riband" accolade, an unofficial acknowledgment of merit given to a passenger liner crossing the Atlantic Ocean at the highest average speed. As a model shipbuilder and a naval architect in training, Harvey must have become captivated by the *Queen Mary* and at least temporarily distracted from his mounting debts.[24]

Pitching In

Impressive achievements like this, however, could not diminish Harvey's continuing concern about his impover-ished condition and his growing indebtedness. Mean-while, an unending stream of bills kept arriving at the family home in Pittsford, including over $80 for Evan's lessons at the Eastman School of Music for the upcoming year. As John and Mabel struggled to make ends meet and take care of family needs at home, their letters to Harvey became less frequent during April and May 1936. Four days after his birthday on May 1, Harvey wrote in his diary that he had received "no mail from home now for almost a month and no money since, when was it?" No letter arrived until May 13. In it, Mabel explained their struggles in general terms, then, as always, ended on a cheery, upbeat note: "Keep well and happy. We are getting in the last lap, and soon you will be home."[25]

Mabel, and especially John, who sometimes failed to share with Mabel the family's precar-ious financial state of affairs, indeed agonized over John's inability to cover Harvey's expenses, along with Evan's. "Many times [we] have almost thought we might better let the

Frank with dogs, Rex and Gyp.

house go," Mabel confessed in a May 1936 letter to Harvey, "then, we pep up again, and decide that if we can stick a little longer, all will be well." As mounting debts for Harvey continued, Mabel tried to ease his concerns by sending buoyant letters filled with optimism and encour-aging words. As she often said in challenging times, she urged Harvey to be patient, keep heart, be cheerful, and smile. "Be positive . . . everything will be OK," Mabel repeated in her letters to Harvey.[26]

In reality, everyone in the Evans household had worked hard to relieve John and Mabel's indebtedness and help pay Harvey's bills. Both John and Evan continued to work at Sibley's. Frank, at age nine, started selling magazines all around Pittsford. By early November 1935, he had four subscriptions. In July 1936, Frank also had a job picking up balls on a driving range at a local golf course, which earned him 50 cents a week.[27] Happily for Harvey, Frank proved to be a cheerful communicator who earnestly tried to send him money. In one letter, he told Harvey that he had received

> a star in writing today [at school]. Well, snow is on the ground. I could not 'pump' the snow today; the snow was so deep and the wind was so strong all together it was very hard. . . . had to stop because my hands were cold; sometimes do your hands get cold? I will have to be going. I am wishing you a Merry Christmas and a Happy New Year.[28]

Mabel also worked to boost the family income by selling some of her much admired hand-knit sweaters. In May 1936, she reported that she was "working every minute on my knitting. I have ten orders now." That fall, Evan and Frank moved into the same second-floor bedroom, thus creating a bedroom upstairs that John and Mabel soon rented to a Mr. Brown. They also hoped to help Harvey pay his university debts and to travel to England to cheer him on at his graduation in 1937. Both John and Mabel often mentioned in their letters how much they wanted to see Harvey receive his degree. Considering that Harvey was the oldest son of a father whose formal education ended around age thirteen, the entire family considered his effort and accomplishment worthy of a grand celebration. Plus, John and Mabel had always encouraged Harvey, as well as Evan and Frank, to pursue their ambitions.[29]

Harvey, like other family members, also attempted to find work in the summer of 1936. His effort coincided with the arrival of a bill from Mrs. Heilbron for the total amount of money he owed: £20. "Wow," Harvey exclaimed in his diary. In early June 1936, Mrs. Heilbron had had enough broken promises from Harvey and evicted him, along with his roommate Frank Graham, from their digs. Since Frank was away at the time, Harvey packed up and carried both of their belongings to their classmate Bob Lynn's digs. Harvey stayed with Bob Lynn while attending welding and other shop classes until mid-July.[30]

Harvey's Good Fortune and Evan's Challenges

Just as more distressing news about his indebtedness arrived on Harvey's doorstep, a fantastic job opportunity materialized. Sometime in the spring or early summer of 1936, as his debts continued to mount, Harvey walked from the university to the India Buildings on historic Water Street in the heart of Liverpool's banking and business district. Here, not far from the River Mersey docks, Harvey stopped by the Elder Dempster Lines offices on the India Buildings' eighth floor. The firm that launched steamship services between Liverpool and China had erected this grand steel-and-stone Beaux-Arts style building for its head offices and rental office space between 1924 and 1932. It was here that Harvey must have applied for work on board the Elder Dempster's British Motor passenger ship MV *Abosso*. In June, he learned with great delight and enormous relief that he was offered a job as a "student engineer" on the *Abosso*.

For five weeks in July and August, the ship routinely traveled down and back up Africa's west coast, delivering passengers and mail to ports in several countries colonized by Great Britain, France, Spain, Germany, and Portugal.

A sobering letter Harvey received from Evan in July, however, tempered his moment of ecstasy as he prepared to leave on the *Abosso*. Evan's letter proved especially poignant since he shared with Harvey, perhaps for the first time, the difficult challenges he faced in Rochester as a gay man. Although the family had become aware of his sexual orientation when he was growing up, it was never mentioned outside the family. Only decades later, a close family friend, Charles Harris, commented on Evan occasionally wearing Mabel's dresses at home. "You can always thank God," Evan began in his letter to Harvey,

> that you aren't a freak of nature. . . . It's rather nice to be distinguished, but not the way I am. Would that the word[s] 'sissy, pansy, Percy, and lily' had never been! You'll never know how dreadfully difficult it is to walk down the street and have people yell from cars in a simpering fashion 'You-hoo' and wave a dainty hand. It's awful! And what makes it worse is that all this isn't my fault. It wasn't my idea to come on earth looking and acting, I suppose, the sissy. When one stops to think, though, it is just a bit unfair. But that's enough of that; I didn't write all this for any pity or sympathy. At this moment, I'm looking at the world through the proverbial rose-colored glasses, so don't let all this worry you. Mom would have a fit if she knew I was writing this. . . . Don't get excited; it's little Evan letting off steam.[31]

Mabel later found Evan's letter to Harvey and "did the sparks fly," Evan reported to Harvey. [32] After Mabel scolded Evan for his letter to Harvey, he decided to keep news of his gender orientation "forevermore" to himself.[33]

Although Mabel, the entire family, and close friends probably all knew Evan was gay, they seemed to appreciate Evan for the kind, generous, tender-hearted, and musically talented man he was. In his lovely baritone voice, he often sang and played the piano at public functions. Around this time, perhaps to save money and maybe also to be in the company of an empathetic musician, Evan stopped his classes at the Eastman School of Music and began taking piano lessons from the talented pianist and Welshman, Francis A. Jones, a graduate of the Royal Academy of Music in London. He, too, was gay. Francis played the piano in concerts and directed musical programs at numerous venues throughout Rochester. He also gave private lessons at his studio at 186 East Avenue, Rochester. Mabel wrote to Harvey that Francis gave Evan great encouragement about his music.[34]

As a gay man, Evan was living in a difficult time and place. In the 1920s and 1930s, America and Britain's acceptance of gay men, particularly in urban cultural centers like New York, Chicago, and London, was not uncommon. Gay clubs openly operated as so-called "pansy clubs." The 1920s witnessed an increase in the number of bohemian enclaves in New York's Greenwich Village, where cheap rents and the possibility of connecting with kindred souls attracted painters, poets, and performers. During this period, homosexuality in New York and London became more open and accepted. Gay performers became the darlings of Broadway. However, an exuberant outpouring from gay performers and artists lasted only until the mid-1930s when the Great Depression and some sensationalized sex crimes resulted in the harsh condemnation of homosexuality. New laws prohibited gay men and any suggestion of homosexuality from being featured in films or on stage. In some places, gay men faced the real risk of arrest, prosecution, and harsh punishment for expressing gay behavior in public. In the mid-1930s, it became extremely demoralizing for Evan or anyone to live openly as a gay or lesbian person.[35]

Anticipating that this would be his last letter to Harvey before his brother left for Africa on the *Abosso*, Evan sent him well wishes for a wonderful trip. "See and do everything possible," Evan encouraged. "Do have a 'swell' time, but please . . . don't forget that the four people who love you the most are living in Long Meadow. And how they're wishing you were sailing for America rather than Africa on the 15th of July."[36]

12

TRAVEL ADVENTURES

1936–1937

O n July 13, with giddy anticipation, Harvey signed on to the MV *Abosso* and carried his bag of belongings onto the ship for his five-week voyage. Launched just one year earlier in June 1935, the *Abosso* was a passenger, mail, and cargo liner built by Cammell Laird, a company in Birkenhead just across the River Mersey from Liverpool. The 11,330-ton *Abosso* became the largest and leading vessel at that time owned by Elder Dempster Lines. The ship boasted two-stroke marine diesel engines driving twin screws that propelled the ship forward at 14.5 knots (16.7 miles per hour). The *Abosso* accommodated 250 first-class, 74 second-class, and 332 third-class passengers. Harvey, one of the two "student engineers" on board, was one of the 182 crew members. On the evening of July 14, he and fellow student engineer, J. F. McKenna, were shown to their second-class stateroom, which Harvey described as "jolly nice."[1]

Harvey immediately recognized that his trip on the *Abosso* along Africa's west coast would be the most memorable adventure of his young life. On this voyage, Harvey would enter the colonial orbits of Great Britain, France,

Germany, Spain, and Portugal, all of which had economic and political interests on Africa's west coast. From the moment he stepped on board, Harvey began recording in detail all of his daily activities, places he visited, and the people he met.

The MV *Abosso* (J. Harvey Evans photo, 1936).

Adventures in Africa and Scotland

On July 15, as the *Abosso* slowly glided away from the River Mersey dock,[2] Harvey penciled the event in his personal diary.

> We left the dock this morning at high tide; we two [with McKenna] viewing the proceedings from the engine room with a peep or two on deck to see how things were going. It was darn interesting. All the engineers were standing by in the engine room. Bells would clang and the hands on large dials would register the orders given on the bridge [the enclosed room on the ship where the captain/officers directed operations]. Then, two of the engineers standing by a set of levers would set the old engines going.[3]

The ship soon moved into position alongside the River Mersey landing stage in front of the Pier Head, where passengers came on board. The *Abosso* set sail that afternoon around 4:00 p.m. and slowly headed north on the River Mersey to the Irish Sea, then south through St. George's Channel separating Ireland from Wales.[4]

During his first day on board, Harvey examined his surroundings and paused to marvel at the *Abosso*'s mechanical equipment.

> She is a very fine ship of some 11,000 tons. This is her sixth voyage, her maiden being in October last. Everything is so up to date, new and fresh looking that she is quite a treat. The engine room, especially with its masses of machinery, stairways, and gear all literally shining is a fine sight.[5]

The next day he described the ship's movements at sea.

> By the morning of the sixteenth we had taken up a slight rolling motion and the steward with kind intentions, but disastrous results brought us both each [Harvey and McKenna] a cup of coffee to start the day. My mate very soon returned his in a most ungentlemanly manner, and on him, I put the blame for my later doing the same. My breakfast fared little better but all in all, I have felt much worse. My mate and the third electrician couldn't be bothered with breakfast at all . . .
>
> Today is a lovely one. The sun shines down with a directness that makes it seem like home on a slightly swelling, beautiful dark blue sea. Lovely little tufts of clouds, fracto cumuli, I think you would call them, are set in a pale blue sky. About me are white boats, white davits [a small crane on a ship used for lowering a lifeboat], white ventilators, white gear of all sorts and above a squat buff funnel pushing out the sound of a distant chugging rumble. Only a very few moments ago a school of porpoises were cavorting directly abeam and

only a hundred yards or less away. They ran us a lovely
race in their sporting. Cleaving both air and water with
the same speed, ease and grace they usually freed themselves of the water in perfect unison in groups of three.[6]

On July 18, the *Abosso* skirted the Bay of Biscay, with
France to the east and Spain to the south. Here, Harvey
wrote that

the sea had a wicked swell and top to it, and kicked us
about quite ruthlessly all afternoon and evening. A husky
wind shoved our equilibrium position over about five
degrees and made the shrouds [ropes supporting the
masts] sing. Then, how we mounted those swells, twisted
over the crest, and dove into the trough! Clouds of spray
swept continually over the forecastle [forward part of a
ship], but we just kept on.[7]

Continuing southwest, the *Abosso* arrived at Portuguese
Madeira, a rocky island west of Morocco, a North African
country with coastlines on the Atlantic Ocean and
Mediterranean Sea. Madeira's capital, Funchal, was notable
for its "scores of white stucco houses and brick red roofs
[which] were planted on the greenish, crescent-shaped
slope before us. Up and up they went until houses, the
crooked roads, and the island itself were lost in the
clouds."[8] Further south, multilingual Senegal, reflecting
the country's many European colonizers over the
centuries, had a very apparent French culture that dated
back to the 1650s. Located on the edge of the Sahara
Desert, Dakar, its capital, was very hot in late July when
Harvey wandered through some of the city's sandy back
streets lined with small "shacks" with thatched roofs,
where women wore bright clothing and old men wove bold
red and yellow fabric on small looms. "It was all just like

the National Geographic magazine come to life," Harvey observed with fascination. In the Senegalese heat, "the engine room temperature reached an unbearably stifling 96 degrees F."[9]

On the morning of July 25, the *Abosso* reached Freetown, Sierra Leone, where locals rowed out to meet the ship in blade-thin canoes and greeted the crew and passengers in English, which had been introduced in the region in 1787. From Freetown, the *Abosso* continued south and southeast to Monrovia, capital of Liberia, arriving there on July 26. On July 28, the ship reached the

Harvey in Dakar, Senegal, Africa, late July, 1936.

small village of Takoradi, Ghana, amidst stiff waves causing the *Abosso* to roll 12 degrees to port and starboard, "sending things off the mess room table." The *Abosso* tied up at a pier lined with warehouses of corrugated iron and concrete blocks. On the morning of August 1, the *Abosso* arrived in Lagos, Nigeria.[10]

In early August, the *Abosso* sailed up the Calabar River to Calabar in southeast Nigeria. On the afternoon of August 4, the ship idled off the southwest shore of the British-German colony of Cameroon, situated in the 1930s between Nigeria and French Equatorial Africa (now Gabon, the Republic of the Congo and the Central African Republic). As the *Abosso* approached land, Harvey spotted "a black mass . . . off to port. Off the stern, the land commences, and with one hop jumps up to the clouds. Low, white wisps only mar the black wall. . . .These are the Kameroons," featuring rugged green mountains.

The next morning, August 5, Harvey went on watch at

4:00 a.m. and, "Through the partial darkness, I could see the black form of Fernando Po sweeping smoothly out of the sea and as smoothly dropping back again." Fernando Po (now known as "Bioko") was named after a Portuguese navigator who, in 1472, explored the West African coast and discovered this island. The pleasantly unexpected sight of Fernando Po marked the end of the *Abosso*'s voyage south.[11]

Early the next morning, the *Abosso* was back in port at Lagos, Nigeria, where Harvey began an adventure to Ibadan, 120 miles inland. Traveling on an uncomfortable lorry, Harvey passed "a hopeless tangle of trees, bushes, vines, and [occasionally] a high palm sticking out above the rest." After many miles, the lorry left the hard-surfaced road and bumped along over a red, dusty, narrow road until it finally arrived in Ibadan. After Harvey met his host, a minister, he bathed and went to sleep under a mosquito netting canopy to the sound of drums beating in the distance. The next morning Harvey toured the town and market and marveled at the vendors' wares—the bones and skulls of goats and horses valued as charms, the carcasses of dead birds smothered with flies, "ghastly" butcher shops with a horrid smell, and chickens and goats everywhere. In the late afternoon, Harvey left on a train from Ibadan to coastal Lagos.[12]

From Lagos, the return trip to Liverpool went quickly. Between August 9 and 16, the *Abosso* stopped briefly at Accra and Takoradi, Ghana, then sailed on to Sierra Leone and past the Portuguese island archipelago of Cape Verde, west of Senegal, before arriving at Las Palmas on the island of Gran Canaria, off the coast of Morocco. On August 17, the ship headed north and revisited Madeira's tiny, rocky island encircled by clear turquoise waters. Harvey kept busy during these final days of his adventure, usually standing two watches a day and looking after the fire hoses. On August 21, the *Abosso* moored at Plymouth on England's southwest coast. Harvey stayed aboard the *Abosso* until it reached Liverpool the next day.

On August 22, after an amazing five and half weeks that had introduced Harvey to a new world so distinctly different from Pittsford, New York, and Liverpool, he signed off the *Abosso*. Waiting for him in Liverpool, however, was a letter from Ferndale banker Mr. Griffith. It served as a harbinger of unresolved financial issues that seemed to follow Harvey everywhere.[13]

Happily, another exciting travel adventure was about to begin for Harvey: a week-long driving tour of Scotland with Frank Graham and Bob Lynn, his engineering class-mates and friends. All three young men realized this might be their last opportunity to explore, together, the cities and outlying areas of Scotland before Harvey returned to America. Frank met Harvey as he disembarked from the *Abosso* and the two drove to Frank's home in Kendal, north of Liverpool. After finalizing a plan for their whirlwind tour of Scotland, they drove north to collect Bob at his home in coastal Workington near the Scottish border.

On August 25, the three then headed northeast into the rural eastern Scottish uplands just north of the English border. For two and a half days, the three men toured an array of sites in Edinburgh. They visited the castle sitting high atop the volcanic Castle Rock and overlooking a steep, expansive green hillside that sloped down to the railroad tracks below. They walked along Princess Street, Edinburgh's main commercial thoroughfare, and toured St. Giles' Cathedral, the "Mother Church" of world Presbyte-rianism; the house of Presbyterian founder John Knox; the home of Robert Louis Stevenson; and the brilliantly engi-neered, cantilevered-steel Forth Bridge, built in 1890, that spanned the Firth of Forth and the Portobello Baths east of Edinburgh. In the late afternoon of August 28, Harvey,

Frank, and Bob headed west into the Forth Valley and across the Scottish central lowlands, through Falkirk and Stirling, to Aberfoyle, where they found a quiet place to park and sleep—sitting up in the car.[14]

On the fifth day of their whirlwind tour, Frank, Bob, and Harvey headed north, beyond several sparkling lochs (Scottish Gaelic for "lakes"), wide-open lush landscapes with deep green forests and small villages, and east through deeply incised hills to Crieff, then Perth, near the mouth of the River Tay. Heading further north from there, they drove through the spectacular domed summits of the sweeping Cairngorms in the Scottish Highlands, with their expansive, open, tundra-like slopes interspersed with ancient woodlands and shallow valleys known as the Caledonian Forest. Finally, Frank, Bob, and Harvey turned east toward Aberdeen at the edge of the North Sea. After a night in their tent, the three headed west the next morning, skirting the northern edge of the Cairngorms and continuing through Alford, Tomintoul, Grantown, and north to Inverness. Here, in this beautifully situated city in the Scottish Highlands, they found a quiet place to park and sleep.[15]

Harvey, Spittal of Glenshee, Scotland, late August, 1936.

The last two days of their tour of Scotland, the three young men drove down the long, narrow Loch Ness—a freshwater lake extending 22 miles through the Scottish Highlands—then on to Fort William and Ballachulish. Finally, they veered southeast to the west shore of Loch Lomond and drove to its southern tip and Balloch's small town, where they again slept in

their car. On their final day, Frank, Bob, and Harvey drove
to Glasgow, then south to Kilmarnock and coastal Ayr in
the low green hills of the Southern Uplands' farming country. They continued to Dumfries and finally to Carlisle in
England before reaching Bob Lynn's home in Workington
on the coast.[16] Harvey must have been amazed by the
variety and beauty of scenery he saw during this grand
circle tour of Scotland. On his 1930s "Philips' Main Road
Map of Great Britain," Harvey carefully plotted every
detail of their 1,125-mile auto trip just as he had done for
his many bicycle trips across England.[17]

Kingsmans Farm Offers Solace as Money Worries Escalate

On September 4, 1936, Harvey arrived back in Liverpool, where he found a letter waiting for him from his
father with eight dollars and a card from ten-year-old
Frank. That night he stayed with friends and packed for
his last bicycle journey across England to Kingsmans Farm.
In two and a half days, with little time or money, Harvey
covered about 260 miles from Liverpool to Huntingdon
near Cambridge, where he stopped to dine with his Uncle
Reg and Aunt Winnie at Paynes Farm before continuing
the last few miles to Kingsmans Farm.[18]

Between September 7 and early October, Kingsmans
Farm once again proved to be a place of comfort and
family warmth, as it had been so many times since Harvey
had arrived in England. This September, as during past
visits, Harvey helped Uncle Frank and Charles Gardner
complete multiple farm chores. They harvested and carted
potatoes; plowed, cut and later carted clover; repaired
gates and stiles; made hay; turned over haycocks; loaded
dung; and operated a threshing machine. "Dobber" Shelley
sometimes lent a hand with the fall chores. Kingsmans

Farm continued to be a gathering place for Stephen and Martha Harvey's children and grandchildren.

During Harvey's September 1936 stay, his Uncle Reg and cousin Vernon came by often, as did his Auntie Bertha Longman, Auntie Ethel Langridge, and some of Harvey's cousins: Patrina Longman and Joan and Stephen Langridge. Auntie Ethel and her daughter, Joan Langridge, came by on some days to pick berries. Occasionally, Mildred Longman (a daughter of Martin Longman from his first marriage) appeared at Kingsmans Farm to paint scenes of the farm and the River Crouch. On another occasion, Auntie Bertha drove Auntie Ethel and Auntie Bea to Rochford with corn samples from the farm. Auntie Maud Gardner and her sons came by on yet another day. On Harvey's last day at Kingsmans Farm before returning to Liverpool, Uncle Reg and Vernon came for dinner, followed afterward by the arrival of Bertha Longman and Maud Gardner, Auntie Ethel and Uncle Maurice Langridge, and their families. Kingsmans Farm had truly become Harvey's home away from home.[19]

Reginald Harvey and Maurice Langridge families,
ca. 1936.

On October 5, as Harvey packed and prepared for his

trip back to Liverpool, he was delighted to receive a letter from his father with $18 enclosed. That evening, Harvey left his bicycle with Uncle Reg and caught a bus from nearby Hullbridge to London, where he boarded a late-night coach to Liverpool. As the coach motored across the Midlands toward Liverpool in the dark of night, money matters remained at the forefront of Harvey's mind. In early September, Mrs. Heilbron had written to him demanding that he pay his long-overdue rent from the previous year.[20]

On the day after arriving in Liverpool, Harvey moved into his new digs with Frank Graham at 22 Limedale Road (2.5 miles from the university), then called on Mrs. Heilbron. She refused to release Harvey's belongings, including his winter coat, until Harvey paid his debt. While there, Harvey managed to collect a few books and a letter from home that assured him money was on the way. Yet, by the end of October, only $3 had arrived from Evan.[21]

Harvey succumbed to a severe head cold just as the weather turned wet, windy, and bitterly cold. In mid-November, he noted in his diary that "it is as cold as I have ever had it in England, and "Mrs. H has my coat, the dog."[22] Meanwhile, Harvey's new landlady, Mrs. Gregson, became increasingly agitated by Harvey's delinquent portion of the rent for the 22 Limedale Road apartment. In late November, she gave him just a couple of days to pay the £5 he owed. Harvey cabled his dad for cash. Only $5 arrived in a letter from his mother, but thankfully Harvey then received £6 from his father on December 1, which immediately went to Mrs. Gregson.[23] Harvey had no money to give Mrs. Heilbron, however, and as December ushered in more frigid temperatures and his end-of-term exams loomed before him, Harvey developed a bad sore throat. Harvey wrote: "I can hardly speak and hardly swallow. Such a rotten day."[24] In early December, Harvey decided he had had enough. He "laid siege . . . on Mrs. Heilbron [the] citadel and though the resistance weakened the fortress did not fall."[25]

Relief: Welsh Singing and Time with Family

Fortunately, Harvey had many distractions during the 1936 fall term that diverted his attention from his impoverished condition and badgering by two landladies. Harvey spent considerable time studying for his fall classes—resistance and propulsion, strength, stability, design, and naval architecture—and, ultimately, preparing for his December term-end examinations.

Most engaging for Harvey, however, was auditioning for and being selected to sing in the Liverpool Welsh Choral Union directed by eminent conductor T. Hopkin Evans. This large Liverpool choir had formed in 1900 when many Welsh chapel choirs sang in the National Eisteddfod of Wales (a Welsh festival of music and poetry) held in Liverpool that particular year. T. Hopkin Evans became one of many well-known composers and conductors who directed this choir. He first attracted widespread attention as the director of the Neath, Wales, choral society. In 1911, he conducted the Welsh national choir at the Crystal Palace in London. Then, in 1917, Evans directed the Birkenhead National Eisteddfod choir in Liverpool. Two years later, he became the conductor of the Liverpool Welsh Choral Union. His magnetic personality and command of both English and Welsh contributed to his esteemed stature at Eisteddfod gatherings. He became a leading figure in the musical life of Wales. [26]

In the fall of 1936, Harvey auditioned to sing with the Liverpool Welsh Choral Union. To his great delight, he received a letter inviting him to sing the part of a second tenor, valued for its romantic character and incredible versatility. Harvey was thrilled to be part of this renowned choir. Immediately, he began faithfully practicing with the choir every Wednesday evening. On November 14, wearing Frank Graham's dinner suit, Harvey went to Liverpool's Grand Central Hall to sing with the Liverpool Welsh Choral Union in a live radio broadcast of *Elijah*. "Magnificent," Harvey penciled in his diary. A local newspaper reported that the performance was "sound and at some points even brilliant."[27]

In mid-November, Harvey also became swept up in his student choir practices for Handel's *Messiah* and Brahms' *Requiem*, scheduled to be sung in the Liverpool Cathedral. Temperatures dropped further, and he continued to brave the cold without a coat. In early December, all personal struggles faded into the background when King Edward VIII announced that he would marry Wallace Simpson. Harvey witnessed the nation's deep sorrow when, on December 10, the King abdicated the throne after ruling England for less than a year. Four days later, Harvey became consumed with his end-of-term exams.[28]

On December 19, Harvey headed to Kingsmans Farm. He arrived when Uncle Frank was fully engaged in early winter farm chores: burning hedges, overseeing the thatching of the stable, and collecting holly. Family members, including Great Aunt Jennie, arrived over the next few days with gifts and holiday cheer. Auntie Ethel and Uncle Maurice Langridge, with their family of four, assisted by Auntie Maud and Uncle Charles Gardner and their family, hosted a Christmas dinner at the Langridge's Hutton House (in Shenfield, near Brentwood, Essex), followed by card games and singing. After Boxing Day (December 26), Harvey continued to help Uncle Frank and some of his male cousins clip hedges around the property and chop and cart wood. On New Year's Eve, Harvey and Uncle Frank welcomed 1937 by candlelight. Harvey regret-

fully realized that this would be his last Christmas in the
United Kingdom with his Harvey and Evans families.
Through darkness and pelting rain on January 6, he
boarded a bus for London and then caught a train to Liverpool for his last six months in Britain.[29]

During the December 1936 holidays, Harvey received
no word or money from home, other than $5 from his
mother and £6 from his father, which only partially
covered rent for his digs at 22 Limedale Road. Despite
Harvey's challenging financial situation, on New Year's
Day 1937, he resolved to adopt his mother's cheerful attitude and "stand up straight and grin." On January 4, a
telegraphed money order for £5 1/6 (5 pounds, one shilling,
and sixpence) arrived. "Whoopee!" Harvey exclaimed in
his diary . . . and undoubtedly smiled, as he had vowed
to do.

The next day, Harvey started the university's winter
term with classes in resistance and propulsion, strength,
stability, and design. Letters from home—without
money—arrived sporadically. A Christmas present for
Harvey from home didn't arrive until January 18, and no
letters came for a month between late January and late
February. As Harvey's concerns about his indebtedness
continued to rise and he received only a small amount of
money from home, he started slipping behind in some of
his classes. He sang, and he read about old ships and their
figureheads for diversion, just as he had often done in the
past. His two close friends, Frank Graham and Bob Lynn,
tried to ease his concerns by occasionally taking him to
the pictures and rugger games.

These activities coincided with dinner events held for
Liverpool engineering students who would be graduating
in June. Harvey had no formal dinner suit for such an
event, so he borrowed a formal suit, tie, Corlett's shirt,
and collar—all but his own socks—from Bob Lynn when

the time came to have photographs taken of the upcoming June 1937 graduation. In one photo of the engineering students dressed in their gowns, only Harvey's smiling face appeared between two classmates' heads. It is clear that he wore no gown.[30]

Harvey without robe and cap with graduating classmates, 1937.

Shortly after this event, Harvey received an ultimatum from his landlady, Mrs. Gregson, in February 1937: "money today or out tomorrow."[31] In response to Harvey's urgent letters to his parents, money from family members and friends began to trickle in. Still, no total amount came close to covering his past debts to the two landladies and the university registrar's office, or his small daily expenses. Finally, on February 12, a letter arrived from Harvey's father with money, as promised. He was shocked, however, to find only £4 in the envelope. Harvey owed his landlady almost £9. "Oh well," Harvey wrote in his diary, "they must have had to scrape at home."[32]

On February 22, his eleven-year-old brother Frank reported that the family had recently purchased a new car. "It is a Dodge, and it is black, four doors, [and with] a big trunk. . . It is very big," Frank wrote.[33] Harvey must have wondered how his family had managed to buy such a significant item and yet could not send him much money to pay for some of his debts that now threatened to render him homeless.[34]

Money Crisis Climaxes

Six weeks into the winter term, all Harvey's efforts to distract himself from mounting money concerns failed. "A major crisis has arisen," Harvey penciled in his diary on February 19, 1937. On that day, he learned that the university accountant had turned down his application for a loan. And his landlady Mrs. Gregson demanded that he find new digs the next day. "Have contemplated sleeping at the varsity [university] or in the park. I can't seem to do much," Harvey anguished.[35]

In desperation, the next day, he wrote to his Uncle Tom in South Wales, begging him for £6. He also shared with him the loss of his accommodations. Tom immediately responded by expressing how "extremely sorry" he and his wife, Liza, were "to hear of your sad position." Tom added that they were pleased that Harvey had enough confidence in them to write about his travails. Tom hurriedly enclosed £7 in a thick envelope and sent it to Harvey via registered mail. In a second letter that Tom wrote a few days later, he invited Harvey to stay with them in Aberaman during the month-long Easter holiday. Tom added that Mr. Griffith at Lloyds Bank was also concerned about Harvey's parents failing to repay Harvey's year-old debt.[36]

Harvey could never have imagined how much worse his financial situation was about to become. Just a few days later, he wrote in his diary: "March 9 is a very bad day."

Was called to see the Register as Mrs. H has written saying I owe £21. He [the accountant] also finds me owing £77 on fees. So now the fun begins. Wrote to Dad. . . . With a dirty collar (all shirts being at the laundry) called on the dean. So I am not to be allowed to take June exams unless £99 is forthcoming. Wrote Dad.[37] [In 1937, £99 equaled roughly £6,788 in early 2020, or $8,767 U.S.]

That day, on the other side of the Atlantic Ocean, John Evans sat down at his desk at Sibley's to compose probably the most serious and sad letter he had ever written to his son. He mailed it to Harvey care of his brother, Tom Evans, at his home in Aberaman, Wales. "I am very much ashamed that I haven't written," John began.

I have been so worried about things that somehow I could not write. I have been carrying a heavy load, and I hate to burden mother or anyone with it. . . . Money matters have been such a burden to me that sometimes I don't know where to turn. . . . One thing on top of another seem to come and upset my plans. I make up my mind to send you a certain amount of money each month & then something comes along and lays me flat again. . . . I know, Harvey boy, you are having a struggle over there & I thank you for the pleasant and cheerful way you always write. . . . Keep happy as usual, and I will do my utmost to send cash which you need so much as often as I can.[38]

John asked Harvey not to tell Mabel that he had written. Tucked in the envelope was £6. John's letter was waiting for Harvey when he arrived at Uncle Tom's and Aunt Liza's for Easter.[39]

On March 20, Harvey set off for Aberdare and Abera-

man, South Wales on the train, and spent the entire Easter
holiday with Uncle Tom, Aunt Liza, their daughter, Hetty,
her ten-month-old baby, Beryl, and son-in-law, Reverend
Rollo Roland. While in Aberaman, Harvey walked into the
town center and bought a much-needed pair of shoes. In
late March, Harvey borrowed Rollo Roland's bicycle on a
lovely sunny day. He set out from Worthing, an elegant
Georgian seaside resort city on England's south coast, and
rode through the rolling green chalk hills of England's
South Downs country to the seaside resort town of
Brighton. Absorbed viewing the passing lovely countryside
from a bicycle, the time quickly flew by. Dusk descended
before Harvey had reached his destination. Suddenly realizing that he had no light on his bicycle or money to catch
a train, he called Rollo and Hetty, in nearby Worthing, and
they immediately rescued him. Soon afterward, Harvey
returned to Aberaman with Hetty and tiny Beryl.[40]

Hetty, Beryl, Rollo Rowland.

For the next two weeks, Harvey studied, went with
Uncle Tom to one of his shop classes, and traveled again
with Uncle Tom to the Evans family home in rural Pentre-
cwrt, Carmarthenshire, where his Aunt Esther still lived.
One night, he and Tom stayed overnight at the Evans
house. The next morning, after Uncle Tom fished in the
nearby River Teifi, just as he had done throughout his life,
Tom and Harvey headed back to Aberaman. To Harvey's

great delight, he received word that his parents had sent £40-15/ (40 pounds, 15 shillings) to a local bank, where he retrieved it shortly before heading back to Liverpool on April 22 to begin his last term at the university.[41]

Four days after the beginning of the spring term, Harvey once again visited the dean of the Engineering Department. Together, the dean and Harvey went to see the registrar, who remained adamant about Harvey's graduation conditions. If all Harvey's registration fees *and* Mrs. Heilbron were not paid in full, the registrar insisted, Harvey could not take his final exams and could not graduate. With a portion of the £40 he had received from his parents while in Aberaman, Harvey immediately paid Mrs. Heilbron the £21-5/10 (21 pounds, 5 shillings, 10 pence) he owed. Finally, after suffering a reoccurring series of persistent colds and sore throats during the winter months, Harvey collected his coat, along with other personal possessions held for months by Mrs. Heilbron as ransom.

At the end of the first week of classes, Harvey went back again to the registrar, who insisted, once again, that Harvey must pay his full university fees or he could not take his final examinations and graduate. That evening Harvey wrote to both his father and Uncle Tom. Harvey made one last attempt to persuade the university registrar to let him take his final exams, even if his fees remained unpaid in full. He also wrote to his Uncle Maurice, begging him for £65-15/ (sixty-five pounds, 15 shillings). Four days later, 10 shillings arrived from Auntie Ethel, Maurice's wife, who promised that more would come later once Maurice returned home.[42]

Remaining ever optimistic and hopeful that, somehow, he might graduate, Harvey went with some classmates to Ravenscroft & Willis to rent a graduation gown from this esteemed 200-year-old tailoring enterprise in London. For decades Ravenscroft & Willis had become distinguished worldwide for its meticulous craftsmanship and the fine quality of its graduation, judiciary, and ceremonial robes. For the quality of its work, Ravenscroft & Willis received commissions to fashion robes for twelve royal coronations (including, most recently, Queen Elizabeth II, Prince Philip the Duke of Edinburgh, and Prince Charles the Prince of Wales.) Harvey felt strongly that if he managed to graduate, he should wear a Ravenscroft & Willis gown.[43]

On the same day that Harvey received money from Ethel, John Evans, filled with shame, composed a difficult, sobering letter to his son.

> You must think I am a fine kind of a Dad not to write to you. Harvey, if you only knew how my heart aches to send you money so I can write something definite to you, I am sure you could to some extent understand. I really am so ashamed I have not written, but usually, I am so full up I cannot write because I only have sad news to tell you. I have borrowed so much already, and, of course, I am trying to pay back what I owe a little each month, so when the first [of the month] comes it is all gone. . . . I can understand your situation, Harvey, & that's why I am so down most of the time hoping & longing to help you & then find I cannot. That's what makes me sad & really the reason for not writing.[44]

John then explained that he had tried to pay a little each month on the money he had borrowed, but when the first of the month [and his pay] came, his money was committed. "I am so down most of the time, hoping and longing to help you and then find I cannot," John wrote with great shame. "These last few months have surely been hard. I only pray for health and strength to work and be able to repay." In closing, John professed,

I admire you & love you for all your splendid ideals, your patience, and fine spirit towards me; all I ask is that you think well of me & keep smiling for the sun will surely shine again tomorrow.[45]

John wired the university accountant a telegram. "Sending money," it affirmed. None ever arrived. Harvey now seriously wondered if all his hard work at the University of Liverpool might be for naught and that he would never graduate from Liverpool with a degree in naval architecture.[46]

On May 19, Harvey learned with disbelief that the registrar had received £25 from John. When Harvey went to the registrar and asked for £5 of the total, the registrar told him to apply to Professor Abell, dean of the Engineering Department, for a loan. Despite Harvey's increasing uncertainty and growing anxiety about how he might have enough money to pay the registrar so he could take his exams, he continued to study diligently. By May 20, however, Harvey's optimism languished. He now expressed great doubts about his future. "It is hard going," he wrote in his diary.[47]

13

FALLING IN LOVE

I t was the pomp and splendor of an upcoming coronation that diverted Harvey's focus from studying and his impoverished condition. The entire nation's attention dramatically shifted from everyday preoccupations to preparing for the coronation of King George VI and his wife, Elizabeth. In cities and towns across the country, government officials planned hundreds of coronation banquets and balls. Liverpool prepared to celebrate the event momentously with a splendid coronation ball given by Lord Derby—Edward George Villiers Stanley, the 17th Earl of Derby. Born in 1865, seventy-three-year-old Lord Derby, formerly a British soldier, Conservative Party politician, diplomat, and racehorse owner, staged a ball at his family home at Knowsley Hall in the Metropolitan Borough of Knowsley on the eastern outskirts of Liverpool. Thousands of Liverpool residents attended the ball on the evening of May 11.

A friend of Harvey's invited him to join a group of young University of Liverpool students going to the coronation ball at Knowsley Hall. Happily, Harvey mingled with many students who danced, ate, and chatted at this gala event. Midway through the evening, Harvey began dancing with a young University of Liverpool student named Phyllis Hargreaves. Late into the evening, Harvey and Phyllis "had some lovely dances together," he later wrote in his diary. Harvey immediately found her light brown hair, clear eyes, sculpted cheekbones, and unblemished skin exceedingly attractive and her thoughtful, caring manner magnetic. After dancing, Harvey and Phyllis went exploring.

Eventually, they climbed onto the roof of Knowsley Hall. Here they sat and talked for a very long time while admiring the expansive view of Liverpool. "We had a lovely time, yes, we had a lovely time," Harvey recalled with delight a few days later. Around 4:30 a.m. the next morning, Phyllis, Harvey, and a small group of friends drove to the Pier Head before continuing to Pitt Street, the first home of Liverpool sailors. Along the way, they admired the elaborate coronation decorations and treated themselves to a hearty breakfast at a café.

On May 12, Harvey buoyantly wrote about the coronation ball and his memorable hours with Phyllis. This event had been

> one of the most enjoyable times I have ever had. How I do hope to have more in the few weeks left to come! And I do think I deserve it. This is more than a wish, it is a prayer. Now at 1 p.m. [May 12] I feel great and have done ever since getting home.[1]

Lord Derby's coronation ball proved to be an event with meaningful consequences for both Harvey and Phyllis. Little could they have imagined that seeds were sown at Lord Derby's ball for an enduring lifetime relationship between them.[2]

During the next seven weeks, Harvey and Phyl met

nearly every day. They studied together, lunched together, attended university events together, went to church and Student Christian Movement events together, sang in the choir together, walked together several times to the university's Walker Art Gallery and the university's enormous Wyncote sports grounds, and walked many times to the Pier Head on the River Mersey. As time went by, Harvey accompanied Phyl across the River Mersey

Phyllis Hargreaves, 1937.

on a ferry to her home, about 20 miles south of Liverpool. Phyllis lived with her mother in Chester, a well-preserved walled medieval city with rows of arcaded, Tudor-style, half-timbered shops. They even tried studying together, accomplished little, and concluded it was an "instructive experiment."[3]

In late May, they walked together to Calderstones Park and sat in the rain together. "I think I saw tears," Harvey wrote in his diary. Their friendship and the warmth between them had developed quickly and deeply. Every day in May, June, and early July, Harvey penned in his diary his visits with Phyl, his preoccupation with her beauty, and the growing friendship and affection they felt for each other. Although they were keenly aware that Harvey would soon return to the United States and they often wrestled with feelings of desire and uncertainty, they both recognized that the profound depth of their feelings for each other was not at all temporary. The passage of time would demonstrate that their affection for each other would be everlasting. On May 24, they went to enquire about sailings to North America for Harvey.[4]

Near the end of May, when Harvey attended his last term-end lectures and when Harvey and Phyl became engrossed in their blossoming relationship, the University of Liverpool's vice-chancellor agreed to give Harvey a loan to pay his remaining university debt. Harvey understood that he would not receive his certificate of graduation until he paid his debt in full.

In the third week of June, Harvey realized he had just 7d (pence) to his name. His roommate, Frank Graham, was in about the same financial predicament. "It is a sorry business," Harvey wrote. "Pawning things is out. We have one pair of trousers besides a suit, one pair of shoes, three pairs of terribly holey socks, and so it goes. I must borrow a suit for degree day."[5]

Even more concerning than his dire financial condition was Harvey's growing dread of the thought of leaving Liverpool and Phyllis. For the first time in months, it now became clear that Harvey would be allowed to take his exams and graduate. Sadly, this meant that his days in Liverpool with Phyllis, Frank, and Bob were numbered. Realizing this, the warmth and feelings of intimacy between Harvey and Phyl grew more intense.

During the second week of June 1937, Harvey and Phyl took all their exams. A week later, Dean Abell told Harvey that he had fallen slightly short of receiving an "honors degree," but, Harvey wrote, he "gave me a wonderful testimonial [saying] that I have an ordinary first-class degree."[6] In a letter of recommendation for Harvey, Naval Architecture, Dean T. B. Abell wrote:

> Mr. Harvey Evans has now completed the full four years' course prescribed for candidates for the degree of Bachelor of Engineering at this University. . . . Throughout his course he has shewn a keen interest in his work and a desire to thoroughly understand the theoretical portions

of the course. . . . He has a knowledge and an equipment which should enable him . . . to examine and solve the problems generally to be met with in ship design and construction and, thus, make him a very useful member of the staff of any shipbuilding firm.

He is a young man of rather outstanding character, good feelings, and charm. He has a pleasant personality and address, and has shewn himself agreeable and able to make contacts with other men of different callings. He also has fairly wide general interests.[7]

Harvey in graduation robe, 1937.

Harvey was now ready to graduate. After seeing Phyl on the evening of July 2 and early the next morning, Harvey attended his degree ceremony and shook hands with Lord Derby and many others. July 4 was a miserable day for many reasons. Wet and windy, it was also the day of Harvey's departure from Liverpool. After packing in the afternoon, he bid "old Frank" Graham, his classmate and good friend for four years, goodbye. That evening, Harvey made his way one last time to Chester to see Phyl. Together they had a "beautiful walk and talk" along the old city walls. It was then "goodbye" to Phyl. "God, it was dreadful," Harvey penned in his diary on July 4.

Farewell to Phyllis, Liverpool, and Britain

The next day, Harvey hurriedly finished packing and caught the 2:15 p.m. train from Liverpool Lime Street station in central Liverpool to London. He arrived at Kingsmans Farm that evening. For the next two weeks, Harvey eagerly awaited money from his father so that he could buy a ticket for a ship to America. As Harvey waited, he helped his Uncle Frank for the last time with farm chores. Harvey also cycled to his many aunts, uncles, and cousins who lived nearby. He presumed that this might be the last time he would ever see his Uncle Reg and Aunt Winnie, Auntie Maud and her husband Charles, Auntie Ethel and Uncle Maurice, Auntie Bertha and Uncle Martin, and Auntie Beatrice, as well as all of their children. Unexpectedly, Marian Jarvis, the oldest daughter of John Harvey (Harvey Evans's great uncle who had immigrated to Saskatchewan, Canada, many years earlier and later moved to Victoria), arrived for a brief visit just days before Harvey would leave Kingsmans Farm.

No matter what he was doing or where he was, Harvey remained continually preoccupied with thoughts of Phyllis. He wrote to her nearly every day.[8]

While visiting Uncle Reg and Aunt Winnie at Sparrows Hill Farm outside Saffron Walden, Harvey completed a job application to the general manager of Bethlehem Shipbuilding Corporation in Quincy, Massachusetts, at his father's urging.[9] John had written a letter to Harvey in late June, suggesting that "Arthur Kettle of Austin-Hastings [in Cambridge, Massachusetts] may be able to help you get into Bethlehem Shipbuilding Company." Harvey's application letter referenced Arthur Kettle:

I should like to refer you to Mr. Arthur Kettle of the
Austin-Hastings Company, Cambridge, Mass. For a
number of years Mr. Kettle's father [Joseph B. Kettle],
was the minister of our church [South Congregation
Church between 1921 and 1926].[10]

In the 1920s, the Kettle family had lived in the church
parsonage on Meigs Street, just two doors away from the
young Evans family. After graduating from high school in
Rochester in the early 1920s, Arthur Kettle had worked
briefly as an "assembler." By 1924, he had moved to Boston
and briefly worked as a "driver" before he began studying
business administration at Boston University, where he
earned a bachelor's degree in 1927. Kettle became associated with the Cambridge-based Austin-Hastings Co. in
1932 and soon became the Machinery Division manager at
that company. It is likely that Kettle, as manager of the
steel division at Austin-Hastings Co., had dealings with
Bethlehem Shipbuilding Corporation when Harvey
applied for a job there in the summer of 1937.[11]

Finally, on July 21, Harvey received money from his
father to pay for his ship passage back to the United
States. He immediately paid for his ticket on the SS *President Roosevelt*, which had begun transatlantic commercial
service in 1922. Harvey hurriedly completed some final
packing before plunging into the River Crouch for one last
swim with his cousin Vernon. The next day, he rose early
and headed into London just for one day to make arrangements for his trunk's shipment and gather information
about the Royal Academy of Music for Evan in anticipation of his enrollment there in the fall of 1937. He wrote
again to Phyllis.

The next morning, July 23, Harvey left the farm at
daybreak for the last time and, with the help of Uncle
Frank and cousin Vernon, caught a bus to Hockley station

before taking a train and taxi to the *President Roosevelt*. The aging ship, crowded with what Harvey described as "a load of typical Ellis Island immigrants speaking in "varieties of tongues"[12] (not unlike the immigrant ship that his father John traveled on in 1911), moved away from the pier at 11:00 a.m.[13]

So, "goodbye to dear old England," Harvey penned as the ship headed out to sea.[14] Once on board, Harvey exchanged his British currency for American dollars. "I hated to part with a 10/ (10 shilling) note this morning to get in return U.S. dollars and cents. I hate even talking of dollars and cents," he wrote regretfully.[15] Just a few hours later, Harvey expounded a little more on his feelings of regret and sadness about leaving a place that had become his home for the past four years, with many supportive family members close by . . . and, of course, his beloved Phyllis.

> It's pretty terrible thinking you've had your last look at England until heaven knows when. All those marvelous people are being left behind and that comfortable life. Last night was a lovely, sad one. We pushed along between the lights of England on the one hand and those of France and a full moon on the other. That was the last of it.[16]

Some things were incredibly hard to leave behind. "I wanted to think of Phyl and write to her," Harvey anguished, "and there is everlastingly a vague wistful feeling that she is the main one I leave behind, but here it is hard to imagine," Harvey penned as the *President Roosevelt* moved out to sea and left England fading in the distance. Nearly every day, Harvey wrote to Phyl in an ongoing letter that evolved as Harvey traveled across the Atlantic.[17]

As he left Phyllis and his friends of four years behind, Harvey brought his indebtedness back to the United States with him. When he left Liverpool in July 1937, he owed myriad people and institutions varying sums of money. His list included: several Harvey and Evans family members (Uncle Maurice and Auntie Ethel, Uncle Frank, Auntie Bertha, and Uncle Tom), the University of Liverpool, the Ravenscroft & Willis company for the purchase of his academic robe, a dentist in Liverpool and Mr. Griffith of Lloyds Bank in Ferndale, Wales. Harvey's total debts upon returning to the United States were around £50 9/6 (50 pounds, 9 shillings, 6 pence), not an insignificant sum in 1937—with inflation, equal to about $4,430 U.S. in 2020. Harvey must have felt a great urgency to get to work immediately after arriving in the United States.[18]

On the morning of July 31, *President Roosevelt* slowly moved up the Hudson River and gently glided into Chelsea Piers. Standing among the excited crowd of greeters was Harvey's family. On the deck and waving excitedly, Harvey observed that Mabel was stouter, John older, and the "boys" (Evan and Frank) seemed "longer."[19] The family spent four days sightseeing in New York City. On their last day, Harvey toured the Brooklyn Navy Yard and looked at a couple of cruisers and destroyers. That afternoon, the Evans family of five climbed into the family's big new Dodge sedan and headed north to their home in Pittsford.

14

APPROACHING WAR

1937–1941

I n the summer of 1937, as Harvey prepared to return to the United States, Liverpool's student newspaper, *The Sphinx,* made an alarming prediction about the inevitability of war. While attending the University of Liverpool in the 1930s, Harvey had become well aware of the growing concern and uncertainty in Britain about the rise of fascism in Europe. The October 1933 issue of the University of Liverpool's *The Sphinx* noted, "We are told that two European countries have adopted fascism and that their populations groan and cower beneath the tyrannous yokes of Hitler and Mussolini."[1] Over the next several months, Liverpool students hotly debated the issue and the accompanying jingoistic nationalism spreading across Europe and repressing democratic principles. In February 1934, *The Sphinx* writer asserted that "the world as a whole seems to be on the brink of imminent war," threatening to bring "western civilization into anarchy and chaos."[2]

In September 1935, when Harvey returned to Britain on the German SS *Europa* from the summer with his family in Pittsford, he had experienced at close range the rise of Adolf Hitler in a German movie entitled *Heil Hitler,* shown to passengers on board. Earlier, in June 1935, *The Sphinx* published an article entitled "The Jew," reporting that "certain new and disturbing features of anti-Semitism . . . which are exclusively a question of European politics, are giving way to venomous attacks on the Jew." The so-called "Jewish Type" and Jewish people became the subject of racial antagonism and the "wildest judgments" fueled by suspicion and scorn.[3]

Two years later, in the summer of 1937, on the eve of Harvey's return to the United States, an article in *The Sphinx* speculated about "the probability of such a [air] raid taking place" on Liverpool, since this bustling industrial city then contained one-third of the nation's food supplies. Although London would be the main target of attacks, Germany might send fifty or more planes to drop bombs on Liverpool. This article speculated that the attacking fleet would be divided into three squadrons, each carrying high explosives, poison gas, and incendiary bombs. It concluded by speculating that the simultaneous use of gas and thermite would be deadly. Inhabitants of a targeted area could either go outside and be gassed or stay indoors and get roasted.[4] Counterbalancing this gloomy prediction was the economic boom that England experienced after an enormous increase in war materials production.[5]

When Harvey celebrated receiving his bachelor's degree in late July 1937 and returned to the United States, he could have never imagined that *The Sphinx* prediction about the possibility of war between Germany and the United Kingdom would ever become a reality. He also most likely felt that this prediction had no relevance to the United States or him. In the late 1930s, America, still struggling to recover from the devastating decade-long Great Depression, was ill-prepared for war. Americans were reluctant to participate in any military conflict that threatened to engulf much of Europe and Asia. When

Harvey arrived back in the United States, America's military preparedness fell far short of a nation anticipating involvement in a war. America remained decidedly isolationist, just as it had at the outbreak of World War I.

This stance would all radically change, however, over the next three years. The entire Evans family—John and Mabel, along with Harvey and his younger brothers, Evan and Frank—would each become significantly transformed by the Second World War and its aftermath.

A New Beginning in Boston

The day after Harvey returned to Pittsford after spending four years in Liverpool, he received a letter from Bethlehem Shipbuilding Corporation in Quincy, Massachusetts, replying to the letter he had written at Uncle Reginald's and Aunt Winnie's home just before leaving England. Bethlehem Shipbuilding Corporation offered him a job; he immediately accepted. His time in Pittsford was now short. He spent the next two weeks with his family and many friends, doing chores at home, adding mementos to his scrapbook, shopping for clothes, and, finally, packing for a trip to Boston to meet his prospective Bethlehem Shipbuilding Corporation managers and co-workers.

On the evening of August 19, Harvey climbed aboard a train bound for Boston. The next oppressive day, Harvey walked along the narrow, winding Boston streets before heading a few miles south to Quincy and the Bethlehem Shipbuilding Corporation offices. Harvey and Bethlehem division managers discussed the naval architecture job offered to him. "Looks marvelous," Harvey effused in his diary. That night he boarded a train and headed back to Pittsford to prepare for his move to Boston.[6]

During his final two weeks at home, Harvey did chores

around the Evans's home—cutting the lawn, chopping wood, and polishing the car—and spent more days visiting and talking with his family and friends late into the night. On August 25, his trunk arrived from England with the rest of his possessions.

At the end of August, Harvey and a contingent of First Congregational Church members drove to the Erie Canal village of Holley, northwest of Rochester. Here, they celebrated the contributions of seventy-year-old Joseph B. Kettle, who had served as the minister at First Congregational Church of Rochester in the 1920s and retired a few months earlier from the nearby Spencerport Congregational Church. Harvey eagerly joined the entourage of well-wishers. He felt an outstanding debt of gratitude to Joseph Kettle for his suggestion that Harvey contact his son, Arthur B. Kettle, a division manager at Austin-Hastings in Cambridge Co., about securing a job at Bethlehem Shipbuilding Corporation in Quincy. During Harvey's last few hurried days at home, the Evans's home buzzed with activity—teas and dinners with friends, picnics outdoors, games of bridge, and many late-night conversations.[7]

The day after a long train trip back to Boston on September 6, 1937, Harvey began his first day of work at Bethlehem Shipbuilding Corporation in Quincy. Most of the first day, he talked to his boss and co-workers about his job details. He then looked for housing in the Fore River area. In little more than one day, Harvey found a place to live with the family of a minister who had presided over the First Baptist Church in nearby Weymouth, Massachusetts, from 1919 to 1929. The Reverend Charles Wesley Allen, his wife Malinda Burton Allen, and Malinda's aunt, Eliza Harriet Burton ("Aunt Lyda"), had moved to New England several years earlier. They were renting out a combined sitting-bedroom in the rear of their home.[8]

Charles, Malinda, and Eliza had been born in Nova Scotia, Canada, between 1868 and 1874 and immigrated to the United States in the late 1890s. Charles W. Allen, born in January 1872, grew to adulthood in Hantsport, Kings County, south of the Bay of Fundy. He graduated from Acadia University in nearby Wolfville, where he set his sights on becoming a minister. Malinda Burton, born in 1874, grew up about 250 miles to the northeast in Margaree, Inverness County, Cape Breton Island. Sometime in the 1890s, Malinda and Charles had met. In 1897, twenty-five-year-old Charles immigrated to the United States and entered the Newton Theological Institution, an evangelical Baptist theological seminary in Newton Centre west of Boston. On September 5, 1899, Charles married twenty-six-year-old Malinda in Newton. The 1900 U.S. census listed Charles as "Reverend Charles W. Allen."[9]

For the next nineteen years, Charles and Malinda lived in several different towns south of Boston. Charles served briefly as minister at the Second Baptist Church in the Upper Falls Village of Newton. Soon afterward he accepted a position at the Third Calvinistic Baptist Church in Middleboro, Massachusetts, several miles south of Newton. Founded in 1761 at a crossroads known as "Rock," Allen arrived at the Rock Church in 1900.[10]

In Middleboro, Charles and Malinda began their family; Eugene Edward arrived in 1901, Gladys Burton in 1902, and Herman Loring and his twin brother, Fred Wesley, were born in 1906. In March 1910, Charles W. Allen accepted a call to the Baptist Church in Milford, Massachusetts, northwest of Middleboro, and remained there until 1915. In March that year, Charles moved to the First Baptist Church in Dedham, just south of Newton. After four years in Dedham, Charles and his family moved to nearby Weymouth, Massachusetts, where he became the minister of the First Baptist Church and served from

1919 to 1929. He then accepted the position of librarian at the New England Baptist Library.[11]

When Harvey moved into the Allens' Weymouth home at 15 Arcadia Road, Charles was sixty-five-years-old, Malinda sixty-three, and Herman thirty-one. The Allens' two oldest children, Eugene and Gladys, had married and had their own homes. The Allens' house stood not only a stone's throw south of Fore River, where Harvey worked at the Bethlehem Shipbuilding Corporation shipyard, but also in an idyllic setting at the end of a wooded, dead-end street just above tranquil Cranberry Pond.

Two miles to the north of the Allens' house, Fore River, a twisting seven-and-a-half-mile tidal estuary, emptied into the Atlantic Ocean 12 miles south of Boston Harbor. Here, in 1622, a trading colony known as the Wessagusset Colony was first settled by sixty immigrants from Weymouth, England, after SS *Mayflower* Pilgrims had briefly anchored and founded the Plymouth colony. In 1635, Wessagusset became Weymouth, which slowly evolved from a fishing and farming community into an industrial town with ironworks, steel mills, and, later, shoe factories. In 1886, Thomas Watson, Alexander Graham Bell's well-known assistant, founded a small shipyard near Fore River's mouth.[12]

From 1937 to 1943, the Allen home became Harvey's home. Charles, Malinda, and their youngest son, Herman, akin to Harvey's older brother, supported Harvey as he began a new life in Quincy and got to know the town and greater Boston area. Harvey shared the Allens' common living space, ate meals with them, and attended the Baptist Church in Weymouth.

The Allens' influence on Harvey and the Evans family was immediate and long-lasting. It happened that Herman Allen and his sister Gladys were extremely musical; they played the piano, organ, and violin masterfully. Gladys had an affiliation with the New England Conservatory of Music in the mid-1930s. It may have been no accident that Harvey's brother, Evan, a talented young pianist, later applied to and was accepted at the New England Conservatory.

Emerging Passion for the White Mountains

Equally significant during Harvey's early days in Weymouth was the influence of the minister who followed Charles Allen at the Weymouth Baptist Church. The Reverend Nathan Warwick Wood presided over the church from 1929 until just a few weeks before Harvey arrived in the fall of 1937. Nathan Wood, son of Nathan Robinson Wood and grandson of Nathan Eusebius Wood —both well-known Baptist ministers, scholars, educators, and administrators—was an inspiring preacher and leader.[13] Nathan had also introduced the young people of the Baptist Church to New Hampshire's White Mountains.

Nathan's parents, Nathan Robinson Wood and Isabel Warwick Bliss Wood, honeymooned in Jackson, New Hampshire in 1900. They spent many summer vacations in this picturesque small farming community southeast of the highest White Mountain peaks,[14] where painters, poets, and vacationers had come since the mid-1800s. Young Nathan Warwick Wood and his parents and grandparents boarded in Jackson at Brookside Farm, home of Eva May Davis Fernald, Leonard Fernald, and their daughter Doris, and sometimes stayed at the nearby Wilson Cottages. After Nathan and Doris married, the young couple stayed in a small log cabin at the end of a trail behind Brookside Farm built by Leonard Fernald around 1933-1934. Harvey and his family would continue to vacation in this cabin for almost a decade.[15]

Nathan often invited the young people at the Weymouth Baptist Church to Jackson, where he guided them on contemplative hikes across brooks, farm fields, and mountain trails. Harvey, who had always loved hiking with his family in the Adirondacks and, later, in northern England and Scotland, found White Mountain hikes refreshing and inspiring. In a letter to a dear friend in England, Harvey described his first hike in the White Mountains with great enthusiasm after summiting the 3,168-foot Mount Monadnock in early November 1937 with church companions Marion Custance, Jack Baley, Lenny Arnold, and Edith Meriam Price.[16]

Harvey hiking Mount Monadnock, New Hampshire,
ca. 1938-39.

Less than a year later, on October 8, 1938, Harvey set out in the early afternoon with a friend, Edith Price, on a trail leading up and over the very steep, barren headwall leading to the summit of 5,793 foot Mount Adams. After a steep, exhausting two-hour climb, they stood on the summit, where temperatures hovered around freezing. Harvey described the calm, crystal clear air and view from the top as simply "marvelous."

Since the sun was rapidly setting on the western horizon, they immediately started their descent. "Just below timberline, all trees [were] flattened like jackstraws [from frequent gale-force winds]. . . . Climbed under, over, and through the trees," Harvey wrote. "Trail completely obliterated" as the sun disappeared. "Came darkness [and] we were lost." Edith "couldn't be held back," Harvey later wrote, as she determinedly searched for the trail. Many times they fell into large holes made by uprooted trees. Finally, they sighted lights in the valley below. After an hour and a half of trudging, Edith and Harvey emerged from the forest at the camp of their anxious friends. Over the next fifteen years, Harvey, Edith, and their friends climbed nearly forty-five peaks in the White Mountains.

Hiking with Nathan Wood and spending relaxing vacations in Jackson ultimately became a life-long passion of Harvey and Edith Price. Over the next decades, Harvey invited family and friends from New England and Great Britain to hike in these stunning mountains and swim in its chilly, clear brooks and rivers.

Harvey and Edith introduced my brother, David, and me to the White Mountains in the mid- and late 1940s. Even before we walked, they pulled us up trails in a "billy cart." Later, they carried us piggyback-style until we could walk. Into the 2020s, the Evans family developed an intimate relationship with Jackson and the White Mountains —its trails, rivers—Doris Fernald Wood and her relatives, the dairy-farming Davis family.[17]

Boston Becomes Home

Harvey moved into his small sitting-bedroom in the

Allens' home on September 9, 1937. He entered his fully-furnished, self-contained room at the rear of the house through a private entrance on the side. Harvey enjoyed meals and the pleasant company of the Allens. He became an intimate, life-long member the family. Herman, eight years his senior, immediately welcomed Harvey, and the two men soon discovered they shared a deep interest in music. Arcadia Road was only about a two-mile walk south of Bethlehem Shipbuilding Corporation.[18]

Only four days after Harvey moved into the Allens' home, Herman took him to what Harvey envisaged as a "real New England church." He met many young people who welcomed Harvey, and the organist and choir director, Helen Bryant. By the end of September, Harvey began attending the Weymouth First Baptist Church choir rehearsals and singing in the choir. In mid-October 1937, Harvey sang his first solo in the choir, with Herman accompanying him on the organ. Soon, Harvey began singing in a quartet comprised of Ted Tabor, Kenneth Arnold, and Leonard Arnold. Harvey also attended church suppers and Bible study classes.[19]

Early on, Harvey began to explore historic places, cultural events, and large department stores in and around Boston. He soon became familiar with the Massachusetts State House, the Boston Symphony Orchestra Hall, and Filenes, Jordan Marsh, and Gilchrist department stores. With Herman and Herman's sister Gladys—who lived in nearby Wellesley—he went to Boston to see a performance of the Russian ballerina Tatiana Riabouchinska, whom Evan had met in Rochester. In December 1937, Harvey and the choir members later went to Boston to hear a Handel's *Messiah* performance. Harvey also went with Herman to see the Brainway Players' performance of *The Lion and the Mouse*.

Soon, Harvey began acting in church plays, just as he

had done in Rochester. Harvey also began attending Boston Symphony Orchestra concerts and the opera in Boston, took dance lessons, sang with a glee club, and had dinners with new friends. Once again, Harvey began building model ships, just as he had done as a youngster and in Liverpool. In November 1937, he ordered a model kit and began assembling *Old Ironsides*/USS *Constitution*. In 1938, Harvey's life had become full and rich.[20]

As Harvey settled into his new life in Weymouth, he became increasingly familiar with members of the Baptist Church who were in the church choir, in plays, and who also hiked in the White Mountains with Nathan Wood. Early on, Harvey came to know Edith Price well; she sang in the choir and hiked with Nathan Wood. Edith had graduated from Burdett College in downtown Boston in 1930 after taking a two-year curriculum in business and secretarial skills. Soon afterward she secured a job working at the well-established Boston investment firm of Studley Schubert, which had survived the Great Depression. She lived at home with her parents and two younger sisters, Avril and Arlene. Edith and Harvey frequently walked home from the Baptist Church to the Allens' house on Arcadia Street, just two blocks from the Price home at 69 Webb Street. Sometimes Edith offered Harvey a ride home in her car.

One evening after choir practice in the early summer of 1938, Harvey walked Edith home and kissed her. She is "the first girl since Phyl," Harvey wrote in his diary. In the subsequent weeks and months, however, Harvey began distancing himself from Edith, perhaps because she seemed too eager to develop a relationship with him. He soon attempted to dodge her whenever possible. "There was no kissing Edith," Harvey wrote in his diary in early April 1938. He continued to remain aloof and chose to interact with Edith only as part of a group rather than alone.[21] After several months of stepping back from Edith, in October 1938, he shared with his diary that, "I miss seeing Edith, but don't love her by a long way."[22]

Missing Phyl While Making New Friends

For many months after leaving England, Harvey terribly missed his brief but very intimate relationship with Phyllis Hargreaves. He often wrote to Phyl after arriving back in the United States. She, too, wrote to Harvey. His diary never failed to mention the long letters he received from Phyl. Harvey continued to hold deep feelings of affection for Phyllis Hargreaves.

In a long letter he sent to her before leaving England, he professed his desire to deepen their relationship. He promised to return to England in two years. She responded openly, gently explaining that she thought the distance between them would not allow their relationship to develop and that only friendship might be possible. "I value your friendship highly," she wrote, "and will look forward to seeing you whenever you come back to England."[23] After Phyl let Harvey know the great pleasure she received from their deep friendship , the two sent future letters exchanging news about their evolving lives. They wrote about encounters they had with family and friends, their thoughts about the differences between men and women, their friendship, and the beautiful times they had shared in Liverpool. They vowed to help each other whenever each one needed support, even across the great distance that now separated them. In their letters, they shared much about themselves.[24]

As 1937 drew to a close and just as their letters gradually became briefer and further apart, Phyl let Harvey know that she would love to see him again. In early 1938 many weeks elapsed between their letters. In March 1938,

Phyl observed that Harvey owed her two letters. In early May, Phyl shared her worry that Harvey might never write to her again.[25]

There was indeed a long hiatus in their communication during this period. Harvey's life had become increasingly busy with work and an array of social and cultural activities. Although his job as a naval architect for Bethlehem Shipbuilding Corporation was slow at first and somewhat dull, Harvey had become immersed in an increasingly rich and varied church and social life.

John, Harvey, Frank in Pittsford, 1937-38.

Harvey also made frequent trips back to Pittsford to see his parents, Frank, and his friends. At first, he returned to Pittsford once a month, leaving on a Friday evening coach from Boston, spending the weekend with his family and then returning to Weymouth on Sunday night. While in Pittsford, Harvey and Evan would visit long-time friends (the Harris, Cain, and Dumas families) during the day. More friends would come to the Evanses's house in the evening for supper, games, and singing. Over Christmas 1937, Harvey spent four days in Pittsford, then, on December 27, drove his father and Evan to work at Sibley's before leaving on an evening coach to Boston. In his diary, Harvey confessed that he felt sad to leave his family and friends behind. However, back in Weymouth, Harvey welcomed the arrival of 1938 at the Baptist Church, where he made several new friends.[26]

Harvey also spent time writing to his families in England and Wales. He regularly wrote to Auntie Bea, Auntie Bertha, Uncle Frank, Uncle Reg and Aunt Winnie, and Auntie Ethel and Uncle Maurice in Essex. He faithfully wrote to Uncle Tom Evans and Aunt Liza in Aberaman, Wales, and to Hetty and Rollo Roland. Harvey exchanged letters with former classmates Bob Lynn, Frank Graham, and Tristram. Harvey's practice of communicating with friends and family on both sides of the Atlantic Ocean and those he met later from around the world continued throughout his life.

In 1938, the Evans family began to meet less in Pittsford and more at Harvey's home in Weymouth. That summer, his younger brother, Evan, still contemplated entering the Royal Academy of Music in London, which Francis Jones, Evan's private piano teacher in Rochester, had attended years earlier. He eventually abandoned this idea, however. Instead, an opportunity arose for Evan to attend the New England Conservatory of Music in Boston. Perhaps with the encouragement of Charles and Malinda Allen's daughter, Gladys Allen MacGregor, who had an association with the New England Conservatory, Evan went to Boston along with John, Mabel, and Frank in 1938.

Harvey made reservations for them to stay nearby at vacation accommodations on Brant Rock Beach south of Quincy. In August, Evan enrolled in a five-year curriculum at the New England Conservatory of Music; he began classes in mid-September 1938. Although Evan stayed in a conservatory dormitory during the week, he often came out from Boston to Weymouth on weekends to visit Harvey and stay overnight at the Allens' home. Harvey, who had recently begun taking voice lessons twice a week at the New England Conservatory, often stopped to see Evan in his dormitory. Evan sometimes joined Harvey and his Baptist Church friends on hikes in the White Mountains.[27]

Evan in Boston, ca.1938.

On the Eve of War

In late 1937, Harvey began making brief but descriptive entries in his diary about the early days of practicing naval architecture at Fore River Shipyard. Between late 1937 and December 7, 1941, Harvey became fully engaged in a range of projects that applied his naval architecture education. Fore River Shipyard proved to be a perfect training ground for a young naval architect.

Fore River Shipyard had a long history of shipbuilding. As early as the 1600s, boat builders swung their hammers in a small boatyard along the Fore River's deep-water channels and the nearby Town River. A ketch (a two-masted sailboat) named SS *Unity* was the first recorded vessel launched at Ship Cove in Fore River in 1696. In 1913, Bethlehem Steel Corporation founded a shipbuilding division in Quincy when it purchased the 110-acre Fore

River Engine Company. During the First World War, Bethlehem Steel Corporation expanded the Fore River Shipyard and initiated a critical ship building division there for the Navy and Merchant Marine. The Great Depression precipitated a great lull in shipbuilding contracts and caused a reduction in Bethlehem Corporation's workforce. During this period, Fore River Shipyard produced only ten ocean liners, thirteen trawlers, eleven miscellaneous freighters and barges, and just thirteen ships for the U.S. Navy.[28]

When Harvey arrived in September 1937, there were only around 800 employees at the Fore River Shipyard. Early on, Harvey's work assignments proved slow and somewhat dull. During his first months, he spent considerable time calculating and drawing bulkheads (walls separating ship compartments) for small destroyers. He watched the launching of three 147-foot trawlers. For several weeks, he also calculated the tank capacities of Army Corps of Engineers' dredges that maintained adequate depths to navigate in rivers and harbors. In March 1938, the University of Liverpool's *Journal of the Engineering Society* noted that Harvey was an "engineering assistant" at Bethlehem Shipbuilding Corporation.

Starting early 1938 and continuing for several months, Harvey worked on an 18-knot tanker's lines for the shipyard's model basin. He then completed work on the twin propeller of the Sun Shipbuilding & Drydock Company's 18-knot tanker. Harvey also designed aspects of the SS *Panama*, whose workers laid down the keel (placement of the backbone of a vessel) in late October 1937. On September 24, 1938, both Harvey and Evan witnessed the *Panama's* launching at Fore River. This 493-foot, 326-ton freighter, completed for the Panama Railroad Company in April 1939, was distinguished by its fire-proof construction from stem to stern. Harvey also designed parts of the USS

Wasp (CV 7), a Navy aircraft carrier launched at Fore River Shipyard in April 1939.[29]

Not only was Harvey's work at Fore River Shipyard gratifying, but so, too, was his ability to finally pay off the debts he had accumulated during his four years at the University of Liverpool. Between July 1938 and September 1940, he paid, in five installments, all of his debt to the University of Liverpool. His graduation certificate finally arrived in the mail.

Harvey, the naval architect, Allens' house, Weymouth, Mass.

Paying off this debt also meant that Harvey could become an associate member of the Institution of Naval Architects of Great Britain, which he joined in April 1941. In June 1940, Harvey also paid the large amount he had promised to pay Mr. Griffith at the Lloyds Bank in Ferndale, Wales. Griffith included a personal note that included a pithy observation about Germany's recent arrival in Paris.[30]

> What an achievement for old Hitler. Won't he be pleased to go through the arc de triumphe and on to Versailles to the "X" room in which that treaty was signed in 1918. We wonder if the U.S.A. will send over their Army and Navy now, or if they will wait until it is too late. . . . We are going to win in the end, but it is a great pity that so many lives are being lost for the sake of democracy.[31]

In September 1940, Harvey also paid his final debt to Ravenscroft & Willis in Liverpool for his long, black graduation gown with hood encircled with rabbit fur.[32]

Although shipbuilding languished during Harvey's early years at Fore River Shipyard, President Franklin D. Roosevelt made many decisions behind the scenes that slowly moved the United States toward naval preparedness for war. Many government leaders became increasingly determined not to repeat the same mistakes made before World War I when the United States resisted building up its military until it became necessary. To prepare for a possible future conflict with the Axis powers, in 1936 the Maritime Commission and the U.S. Navy coordinated their efforts to construct new and expand old shipyards on the Gulf, Pacific, and Atlantic coasts. This suggested a shift away from the United States' post-World War I isolationism.[33]

Around the same time, the Naval Act of 1936 authorized constructing the first new battleship since 1921. In response to the Japanese invasion of China in late 1937 and the German annexation of Austria in March 1938, Congress passed the Naval Expansion Act in May 1938, mandating a 20 percent increase in the U.S. Navy's fleet. This act called for constructing a specified number of battleships, cruisers, destroyers, and submarines.[34]

These steps taken to prepare the United States for military engagement proved timely. In October 1938, Germany annexed the Sudetenland of Czechoslovakia, home of many ethnic Germans. In late September, government leaders in Germany, Great Britain, France, and Italy provided for the cession of the Sudeten German territory of Czechoslovakia to Germany in the Munich Agreement to prevent a war threatened by Adolf Hitler.

Harvey expressed outrage at this agreement. "That fool Hitler needs kicking," he lamented in his diary. Despite Hitler's advances, Harvey, like many in the United States, optimistically believed that "we will not have war."[35] This wishful thinking soon exploded, however. In the spring of 1939, Hitler's German Army seized the rest of Czechoslovakia, and, in September, Germany invaded Poland. Great Britain and France declared war against Germany in September 1939, marking the beginning of the Second World War.[36]

These events moved American public sentiment ever closer to supporting military preparedness. On June 10, 1940, President Roosevelt declared that it was time to "proclaim certain truths." America could no longer pretend to be "a lone island in a world of force. . . . Our sympathies lie with those nations that are giving their lifeblood in combat against these forces."[37] Following Roosevelt's address, Congress passed the Two-Ocean Navy Act in July 1940, authorizing an 11 percent increase in naval tonnage and the procurement of 115 destroyers, 43 submarines, 27 cruisers, and 18 aircraft carriers. The U.S. Navy concluded that modern aircraft designs had demonstrated that carriers should be the Navy's backbone, with destroyers, cruisers, and submarines providing critical support.[38]

Fore River Shipyard, Braintree, Mass.

President Roosevelt's vehement advocacy of wartime preparedness and Congress's passage of acts requesting the addition of many new naval vessels profoundly impacted Harvey's work at Fore River Shipyard. By 1941 employees at Bethlehem Shipbuilding Corporation had completed about thirty-five ships (freighters, tankers, trawlers, and dredges) for petroleum and other companies and the United States Navy.[39]

In early January 1941, Roosevelt announced the "Emergency Shipbuilding Program," mandating the rapid completion of 200 large-capacity "emergency ships" designed to send cargo to the Allies. These ships became part of the so-called "Liberty Fleet." On September 27, 1941, Bethlehem Shipbuilding Corporation launched its first Liberty ship, the SS *Patrick Henry,* at its Baltimore shipyard. Liberty ships became the first mass-produced cargo ships built in response to the staggering loss of Allied ships to German submarine attacks early in the war. Harvey never designed any Liberty ships; however, he witnessed their construction at Bethlehem Shipbuilding Corporation and was well aware of their critical role in providing vital food and military supplies to his Harvey and Evans families and all of Great Britain.[40]

In 1939, and accelerating in 1940 and 1941, the United States moved ever closer to total engagement in the war. Harvey's career as a young naval architect became increasingly varied, engaging, and purposeful. When Great Britain entered the war in September 1939, Harvey had professional and personal reasons to energetically pursue his chosen career as a naval architect. The Selective Service System indeed agreed that his training and skills as a naval architect transcended any service he might contribute as an enlisted soldier. After the draft began in October 1940, Harvey registered with his Local Board of the Selective Service every year, yet he always received a 2-B classification: "deferred war production."[41]

Phyllis and a "Land of Heros"

In August 1937, Harvey had assured Phyllis Hargreaves that he would return to England in two years to pursue their relationship. Neither of them could have imagined, however, the explosive global developments that would envelop Britain, France, and their allies. After Britain declared war on Germany in September 1939, they both realized that his return to England would not be possible until the war was over. They also did not fully acknowledge the real possibility that one or both of them might meet another person who would attract their attention. By chance, this happened to Phyllis first. In July 1940, Harvey received an invitation from Phyl to attend her wedding at St. Stephens Church in Prenton near Liverpool on July 27, 1940, to Robert Crossley. Harvey marked the day in bold red ink in his calendar, suggesting the enormous meaning it had for him. One year later, in July 1941, the British Army drafted Robert (Bob) Crossley. Five months later, on December 7, 1941, the Japanese bombed Pearl Harbor, immediately pulling the United States into war. This was the only other event that Harvey wrote in red ink in his calendar.

In early 1943, Harvey received another letter from Phyl, who was now living in Hoylake, about 10 miles west of Liverpool, and caring for her five-month-old baby while her husband, Bob, served in the Royal Air Force. Phyl grimly described the period between mid-1940 and mid-1941, when she and her son Bobby were "bombed and blitzed and never went to bed knowing whether we would ever be alive again. You would have . . . [an] awful shock to see Liverpool now and the wide-open spaces!"[42] On March 13, 1941, during a nighttime German bombing raid, London, Liverpool, and other major industrial cities in Britain became prime targets. The Harrison Hughes Building, where Harvey had attended his engineering classes at the University of Liverpool, suffered devastating damage. Firewatchers stationed in the clock tower of the nearby Victoria Building watched the parachute landmine drifting past them into the quadrangle near the Harrison Hughes Building but were helpless to do anything to prevent its explosion.[43]

Harrison Hughes Building bombed, Liverpool, ca. 1940.

With her husband away in Libya and Egypt and, later, Tunisia and Cairo, Egypt, for nearly the entire war, Phyl carried on alone during long, horrifyingly black nights with all windows blacked out and sirens screaming, wondering if she and her baby would survive to see her husband again. Phyl's health began to deteriorate as the terrifying nighttime bombings continued. In late 1943 she suffered a "nervous collapse."[44]

After hearing from Phyllis about the many trials she and her friends and family in Britain had faced, Harvey shared his most poignant feelings with her. I have such "great admiration for you and all my good British friends and relatives. They fill me too with a great feeling of smallness. . . . You are a land of heroes to me and, I must confess, that coming away from a movie like *In Which We Serve* [a 1942 patriotic British war film] I fairly burst with pride and love for you all."[45]

15

HARVEY AND EVANS FAMILIES
TOGETHER AT WAR

1940–1945

Harvey soon learned about the tremendous role that Phyllis, some of his aunts and female cousins, and thousands of other British women were playing to support Britain's Home Front during Germany's endless bombings. Women's roles in the wartime workforce shifted from characteristic domestic activities to jobs requiring more physical strength and technical knowledge. Women now worked in munitions, chemicals, metals and shipbuilding industries, skilled and semi-skilled engineering jobs, and mechanical occupations. They volunteered to transport munitions and coal by barge on Britain's inland waterways. Tens of thousands of young women joined the Women's Land Army and were moved from the cities to rural farms to raise vegetables, fruits, and herbs to help feed British civilians and boost civilian morale. Betty Harvey, daughter of World War I veteran Reginald Harvey, considered joining the Women's Land Army but decided against it and worked instead in a bank throughout most of the war.[1]

Women began working in many areas that required intellectual acuity, unwavering focus, and the ability to endure prolonged stress. One Harvey family member,

Hilda Ellen Harber, became one of 8,000 women who worked at Bletchley Park, the principal center of Allied code-breaking cryptanalysis.[2] Unmarried women between the ages of twenty and thirty also undertook military jobs such as searchlight operators, and were trained to use anti-aircraft guns. After December 1941, women joined many auxiliary military branches, such as the Women's Royal Naval Service, Women's Auxiliary Air Force, Air Auxiliary Service, and the Air Transport Auxiliary. Over 640,000 British women served in various auxiliary services. Women became the heroes of war at home in Great Britain.[3]

The Harvey and Evans Families in Wartime

As the United States moved closer to total engagement in World War II, Harvey's sympathies lay unreservedly with the British people, especially his Harvey and Evans families, which he had come to know intimately during his four years at the University of Liverpool. Harvey had a very close personal connection to his many relatives, who were now experiencing war at close range. The English Harveys and Welsh Evanses were his people and were now, in the 1940 words of President Franklin D. Roosevelt, "giving their lifeblood in combat against these forces."

In letters from his English family, Harvey soon learned about the conscription of Harvey men—two of his cousins, Vernon Harvey and Desmond Langridge. In the 1930s, Vernon Sylvester Harvey, son of World War I veteran Reginald Harvey, spent considerable time with Harvey Evans when he stayed at Kingsmans Farm and visited Vernon's parents, his Uncle Reginald and Aunt Winnie, at Paynes Farm. Vernon Harvey entered the civilian British Merchant Navy just before the United Kingdom declared war against Germany in 1939. His keen interest in and experience working with wireless radios from a young age made Vernon well qualified to become a wireless operator in the Merchant Navy and, ultimately, a "first radio officer" by age twenty-four in 1944.

Vernon Harvey (courtesy Nick Hards).

Radio officers often performed extraordinary acts of bravery and self-sacrifice since they and the ship captain would be the last to leave a sinking ship. In late 1939, Vernon's cargo ship, the 405-foot-long SS *Boulderpool*, made a north-westerly arc from England across the Atlantic through icebergs just south of Newfoundland. It then moved up the St. Lawrence River to Montreal. (Seventeen months later, on March 7, 1941, after Vernon had left the *Boulderpool*, a flotilla of German E-boats sank the *Boulderpool* along with a convoy of five other ships off the coast of Cromer, Norfolk.) During the war, Vernon went in and out of Alexandria, Egypt, several times. In the early 1940s, Vernon was in the Aegean Sea, between Greece and Turkey, when a devastating Turkish earthquake caused extensive flooding across much of the country.[4]

In June 1942, after ten months at sea, he returned home to his family for three weeks. In a letter to Harvey, Vernon's sister, Betty, observed that he "looked marvelously tanned and well, and, gosh, we're all pleased to see him!"[5] In August 1942, Vernon found himself in the Caribbean Sea on a British freighter torpedoed by a German submarine near Jamaica.[6] The ship listed starboard and the crew could get only one lifeboat free from the vessel. As the German submarine moved menacingly among the men floundering in the sea, Vernon and several other crew members bailed out the one lifeboat they had

freed from the ship so that it could accommodate thirty-
one men who had survived the attack. They drifted for
thirty hours before washing up on a Jamaican beach. From
there, the men made their way overland to Kingston, the
Jamaican capital. Despite this harrowing experience,
Vernon and his crew were "anxious to get another ship as
quickly as possible." In September, soon after Vernon
reached Kingston, he sent a telegram to his sister, Betty:
"Happy returns safe and sound."[7] Vernon likely may have
been torpedoed at least once more before he left the
Caribbean.

Near the end of the war, Vernon also went to Russia as
part of a convoy of several British merchant ships delivering equipment, material, ammunition, combat vehicles,
and food to Allied ports on Russia's northern coast. The
convoys, traveling for ten to fourteen days, often encountered rough weather in the Norwegian and Barents Seas
north of Norway and Russia and routinely navigated
through fierce storms and thick fog. German airplanes and
submarines usually learned about these convoys and sometimes bombed or torpedoed them. Despite all the action
he saw, Vernon survived his World War II adventures and
returned to England at the end of the war with a Russian
samovar (a sizeable metal container used to heat and boil
water) and knowledge of skiing. For his service in the
Merchant Navy, Vernon received a "Civil Commendation
for brave conduct."[8]

Although not conscripted into the military, Raymond
Harvey Langridge, born in 1917, served in the Home
Guard. Organized in May 1940, the Home Guard was
considered Britain's last defense against a feared German
invasion. Raymond also continued to farm, and thus he
provided both civilians and military personnel in Great
Britain with much-needed food.[9]

Raymond's brother, Desmond Henry Langridge, born

in 1920, was called up in 1940. "Citizen Soldiers" like
Desmond, a farmer, were recruited from many different
civilian backgrounds to defend their homes, country, and
way of life. Trained early on as a ground-based anti-aircraft
gunner, Desmond often moved to dangerous locations
throughout Britain as the war progressed. He first went to
Oswestry, Shropshire, near the Welsh–English border, for
the base training. He then joined heavy artillery "Ack-Ack
Battery," where he received training on a "Predictor," an
instrument that precisely calculated and followed the position of approaching enemy planes while artillery personnel
were preparing to shoot them down. Desmond's Ack-Ack
Battery's primary goal was to protect British towns, cities,
and industrial areas from German bombing attacks.[10]

After receiving training in Oswestry, he then moved to
Camp Weybourne in Norfolk, on the east coast of
England, to practice his training before being posted to
Birmingham for several months. While in Birmingham,
Desmond became a Lance Bombardier (a non-commis-
sioned officer in an artillery regiment of the British Army)
before moving to a Wolverhampton gun site. In 1942,
Desmond moved to Aberdeen, Scotland, and, then, by
boat to gun sites near Kirkwall in the Orkney Islands. At
these gun sites, Desmond protected a British fleet
anchored in a nearby harbor. Desmond may have barely
missed traveling on an ill-fated boat to the Orkneys, which
was sunk by German bombers.

Harvey received periodic news of Desmond from his
cousin Betty. In mid-1942, Harvey learned in a letter from
Betty that Desmond had been home on leave from the
Orkneys. In March 1943, Harvey reported to Phyl that
Desmond had "served in the Orkneys and Birmingham
during [their] worst raids as an anti-aircraft gunner."[11]
Around this time, Desmond received a promotion from
bombardier (corporal) to sergeant. After sixteen months,

his regiment moved to the Isle of Wight and then to Dartmouth on England's south coast to defend a U.S. Army invasion practice area.[12]

Desmond was at Dartmouth on D-Day, June 6, 1944, when British, American, and Canadian forces landed on France's Normandy coast and pushed back the Germans, marking a pivotal event in the war. Desmond later moved to Brighton on England's south coast, then to the Isle of Sheppey near the mouth of the River Thames to fire on "doodle bugs" (German flying bombs). Finally, he attended an officer training course near Towyn, Wales. When the war in Europe ended in mid-1945, Desmond went to Kenya to train African soldiers to fight in the Far East. He left Mombasa, Kenya, after the war in the Far East ended in 1946 and returned to England to work for a time on his Uncle Reginald's farm in Great Chishill, just south of Cambridge.[13]

Desmond Langridge, sergeant, ca. 1945 (courtesy David Langridge).

Other Harvey family members also became fully engaged in World War II. The Harvey family's fishing and maritime branch, descendants of William Harvey, the brother of Stephen Harvey, participated in the Dunkirk evacuation in late May and early June 1940. Grandchildren of William Harvey and their spouses assembled small fishing boats, barges, and pleasure craft at Leigh on the River Thames. They crossed the English Channel to take part in the treacherous and heroic rescue of over 330,000 Allied soldiers under attack by the Germans on France's Dunkirk beaches.[14]

Even Harvey Evans's uncle, Tom Evans, contributed to the war effort on the home front in Wales. Then in his early sixties, Tom volunteered to serve as an Air Raid Precautions (ARP) warden. Set up in 1937 by local government councils, ARP wardens reported bombing incidents. In September 1939, when heavy German bombing during the Blitz caused horrific deaths and devastating damage to buildings, wardens like Tom patrolled the streets at night, enforcing "blackout" rules.[15]

Harvey felt pangs of anxiety when his own brother—sensitive, kind Evan—decided to join the U.S. Army. Undoubtedly, Evan must have felt torn between pursuing his musical education and contributing in a small way to the fight for the birthplace of his parents—England and Wales—and the home of so many of his relatives.

In the summer and fall of 1940, after repeated bombings by the German *Luftwaffe* over the English Channel and ports and airfields in England, Churchill and Roosevelt met on September 2 and agreed that the U.S. would give Britain 50 obsolete destroyers in exchange for a 99-year lease to territory in the Caribbean and Newfoundland. This agreement confirmed that airfields in Bermuda, constructed by the United States, would be shared with the British Royal Air Force. Churchill warned Roosevelt that if Britain fell, British colonial islands close to U.S. shores, such as Bermuda, would be vulnerable to German attack and occupation. Eventually, the U.S. Army Air Force airfield at Fort Bell and the U.S. Naval Operations Base joined forces with British air stations already operating in Bermuda. The United States thus became responsible in part for the security of British Bermuda.

Two weeks later, in mid-September 1940, U.S. Congress passed the Selective Training and Service Act, requiring all men between the ages of twenty-one and thirty-six to register with their local draft board. Anticipating the inevitability of his recruitment, Evan decided not to continue his music studies in the fall, but withdrew from the New England Conservatory in June 1940 after working for two years toward a five-year degree. Over the next few months, Evan prepared for his induction in the U.S. Army.

Evan waited five months. On February 24, 1941, before the United States had entered the war, the Selective Service called up Evan. He entered the Army as a private in the Warrant Officer Corps (highly trained specialists who served as technical experts). Two months later, Evan, along with many young recruits, left the Army base in Brooklyn, New York, on the Army's SS *American Legion* transport ship. Private Evans, one of 860 men in the 52nd Coast Artillery, F Battery, became one of the first to arrive on Bermuda on April 20, 1941—nearly eight months before the United States officially entered the war. Immediately upon arrival, Evan and other U.S. Army soldiers mingled routinely with British soldiers.[16]

Private Evans was given an array of tasks when he first arrived. After the 6:00 a.m. reveille bugle call, depending on the day of the week, Evan had police duty, guard duty, cleaning, drills, kitchen patrol, preparation for inspections, plotting tedious marches through forests and across fields, and many other tasks.

Within the first year of his service in Bermuda, Evan developed a close relationship with Philip H. Conine. Although sentiments about gays in the United States reached a high pitch during World War II, gay men managed to build a protected world inside the U.S. Army. In Great Britain, possibly 250,000 military men were gay or bisexual. During the war, attitudes towards gay men in the military relaxed, and many men were open about their sexuality. Negative attitudes towards gays and lesbians in the military continued to resurface for many decades after World War II. Evan and Philip Conine, who later married a woman and had a family, kept in touch for many years.[17]

Evan, the announcer, U.S. Army, Bermuda, ca. 1944.

Towards the end of 1941, Evan and others in his unit spent long hours on the shooting range.[18] In a 1943 letter to his dear friend Phyl in England, Harvey reported that Evan "turned out to be the best rifle marksman of his battery, and . . . is the plotter of the gun crew which has set up the best record for accuracy of the whole U.S. Army for their type of heavy coast defense common."[19] Later, Evan also served as an "entertainment specialist 442" (someone with professional music training). He then became the station manager and head announcer for the U.S. Armed Forces radio station WXLQ of Bermuda Base Command. By the end of the war, many Americans knew Corporal Evans as "the announcer," who scheduled both live and pre-recorded radio programs, handled station publicity, and served as master of ceremonies for radio programs. Even after an eight-inch projectile smashed one of Evan's fingers, he served as his regiment's organist and pianist. He assisted the Base Commander's senior chaplain with pastoral music at chapel services and directed a men and women's chorus. In 1944, towards the end of the war, Evan received recognition as a "Marksman," Carbine, First C1 Gunner, received a Good Conduct Medal, and was awarded an American Defense Service Medal and American Theatre Campaign ribbon.[20]

In letters to his family, Evan sometimes shared his fear of German U-boat attacks every time the shriek of air sirens blasted across Bermuda, and blimps drifted through the sky like enormous floating eggs in search of U-boats. The threat of German U-boat attacks on Bermuda remained inescapable until the very end of the war. Life continued to be uncertain and tense for Evan during nearly his entire 51 months stationed on Bermuda.[21]

Several of Harvey's closest friends also served in the military. Herman Allen, akin to Harvey's older brother, served as a private in the U.S. Army and was stationed at Camp Beale, a training site for the 13th Armored and the 81st and 96th Infantry divisions. Located north of Sacramento, this was the home of 60,000 soldiers, a prisoner of war camp, and a hospital. Later, Herman wore the crossed flag insignia of the 232nd Signal Corps based in San Francisco. In his early forties, Herman's older brother, Eugene, became a major in the Medical Corps' Evacuation Hospital in New York City.[22]

Designing Ships for War

Harvey, unlike Evan, was never called to serve in the military since his Local Board of the Selective Service System gave him a 2-B classification ("deferred war production") every year that he registered to enlist. His highly valued knowledge and skills as a naval architect far outweighed any contribution he may have made serving in the military. Before and during U.S. engagement in the war, the Allies needed a continuous supply of different ships: light and heavy cruisers, destroyers, battleships, and aircraft carriers for the U.S. Navy as well as numerous other vessels for Britain, to replace the many ships that German U-boats sank. On the eve of United States entry in the war in late 1941, the pace of production at Fore River Shipyard, along with fifteen other Bethlehem Shipbuilding Corporation shipyards on the East, West, and Gulf coasts of the United States, greatly accelerated. By December 1941, employment at Fore River Shipyard rose to 17,000. In January 1943, Bethlehem Shipbuilding Corporation employed 32,000 workers at its Fore River Shipyard. Employees like Harvey worked busy days and often three nights a week to keep up with the enormous demand for ships.[23]

By the spring of 1943, Bethlehem Shipbuilding Corporation had hired thousands more men and women to design and build an increasing number of U.S. Navy ships. Roughly 2,000 women took the place of men who had been drafted into the military. Many of these women became proficient at welding large steel panels used in different sections of ships. They soon became known as "Winnie the Welder."

In November 1941, the British Admiralty sent a small delegation of naval architects to collaborate with the U.S. Navy's Bureau of Ships to determine the best design for lightly armored, fast-moving Landing Ship Tanks (LST) designed to carry infantry, tanks, and supplies to landings on French beaches. In 1942 and 1943, Congress passed three acts that mandated the construction of LSTs, along with destroyer escorts and other assorted landing craft. Workmen laid down the first LST keel at Fore River Shipyard in June 1942. Between November 1942 and June 1944, employees at Bethlehem Shipbuilding Corporation delivered forty-six LSTs[24] and contributed significantly to the success of D-Day landings in France. [25]

Harvey's work as a naval architect no longer seemed the least bit dull, but enormously varied, engaging, and purposeful. As one of about seventy-five men working in the design department, Harvey helped draw up the lines of many ships—battleships like the USS *Massachusetts* and aircraft carriers like the USS *Lexington* (CV-16), along with her sister ship the USS *Bunker Hill* (CV-17).

In a March 23, 1943, letter to Phyl, Harvey described his work this way: "I am in the basic design department of Bethlehem Steel Company's Fore River Shipyard where I have been ever since I started work." In the Central Technical Department, Harvey worked entirely on basic design in its first stages. He, therefore, "settled on a ship's dimensions, lines, and subdivision from an examination of resistance and propulsion and stability in damaged and undamaged conditions." Harvey proudly reported to Phyllis that Bethlehem Shipbuilding Corporation had built numerous smaller vessels, primarily for Britain.

In this same letter to Phyl, he described designing a "forward poppet," the high forward end of a cradle that supports about 25 percent of a ship's weight when its stern lifts up and the bow points downward during its launching. In September 1942, at the launching of the USS *Lexington,* the forward poppet that Harvey helped design supported around 6,750 tons (one quarter) of the ship's total weight of 27,500 tons. "If you have seen any photos of the launching of our latest aircraft carriers *Lexington* and *Bunker Hill,*" Harvey wrote Phyl, "you will have seen a piece of my handiwork in the form of the steel structure supporting the forward end of the ship." Many years later, Harvey recalled how "thrilling" it was to be involved in many different aspects of a ship's launching.[26] Harvey closed his letter to Phyl by reflecting on his varied experiences as a naval architect. "In the past five years, I have acquired a wonderfully well-rounded experience in this, the office of one of our country's largest and finest ship-builders. It has been like a rotating internship."[27]

Beginning a Life and Family during Wartime

As the war turned decidedly in favor of the Allies, Harvey's life remained hectic. He worked many long days between late April and early September 1943, sometimes until late into the evening. Despite his continuing long-distance friendship with Phyl, twenty-nine-year-old Harvey and thirty-two-year-old Edith, who had continued to see each other and hike together in the White Mountains, decided to marry.

Edith and Harvey, Fernald Brook, Jackson, NH, ca. 1942.

On July 3, 1943, Reverend Charles Allen married Harvey and Edith at the First Baptist Church in Weymouth. Mabel and John came from Rochester for their son's wedding as well as a few Rochester friends, notably life-time friend Charles Harris and his new wife, Justine. After collecting gasoline ration coupons for weeks, Harvey and Edith drove to New Hampshire and honeymooned in the White Mountains for a week. Harvey then immediately returned to his job at Fore River shipyard. Harvey and Edith settled into a rented gambrel-roof house (at 555 North Street) not far from the Fore River Shipyard.[28]

Wedding of Harvey and Edith, July 3, 1943.

Harvey and Edith began married life in a world of great uncertainty as World War II continued. In June 1944, the cruiser USS *Quincy II,* built by the Bethlehem Shipbuilding Corporation, and three other cruisers, fired on German installations at Cherbourg, France. Their successful bombardment marked a critical turning point in the war.

Following this event, Admiral Edward L. Cochran, Chief of the Bureau of Ships, United States Navy, telegraphed the Fore River Shipyard with words of tremendous praise. The *Quincy II* performed well, making a "splendid account of herself in support of the Allied invasion of Western Europe," Cochrane affirmed.[29] Fore River Shipyard employees, including Harvey, must have swelled with pride.

Less than five months later, on October 7, 1944, Edith gave birth to a son, Harvey David Evans, named after his grandmother's Harvey family and his grandfather's older brother, David Evans, who encouraged John to become a draper. Dr. Butler, the attending physician, noted that the birth had been extremely difficult for both Edith and David and insisted that they both stay thirteen days at Milton Hospital. Harvey visited Edith and David every day after working long hours at the shipyard. In mid-November, Evan arrived on leave from Bermuda and stopped briefly to see Harvey, Edith, and David before taking the train to Rochester to visit John and Mabel. In late November, Harvey, Edith, and David moved from 555 North Street to 31 Totnes Road, where they settled into a small, cozy rental house at the end of a quiet street in Braintree.[30]

Throughout the war, the Fore River Shipyard employees continued to receive high praise for their many design accomplishments and production records. Harvey contributed to the shipyard's growing reputation for outstanding quality, design, and production. On May 15, 1942, Fore River Shipyard received the highly esteemed Navy "E" award for production excellence. During 1944, they launched thirty-seven ships, the equivalent of about one ship every ten days.

On June 8, 1944, a record was set by Bethlehem Ship-building Corporation when three ships were launched at Fore River Shipyard in one day. Near the end of the war, workers at both Fore River and the nearby Hingham ship-yard constructed a total of 227 ships and set a world record for delivering five ships in fifty hours. By the end of 1945, the Bethlehem Shipbuilding Corporation had launched 1,121 vessels of all kinds: "No other shipyard in the United States built such a diverse array of naval vessels."[31] In terms of tonnage, speed of delivery, and the quality of construction, the Fore River Shipyard at Quincy became known as "the Greatest Shipyard of World War II."[32]

Military Service at War's End

In the fall of 1944, World War II began winding down in Europe. Despite this, the United States and Great Britain still enlisted young men. In July 1944, John and Mabel's youngest son, eighteen-year-old Frank, enlisted in the U.S. Army Air Force.

All through high school in the small town of Pittsford, Frank had learned about Evan's war experiences in Bermuda. Frank thought seriously about training to become an aviation cadet. In mid-1943, at age seventeen and still in high school, Frank successfully passed all the requirements to begin his Air Force training. Attempting to keep all of this from his parents, he sent his exam results to Harvey in Weymouth. "What should I do?" Frank asked Harvey in a letter. Harvey must have advised Frank to finish high school, where Frank was totally immersed in acting, singing in the chorus, serving as the president of his junior class, presiding over of the school's Alpha Chi (national honor society), and working as the business manager of his high school yearbook. He also played baseball with great enthusiasm. He attended the Christ Episcopal Church in Pittsford. On January 23, 1944, the Rochester diocesan bishop confirmed Frank and nine-teen others at Christ Episcopal Church. After consulting with the diocese bishop, in late May 1944, Bishop Bartel H. Reinheimer admitted Frank as a postulant (a candidate for priesthood training) in the Diocese of Rochester.[33]

On the eve of his high school graduation, Frank enlisted in the U.S. Air Force and soon joined the Air Combat Crew. On July 5, Frank left Pittsford and entered the Air Force at Fort Dix, New Jersey, for initial training.

He then went to Keesler Field in Biloxi, Mississippi. In October 1944, Frank moved to the smaller Greenwood Air Force Base at Greenwood, Mississippi, where he continued his pilot training. Later, as part of Squadron C, 2132nd Army Air Force Base Unit, Frank moved to Maxwell Air Force Base in Montgomery, Alabama.

Frank Evans, Air Force, Tennessee.

Toward the end of 1944, he transferred to a Pilot School at Smyrna Army Airfield near Nashville, Tennessee. Frank eventually returned to Keesler Field in July 1944 and remained there until Japan surrendered in mid-1945, and World War II officially ended. A month later, when Army Air Force pilots were no longer needed, Private First Class Frank H. Evans became a clerk typist. By then, he had been recognized as a sharpshooter (Carbine M 1). He was awarded a World War II Victory Medal and American Theater Ribbon before being discharged from the Air Force at Rome, New York, on November 2, 1945.[34]

Just as World War II ended, Stephen Geoffrey Harvey, six months younger than Frank and the youngest son of Reginald and Winnie Harvey, also joined the British military. Like his cousin Frank, Stephen had been in high school when the war began. He then entered Magdalene College at Cambridge University, where he took short, less rigorous courses open to the general public. Although Stephen, like Frank Evans, had aspired to join the Air Force and took an exam to qualify as a rear gunner, he became ill and failed the exam. Instead, around his twentieth birthday, he joined the Royal Norfolk Regiment, a line infantry regiment dating back to 1685. The Royal Norfolk Regiment had already fought with distinction in the invasion of Europe and the Far East. Stephen probably joined the Royal Norfolk Regiment in mid-1945 as the war wound down.

In December 1945, Stephen went to India. Stephen's location in India can only be roughly reconstructed by the dates and mailing addresses of letters written to him by family members. Beginning in early 1946, Stephen received his mail in Agram, Bangalore (now Bengaluru), India, as an officer cadet in training to become a commissioned officer in the India Command. In this role, he helped maintain the internal security of India, then Burma (Myanmar) in 1941 followed by Ceylon (Sri Lanka) in 1943. By mid-June 1946, five-foot-seven-inch-tall Stephen had become a second lieutenant in the Royal Norfolk Regiment, by then attached to the Fourth GR (Gurkha Rifles), according to Stephen's identification card.

In October 1946, Reginald, his father, congratulated Stephen for his rank advancement. "Dear Gurkha," Reginald began, "was glad to hear that you had managed to become an officer and a gentleman . . . as your father before you," referring to Reginald's commission as a second lieutenant in a reserve Irish Cavalry regiment during the First World War.[35]

Stephen Harvey, Fourth Gurkha Rifles.

The Gurkhas of Nepal had a reputation for being the world's most legendary fighters—men of fearless courage and military prowess. For 200 years, the British valued the Gurkhas for their character and camaraderie. During the Second World War, 250,000 Gurkhas joined British regiments in numerous theatres in the Eastern hemisphere. The traditional 18-inch-long curved blade in the *kukri* knife represented the Gurkhas' ferocity in battle. As a testament to their extraordinary courage, the Gurkhas received more Victoria Crosses—the most prestigious award for valor in the British honors system—than any other regiment. By the end of the Second World War, forty-three Gurkha battalions had fought for Britain in multiple theatres—Syria, North Africa, Italy, Greece, and countries then part of the British Empire including Burma, northeast India, and Singapore.[36]

After the war ended, the Gurkhas continued to play an essential role in peace-keeping after India was partitioned into two states—the Dominion of Pakistan and the Union of India—on August 15, 1947. Partition sparked riots, violence, and an unprecedented wave of migration. Roughly 4.5 million Sikhs and Hindus migrated from

Pakistan into India, and 5.5 million Muslims headed from India to Pakistan. This "partition holocaust" required enormous peace-keeping efforts by the Gurkhas, including the Fourth Gurkha Rifles fighting with the Royal Norfolk Regiment. Adding to the explosive tensions caused by partition were post-war nationalist demands for independence from the British Empire. These erupted in both Burma and Ceylon during and after the war. Stephen Harvey helped lead the Fourth Gurkha Rifles in peace-keeping missions southeast Asia during this turbulent time. Stephen may have remained in India until the final stages of partition, which ended in August 1947 and early 1948.[37]

Stephen Harvey eventually became part of Company 154 in the Royal Indian Army Service Corps (RIASC), comprised of both the Indian Army and British Army in India. Stephen trained in a RIASC center located in India's southern region at Avadi, Madras presidency, east of Bangalore on the Bay of Bengal coast. The Royal Indian Army Service Corps was responsible for providing and transporting food, fuels and lubricants, ammunition, and hospital items to the Army, Air Force, and Navy.[38]

Like Stephen Harvey, Peter Gardner, another grandchild of Stephen and Martha Harvey and the son of Maud Harvey and Charles Gardner, also participated in British peace-keeping activities after the war ended. British sympathy for the Jews, which grew during the genocide of European Jews in the Holocaust, strongly supported the creation of a Jewish state in the Holy Land. In early 1947, eighteen-year-old Peter Gardner joined the Palestine Police Force (PPF) charged with countering the Jewish underground organizations that resisted British control of Palestine after the war. Peter Gardner remained in the PPF for eight months. After the newly created United Nations drafted a Partition Plan dividing Palestine into

Jewish and Arab sections, Peter and all 4,000 PPF men withdrew from Palestine in late 1947.[39]

World War II created a common thread of military service that involved the Harvey and Evans families on both sides of the Atlantic. Although Mabel Evans's nephews—Raymond and Desmond Langridge, Vernon and Stephen Harvey, and Peter Gardner—had never met Evan and Frank Evans, their experiences serving in the Allied Forces brought them together.

Peter Gardner in Israel, 1946 (courtesy Wayne Gardner).

Evan in England with Liza Evans, Rollo Rowland, and Hetty Evans Rowland, ca. 1946.

Harvey's role as a naval architect during the war also contributed to his sense of kinship and shared purpose with his Harvey and Evans families in Britain. It was Harvey's generation of family members—people that he came to know well during his four years at the University of Liverpool—that now fought to defeat the Axis Powers. Throughout the war, both Harvey and Mabel exchanged letters with family members serving in the military. All Harvey family members now felt united by a common purpose. Betty, in a 1942 letter to Harvey, wondered if Evan might come over after the war. Her hope soon became realized: Evan visited family members in England for the first time shortly after the war ended.[40]

John and Mabel: Challenged at Home

The war brought a different kind of struggle and hardship to John and Mabel in Pittsford. Their comfortable life during the 1930s and early 1940s gradually diminished. When John's job as a buyer at Sibley's became precarious, and he witnessed the departure of many of his long-time co-workers, he worried about his own job. At the same time, he struggled to make monthly home mortgage and car payments. John Evans worried silently about the possible loss of his job at Sibley's as he watched others around him leave. Despite these stresses, John did his best to hide his concerns from Mabel and his family. Such a heavy burden was hard to conceal.[41]

Somehow, for a while, John managed to juggle these many overwhelming financial demands, described vaguely in his letters to Harvey as a "heavy load."[42] Probably he overlooked debts and borrowed money to pay essential expenses. On the eve of U.S. entry in World War II, two enormous balloon payments on the Evans's house became due: $4,000 and $7,000. John and Mabel were completely unprepared to make these large payments.

For John, the worst imaginable events converged. In addition to balloon payments for the Evans house, John's hours at Sibley's may have been drastically cut back. No letter or Sibley records still exist to shed light on John's eventual separation from Sibley, Lindsay & Curr. On the verge of entering the war, the U.S. may have already begun to ration many fabrics, including silk and nylon blends, before Japan banned the export of silk altogether.

On June 25, 1940, the Supreme Court of the State of New York summoned John and Mabel (plus two others) to court in Rochester. The next day, the court filed a "Notice of Pendency of Action" stating that a real property claim was alleged and warning against any attempt to acquire any legal interest in the Evans property at 179 East Brook Road in Pittsford.[43]

Several months later, in September 1941, John and Mabel, still residing at 179 East Brook Road, signed a deed of trust (indenture) agreeing to pay their debt. Undoubtedly feeling enormous shame, and unable to offer friends a reasonable explanation for the loss of their lovely home at 179 East Brook Road, John, Mabel, and Frank moved in late 1941 to a nearby two-story rental house on a street with a similar name—Brook Road—a quarter-mile away. This rental house, built in 1920, was one thousand square feet smaller than their East Brook Road home and stood on a lot one-third the size of their foreclosed property.[44]

John and Mabel shared few details of their financial woes with their friends or with Harvey and Evan. In the fall of 1941, when the Evans family lost their East Brook Road home, Harvey was immersed in designing ships for the war, Evan was thousands of miles from home in Bermuda, Frank was preparing to enter his sophomore year at Pittsford High School, and the United States teetered on the brink of war.

Only Mabel knew of the final demoralizing blow that overwhelmed John in 1941: he lost his job at Sibley, Lindsay & Curr. Feeling great shame, John never shared with anyone, perhaps not even Mabel, the precise details of what happened. His sons knew only vaguely about John's job loss. Fifty years later, Harvey recalled that his father was "the last of the 'old help' to be let go from

Sibley's."[45] Whether anticipated or not, the blow to John could not have caused more profound anguish and shame. At the age of fifty-eight, John managed to find a job as a salesman in Pittsford, according to a 1943 Pittsford city directory. The employer's address, however, does not appear in that city directory. John's usual cheerful disposition withered, his mood turned somber, his shoulders slumped. Mabel's characteristic buoyancy could not diminish John's sense of defeat and loss.

Over the next three to four years, life in the Evans home became subdued and somber. Evan and Harvey infrequently came to visit since Evan was in Bermuda, and Harvey worked long hours at Bethlehem Shipbuilding Corporation, then married and started a family. Frank's activities in Pittsford High School kept Mabel and John engaged. John continued to participate in the Cambrian Welsh Society and the life of the South Congregational Church until nearly the end of World War II. But life had changed for John and Mabel and would never again be the same.[46]

16

AN END AND A BEGINNING

1944–1967

The birth of Harvey David Evans (known as David) in October 1944 must have brought a sparkle to John's eyes even as he tried to reconcile the loss of the family's home. He certainly delighted in knowing that the Evans family would continue in America with a new family member that carried his and Mabel's family names. Regrettably, John would never meet David. Just two and a half months after David's birth, John walked "a quarter of a mile to work through knee-deep snow" in mid-December. Then, "after resting [at work] he did the same in reverse." The exertion was too much for his weak heart.

After being bedridden for five days at home, Dr. Roland C. Harris, a long-time family friend who had helped deliver Harvey in 1914, came to visit John on December 17 and 19. In a letter he sent to Harvey in Massachusetts, Dr. Harris explained, "I consider John a very seriously and dangerously ill man. I am not sure whether he has a coronary occlusion or angina pectoris." Two years earlier, John had been diagnosed with arteriosclerotic heart disease; a coronary infarction followed in November

1944. Dr. Harris advised calling a heart specialist to make a precise diagnosis and admit John to a hospital.[1]

On December 17, 1944, Harvey suddenly stopped recording his daily activities in his small diary, perhaps after receiving Dr. Harris's grim prognosis. On Christmas Eve, Harvey received word that he "had better come home to Pittsford."[2] On Christmas Day, uniformed soldiers and festive vacationers packed the train with holiday cheer. When Harvey arrived in Rochester, Evan and Frank were already there with John at Park Avenue Hospital in Rochester. Grievously ill, John only lived for two more days; he died on the morning of December 28, 1944, his sixty-second birthday.[3]

Remembering John

John's death stunned everyone. Few people knew of the financial struggles John had silently endured during the past decade. John's friends and even Mabel could not comprehend the tremendous toll that his financial worries and job insecurity had taken on his health. Few also realized that John was genetically predisposed to suffer from heart ailments. Two of his older brothers, David and Ben, had both died of heart failure at ages forty-six and fifty-six, respectively. Whatever the causes of John's passing, John's determined effort to create a secure and satisfying life for his family had finally ended. Now he could finally rest. On New Year's Eve, while John laid still in the Zornow Funeral Home in Pittsford, Harvey came to Zornow's alone and, with a heavy heart, sketched his father's tranquil face.[4]

John deceased in funeral home (sketch by J.
Harvey Evans, Dec. 1944).

At 2:30pm on the chilly afternoon of January 1, 1945,
John Evans's family and friends remembered him at a
memorial service. Reverend Robert Brown delivered a
sermon entitled "The Father and Three Sons." John's three
sons: John Harvey Evans, a naval architect in Braintree,
Massachusetts; Corporal Evan Reginald Evans, stationed
in Bermuda; and Cadet Frank Harold Evans, stationed in
Greenwood, Mississippi. Reverend Brown delivered a
short but poignant eulogy capturing the essence of John's
character and presence in the church for thirty years.

> South Congregational Church has lost a faithful and
> sincere member. His presence among us was always
> inspiring to both young and old, and his devoted service
> constituted an example of loyal, willing Christian charac-
> ter. . . . He was a good friend and wise counselor to us all.
> . . . Our memory of him will always be a pleasant one,
> and his faithfulness will ever be an inspiration to our
> members. . . . To Mrs. Evans, and to his three sons,
> Harvey, Evan, and Frank, the congregation of South
> Church extend their deepest sympathy.[5]

Many long-time friends from the South Congregational Church, where John had served as a deacon since

1918 and been a devoted member of the choir for decades, gathered to remember him and support his family. As the sun dropped low in the late afternoon and temperatures hovered around freezing, John Evans was laid to rest in White Haven Memorial Park, a large pastoral grassy cemetery, just a mile from their Pittsford home. Beside John were the future gravesites of Egbert and Auley Cain, who had been John and Mabel's closest friends ever since John had arrived in Rochester from Great Britain in 1912.

Harvey, the eldest son, found himself thrust into the role of surrogate head of the Evans family at this profoundly sad time. Harvey read a few heartfelt words at John's gravesite.

> Always you have been among our dearest friends on so many happy occasions in the past. . . . Now you also seem to have chosen to bear with us the sorrow of John's passing. We cannot with words describe the huge emptiness we feel, but John, being a part of you, as he was, know[s] you understand. Nothing can convey our feelings regarding your devoted friendship . . .[6]

The loss of the family's bright light and uplifting spirit rained great sadness over those who gathered to celebrate his life. Enormous adjustments needed to be made in a world without John as World War II wound down. Not long after John's burial, Mabel left Pittsford, never to return, except for occasional visits with long-time friends. Six months later, World War II ended, and the Evans family, like hundreds of thousands of others, looked ahead, in anticipation of a new beginning. Just as John and Mabel had opened a new chapter in their lives as immigrants in America, now each Evans family member would experience new beginnings in their own lives. All of John and Mabel's sons turned a corner and headed in a new direction after the war and after John's death, sometimes more than once, as they adapted to changes and made choices about their future.

Mabel Carries On

Following John's death, Mabel lost her bearings; her husband of thirty-one years, and her source of moral support and income, were suddenly vanished. Without John's income, Mabel could not afford to keep their rental house at 13 Brook Road. Mabel soon made arrangements to remove her and John's possessions from their home and leave Pittsford. In January 1945, nineteen-year-old Frank, with Harvey's assistance, completed the necessary paperwork for Mabel to receive Frank's military dependency benefits from the War Department. (Harvey's penciled handwriting on the original form discloses his contribution to completing this form.)

On February 18, 1945, Mabel reported that she had just been granted a class B allotment for financial support. On her application, she reported that "section 5 of my application for an allotment in the name of my son Corporal Evan R. Evans should be amended to include this measure of support. . . . My husband has just passed away, and these two sons (Frank and Evan) are my only anticipated means of support," Mabel wrote. To qualify for dependency benefits from the War Department, one of Mabel's sons, Frank, probably needed to be living at her same address. Harvey and Edith's home now became the address for Mabel and Frank. It also became the gathering place for the entire Evans family since no Evans home remained in Pittsford.[7]

For a year or so after John's death, Mabel sometimes lived with Harvey, Edith, and David in Braintree. She then moved erratically from place to place for several months, trying to find her footing without John. In the fall of 1945,

314 GAIL E. EVANS

Mabel lived with her dear, long-time friends, Auley and Egbert Cain, at 50 Mulberry Street in Rochester. When Frank left the Air Force in the fall of 1945, he also went to live with the Cains. As Mabel grieved over John's passing, she lived in a world turned upside down with neither an anchor nor a paddle to help give her stability and a new direction.

Sometime in 1946, Mabel moved to Massachusetts and settled into the sitting-bedroom at the rear of the Allens' home at 15 Arcadia Road in Weymouth, where Harvey had lived for six years after he returned to the United States from Liverpool. Mabel continued living in the Allens' home until the mid-1950s, when Harvey, Edith, and their family moved from Weymouth. Mabel, at Harvey's encouragement, later moved closer to their new home in Lexington, Massachusetts.[8]

Gail, Mabel, and David, Braintree, Mass., ca. 1947.

Frank Changes Course

Private First Class Frank Harold Evans, in the 2140th Army Air Force, ended his military service at Keesler Field in Biloxi, Mississippi after the war ended. In early November 1945, he received his separation orders at Rome, New York. A new chapter in his life began soon afterward.

In 1944, Bishop Bartel H. Reinheimer, head of the Episcopal Diocese of Rochester, had been "favorably impressed" with Frank and received him as a postulant on May 26, 1944, on the eve of Frank's high school graduation. When Frank left the Air Force in November 1945, he remained determined to become an Episcopal priest. He had been accepted at Hobart and William Smith Colleges, a private co-educational college in Geneva, New York. Fall classes at Hobart, however, had already begun. During the next three months, Frank probably divided his time between Rochester, where he stayed with Mabel at Auley and Egbert Cain's home, and Braintree, where he lived with Harvey, Edith, and baby David.[9]

On February 7, 1946, Frank entered Hobart and pursued a general liberal arts degree with an emphasis on the history of Christianity. Bishop Reinheimer had an intimate connection with Hobart, having received his Doctor of Law degree there in 1936. Later, he became a trustee, a chancellor, and a member of the Hobart Alumni Association. Like Reinheimer, the majority of the faculty at Hobart was Episcopalian. By the late 1940s, Hobart and William Smith Colleges had graduated many students who had become bishops; nearly 450 others had become priests. Frank very likely had part or all of his tuition and expenses paid by the GI Bill (created by the Servicemen's Readjustment Act of 1944). In 1945–46, the GI Bill of Rights and other state and federal laws provided white women and men veterans with financial assistance to further their education, receive low-cost loans for home ownership, and obtain skilled jobs. (In contrast, intimidation kept black veterans from enjoying GI benefits and

ultimately widened the racial gap in post-war America.)
Frank found housing available on campus at Medery Hall,
bordering the expansive Hobart-Smith Quad near the St.
John's Chapel.[10]

Between February 1946 and June 1947, Frank took
fifteen months of courses, with only a short break of two
to three weeks between the terms. His classes ranged from
U.S. and English history to math, Latin, composition,
Hebraic religious literature, Greek and Latin literature,
ethics, and several Bible classes. In the summer of 1947,
Frank took three much-needed weeks off.

During the 1947–1948 academic year Frank enrolled in
another heavy load of classes: physics, chemistry, political
science, Christian symbolism in architecture, and U.S.
history. Between October 1948 and January 1949, he took
six history and religion classes. Frank also participated in
the century-old Theta Delta Chi fraternity, whose past
members had included top Hobart scholars. Frank also
belonged to the Motet Choir, Schola Cantorum choir, St.
John's Guild, and the Canterbury Club. Like Harvey and
Evan, Frank enjoyed singing and joined the choir at Trinity
Church on South Main Street in Geneva.[11]

Frank also met and dated a woman at Hobart and
William Smith Colleges. By the end of 1948, he had developed a serious relationship with eighteen-year-old Barbara
Joyce Turck from Buffalo. In December 1948, an
announcement of their engagement appeared on the
society page of a local newspaper.[12]

Considering all that Frank attempted to juggle in his
life at Hobart, it's not surprising that his grades were less
than stellar, except in music and history, his favorite
subjects. In February 1948, Frank failed a couple of courses. He ranked sixteenth in his class of thirty-one. In 1949,
Harvey received Frank's first semester "Grade Report"
from Hobart, which reported he received an F in philos-

ophy and two D's in history and music. Despite Frank's less than impressive grades, in late 1948 and early 1949, he remained hopeful that he could go on to divinity school. Frank had his transcripts sent to both the Berkeley Divinity School, affiliated with Yale Divinity School in New Haven, Connecticut, and to the Protestant Episcopal Theological Seminary in Alexandria, Virginia. He also sent his transcripts to the Rochester Rotary Club, presumably hoping to receive scholarship money.[13]

For reasons that are unclear seventy years later, Frank Evans abruptly changed his life course in early 1949. He may have done too poorly in many of his classes or fallen short of earning the 120 semester hours required to graduate in the spring of 1949. He may also have failed to gain acceptance to either Berkeley Divinity School or the Protestant Episcopal Theological Seminary. Additionally, Frank may have exhausted funding from his GI Bill. He may have also learned that Rochester's Rotary Club would no longer award him money for his education.

Finally, Frank may have lost the support of Bishop Bartel H. Reinheimer, who had initially received him as a postulant in 1944. While at Hobart, Frank probably learned that Reinheimer had been diagnosed in 1947 with a weak heart and that his health was precarious. In the summer of 1949, Reinheimer's heart condition worsened and became so disabling that he resigned as bishop of the Diocese of Rochester. All of this disturbing news undoubtedly disheartened Frank and forced him to reconsider his future. Around February 1949, he abruptly broke his engagement with Barbara Joyce Turck, left Hobart and William Smith Colleges, and moved to Boston, where all his family now lived.[14]

On November 12, 1949, ten months after Frank left Hobart, the Right Reverend Bartel H. Reinheimer died in Rochester's Genesee Hospital. He was sixty years old, two years younger than Frank's father when he had passed away in late December 1944. After Reinheimer's funeral service at Christ Church in Rochester, his burial took place at Glenwood Cemetery in Geneva, one mile south of the Hobart and William Smith Colleges' campus. Frank must have been tremendously saddened both by Reinheimer's passing and the decisive end of his long-time ambition to become a priest.[15]

Perhaps anticipating Reinheimer's death, Frank had turned in a different direction and begun a new chapter in his life. After arriving in Massachusetts, Frank stayed briefly with Harvey, Edith, and David at 31 Totnes Road in Braintree. He then went to live at the home of Charles and Malinda Allen at 14 Arcadia Road in Weymouth, where Mabel had lived since around 1946. Frank began taking classes in the fall of 1949 (on the history of England since 1815, plane trigonometry, and Latin American history) at Boston University (BU). Compelled also to work and earn an income, Frank took a job at the BU library. His life once again became full.

At the BU library, Frank met and began dating Avis Holmstrand, the daughter of Swedish immigrant grandparents and parents born in Brockton, Massachusetts. Avis received a bachelor's degree in English from Boston University in 1949. Struggling to pursue his coursework, his job at the BU library, *and* date Avis, Frank soon decided against taking his final exams in trigonometry and Latin American history. He also stopped taking any future classes at BU. For the next year and a half, he focused his attention on his BU library job and dating Avis.[16]

On July 28, 1951, Frank and Avis married at the Swedish Congregational Church (now the Covenant Congregational Church) in North Easton, west of Brockton, Massachusetts. They began their life together in a four-room Cape Code style house at 65 Thomas Road in Weymouth, enlarged by Frank and his father-in-law when they built a dormer window on the garage roof. Their first and only child, Christine, was born on February 27, 1957.[17]

Frank's married life demanded that he find a reliable, higher-paying job than his BU library position offered. How to achieve this without a degree from Hobart and William Smith Colleges or Boston University required some creative thinking. Amazingly, Frank's search for a new job sprang from a relationship with the son of a former minister at the South Congregational Church in Rochester. Nearly fifteen years earlier in 1937, John Evans had urged Harvey to contact Arthur Kettle and inquire about securing a job at the Bethlehem Steel Corporation. Just before Harvey returned to the United States in the fall of 1937, Arthur Kettle agreed to be a reference for him when Harvey applied for and received a job offer from Bethlehem Shipbuilding Corporation. Now, Harvey hoped that Arthur Kettle, currently the manager of the "Machinery Division" of Austin-Hastings, a sheet metal and pipe supplier in Cambridge, might help Frank secure a job at Austin-Hastings.

Harvey, eager to help his younger brother, probably contacted Arthur Kettle. Located in Cambridge since 1926, Austin-Hastings Co. had greatly expanded its warehouse and office building at 226 Binney Street in 1947, just as Harvey began working at a new job nearby in Cambridge. That year, Arthur Kettle served as executive vice-president and general manager of Austin-Hastings Co.[18] At Harvey's suggestion, Kettle decided to hire Frank.

In late 1950 or early 1951, Frank began working at Austin-Hastings Co. as a clerk. Ten years later, thirty-four-year-old Frank received a promotion to office manager, which paved the way for Frank's eventual advancement to the firm's "data processing manager." As the data processing manager, Frank learned everything he could about computers and their advancing capability to manipulate data. It may have been around this time that Frank's growing expertise in this area earned him the moniker of "computer jock."[19]

Frank's promotion may have prompted Frank, Avis, and daughter Chris to move to a slightly larger house at 19 Governor Winthrop Lane, half a mile from their home on Thomas Road in Weymouth. Frank continued as the Austin-Hastings Co. office manager until around 1967 when the City of Cambridge ordered the company (and other businesses on neighboring blocks) to vacate their buildings to allow a planned urban renewal project development involving NASA (National Aeronautics and Space Administration). In 1967, Austin-Hastings Co., forced to leave Binney Street in Cambridge, moved ten miles north to East Woburn. That year, Frank and his family moved to Lynnfield (14 Fletcher Road) so that Frank could be closer to work.[20]

Frank and Harvey, Braintree, ca. 1944.

Evan Begins a New Life Chapter

Frank's older brother, Evan, welcomed the end of World War II after serving four years and four months with the 52nd Coast Artillery F Battery of the U.S. Army in Bermuda. On June 30, 1945, Evan received an "honorable discharge" and left the Army as an "Army Technician Fifth Grade" (called T/5 or "Tech Corporal"). At that time, he also received a final disbursement of $11,770 (equal to

$169,147 U.S. in 2020) that he collected at Fort Devens, Massachusetts, not far from the home of Harvey, Edith, and David in Braintree. In mid-1945, Evan knew that he could never realize his pre-war dream of becoming a concert pianist since he had been away from his training at the New England Conservatory of Music for five years. At age twenty-nine, it was too late to pick up where he had left off. Like Frank, Evan faced a world and life much altered by the war, which demanded a revised plan for the future.[21]

Evan and Harvey, Braintree, Mass., ca. 1944.

As the war wound down, Evan gave considerable thought to the next chapter in his life. From a young age, Evan was aware of the Red Cross and its humanitarian pursuits. This resonated deeply with Evan, known for his gentle temperament and kind spirit of giving to those in need. Founded in Switzerland in 1863, Clara Barton, a nurse in the American Civil War (1860-1865) and some of her friends organized the first chapter of the American Red Cross after the war in 1881 in Dansville, New York, near Rochester. In the 1890s, the American Red Cross aided the United States military during the Spanish-American War. It also provided disaster relief to victims of forest fires, floods, and hurricanes in the United States. The Red Cross later gave aid to survivors of the 1912 RMS *Titanic*, and, during World War I, the American Red Cross sent the USNS *Mercy Ship* to Europe with medical staff and supplies.[22]

In 1917, when the influenza epidemic at the end of World War I engulfed Europe and America, Rochester's American Red Cross chapter instantly went into action. In 1918, after hundreds of Rochester residents came down with the flu and overwhelmed the city's hospitals, the Red Cross helped open and equip several emergency hospitals throughout the city. Additionally, over 100,000 city residents began collecting surgical supplies, clothing, and knitted socks for the Red Cross. Making over 2,000 socks a week, the Rochester Red Cross led the nation in sock production. Mabel, known for her skillful knitting, undoubtedly contributed to the campaign to knit hundreds of socks while looking after infant Evan and toddler Harvey. The South Congregational Church, the Evans family's church, initiated regular collections for the Red Cross. As the years went by, Rochester continued its loyal support of the American Red Cross. Evan certainly must have known of his parents' support of the American Red Cross's extraordinary generosity and countless humanitarian pursuits.[23]

After entering the U.S. Army, Evan became even more familiar with the good works of the Red Cross. He knew of the Bermuda Red Cross, an offspring of the British Red Cross, which worked in hospitals, care homes, nurseries, ambulance units, and rest stations across Bermuda. During the war, the number of Red Cross volunteers grew exponentially. In 1945, 7.5 million volunteers and 39,000 staff members attended to 16 million military men and women. The Red Cross collected 13.3 million units of blood for the American military. Red Cross workers provided compassionate support to all men and women in the military wherever they were stationed. Evan's own caring nature aligned perfectly with the Red Cross's compassionate and generous core values and activities. In October 1945, Evan joined the American Red Cross.[24]

For nearly thirteen years, the American Red Cross gave Evan meaningful employment, worldwide travel experiences, and a strong sense of belonging to a worthwhile organization. After first receiving Red Cross training in late November 1945, Evan (soon nicknamed "Si") arrived in France to begin work as assistant field director at "Camp Service" field offices. Closely associated with the military after the war, Red Cross Field Service offices were located in the U.S. European Command Headquarters. Red Cross employees all wore Army officers' uniforms with the emblem of a red cross, instead of military insignia, below the left shoulder.

Evan in the Red Cross, ca. 1946.

When Evan joined the American Red Cross, his job included an array of personnel duties. He counseled military service people, helped facilitate communication between soldiers and their families, and helped military servicemen and women receive financial assistance. Evan also helped exchange messages between family members separated by the war. He also undertook the sometimes heart-wrenching task of researching the fate of missing or deceased family members. In 1946, he moved between the American Red Cross Field Service offices in Metz, France, and Wiesbaden and Frankfurt, Germany. Over the next several months, Evan learned to speak and write both French and German.

Evan also traveled widely through Europe when he had days off from his work. Often he sent postcards to Harvey and Edith from well-known cities and sites he had visited. "Arrived in Milan last evening," he wrote in November 1947.[25] "Visited the cathedral (Duomo di Milano) this morning. . . . Leave this afternoon for Florence, then on to Rome. Details when I see you all in January."[26]

In late January 1948, Evan sailed from Bremerhaven, Germany, to New York City on the USAHS *Blanche F. Sigman*, originally a Liberty ship converted into a hospital ship used for transporting nurses and military personnel between European cities and New York City. He made a second trip to the U.S. in September 1948 after visiting Great Britain to meet Evans and Harvey family members for the very first time. In early December 1949, Evan returned to the United States, sailing on the USNS *General R. E. Callan* from Bremerhaven, Germany, via Southampton, England, to New York City. In 1948 and 1949, Evan visited Harvey, Edith, David, and Gail (born in May 1947) on Totnes Road in Braintree. Mabel and Frank lived on nearby Arcadia Road with the Allen family. Evan continued to work in the Red Cross Field Director's office in Frankfurt in 1949.[27]

In the early 1950s, Evan's American Red Cross assignments took him to several Atlantic seaboard states. Between 1950 and mid-1954, Evan worked at a Navy installation in Little Creek, Virginia, near Norfolk, then in Rhode Island, then in the New York City Field Office (1952), then at Fort Devens, Massachusetts (1952–1953), and, finally, at Limestone Air Force Base in northern Maine (1953–1954). When Evan left Fort Devens in 1953, the local newspaper noted his departure.

Mr. Si Evans, popular Red Cross Assistant Field Director, departed last week for his new assignment at Limestone Air Force Base in northern Maine after completing a two-year tour at Devens. During his stay at Devens, Mr. Evans had established himself as a sincere friend of those in need, and was never too busy day or night to lend a helping hand. Mr. Evans assisted personnel with all types of problems, ranging from emergency leaves to financial assistance and because of his sincere interest was highly regarded by all who looked to him for aid.[28]

In May 1954, the American Red Cross sent Evan to Asia, where, for the next four years, he served with the 32nd Infantry, Seventh Infantry Division as the field director of the Red Cross in Korea. This occurred after President Truman sent U.S. troops there to push back North Korean forces from invading South Korea in 1950. While in Korea, Evan received a "service bar," recognizing his tenth anniversary (1945–1955) of employment in the American Red Cross.[29]

Evan spent his last two years (1956–1958) in Japan as field director, where he had a range of responsibilities: personal counseling, carrying out Red Cross financial programs, instructing First Aid and water safety courses, and staffing Gray Lady programs in hospitals and health care facilities. In his final year in Asia, Evan oversaw a professional staff of eight Red Cross employees based at Japan's largest Air Force military installation. After thirteen years of living and traveling in Europe, America, and Asia, Evan left the American Red Cross in August 1958, emotionally exhausted and ready for a change.[30]

During his time in the American Red Cross, Evan made and maintained friendships with people he met from around the world: a former German prisoner of war, who worked for Evan in France; a Czechoslovakian fellow whom he helped bring to America after the Russians occupied his country; as well as dozens of other people he met and corresponded with from France, Germany, the United States, Korea, and Japan.[31]

After nearly two decades of memorable years of travel, challenging work, and building worldwide friendships, Evan, at the age of forty-two, felt the need to become more firmly rooted in culturally rich Boston and be closer to his family. It was time, Evan felt, to turn a corner and head down a new path that would apply his knowledge and skills in social services and administration.

In early December 1958, Evan became the executive director of the Deaconess Home and Community Center in Fall River, Massachusetts, a place for emotionally disturbed teenage girls. During three years there, Evan succeeded in expanding the number of personnel at the Deaconess Home. When funding for personnel and property improvements proved insufficient, however, he resigned in August 1961.[32]

Evan then decided to return to a job that he had come to know well as a teenager in Rochester, with far less responsibility and less personal stress. Putting to use his experience working as a stock and sales clerk at Sibley's in the 1930s, Evan, in February 1962, took a job as a retail clerk at Filene's Sons and Co. department store at Downtown Crossing in Boston. He remained in this job until September 1965. While working at Filene's, Evan rented an apartment in a three-story, wood-frame apartment building not far away. After he left Filene's, Evan began working at an upscale men's clothing store (Roger Kent) in a shopping mall in the new Prudential Center, completed in 1965 in Boston's Back Bay.[33]

Evan's life seemed full, engaging, and culturally rich in the mid-1960s. He delighted in sharing with me, his niece, his great fondness for Dionne Warwick's famous *People Who Need People,* as well as the talented ballet dancer Edward Villella, who Evan took me to see in Boston in 1964. In a letter to his niece Chris Evans that same year, Evan enthusiastically shared his tremendous love of orchestral music (Brahms, Schumann, Mahler, and Prokofiev) and piano composers Chopin, Rachmaninoff, Ravel, and Debussy. Evan read voraciously on a wide array of subjects: Chinese porcelain, early English history,

French music and art, South America, prison reform, and the rehabilitation of prisoners in Massachusetts. Evan wrote to Chris that his "happy home looks like a branch of the Boston Public Library."[34]

Evan's job at Roger Kent lasted only a few weeks, however. Its brevity seemed to portend mounting challenges for Evan. In the fall of 1965, Evan moved into the Beacon Chambers (now "Beacon House," 19 Myrtle Street) just above the Boston Common, which rented affordable apartments and hosted Alcoholics Anonymous meetings. As a teenager, I was told, but knew little, about Evan's struggle to moderate his consumption of alcohol. Now, however, his struggle to control drinking became apparent.

During the next few months, Evan began working at the McLean Hospital, a psychiatric hospital in Belmont (a suburb northwest of Boston), and moved to a fifth-floor apartment at 23 Pinckney Street near the Boston Common. In the fall of 1966, Evan broke his leg in several places in an accident, could not work for several weeks, and went to live with Harvey and Edith in Lexington while his leg healed. Eventually, he moved into the nurses' living quarters at McLean Hospital and resumed working there. Evan continued to struggle with alcohol and, in 1967, went to live at the Stetson Home in Barre, Massachusetts, where he received alcohol and psychiatric treatment.

Harvey Turns a Corner

Harvey, like Frank and Evan, also changed his career path after the war. When World War II ended in early September 1945, the Bethlehem Shipbuilding Corporation completed a few wartime orders, began to overhaul other ships, and also sought to diversify its ship contracts. Harvey probably contributed to the completion of heavy cruisers already underway, including the USS *Des Moines* launched in September 1946 and the USS *Salem* launched in March the following year. Work for the U.S. Navy steadily declined, and orders for several other cruisers were canceled. Bethlehem Shipbuilding Corporation now began contracting with the U.S. Maritime Commission for the design and construction of oil tankers. Harvey must have wondered how his future might unfold as a naval architect in this post-war era.[35]

Never could he have anticipated an unimagined opportunity that presented itself to him in 1947 when Harvey was then a supervisor in the Central Technical Department at the Shipbuilding Division of Bethlehem Steel Company. Probably the convergence of many factors—Harvey's ten years of ship-design experience at Fore River Shipyard during a critical time in history, his likable personality, and the presence of a handful of particular individuals—presented Harvey with an unimagined opportunity.[36]

In 1947, Navy Admiral Edward Lull Cochrane, Chief of the Navy's Bureau of Ships from November 1942 to November 1946, retired from the Navy and joined the faculty at Massachusetts Institute of Technology (MIT). During the war, Cochrane had been directly responsible for the Navy's massive wartime shipbuilding program, including the work completed by Bethlehem Shipbuilding Corporation employees. Also trained as a naval architect, Cochrane had served at the Philadelphia Naval Shipyard during World War I. In 1920, he had graduated from MIT with a Master of Science degree in naval architecture. When Cochrane came to his job as head of MIT's Naval Architecture Department after World War II, he arrived with a clear vision of how he wanted to strengthen the department and where he might find the people to accomplish this. Along with his sterling qualifications, Cochrane brought to his job a keen judgment of people.[37]

In early September 1947, Cochrane contacted Fore River Shipyard's Technical Manager, J. E. Burkhardt, and asked for his recommendations of a suitable person to join the naval architecture faculty at MIT. The ideal candidate, Cochrane believed, would be a young man, able to serve as an assistant professor for three years at a salary of $4,500 a year. The candidate should have about five years of drafting experience, be familiar with basic design, do class-work with the students in the department's Drafting Room, help mark student papers that examined design problems, and, after a year, be able to lecture. Burkhardt recommended two possible men for the job; one was J. Harvey Evans.

When Burkhardt presented Harvey's background and qualifications to Cochrane in September 1947, he noted Harvey's naval architecture degree from the University of Liverpool and his ten-year employment in the Central Technical Department of the Shipbuilding Division of Bethlehem Steel Corporation. This division, Burkhardt explained, has

> prepared preliminary designs, guidance plans, and calcu-lations for new naval and merchant vessels, and major conversions for all Bethlehem yards. . . . At the present time, Evans is in charge of a small group doing hull form calculations and plans. His formal experience with us, however, has been quite broad. His work is of a high order. He makes a good verbal presentation of his work. Good personality and quiet disposition.[38]

Admiral Cochrane expressed interest in Harvey and interviewed him soon after receiving Burkhardt's recom-mendation. When interviewed, Cochrane found Harvey "keen and alert mentally, frank in his discussion, and [he] makes an excellent verbal presentation," just as Burkhardt had reported. Cochrane concluded that Harvey would be a "very satisfactory addition to the staff of MIT's Department of Naval Architecture and Marine Engineering."[39]

In October, Cochrane invited Harvey to join MIT's faculty, whose naval architecture department, founded in 1893, was the oldest in the United States. Delighted, Harvey accepted Cochrane's invitation and began teaching in late 1947 as a temporary instructor. In addition to working with students in the Drafting Room, Harvey soon became an assistant instructor in the design of warships. His classes included many Naval Academy graduates and Naval Reserve officers.[40]

Harvey must have felt enormously gratified to learn that the many challenges he had faced at the University of Liverpool and the effort he made to apply his Liverpool education at Bethlehem Shipbuilding Corporation now had opened a new door for him. Harvey had no time, then, to record his thoughts and daily experiences in his diary; he must have become consumed with the challenges of his job to teach, research, and engage in professional service activities at such a prestigious university.

Between 1947 and mid-1949, Harvey worked hard to fulfill the demands made on him in his new job at MIT. His efforts were well rewarded. Based on his "aptitude and achievement in research, in pure or applied science," he was elected a member of the MIT chapter of Sigma Xi, an international honor society of science and engineering.[41] In the spring of 1949, Harvey and Edith received an invitation to MIT's grand "Mid-Century Convocation" developed around the theme of "Social Implications of Scientific Progress." Nearly fifty prominent scientists, engineers, statesmen, attorneys, architects, chemists, historians, and philosophers assembled from around the world to discuss this theme at some of Boston's most prestigious and elegant assembly halls and restaurants. Among the featured speakers were President Harry Truman and Winston Churchill, the former Prime Minister of Great Britain and exalted wartime hero in Harvey's eyes. Harvey and Edith attended a black-tie dinner at the historic, elegant 1927 Hotel Statler in downtown Boston. Harvey must have been amazed to find himself in this grand setting with an array of luminaries.[42]

Harvey soon found the combination of teaching, research, and writing wonderfully fascinating and rewarding. "The majority of the students I have had have been graduates, and their seriousness of purpose and evident interest has made my teaching . . . extremely fulfilling," Harvey observed.[43] He also received the support of Admiral Cochrane and Laurens Troost, a visiting professor from the University of Delft, who became the department chair in 1952. In 1949, Harvey became an assistant professor, followed by a promotion to associate professor with tenure in 1952.[44]

Harvey teaching at MIT, ca. 1949.

During the 1950s, the majority of Harvey's students continued to be highly motivated graduates from the U.S.

Naval Academy, as well as from various engineering schools. Harvey taught both introductory and advanced naval architecture courses focusing on ships' structural design. His classes addressed the critical components of stability, strength, and rigidity of structures, all aimed at accommodating heavy loads and preventing structural failure.

By the late 1950s, Harvey taught all the courses on design and structures offered during the academic year and summers. He became a vocal advocate of creating a marine biological laboratory at MIT that tested structural issues. Harvey's research resulted in several articles on various structural design topics, published in British and American engineering journals. Since current textbooks on the subject didn't exist, Harvey, with others, wrote mono-graphs for his students that eventually became published as a weighty textbook, *Ship Structural Design Concepts* (1974).[45] His list of publications continued to grow.

In his early years at MIT, Harvey joined several naval architecture societies: the Society of Naval Architects and Marine Engineers (SNAME), where he became the chairman of the New England section; the Institution of Naval Architects in Great Britain; the British North East Coast Institution of Engineers and Shipbuilders; the American Society of Naval Architects; and the Society for Experimental Stress Analysis. He also began consulting at the Design Division of the Boston Naval Shipyard. The list of consulting companies and occasional attorneys that hired him grew longer in the 1950s and 1960s and took him to cities throughout the United States, as well as Buenos Aires and Havana.[46]

Throughout his early years at MIT, Harvey combined teaching, research, and writing with his life-long love of travel in the United States, Great Britain, and around the world. It was a love initially stimulated by a curiosity about his parents' heritage and, later, by his four years in England at the University of Liverpool. In the summer of 1956, Harvey taught naval architecture courses at the University of California at Berkeley. On this occasion and later, he combined his teaching with travel to fascinating places, which he carefully planned and plotted on maps. A trip to Berkeley from Boston and back involved a two- to three-week driving tour that featured stops in numerous historical and cultural sites and many national parks. This trip left life-long impressions on his children, David and me. Traveling became an important pursuit in our family when we were young and was a regular activity in our adult lives.[47]

The following year Harvey taught naval architecture for four months (March to July 1957) in the College of Engineering at Seoul National University in Korea. In planning his return to Boston in July 1957, Harvey put together a round-the-world trip that included stops in fifteen cities in Asia, the Middle East, and Europe before finally landing in England to visit English and Welsh relatives, whom he had not seen for twenty years. These trips greatly intensified his already strong love of exploring new places, people, and cultures, first kindled in the 1930s when he traveled across England and Wales and along the west coast of Africa as a student engineer on the MV *Abosso*.

In the early 1960s, Harvey's developing career at MIT hit a bump in the road. After serving as the department chair for one year (1960–1961), Horton Guyford Stever, an electrical engineer with limited naval architecture knowledge, became the new department chair. Stever seemed to question the value of Harvey's teaching, graduate student advising, and research. He gave Harvey the definite impression that he doubted his future contributions to MIT's naval architecture department. This, plus the department's shifting focus, proposed downsizing, and even potential closure, caused Harvey great concern. His growing uncertainty about the department and his future prompted Harvey to investigate employment at the University of Michigan in Ann Arbor. With its emphasis on applied design (relating to hull structures) rather than basic theoretical science, the Michigan naval architecture department seemed much more compatible with Harvey's professional training, teaching, and interests. In confidence, Harvey wrote to the University of Michigan naval architect Harry Benford, who agreed to explore, with the current department chair, Harvey's possible future at Michigan. The outcome of Benford's inquiry is not known.[48]

Despite Harvey's uncertainties about his future at MIT, he never moved from New England to Michigan. He may have found a satisfying avenue to pursue with his teaching, research, and consulting in structural design at MIT. Plus, during the 1950s and early 1960s, Harvey's teaching, research, and publishing garnered a promotion to full professor in 1961 (around the time he wrote to Benford). Family reasons could have also factored heavily in his decision. David was seventeen, and I was fourteen, in 1961, and our coming of age proved challenging for us all . . . something that Harvey didn't want to walk away from. Edith had also become engaged in her job as the secretary in a doctor's office. She had also taken up and excelled at weaving.

Additionally, Evan was struggling to find and keep permanent work and to grapple with his continuing battle with alcoholism. He and Mabel increasingly confronted age-related health issues. Finally, both Edith and Harvey had long, enduring relationships with family and friends in Boston and Jackson, New Hampshire, where they had vacationed since the 1930s and later bought property. All this may have convinced Harvey and Edith not to move to Michigan.[49]

By the mid-1960s, Harvey, the son of a Welsh draper and an English landowning farmer's daughter who had immigrated to the United States just fifty years earlier, had managed to make a new life for himself. He had progressed in his career beyond his own and everyone's expectations. Yet life continued to present uncertainties and challenges for Harvey, Evan, Frank, and their families.

Mabel and John Reunited

Evan's health challenges intensified and coincided with his mother's declining health. After Mabel moved from the Allens' home in Weymouth in the mid-1950s, Harvey and Edith found a succession of comfortable accommodations for her close to their Lexington home. Often Mabel joined family gatherings at the Evanses' Lexington home and periodically at Frank, Avis, and Chris's house. As she moved into her seventies and needed more support, Harvey moved her in late 1966 to an assisted living unit at Llewsac Lodge (Carleton-Willard's Llewsac Lodge) in nearby Bedford.[50]

Mabel's health continued to decline, and her care needs grew. In 1967, she moved to Pine Knoll Nursing Center in Lexington. Then, in September, she entered the hospital, where she was diagnosed with multiple health issues—congestive heart failure, acute myocardial infarction, arteriosclerotic heart disease, diabetes, and multiple myeloma. On October 29, 1967, Mabel Ida Harvey Evans died at the age of seventy-nine.

Not long afterward, Harvey, Edith, Frank, Avis, and Evan traveled to Rochester, New York, to be present at her funeral and burial next to John at White Haven Memorial Park in Pittsford. Many years later, ten-year-old

Chris Evans recalled that her parents went away for a few days to Rochester right around Halloween on October 31 that year.[51] Mabel's passing marked the end of her and John's joint decision to leave Britain and immigrate to America and chart a new life course together for themselves and their family.

17
———

EPILOGUE

Three days after Mabel died, Harvey, Evan, and Frank drove to Rochester for their mother's burial next to John, who had been laid to rest twenty-two years earlier. On October 31, friends of Mabel's and the Evans family gathered at the Zornow Funeral Home in Pittsford, just as they had done when John died. The following morning, a mild day with gentle rain falling, the family and a handful of long-time Evans family friends gathered around for a graveside service at White Haven Memorial Park in Pittsford. Nearby was the gravesite of Egbert Cain, a long-time Evans family friend, who had died in 1952. Auley M. Cain, the widow of Egbert and dear friend of Mabel's, and her daughter Doris Cain McConnell were probably present at Mabel's burial.

The gathering of such dear family friends brought back fond memories of Harvey, Evan, and Frank's childhood in Rochester and Pittsford, making the gathering at the cemetery both solemn and nostalgic. After the service at White Haven, Mabel and John's three sons probably drove by their gracious former home at 179 East Brook Road, less than a mile from the cemetery, and their nearby Brook Road home that John, Mabel, and Frank had occupied for about three years during World War II.[1]

The drive back to Boston was undoubtedly a time of quiet reflection for all three brothers. Mabel's burial, and the sight of old friends, must have aroused fond memories for the three Evans men. Mabel's stories and distinctive sense of humor would now just be memories. Her burial next to John in Pittsford marked the end of their parents' new lives in America after immigration. Their three sons embodied many of their parents' core values of honesty, openness, optimism, and compassion for others. Yet, their lives had been just as influenced by momentous historical events—1920s gay frivolity, the immobilizing Great Depression, and a shattering world war—in the first half of the twentieth century.

Slowly as they traveled back to Boston, the three sons now shifted their attention to their own lives in the mid-1960s. When Mabel died in October 1967, Evan, always generously offering to give to those in need, lived at the Stetson Home in Barre, Massachusetts, where he received counseling for his alcohol and psychiatric needs. In 1968, Evan began working at the Metropolitan State Hospital, which had opened in 1930 in Waltham near Lexington. Patients here received treatment for mental health disorders.[2] In July 1973, Evan's failing eyesight required cataract surgery at Mount Auburn Hospital in Cambridge, Massachusetts, followed by a recovery period at Harvey and Edith's home in Lexington.

In 1974, he was diagnosed with cancer of the mouth and throat (oropharynx), perhaps caused by decades of smoking and alcohol consumption. That year Evan entered Pondville State Hospital in Norfolk, Massachusetts, where he received radiation treatment. In early 1975, he moved to the Veterans Administration Hospital in Bedford. Unable to swallow, he began receiving food through a tube fed into his stomach. On August 12, 1975, Evan Reginald Evans died at the age of sixty.[3]

Sadly, Harvey reported his death in a letter to Aunt Winnie and cousins Vernon and Audrey Harvey in England. "In so many ways," Harvey wrote, "his last years were his noblest of all, and we simply pray 'waft him, angels through the skies,'" a prayer uttered after the tragic death of Iphis, daughter of Jephtha and biblical leader of the Israelites, as depicted in Handel's oratorio *Jephtha*. Evan had requested that his body be donated to Harvard Medical School for teaching, study, and research. Months later, he was buried in Pine Hill Cemetery (also known as the Harvard University Cemetery) in Tewksbury, Mass-achusetts.[4]

Following Mabel and Evan's deaths, Harvey's MIT work and the rewards he received from it intensified as he approached retirement. He continued to teach and present research papers at professional conferences, particularly at national and international meetings of the Society of Naval Architects and Marine Engineers. In mid-1976, Harvey organized a meeting of the Sixth International Ship Structures Congress at MIT, the first ISSC meeting ever held in the United States.

In November 1976, a year after Evan's death, Harvey, age sixty-two, suffered a severe heart attack at precisely the same age and almost the same date that his father had died of heart disease. Harvey survived and recovered but decided to semi-retire from MIT. He soon focused on researching the computer-aided design of marine vessels, principally submarines operating at great depths. He also devoted time to the design and development of reinforced concrete ships used for transporting liquid natural gas. In

December of that year, the Society of Naval Architects and Marine Engineers awarded Harvey the distinguished Davidson Medal for his "outstanding scientific accomplishments in ship research."[5]

Harvey in red jacket, ca. 1982 (G. Evans photo).

In 1978, after teaching at MIT for thirty-one years, Harvey fully retired and received an appointment as an emeritus professor, which came with a small office in MIT's Naval Architecture and Marine Engineering department overlooking busy Massachusetts Avenue. He continued to consult and travel.

Harvey's love of travel and photography took him, Edith, and me to Alaska in 1977 to visit David. For ten years, David and his wife, Sage, lived along the upper Yukon River and Nation River tributary, 60 miles downstream from the remote village of Eagle, Alaska. They made their living from fishing, hunting, and trapping in frigid winter temperatures that occasionally dipped to minus 70 degrees Fahrenheit (minus 56 degrees Celsius). For two weeks, Harvey and Edith (then in their mid-sixties) and I slept in tents pitched on a sandy beach along the expansive Yukon River. During our visit, we participated in David's daily subsistence activities—gill-net fishing and fish drying, berry picking, wood gathering, and hunting for moose—just as Native Americans had done for centuries.[6]

Harvey and Edith, c. 1991 (D. Evans photo).

Over the next fifteen years, Harvey and Edith traveled several times to Oregon, Washington, and California to visit me, where I had lived since 1973. In June 1992, after Harvey made a remarkable partial recovery from a severe stroke the previous year, they traveled to California to witness my receipt of a PhD in history at commencement ceremonies at the University of California at Santa Barbara. Only five months later, Harvey again succumbed to heart disease. His significantly weakened heart caused his death on November 23, 1992, at the age of seventy-eight. As he had requested, Edith, David, and I spread his ashes on the scenic rural property that he and Edith had owned for nearly thirty-five years in Jackson, New Hampshire, where they had enjoyed hiking and relaxing in the White Mountains since the 1930s.[7]

Mabel and John's youngest son, Frank, continued to work as the office and data processing manager at Austin-Hastings Co. in its new Woburn location. After nearly twenty-five years as their office manager and "computer jock," Frank's job at Austin-Hastings Co. ended in the mid-1970s, around the time the company declared bankruptcy. Frank then secured a position as a computer specialist at an insurance company in Boston and continued working there for about five years.

Around 1983, Frank became the director of data processing for the Town of Wellesley. Frank retired from this job in 1989, after a heart attack at age sixty-three. However, about a year later, Frank joined a fact-finding committee for the Town of Lynnfield, the family's home town, that examined its computer systems. Other health issues challenged Frank in the late 1990s.

After a herculean effort to overcome multiple health challenges, in June 2003, Frank died at age seventy-seven. Frank was the youngest and last remaining child of John and Mabel Harvey Evans, who had immigrated ninety years earlier to America from Wales and England. Their story was carried forward in their three sons, whose own choices, together with the force of historical events, influenced their future and the futures of their children.[8]

PASSAGES CHRONICLES the story of one family that lived during a remarkable period in American and world history. The Harvey-Evans family and thousands of others like it experienced a half century of momentous changes: global immigration between the 1890s and 1920, the Great War and a global flu pandemic, the Great Depression of the 1930s, World War II, and the beginning of the Cold War.

This tumultuous history forever altered the world and challenged the lives of those living through this epic period. Considered the "Greatest Generation" by American journalist Tom Brokaw in his 1998 book, those who came of age and grew to adulthood during this time of seismic upheavals learned how to overcome numerous obstacles, solve problems, develop self-reliance and resilience, and prioritize life choices.

All five Evans family members embraced the vision of America as a place of new beginnings and endless possibilities. John and Mabel's high hopes for achieving a satisfying middle-class life continued even as the world around them went through periods of great distress and uncertainty. As their children grew and matured in the 1920s and 1930s, John and Mabel encouraged their sons to set high goals, be optimistic about their futures, and pursue aspirational careers. Consequently, Harvey envisioned becoming a naval architect, Evan a concert pianist, and Frank a priest.

Despite the Evans family's high expectations and positive outlook, obstacles large and small—overwhelming historical events and confounding personal disappointments—confronted John and Mabel and each of their sons in the 1930s and 1940s. For thirty years, John and Mabel worked hard to earn a reasonable income and create a secure, loving, and welcoming home in Rochester, then in Pittsfield, for their family. Their dreams suddenly shattered when John's company laid him off and the family lost their Pittsford home on the eve of U.S. entry into World War II.

Each family member confronted and surmounted great challenges during their lifetime. Harvey struggled as a young man with sometimes average grades and, then, a desperate financial situation at the University of Liverpool, which almost kept him from graduating and fulfilling his dream of becoming a naval architect. Evan's largest obstacles were coming of age during World War II and living when gay men were viewed as odd and often became targets of ridicule. Evan's poor health at the end of his life presented him with a final monumental challenge. For Frank, after serving in the U.S. Army Air Force at the end of World War II and then working hard for nearly four years at Hobart and William Smith colleges, his combined mediocre grades, his mentor's death, and his limited funds abruptly ended his ambition to become a priest. Consequently, Frank needed to reimagine a different life.

Recounting the story of Harvey's challenging cycling adventures across England on a one-speed bicycle drew me into the much larger story of his life and his family history. I eventually realized that this history was much more than a dry narrative of Harvey's travels between the University of Liverpool and Kingsmans Farm. The initiative and endurance it took to cycle across England multiple times revealed notable aspects of my father's developing character that I never recognized and barely appreciated as a child. His cycling suggested his great resolve and resilience at a challenging time in his life. The determination and grit he mobilized to cycle great distances during all kinds of weather served as a lodestone—a guiding principle— that helped him find his way not only on his bicycle but throughout his life. His cycling challenges not only boosted his physical stamina but also developed his strength of spirit. Difficult cycling challenges that he endured served as a rite of passage—an initiation into adulthood.

As I learned more about my father's two brothers, Evan and Frank, I discovered that they had similar transformative experiences and rites of passage that developed and affirmed their strengths. Evan's experience as a popular radio host on the Armed Forces Network in Bermuda bolstered his self-esteem. Colliding sobering events in Frank's life—the death of his father at age nineteen, an abrupt break from Hobart and William Smith Colleges and the woman he intended to marry, the death of his Episcopalian bishop mentor, and the need to start his life over again—became a transformative strengthening time for him at a young age.

Historical circumstances provided the context within which each Evans family member had life-altering experiences and made significant choices about their futures. If their choices failed to achieve one desired goal—as they sometimes did—they paused and chose an alternative way forward. Several times, of necessity, they learned to stand up when knocked down by unexpected distressing events.

As the famous first-century Greek philosopher and teacher Epictetus prophetically observed, "We cannot choose our external circumstances, but we can always choose how we respond to them." Many centuries later, celebrated Austrian psychiatrist and Holocaust survivor Viktor Frankl (1905–1997) famously wrote in *Man's Search for Meaning* (1946), "Everything can be taken from a man [person] but one thing: the last of the human freedoms—to choose one's attitude . . . to choose one's own way." In the words of Mahatma Gandhi, "Keep your values positive because your values become your destiny." These became approaches to life that the Evans family learned and embraced.[9]

My father expressed one aspect of his philosophy of life in a personal letter he wrote to me in the late 1960s, after I was forced to abandon a future in competitive gymnastics due to a severe injury.

> You and I live on the assumption that anything is possible if we just set about going after it. We just expect

things will work out the way we want them to. . . . Often
this buoyant attitude is almost enough by itself, and that
kind of faith leads us to attempt things we never would
otherwise.[10]

Remaining positive contributed to the resilience, optimism, and strength that each Evans family member developed during their lives when confronting adversities.

It is impossible to write a story about the Evans-
Harvey family without wondering what legacies we, the
descendants of John and Mabel and their ancestors, might
have noticed and acquired. While writing this history and
giving this question considerable thought, my final non-
objective thoughts are these. Certain experiences and
events in David's and my lives instilled in us a life-long
fascination with travel and discovery.

As teenagers and young adults, David and I also
became avid travelers. We visited many of our British and
Welsh aunts, uncles, and cousins and explored their
history in cemeteries, libraries, and conversations we had
with our relatives. Between 1969 and 1971, David traveled
widely and held many different jobs. He worked as a logger
in Ketchikan, Alaska, a parcel-sorter in Amsterdam,
Netherlands, a copper mine laborer in Timna Valley, Israel,
an apple picker in Chelan, Washington, a dock worker in
New Orleans, and a river rafting guide in Jackson,
Wyoming. In 1971-72, I spent a year working and traveling
in Japan and Korea, then crossed the Soviet Union's broad
expanse on the Trans Siberian Railway, extending 5,775
miles (9,289 km) from Vladivostok on the Sea of Japan to
Moscow. I made a final stop in Britain to visit English relatives before returning to Boston. My brother, David, and I
inherited a great love of travel and new adventures from
our father.

Eventually, David settled in Alaska, where he lived and

trapped marten in the remote bush country for a decade. Later, he worked for the National Park Service, first in Alaska, then in Arizona, as a specialist in log cabin construction. He didn't return to New England until later in life when he was in his sixties. I also moved away from New England to Oregon, California, and then Washington before immigrating to Canada in 2006. After first making my home on the West Coast in the 1970s, I continued to travel and led tours to England and Istanbul, Turkey. My father's great fascination with travel and meeting new people profoundly influenced us both.

Maintaining relationships with family and also close friends over many years is yet another practice that I, in particular, learned from our father. Phyllis Hargreaves Crossley, once the love of Harvey's young life, and her husband, Robert Crossley, met and traveled with Harvey and Edith in England several times in the 1970s. Harvey and Phyllis remained life-long soul mates, and their spouses became friends. Harvey stayed in touch with Phyllis until he died in 1992.

Before his death, I also developed a friendship with Phyllis, staying in touch with and getting to know her in Christmas cards and letters. In 2002, Phyllis and I finally met in Ipswich, England, where she then lived. Together we swam in a local pool and enjoyed long conversations over meals. Her fondness for Harvey was still very much evident in the sincere caring, and generous spirit she showed me.

I continue to travel to England and Wales to spend time with many Harvey relatives at the annual family reunion near Kingsmans Farm. I've also spent time with Welsh relatives. Like my father, my computerized version of his Rolodex file includes dozens of Welsh and British family members whom I've written to and sometimes visited over the years. Visiting my Evans and Harvey ancestors' homes and countryside has connected me to a place and a past that feels familiar and comfortable. I am delighted to be a member of the families of my ancestors.

Harvey family reunion, Hullbridge, Essex, near Kingsmans Farm, 2018.

Sally& Bob Vernall & Pam Powell, 2016.

Carol Driscoll and Gail, 2016.

ACKNOWLEDGEMENTS

Fifteen years ago, I imagined writing a family history. This dream eventually became a reality between 2015 and 2021 and has taken shape in *Passages*. In this family history, I have drawn on a massive amount of material that my father collected over many decades. I explored at numerous libraries and archives in the United States and Great Britain, interviewing dozens of family members in both countries, and traveling to places in the United States and United Kingdom where they were born, lived, worked, and are buried. This project has taken more time than I ever imagined it would. Editing, designing, and printing this book proved to be a protracted endeavor. As a trained historian with a PhD in history, I was determined to make this book historically accurate, as well as fascinating reading. I hope that my efforts have succeeded in making *Passages* a true-life story that is totally engaging.

Individuals in numerous libraries, archives, and government offices have played a critical role in bringing this project to fruition. Among the many items retrieved were maps, photographs, government documents, business records, and abundant personal papers. In England, I was aided by numerous librarians during several trips I made to The National Archives at Kew, London. At the Essex Record Office in Chelmsford, staff retrieved fascinating tithe maps (English and Welsh parish maps prepared after 1836), and documents related to the history and agriculture of low-lying southeast Essex near the River Crouch. At the National Archives of Wales in Aberystwyth, Mark Strong, Gwllym Tawy, and several other librarians were exceedingly helpful in interpreting details on 1880s maps of Parke in the village of Pentrecwrt, the home of at least three generations of the Evans family. At the Glamorgan Archives in Cardiff, Jenny Jones was enormously helpful in locating useful information that had been temporarily relocated from the Carmarthenshire archives to the Glamorgan Archives. Via email and telephone, I received thorough and prompt assistance from Eric Davies at the Dyfed Family History Society in Tenby, Pembrokeshire, from Helen Palmer at the Ceredigion Archives in Aberystwyth, and from Catrin Simon at the Carmarthen Library in Carmarthenshire.

In Rochester, New York, I received excellent guidance from David Peter Coppen, librarian and archivist in Special Collections of the Sibley Music Library at the Eastman School of Music, where Evan Evans took piano lessons for roughly two years. At the Rochester Historical Society, William Keeler, librarian and archivist, quickly and efficiently retrieved many pertinent records about the South Congregational Church and other aspects of Rochester history dating from the 1910s to the 1940s. Library administrator Christy Lou Zuhlke encouraged and publicized my use of the library and my family history project. At the University of Rochester, Melissa S. Mead in the Department of Rare Books and Special Collections at the Rush Rhees Library, helped me locate the records of

Sibley, Lindsay & Curr, where John Evans worked for nearly thirty years.

At the Monroe County Courthouse in downtown Rochester, Irwin Harris, and especially Nese Baykal, gave me their undivided attention when I asked for help locating deeds and other property records of the Evans home in Pittsford. Nese found a document I never knew existed—the early 1940s foreclosure proceedings for the Evans's home at 179 East Brook Road in Pittsford. Her investigative skills unearthed a secret that the family knew nothing about.

At the tree-shaded pastoral White Haven Memorial Park in Pittsford, where both John Evans and Mabel Harvey Evans are buried, both the office personnel and a groundskeeper offered their assistance in finding their gravesites in this vast cemetery. Locating John's and Mabel's "grass masters," flush with the grass after more than fifty years, would have been impossible without their help.

Countless individuals—friends and family members in the United States, Canada, and Great Britain—contributed in so many ways to the development and production of this family history. In Canada, Welsh-born John Andrew Owen Jones, who emigrated from Wales to Canada as a young man, kindly translated into English parts of a Welsh local history of a nineteenth-century community in South Wales near my grandfather's birthplace. Since I could find no English version of this book, I was thrilled by Andy's willingness and ability to translate a relevant part of it.

At St. Paul's Anglican Church in Vancouver, two individuals aided me in writing this family history. Retired history professor David Facey-Crowther read and made helpful suggestions about several sections of *Passages*. British-born psychologist, writer, and editor Leslie Buck reviewed and thoughtfully proofread my entire book and guided me in placing the images. Throughout the arduous writing and revision of my book, Leslie, an author himself, gave me advice and endless encouragement.

Sharon Connaughty graciously offered to apply her knowledge and expertise using Photoshop to enhance the resolution of roughly seventy-five images I included in *Passages*. Huge thanks are owed Sharon for her untiring efforts.

At the outset of this project, author and long-time friend Cynthia Stowell, in Portland, Oregon, spent hours sharing her instructive thoughts about the form and shape that my family history might take. Her guidance was invaluable at the critical formative stages of my project. On the West Coast of the United States, a good friend and former real estate guru, Dorene Gould of Bellingham, Washington, helped interpret the foreclosure documents of my grandparents' home in Pittsford. She and I also became avid genealogical research companions. We spent endless hours at the Bellingham, Washington, Family History Center poring over hundreds of online births, deaths, marriages, and other family history records.

Both Dorene, along with life-long friend Margaret Hallett in Sausalito, California, patiently listened to my endless tales of research delights, frustrations, and the ongoing adventures of writing *Passages*. Margaret's and Dorene's abiding interest, patience, and encouragement affirmed their friendship many times over.

Stephanie Harris, the daughter of Charles Harris, my father's childhood and life-long friend, assisted with my research at the Rochester Historical Society, the Rush Rhees Library at the University of Rochester, and the White Haven Memorial Park cemetery. Stephanie's extensive knowledge of our shared family history extending back two generations, her research insights, and her wonderful sense of humor was much appreciated and tremendously enjoyed. Steph also kindly offered me her couch to sleep on while I stayed for days of research in Rochester. She never grumbled, either, when I asked if she could deliver me to a bus station so I could catch a 5:00 a.m. bus to Boston.

Although sparse in number, my Welsh relatives encouraged and contributed to my research and writing efforts in numerous ways. I visited Beryl Cooke, daughter of my father's cousin Hetty Evans and Rollo Rowland, in England and the United States and Canada many times. She was an astute and eager contributor and an enthusiastic supporter of my project. Her knowledge and memory of Evans family history have been without equal. Now living at Poundbury in Dorchester near the south coast of England, Beryl and her late husband, Graham, have welcomed me to their home numerous times over the years. Beryl and Graham's daughter, Sally Cooke, forever an avid genealogist, have continued to uncover details of the Evans family's history and inspired me to push forward with my historical research.

Carol Driscoll, a distant Evans relative, and her partner, Gary, of Gorseinon near Swansea in South Wales, welcomed me to their home in 2016. They gave me a grand tour of the stunning nearby Gower Peninsula before taking me to the Evanses' birthplace in Pentre-cwrt and to the nearby Saron Chapel cemetery where so many Evans family members are buried. Their tour ended in the market town of Newcastle Emlyn on the River Teifi, not far from Pentre-cwrt. Carol eagerly shared her family photographs and the history of her branch of the Evans family. Sally Vernal and husband Bob, as well as Sally's sister, Pam Powell, met and shared their knowledge of their branch of the Evans family with me over lunch in Hereford, England.

My many Harvey family relatives have shown me tremendous warmth and many kindnesses. In 2018, second cousin Wayne Gardner, a grandchild of Maud, one of my grandmother Mabel's sisters, met me at the Shrewsbury train station in central England, after I arrived from Aberystwyth, Wales. He then drove me north to visit a second cousin Nick Hards, a grandson of Reginald Harvey.

Wayne continued driving me across England to Bury St. Edmunds, Suffolk, where a Harvey family second cousin, Julia Read, served us a memorable dinner and shared family history stories of her mother, Patrina Adele Longman Read. Patrina was the last living granddaughter of Stephen and Martha Harvey.

The next day, Wayne drove me south to Hockley, Essex, where many descendants of Stephen and Martha gathered at the cemetery at St. Peter and St. Paul's Anglican Church. Here we found and cleaned the gravesites of Stephen and Martha Harvey. From the hilltop church cemetery, we looked north across the former fields of Kingsmans Farm to the River Crouch. We then continued a short distance to the Kingsmans Farm Harvey family home. At a restaurant in nearby Hullbridge, we shared a lovely lunch and endless conversation about our shared family history. We all had Wayne Gardner to thank for organizing this memorable Harvey family reunion.

For months afterward, other Harvey second cousins, including Tim Harvey and Geraldine Hards Newmark (grandchildren of Reginald Harvey) and Jenny Langridge Bibby and Sheil Langridge Ouzerdine (grandchildren of Ethel Harvey and Maurice Langridge), continued to share with me detailed knowledge of their branch of the Harvey family. Clare Harvey Frederick, avid family historian and a second cousin of my father, also kindly sent me a copy of the detailed history of her branch of the Harvey family.

Two other grandchildren of Ethel Harvey and Maurice

Langridge—David Langridge and Sarah Oakley—who were not able to be at the 2018 annual Harvey family reunion, have also shared their knowledge of Harvey family history. Also unable to attend was Vivienne Salmon, a descendant of William and Ann Alice Harvey, born in the 1780s. She kindly sent me a copy of her meticulously researched Harvey family history. All of these Harvey family members have been extremely generous with their knowledge, family histories, and photographs passed down to them.

Finally, I am exceedingly grateful to my Evans–Harvey families in the United States—my brother, Harvey David Evans, and my cousin, Christine Evans Gehret—for supporting my five-year-long research and writing efforts with interest, encouragement, and patience. David has carefully edited many sections of my book. Both David and Chris have remained patient when I've asked them endless questions about their knowledge of certain aspects of our family history. The time and suggestions Dave and Chris have offered have greatly improved the stories told in *Passages*. I am enormously grateful for their many contributions and loving support.

I am greatly indebted to those who carried this project beyond the writing stage and magically turned it into a readable and attractive book. In Kyiv, Ukraine, Anton Pshinka did a superb job designing the book's front and back covers and spine. He was receptive to my suggestions, completed his skilled design work quickly, and continued to answer my endless questions after he finished the covers.

In the final stages of transforming the manuscript into a book, I received invaluable assistance from editors and a formatter. London, England, editor Tatiana Wilde completed an editorial assessment and copy editing in the summer of 2020. British Columbian editors and a skilled formatter joined the team, bringing *Passages* to completion in late 2020 and early 2021. The competent and generous-spirited Stephanie Candiago laid out the text and photos while Jo-Anne Gordon's fine-tuning and proofreading were woven into the process of formatting. I called upon one more editor to carefully comb the book before sending it off for printing. Experienced Amanda Bidnall, writer, editor, and historian in Langley, British Columbia, completed the last thorough proofread in early 2021. I am so very grateful to all the skilled, talented, and generous contributions that each of these individuals made to making *Passages* a reality.

ABOUT THE AUTHOR

Gail E. Evans is a historian, author, and former athlete. As a teenager she excelled in gymnastics, then, influenced by her father's stories of living and traveling in Great Britain and visiting Europe, she became enamored with traveling to new places. Early on she lived in Japan, traveled across the former Soviet Union, and later led tours to gardens in the  northern Cotswolds of England, and Istanbul, Turkey. She has traveled many times to visit Harvey and Evans family members in England and Wales. Gail has worked professionally in the field of historic preservation (heritage conservation), researched and written histories on wide-ranging topics for the U.S. National Park Service and Parks Canada with D. Michael Hatch, and taught history at the university level. She immigrated to Canada in 2006. Gail received a BS in historical geography from the University of Oregon and a PhD in history from the University of California, Santa Barbara.

NOTES

1. From Different Worlds

1. Neville Williams, *The Life and Times of Henry VII* (London: Weidenfeld & Nicolson, 1994), 17.

2. David Williams, *A Short History of Modern Wales: 1485 to the Present Day* (London: John Murray, 1976), 71-73.

3. Letter from Thomas Evans, grandson of David and Hannah Evans, to John Harvey Evans (hereafter "JHE"), a nephew of Tom Evans, 19 February 1945.

4. Tom Evans, letter to JHE, 3 July 1940, G. Evans Papers.

5. Ben Johnson, "Merthyr Tydfil and the Welsh Men of Steel," *Historic UK* magazine.

6. Ronald L. Lewis, "Reconstructing Welsh Identity in the American Colonies," *North American Journal of Welsh Studies* 6: 1 (Winter 2011), 44; Russell Davies, *Secret Sins: Sex, Violence and Society in Carmarthenshire, 1870-1920* (University of Wales Press, 1996) 186.

7. Bert J. Rawlins, "Economic, Religious, and Social Change in Industrial Wales," *World Conference Records*, 1980.

8. Daniel Parry-Jones, *Welsh Country Upbringing* (London: B. T. Batsford Ltd., 1949), 25-27.

9. Tom Evans, letter to JHE, 19 February 1945, which listed the names and birth dates of the children of Evan and Frances Evans, G. Evans Papers; David Evans, *1841 Wales Census*, Ancestry.com. Also see: Pentre-cwrt, Llangeler Parish, "Welsh Tithe Map—Places of Wales," 1840s, National Library of Wales, Aberystwyth.

10. *1861 England, Wales, & Scotland Census*, transcription, Parke, Llangeler, Newcastle-in-Emlyn, Ceredigion, Wales.

11. Hetty Evans Rowland, granddaughter of Frances and Evan Evans, interviewed by Gail E. Evans, 2 April 2005, G. Evans Papers.

12. *Ibid.*

13. JHE, photos of Parke, taken in April 1934 and April 1937, G. Evans Papers.

14. JHE, "Family Folklore," hereafter cited as: JHE, "Family Folklore," 31 January 1985, G. Evans Papers. ("Family Folklore" consists of about thirty pages written by J. Harvey Evans recounting his memories of the Evans and Harvey families in 1920 and then from 1933-1937 when he attended the University of Liverpool.)

15. Beryl Cooke (great-granddaughter of Evan and Frances Evans), phone interview by G. Evans, 18 May 2015.

16. Nick Catford, "Station Name: Pentrecourt Platform," Disused Stations, at http://www.disused-stations.org.uk/p/pentrecourt_platform/.

17. *1902 England, Wales & Scotland Census,* transcript, "Dancapel, Llangeler (Carmarthen), Newcastle in Emlyn, Cardiganshire, Wales," *1901 Wales Census,* John Evans; David Jenkins, *The Agricultural Community in South-West Wales at the Turn of the Twentieth Century* (Cardiff: University of Wales Press, 1971), 36.

18. JHE, "Family Folklore," 31 January 1985, G. Evans Family Papers.

19. One hundred and fourteen Roman archaeological sites have been found within 10 km of Hockley, Essex, according to the ARCHI database, from the British Archaeological Records, Historic Sites and Monument Databases, Local History Sources and Archaeology Research Reports.

20. Stephen Rippon, "The Rayleigh Hills in South-east Essex: Patterns in Exploitation of a Woodland," *The Essex Landscape, in Search of Its History* (Chelmsford: Essex County Council, 1999), 20-28; Stephen Rippon, Adam Wainwright, and Chris Smart, "Farming Regions in Medieval England: The Archaeobotanical and Zooarchaeolgical Evidence," *Medieval Archaeology Journal,* Vol. 50 (2014—Issue 1), 195-255; E. H. Hunt and S. J. Pam, "Essex Agriculture in the 'Golden Age,' 1850-73," *Agricultural History Review* 43: II; Stephen Murray, "Landscape, Agriculture and the Rural Economy of Hockley, Essex, 1814-1916"; "Agriculture of the County of Essex, 1794—part 1," *Rural History,* 26: 2 (October 2015), 201-26.

21. N. V. Scarfe, *The Land of Britain: The Report of Land Utilisation Survey of Britain* (London: Survey by Geographical Publications, Ltd., 1942), 405-408, 454-55; Vivienne Salmon, Harvey family historian, email communication with G. Evans, 10 December 2018.

22. R.G.E. Wood, compiler, *Agriculture in Essex, c. 1840-1900* (Chelmsford: Essex Record Office Publications No. 67, 1975), "Introduction," p. 1.

23. Salmon, email to G. Evans, 10 December 2018.

24. T. W. Flethcer, "The Great Depression of English Agriculture, 1873-1896, in P. J. Perry, ed., *British Agriculture, 1875-1914* (London: Methuen, 1973), 31; David Cannadine, *The Decline and Fall of the British Aristocracy* (London: Pan, 1992), 92; E. H. Hunt and S. J. Pam, "Responding to Agricultural Depression, 1873-96; Managerial Success, Entrepreneurial Failure?," *Agricultural History Review* 50: 2 (2002), 225-34; Sir William Gavin, CBE, *Ninety Years of Family Farming: The Story of Lord Rayleigh's and Strutt & Parker Farms* (London: Hutchinson & Co., 1967), 96-97.

25. Hunt and Pam, "Responding to Agricultural Depression, 1873-96," 231, 233-38.

26. Communication from Carol Davey, Wayne Gardner, Peter Gardner (descendants of Maud Harvey Gardner and Charles Edward Gard-

ner), 6, 7, 8 February 2022, who provided census and christening data and family history notes pertaining to the Stephen and Martha Harvey family and the "black boarded cottage"; communication with Vivienne Salmon (Harvey family descendent) and author: 23 July 2017, 16 February 2019, 25, 26, and 27 January 2022, 6 February 2022; Vivienne Salmon, *The Harveys: A Farming Family in Thundersley, Hadleigh & and Faraway Places* (Hadleigh & Thundersley Community Archives, Hadleigh, Benfleet, Essex, 2021, pp. 19-20; Hadleigh & Thundersley Community Archives, Hadleigh, Benfleet, Essex, photograph of the "black boarded" cottage, ca. 1912; and E.H. Hunt and S.J. Pam, "Agricultural Depression in England, 1873-96: Skills Transfer and the 'Redeeming Scots,'" *Agricultural History Review*, Vol. 59, Part I, 2011.

27. Historic England, "Kingsmans Farmhouse," Listed Building, Grade II, List Entry Number 1147823, listed 7 October 1981; A. Doull Chatham, "Plan of the Parish of Hockley, County of Essex," 1840 Tithe Map; Ordinance Survey map, 1873, Southern Division, Sheet LXIX 4; Ordinance Survey map, 1896, Essex, Sheet LXIX 4. All three maps at Essex County Record Office, Chelmsford, Essex, England.

28. According to JHE, the farm received its name when a British king's soldier was stationed near this location on the River Crouch in the early 1800s to warn local residents of the "threat of invasion by the French during Napoleon's reign," JHE, "Family Folklore," 31 January 1985.

29. S. J. Pam, "Essex Agriculture: Landowners' and Farmers' Responses to Economic Change, 1850-1914," Ph.D. dissertation, University of London, 2004; Stephen Harvey served as chairman of the Hockley Parish Council from 1902-1908 and 1910-1931, according the plaque listing parish council chairs in the Hockley firehouse. Address by The Rev. T. W. Mason at the Funeral of Stephen Harvey, September 19th, 1931, G. Evans Papers.

2. Becoming Drapers

1. George S. Cole, *Cole's Encyclopedia of Dry Goods: A Reference Book for the Wholesale and Retail Dry Goods Trade of the United States* (New York: Root Newspaper Association, 1900), 148, 154. George S. Cole, *Revised Edition. A Complete Dictionary of Dry Goods and History of Silk, Cotton, Linen, Wool and Other Fibrous Substances* (Chicago : W.B. Conkey company, 1892), 116-118.

2. England and Wales Census, 1861 and 1871.

3. Wales Census, 1841, 1851, 1861, 1871, and 1881, online at Ancestry.com; New York Passenger Lists, 1820-1957 (1868) online at Ancestry.com; David Evans, Certified Copy of an Entry of Death,

Pontypool, Mounmoutshire, subdistrict of Marwolaeth, General Register Office, London, England; Tom Evans, letter to JHE, 20 November 1947, G. Evans Papers.

4. England and Wales Census, 1891; David Morgan Ltd., Department Store, Cardiff Records, Glamorgan Archives, Archives Wales, 2 December 2015.

5. Wales Census, 1891 and 1901, at Ancestry.com; "England Mercantile Occupations, Merchants, Retailers, Clothing Materials, Dress, Drapers, Haberdashers (National Institute)," excerpted from the course "English: Occupation Records-Professions and Trades."

6. Wales Census, 1901.

7. "Oxford Street," *Survey of London*, Bartlett School of Architecture, University College London, Yale University Press, 2017; Deborah Wynne, "The 'Despised Trade' in Textiles: H.G. Wells, Willian Paine, Charles Cavers, and the Male Draper's Life, 1870-1914," *Textile History* 46: 1 (May 2015), 99.

8. *Post Office London Directory, 1899, Official, Street, Commercial, Trades, Law, Court, . . .* (London: Kelly's Directories, Ltd., 1899), 632; *Post Office London Directory, 1910 [Vol. 1, Part 2, Street Directory]* (London: Kelly's Directories, Ltd. 1910), 522.

9. "Drapers Assistant," RootsChat Aristocrat, 31 December 2015; "The Drapers' Company," www.thedrapers.comuk/Company/History-And-Heritage; Marshall & Snelgrove—100 Years of Luxury," https://vintagefashionguild.org/label-resource/marshall-snelgrove/.

10. *Post Office London Directory, 1910 [Vol. 1, Part 2, Street Directory]* (London: Kelly's Directory, Ltd, 1910), 472; England Census, 1911, at Ancestry.com; England and Wales Census, 1871.

11. England Census, 1861, at Ancestry.com; England Census 1881, at Ancestry.com; England and Wales Births, 1837-2006, transcript; England and Wales & Scotland Census, 1901.

12. Later bought by another department store, Derry and Toms, built in an Art Deco style with a 1.5-acre roof garden, retained its name and remained open until 1973. *England and Wales Census*, 1911, noted in Vivienne Salmon, "Following the Life of Ethel Millicent Harvey, 1886-1960 . . ., April 2016, typescript.

13. Mary Higgs and Edward E. Hayward, *Where Shall She Live: The Homelessness of the Women Worker* (London: P.S. King & Son, 1910), 5-6.

14. *Post Office London Directory, 1910 [Vol.1, Part 2, Street Directory]* (London: Kelly's Directories, Ltd., 1910), 472, 676; "Mabel Ida Harvey," England Census, 1911; "Mabel Ida Harvey," England Census, 1911; Bartlett School of Architecture, University College London, "South-East Marylebone," *Survey of London, Vols. 51 & 52,* (New Haven: Yale University Press, 2017), 1, 65-67.

15. Joslyn McCraw VonKaenel, "Conspicuous Consumers: The Victorian Department Store and the Women's Movement" (2015). The

1900 *Cole's Encyclopedia of Dry Goods*, defined "draper" as one who deals in cloth or clothing.

16. JHE, "Family Folklore," 31 January 1985.

17. Victoria and Albert Museum, "History of Fashion 1900-1970"; Dolores Monet, "Women's Fashion During WW I: 1914-1920;.Geofrey Wheatcroft, "The Making of the English Middle Class, *The Atlantic*, 283: 6 (June 1999), 128-29.

18. Donna Loftus, "The Rise of the Victorian Middle Class."

19. John Evans, "Declaration of Intention," 18 January 1912, Youngstown, Mahoning, Ohio, 18 January 2018; Mabel I. Evans,"US Passport Applications, 1795-1925," 5 March 1920; Evans photos of John and Mabel in their twenties, G. Evans Papers.

20. United States of America, "Certificate of Naturalization," 27 November 1917, 515 Meigs Street, Rochester, NY, Monroe County; John Evans, "U.S. Petition for Naturalization," 27 November 1917, G. Evans Papers.

21. JHE, "Family Folklore," 31 January 1985, 25, G. Evans Papers.

22. JHE, "Family Folklore," 31 January 1985, G. Evans Papers.

23. Deborah Wynne, "The 'Despised Trade' in Textiles," *Textile History* 46: 1 (May 2015), 99-108.

24. *Historic England*, "The Fashion for Shopping," online.

25. Wayne Gardner, grandson of Maud Harvey and Charles Gardner, email to G. Evans, 27 September 2017.

26. JHE, "Family Folklore," 31 January 1985.

27. JHE, "Census of Canada, 1891, at Ancestry.com; "John Harvey," Canadian Passenger Lists, 1865-1935, online; John Harvey's obituary notes his arrival in Victoria in 1907. Peter Harvey Gardner, Maud's son, recorded this aborted immigration plan by Stephen and Martha Harvey on a "Certified Copy of an Entry of Birth," Billericay Registration District, on 12 February 1960, of Maud Elsie Harvey, born on 23 April 1892.

28. Roger Daniels, *Coming to America* (New York: Harper Perennial, 2002), 216.

29. Excerpt from Arthur Meier Schlesinger, "The Significance of Immigration in American History," *American Journal of Sociology* 27: 2 (July 1921), 71-85.

3. Immigrating to a New World

1. "Average Weather on October 3rd in Southampton," https://weatherspark.com/d/41541/10/3/Average-Weather-on-October-3-in-Southampton-United-Kingdom

2. "The Huge New Dock at Southampton," *Scientific American Supplement*, 19 August 1911. It is not positively known if Mabel and Ethel saw John off on the *Ascania*.

3. "Cunard Line," Out-going Passengers, Date of Departure, 3rd October 1911, Port of Departure, Southampton, Ship Name *Ascania*.

4. "S.S. Ascania (1), Cunard Line," Norway-Heritage, Hands across the Sea, Bradford Hudson, Ph.D., "Cunard in Boston," *Boston Hospitality Review*, 1 February 2015; "The Cunard Line: Passenger Lists and Emigrant Ships from Norway: The Cunard Line."

5. Marian L. Smith, "By Way of Canada: U.S. Records of Immigration across the U.S.-Canadian Border, 1895-1954 (St. Albans Lists)," *Genealogy Notes* (National Archives of Canada), 32: 3 (Fall 2000).

6. Desmond Glynn, "'Exporting Outcast London': Assisted Emigration to Canada, 1886-1914," *Histoire sociale—Social History*, Vol. XV (May 1982), 215-17; "The Last Best West: Advertising for Immigrants to Western Canada, 1870-1930."

7. "Norway-Heritage, Hands Across the Sea, The Cunard Line"; Canadian Immigration-Early 1900s, Some Canadian Immigration Statistics"; "Clifford Sifton and Canada's Immigration Policy"; "A Hundred Years of Immigration to Canada, 1900-1999."

8. Jonathan Schneer, *London 1900: The Imperial Metropolis* (New Haven: Yale University Press, 1999), 28.

9. The *Ascania* had a short life. During the First World War, the ship sailed across the North Atlantic as an Armed Merchant Cruiser. In May 1918, a detachment of the US 119th Infantry made up a transatlantic convoy to Liverpool, England, where submarines attacked the ship. Less than a month later, the *Ascania* was wrecked in the Breton Strait, 20 miles east of Cape Ray, Newfoundland. Also see: "*Ascania* (1)," Shipwrecks of the Cunard.

10. Angelo M. Pellegrini's description, in Ronald Sanders, *Shores of Refuge: a Hundred Years of Jewish Emigration* (New York City: Henry Holt, 1988), and quoted in David Laskin's *The Long Way Home: An American Journey from Ellis Island to the Great War I* (New York: Harper Perennial, 2010), 33.

11. "Steerage Class – Conditions - A Report of the Immigration Commission—1911.

12. Scott Thompson, "The Voyage: A Voyage from Norway to America in 1911."

13. "Steerage Class – Conditions - A Report of the Immigration Commission—1911"; "Border Crossings: from Canada to U.S., 1895-1956, The Generations Network, Inc., 2007.

14. Lisa Chilton, "Receiving Canada's Immigrants: The Work of the State Before 1930" (Ottawa: The Canadian Historical Association, 1916), 21-24.

15. Marian L. Smith, "By Way of Canada: U.S. Records of Immigration Across the U.S.-Canadian Border, 1895-1954" (St. Albans Lists), *Genealogy Notes* 32: 3 (Fall 2000); Arian L. Smith, "By Way of Canada: U.S. Records of Immigration across the U.S.-Canadian Border, 1895-1954" (St. Albans Lists)," *Prologue: Selected Articles* (U.S.

National Archives publication) 32: 3 (Fall 2000). John Evans, "List or Manifest of Alien Passengers for the United States," S.S. *Ascania* sailing from Southampton, 3 October 1911.

16. Marion L. Smith, "By Way of Canada: U.S. Records of Immigration across the U.S.-Canadian Border, 1895-1954 (St. Albans Lists)," *Genealogy Notes* 32: 3 (Fall 2000). Also see: *Prologue: Selected Articles* (U.S. National Archives publication; and John Evans, "List of Manifest of Alien Passengers for the United States," S.S. *Ascania* sailing from Southampton, 3 October 1911.

17. Canada-rail, "Grand Trunk Railway Reporting mark: GT"; Jan Raska, "Port of Precedence: A History of the Port of Quebec, Part 1 —Establishing the Port of Quebec"; "Ville de Quebec: Heritage: The Modernization of the Port in the 19th Century"; Samuel Veniere, "Port of Quebec," 18 October 2018,; John Evans, Cunard Line, "Out-going Passengers," images reproduced by courtesy of The National Archives, London, England. Also see: "Declaration of Intention," John Evans, 15 January 1912, Youngstown, Ohio, and Michigan Government, SOM/Places, "Saint Clair River Tunnel (Saint Clair Railroad Tunnel, First International Tunnel, Grand Trunk Tunnel)."

18. *Youngstown City Directory* (Akron: Burch Directory Company), 1911, 1912, 1066; 1913, 469; 1915, 1916.

19. John Evans, "Declaration of Intention," 15 January 1912, G. Evans Papers.

20. *Youngstown Official City Directory* (Akron: Burch Directory Company, 1912), 455, 1066.

21. Ronald L. Lewis, "Reconstructing Welsh Identity in the American Coalfields," *North American Journal of Welsh Studies* 6: 1 (Winter 2011), 32-33. The actual numbers of Welsh in Ohio may have been more than 100,000 in 1900, since the Welsh county of Monmouthshire was then administered by England and the Welsh were not counted. Judy Williams, Benjamin D. Rickey & Co., "Downtown Youngstown Multiple Resource Area (History/Architecture)," National Register of Historic Places Inventory-Nomination Form, 1985.

22. *Youngstown Official City Directory* (Akron: Burch Directory Company, 1913); "Erie's History and Memorabilia—Boston Store, State Street."

23. Blake McKelvey, "Indian Allan's Mills," *Rochester History* 1: 4 (October 1939), 1-4.

24. "History of Rochester, New York; Post-war Industrial Boom"; Wilfred H. Schoff, "The New York State Barge Canal," *Bulletin of the American Geographical Society,* 47: 5 (1915), 321-333.

25. "The Architectural Heritage of the Warners in Rochester, NY, Biographical Information," and "Their Work" Robert G. Hill, *Biographical Dictionary of Architects in Canada, 1800-1950* (Robert G. Hill, 2009).

26. Karen McCally, "Rochester Goes Shopping: Sibley's and the Rise of 'Consumer Culture'"; Andrew D. Wolfe, *Bold Century, 1868-1968: 100 Adventurous and Happy Years of Merchandising/The Story of Sibley, Lindsay, and Curr Company of Rochester, Monroe County, New York* (Rochester: Rochester Historical Society, 1968), 9, 25.
27. Wolfe, *Bold Century, 1868-1968*, 9.
28. *Ibid.*, 17.
29. Noted architect J. Foster Warner designed the Granite Building for Sibley, Lindsay & Curr in the Beaux-Arts style. Emily Morry, "Unshakable Roots: Granite Building Faces Metamorphosis," *Democrat and Chronicle*, 13 October 2016; "The Architectural Heritage of the Warners in Rochester, NY, Their Work"; Wolfe, *Bold Century, 1868-1968*, 14-18.
30. Wolfe, *Bold Century, 1868-1968*, 15, 32.
31. *Ibid.*, 34-35, 37.
32. *Ibid.*, 36.
33. Donovan A. Shilling, *Rochester's Downtown* (Charleston, SC: Arcadia Publishing, 2001), Chapter Five, "East Main"; Wolfe, *Bold Century, 1868-1968*, 21, 36-38.
34. Wolfe, *Bold Century, 1868-1968*, 21, 36-38; "What Happened to . . . Sibley's," *Democrat and Chronicle*, 19 July 2014.
35. Wolfe, *Bold Century, 1868-1968*, 34.
36. J.M. Lathrop & Co., *Plat Book, City of Rochester, New York* (New York: J.M. Lathrop & Co.), 1900, Plates 6 and 15, Library of Congress; "New York Conference Churches, South Congregational Church, Rochester, New York, organized September 19, 1886," Rochester Historical Society; "Observes 30th Anniversary of Founding Church," *Democrat and Chronicle*, 4 November 1916, Rochester Historical Society.
37. Noyes Bartholomew was not listed in the 1910 and 1911 Rochester Directory, and listed for the first time in 1912. *Rochester Directory, 1912*, Rochester Public Library. Noyes Bartholomew remained at the South Congregational Church until around 1922. He eventually relocated to Milford, New Hampshire. "Family of Noyes Otis Bartholomew and Elva Maude Veazie," Veazie.org – Family of Noyes Otis Bartholomew and Elva Maude Veazie. Also see: *My Heritage* website, "Noyes Otis Bartholomew."
38. *Ibid.*
39. "In Memoriam," 14 January 1945, for the passing of senior deacon John Evans, South Congregational Church, Rochester; "Welsh Congregational Church."

4. Mabel and John Reunite

1. England, General Registry Office, "Certified Copy of an Entry of Death," 1913, Vol. 11a, pg. 454, reported that David Evans died at 1 Llantwit Street, Cardiff (his home), on 6 January 1913 due to "apoplexy, heart failure." David's brother-in-law, John Williams, was present at his death.

2. "Heart of City Threatened by Record Flood," *Democrat and Chronicle*, 29 March 1913, p. 1.

3. *Ibid.*, p. 1 and 12.

4. "Rochester's Great Flood(s)," Rochester Subway; Trudy E. Bell, "The Great Easter 1913 'Midwest' Flood in New York State," accepted for presentation at the 30th Conference on New York State History, SUNY Plattsburgh, June 2009, 1-2.

5. "25th Anniversary, Manual and Membership Roll, South Congregational Church, Rochester, NY," 52, Rochester Historical Society; *Rochester Directory, 1913,* Central Library of Rochester and Monroe County-City Directory Collection; "List of Manifest of Alien Passengers for the United States Immigration Officer at Port of Arrival," arriving on the *Virginian* from Liverpool, departing May 9, arriving at Quebec on 17 May 1913, online at "U.S. Border Crossings from Canada to U.S, 1895-1956."

6. Much later, Mabel recalled that she traveled on the S.S *Cynthia*, although JHE thought that she had sailed on the *Virginian,* which research confirmed; "Passenger Lists Leaving the UK, 1890-1960 Transcription," and also the actual page with the three women's names.

7. "Second Cabin Accommodations—1910 Travel Guide."

8. "History of the Allan Royal Mail Line of Steamers—1914," *Gjenvick-Gjønvik Archives;* "Supplement" to the *Illustrated London News,* 21 September 1912, xii, at GJenvick Archives; "Titanic Inquiry Project, *Virginian,* Allan Line; "Supplement" to the *Illustrated London News,* 21 September 1912, xii; "The Allan Line and Their Turbine Ferry to Canada," *Review of Reviews* 30 (December 1904), 683-86.

9. "Supplement" to the *Illustrated London News,* 21 September 1912, xii, GJenvick Archives; Paul Lee, *The Titanic and the Indifferent Stranger* (London: Paul Lee, 2009); Sean Molony, *Titanic Scandal: The Trial of the Mount Temple* (Gloucestershire: Amberley Publishing, 2012). Also see: "'Bertha Watson' [Margaret Sanger] slept here: The R.M.S. *Virginian,"* Margaret Sanger Papers Project—Research Annex, Tag Archives: R.M.S. *Virginian.*

10. *"Titanic:* 10 Famous People Who Died on the *Titanic";* "George Dennick Wick"; "Largest Ship Afloat, Meets with Accident," *Youngstown Vindicator,"* 15 April 1912, 1 and 16.

11. "Second Cabin Accommodations—1910 Travel Guide," at Gjenvick website.

12. "List or Manifest of Alien Passengers for the United States Immigration Officer at Port of Arrival," on S.S. *Virginian,* sailing from Liverpool on 9 May 1913, arriving at Port of Quebec, 17 May 1913, at U.S. Border Crossings from Canada to U.S., 1895-1956." Many years later, JHE wrote in his November 1982 notes pertaining to legal documents received about his parents that he only assumed Jennie came to Rochester, but did not positively know this; "List of Manifest of Alien Passengers for the United States Immigration Officer at Port of Arrival," arriving on the *Virginian* from Liverpool, departing May 9, arriving at Quebec on 17 May 1913, Ancestry.com, "U.S. Border Crossings from Canada to U.S, 1895-1956."); "Passenger Lists of the *Virginian* Arriving in Quebec, Que. On 1913-05-15," Library and Archives Canada; Betty Harvey, letter to JHE, 15 July 1942, G. Evans Family Papers; "Passenger Lists Leaving UK, 1890-1960, *Virginian,* departed from Liverpool on 9 May 1913, at FindMyPast, at FindMyPast.

13. "Canadian Control of Railroads in the United States," Senate, 66th Congress, 2nd Session, Document 162, United States Congressional Serial Set, Volume 7658 (Washington: Government Printing Office, December 4, 1919), 221.

14. In 1913, around the time Mabel and Ethel traveled across the Adirondacks, the New York Central bought the Mohawk and Malone Railroad (renaming it the "Adirondack Division" of the New York Central Railroad), and began making major upgrades to accommodate heavier engines and to withstand the harsh winters in the mountains. The Old Print Shop, "Mohawk & Malone RY. Adirondack & St. Lawrence Line. The New Route in Connection with the New York Central to the Adirondack Mountains and Montreal"; Adirondack Almanac, "New York Central RR—The Adirondack and St. Lawrence Railroad."

15. "Historic Saranac Lake, Adirondack & St. Lawrence." online.

16. City of Rochester, "Record of Marriage, No. 12166, State of New York," Groom, John Evans, Bride, Mabel Ida Harvey, 19 May 1913; Mabel D [*sic*] Harvey, "New York County Marriages, 1847-1948, 1908-1936, FamilySearch; Sermon: "The Father and Three Sons," In Memoriam, South Congregational Church, Alexander and Pearl Streets, Rochester, NY, Sunday, 14 January 1945. G. Evans Papers.

17. Photos of early childhood and 515 Meigs Street house and friends, JHE Scrapbook, 1910s-c. 1937, G. Evans Papers.

18. *Rochester Directory, 1914,* City Directory Collection, Central Library of Rochester and Monroe County. This is uncertain, however, since there is no Ethel Harvey listed on Meigs Street or elsewhere in Rochester in the 1913 or 1914 *Rochester Directory* of residents.

In late August 2018, when I was photographing 28 Goebel Street, I met an older woman who came out onto the top of the stairs leading from the enclosed front porch. I explained why I was taking photos. She told me that she had lived in the house for over fifty years. She was delighted to learn that my father had been born in the house in 1913.

19. *Rochester Directory, 1914,* Central Library of Rochester and Monroe County—City Directory Collection.

20. "A.C. Harris" is on Harvey's "Transcript of Birth, John Harvey Evans," Monroe County Office of Vital Research, Rochester, New York, created on 19 September 2017. Charles Harris, letter and responses to questions asked by me, 10 October 1999, in G. Evans Papers. In 1999 Charles Harris, a childhood and lifetime friend of J. Harvey Evans, recalled in a letter to me: "I believe my father [a doctor] delivered Harvey on Meigs St., one block from the historic Erie Canal, which was still functioning at that time." Charles's memory about his birthplace and circumstances of it vary from John Harvey Evans's hearsay information about his birth. Also see Central Library of Rochester and Monroe County, City Directory Collection, 1914."

21. Wilford M. Wilson, Weather Bureau, U.S. Department of Agriculture, *Climatological Data: New York Station,* May 1914, 51, 55, and 57; "Weather Forecast," 2 May 1914, *Democrat and Chronicle,* Rochester, New York.

22. "Dance to Aid Suffragists," *Democrat and Chronicle,* 1 May 1914; "To Observe Suffrage Day," *Democrat and Chronicle*; Rochester's Subway, "Today, September 14, in Rochester History: The Seneca Hotel Opens," *Democrat and Chronicle.*

23. *Rochester Directory,* 1914-1915, City Directory Collection, Central Library of Rochester and Monroe County, at http://www3.libraryweb.org/lh.aspx?id=1105. In 1914-1915, the young Evans family occupied the first floor of 515 Meigs Street, owned and occupied on the second floor by Louis H. Jacobs, a builder, and his wife, Clara.

24. *Rochester Directory,* 1915-1920, City Directory Collection, Central Library of Rochester and Monroe County; Daniel A. Graff, "Retail Workers," *Encyclopedia of Chicago.*

5. Troubled Times

1. National Archives of the United Kingdom, "Why Did Britain Go to War?"; Gary Sheffield, "The Origins of World War One," online at http://www.bbc.co.uk/history/worldwars.

2. David Laskin, *The Long Way Home: An American Journey from Ellis Island to the Great War* (New York: Harper Perennial, 2010). Laskin recounts the service of twelve newly arrived immigrants, who served in various branches of the U.S. military during World War I.

3. Black and Naylor, "Rochester and World War I,"2- 3.

4. Stuart Hallifax, "Citizens at War: the Experience of the Great War in Essex, 1914-1918," submitted for examination for D.Phil in History, The Queen's College, Oxford, 2010, 126-28; Bonnie White, "Feeding the War Effort: Agriculture Experiences in First World War Devon, 1914-1917," *Agricultural History Review* 58: 1 (2010), 95-101; National Farmers' Union, "Farming and the First World War: Mechanisation," NFU, online; "The Few that Fed the Many," online.

5. Maurice Olden Langridge, England and Wales, Civil Registration Birth Index, 1837-1915, at Ancestry.com; *England Census, 1911* at Ancestry.com; Maurice Olden Langridge, London and Surrey, England Marriage Bonds and Allegations, 1597-1921.

6. Maurice Olden Langridge, "Report on Cadets, No. 1 ASC Officer Cadet Company," Military Service Record, WO_339_10280_001, National Archives UK; Vivienne Salmon, *The Harveys: A Farming Family in Thundersley, Hadleigh & Faraway Places* (Benfleet, Essex: The Hadleigh & Thundersley Community Archive, 2021); Maurice Olden Langridge, London, England, Church of Marriages and Banns, 1754-1931, at Ancestry.com.

7. Maurice Langridge, "Short Service, Attestation of Maurice Langridge," 2 September 1914; "Statement of the Services of No. . . Name: M. Langridge"; "Proceedings on Discharge," in Military Service Record, WO_339_10280_001, National Archives, Kew, London. By 1918 the Army Service Corps had moved three million men, five-hundred thousand horses, and millions of pounds of meat, bread, and forage to hundreds of army regiments. "The Army Service Corps in the First World War—Long, Long Trail," online; "Unit History: Royal Army Service Corps," online.

8. Maurice Olden Langridge, "Application for Admission to an Officer Cadet Unit," April 1917, Military Service Record, WO_339_10280_001, National Archives, online.

9. Maurice Olden Langridge, "Military History Sheet," from 2 September 1914 to 3 February 1918, Military Service Record, WO_339_10280_001, National Archives, England.

10. "Short Service, Attestation of Harvey, Reginald John," certified on 3 November 1915 and 3 March 1916; also "Medical History of Harvey, Reginald John," 3 December 1915, both pages in the Military Service Record of Reginald John Harvey, National Archives, England. The Waterford Barracks also provided accommodation for several other cavalry regiments (the Fifth Royal Irish Lancers, Ninth Queen's Royal Lancers, 12th Royal Lancers, 16th The Queen's Lancers, and the 21st Lancers); "Statement of the Services of No. 23654, Reginald John Harvey, November 1915—February 1917, Military Service Record of Reginald John Harvey, National Archives, England. The Eighth Reserve Regiment, along with the ninth and tenth reserve regiments, were part of the Third Reserve Cavalry Brigade in the spring of 1916. The Eighth Reserve Regiment was associated with

the 17th Lancers and three other cavalry regiments. In 1917, the Eighth Reserve Regiment was absorbed into the First Reserve Regiment. "Cavalry Reserve Regiments (United Kingdom)."

11. Ciaran Byrne, *The Harp and Crown: The History of the 5th Royal Irish Lancers, 1902-22* (Lulu Books on Demand, 2007), 104-108; "Cavalry Reserve Regiments (United Kingdom)."

12. Nick Hards, email to Wayne Gardner, Tim Harvey, Vivienne Salmon and Gail Evans, 22 November 1917.

13. "Certificate of Recommendation for Admission to an Officer Cadet Unit," 18 August 1916, Reginald J. Harvey's Military Service Record, National Archives, England. "Minute Sheet," 21 September 1916, Reginald J. Harvey's Military Service Record, National Archives, England; *Supplement to the London Gazette*, 15 February 1917, 1625; "The Long, Long Trail, The Reserve Regiments of Cavalry"; "Medical Board Report on a Disabled Officer," Stewart Barracks, Curragh, 10 October 1917; "Medical Board Report on a Disabled Officer, Curragh, 4 December 1917; "Medical Board Report on a Disabled Officer," Curragh, 14 January 1918; "Medical Board Report on Disabled Officer," 14 February 1918, First Reserve Cavalry Regiment, Curragh; all in Medical Service Record for Reginal Harvey, National Archives UK. "Supplement to the London Gazette," 2 March 1918, 2689.

14. Beryl Cooke (granddaughter of Thomas Evans), email to Gail E. Evans, 27 December 2018, G. Evans Papers.

15. Chris Wood, "Keir Hardie: Wales' First World War One Objector," BBC News, 23 August 2017; John Davies, "The Legacy of WW1," at http://www.bbc.co.uk/wales/history/sites/themes/pierods/ww1_background.shtml; Jessica Flynn, Wales Online, "World War One Centenary: How Wales Reported the Start of the Great War," at https://www.salesonline.co.uk/news/wales-news/world-war-one-centenary-how-7555809

16. John Davies, "The Legacy of WW1"; Jessica Flynn, Wales Online, "World War One Centenary: How Wales Reported the Start of the Great War."

17. Flynn, "World War One Centenary."

18. "South Congregational Elect New Officers," *Democrat and Chronicle*, 17 January 1935, at www.DemocratandChronicle.com.

19. Evan Reginald Evans, State of New York, Department of Health, Certification of Birth, 16 July 1916.

20. "U.S. Entry into World War I, 1917," Milestones in the History of U.S. Foreign Policy, Office of the Historian, Department of State, online.

21. Davis Tucker and Jessi Creller, "1917 Immigration Act," online.

22. Black and Naylor, "Rochester and World War I," 4.

23. "U.S. Entry into World War I, 1917," Milestones in the History of U.S. Foreign Policy, Office of the Historian, Department of State;

"U.S. Enters World War I," HISTORY, online; "Wilson Before Congress," online.

24. On December 7, 1917, the United States later declared war on German ally Austria-Hungary. Black and Naylor, "Rochester and World War I," 3-7.

25. Black and Naylor, "Rochester and World War I," 6-7; Sheffield, "The Origins of World War One," online.

26. Until 1922 married women became U.S. citizens by virtue of their marriage to a citizen or to an alien who became a naturalized citizen, like John Evans. After Congress passed act [42 U.S. Stat. 1022], married women who wanted to become citizens needed to follow the requirements of the Naturalization Law, in G. Evans Papers.

27. Al Mancini, "Women on the Homefront," *Rochester History, Rochester during World War One,"* 51: 3 (Summer 1989); Black and Naylor, "Rochester and World War I," 9-11.

28. Black and Naylor, "Rochester and World War I," 12-13.

29. Ibid., 7-9, 14-18.

30. "War Diaries," 5th Lancers, (WO 96/1134/2), digitized, Vol. 2, May and June 1918, 61 and 64, National Archives, England; "Arrival Report," Reginald John Harvey, 18 June 1918, Military Service Record, National Archives, England; Ciaran Byrne, *The Harp and Crown: The History of the 5th (Royal Irish) Lancers, 1902-1922* (Great Britain: Lulu Books, 2008), 103-108, 201.

31. U.S. Department of Health and Human Services, National Institute on Deafness and Other Communication Disorders, Otosclerosis. Otosclerosis is a common cause of hearing loss in young adults caused by an abnormal growth of bone in an ear. Medical Board Report on Disabled Officer," 16 July 1918 and "Medical Report, War Office, Whitehall, London, 18 June 1918; both in Reginald J. Harvey, Military Service Record, National Archives, England; 2nd Lt. Reginald John Harvey, letter to the Secretary, Department F3, War Office, Whitehall, 8 August 1918 and "Minute Sheet No., Register No. 14933," 2nd Lt. R. H. Harvey, 5th Lancers, June 4—August 7, 1918, in Reginald J. Harvey, Military Service Record, National Archives, England.

32. "Medical Board Report on Disabled Officer," 7 October 1918, Reginald J. Harvey Military Service Record, National Archives, England. J. Harvey Evans, who knew Reginald Harvey first in the 1930s, then until his death in 1970, noted his deafness.

33. Jonathan Krause, "Western Front," International Encyclopedia of the First World War," Version 1.0, 1914-1918; Military Service Record, WO_339_10280_001, National Archives, England.

34. Maurice Langridge, letter to Secretary of State for War, War Office, Whitehall, 26 July 1919; Maurice Langridge, "Medical Board Report on a Disabled Officer," 27 November 1918; Letter to The Secretary of State for War, War Office, Whitehall, 26 July 1919; "Protection

Certificate Officer," 27 June 1919; "Army Service Corps, Temporary," Langridge, Maurice Olden, Book No. 2/59, letter from Ld. P. Fruin to M.O. Langridge, at Folley Lane, Hockley, 1 March 1920; all in Military Service Record, WO_339_10280_001, National Archives, England.

35.　John Evans, "U.S., World War I Draft Registration Cards, 1917-1918," Rochester Local Board No. 6. See also: Michelle Lee, "Military Draft Act of 1917"; "Registration Certificate," John Evans, living at 515 Meigs Street, in J. Harvey Evans Scrapbook (1913-1937), G. Evans Papers.

36.　"The Sun Calendar: The Weather," and "British Prelates on War Mission," and "Spanish Influenza Here," all in *The Sun* (New York City), 12 September 1918, 12.

37.　Andrew Preston, *Sword of the Spirit, Shield of Faith, Religion in American War and Diplomacy*, Alfred A. Knopf, 1912, 276.

6. Going Home to England

1.　Rochester Chamber of Commerce, *The Book of Industrial Rochester* (Rochester, NY: Rochester Chamber of Commerce, 1919).

2.　*Ibid.*

3.　"U.S. Entry into World War I, 1917," Milestones in the History of U.S. Foreign Policy, Office of the Historian, Department of State. See also: Center for Immigration Studies, "Historical Overview of Immigration Policy, James Fallows, "Politics: Immigration: How It's Affecting Us," *Atlantic*, "Emergency Quota Act," 1921.

4.　Daniel A. Graff, "Retail Workers," *Encyclopedia of Chicago;* John Evans, Rochester City Directory, 1918, John listed as a "clerk" at 250 Main, E (home of Sibley, Lindsay & Curr); John Evans, "U.S., World War I Draft Registration Cards, 1917-1918," signed 12 September 1918, John Evans was a "silk salesman," Rochester Local Board No. 6; *Rochester Directory,* 1910, City Directory Collection, Central Library of Rochester and Monroe County; "Some of the Angles of Selling through Retail Salesmen," "Ideas that Will Sell January Silks," "Ori ental and Old French Styles," all in *American Silk Journal*, 33: 1 (January 1914), 30, 31, and 39, respectively.

5.　National Archives and Records Administration (NARA), Washington, D.C.: NARA Series: "Passport Applications, January 2, 1906-March 1, 1925," Certificates: 182750-183125, 10 Mar 1920-11 Mar 1920, "Mabel I. Evans."

6.　Kathleen Morgan Drowne, Patrick Huber, *The 1920s* (Westport, CT: Greenwood Publishing Group, 2004), 259-60.

7.　"Chelsea Piers History 101."

8.　New York Architecture, "Chelsea Piers," online at http://www.nyc-architecture.com/CHE/CHE-035.htm.

9. *"Adriatic (II)"* White Star Line History, http://www.whitestarhistory.com/adriatic; Dan Kerins, digital editor, "Berth 44, Ocean Dock, Dock Gate 4, Southampton," 29 December 2011; "UK Incoming Passenger Lists, 1878-1960."

10. "Application for Certificate of Citizenship" for Mabel Ida Evans, October 2, 1959, noted that May 20 was date of departure. J. Harvey Evans Scrapbook, two sepia photos of Mabel, her sons, and others onboard the *Adriatic,* 1920, both in G. Evans Papers.

11. Matthew Fautley and James Garon, *The Essex Coastline—Then and Now* (Winterbourne Down: Potton Publishing, 2004), 131, 146; Alfred J. Padgett photo, "Kingsmans Farms, Hullbridge," No, 6016, Essex Record Office, Chelmsford, Essex.

12. JHE, "Family Folklore," 31 January 1985, in G. Evans Papers.

13. Vivienne Salmon, *The Harveys: A Farming Family in Thundersley, Hadleigh & Faraway Places* (Benfleet, Essex: The Hadleigh & Thundersley Community Archive, 2021).

14. Rev. T. W. Mason, "At the Funeral of Stephen Harvey," 19 September 1931.

15. JHE, "Family Folklore," 31 January 1985.

16. *Ibid.*

17. Both from JHE, "Family Folklore," 31 January 1985.

18. JHE, "Family Folklore," 31 January 1985.

19. Hetty [Evans] Rowland, interview by Gail Evans, 2 April 2005, transcript, p. 7, in G. Evans Papers; Beryl Cooke, daughter of Hetty Evans Rowland, email to Gail Evans, 5 January 2019. "Monthly Weather Report of the Meteorological Office," 45th year, No. 7, July 1920.

20. Goran, "The Interior of RMS *Mauretania*," *News,* May 1, 2016; Richard Cavendish, "Launch of the *Mauretania*," *History Today* 56: 9 (September 2006).

21. "A Ship of Firsts: Cunard's Innovative Developments."

22. J. Harvey Evans, interview by Robbie Mason at 8 Doran Farm Lane, Lexington, Massachusetts, February 1989, in G. Evans Papers. Cavendish, "Launch of the *Mauretania*"; "On the Water: Comfort, Courtesy, Safety, Speed," American History, Smithsonian Institution. The *Mauretania* made its last voyage in 1934; it was broken up for scrap the following year. Cunard launched a second *Mauretania* (*"Mauretania," Encyclopedia Britannica,* "Mauretania-ship-1906-1935.")

23. "Chelsea Piers History 101"; "Mabel Ida Evans," New York, Passenger Lists, 1820-1957" and "List or Manifest of Alien Passengers for the United States" on the *Mauretania*, departing Southampton on September 18, 1920.

7. At Home on Meigs Street

1. "Introduction to Prosperity and Thrift: The Coolidge Era and the Consumer Economy, 1921-1929," online; "Introduction to Prosperity and Thrift: Merchandising and Advertising," online.
2. *U.S. Census 1920* reported that John Evans was a "salesman" in a dry goods store, Rochester City Directory, 1920.
3. Rochester City Directories, 1920s.
4. Landmarks Preservation Commission, "Madison Belmont Building" (181 Madison Avenue, New York City), 20 September 2011, Madison Bel mont Building.
5. Jacqueline Field, Marjorie Senechal, and Madelyn Shaw, *American Silk, 1830-1930: Entrepreneurs and Artifacts* (Lubbock, Texas Tech University, 2007), xxii.
6. "Fact and Comment," *The American Silk Journal* 33: 2 (February 1914), 25-26.
7. C. R. Clifford, "When the Silk Journal Was Started," and "Forty Years Ago and Now," both in *The American Silk Journal* 41: 1 (January 1922), 67-68 & 65-66. Quote from p. 67.
8. "Fact and Comment," *The American Silk Journal* (February 1914), 33: 2 (February 1914), 25-26; "Fact and Comment," and "For Whom Does the Buyer Buy," *The American Silk Journal*, 33:1 (January 1914), 23-24 and 2 (respectively).
9. Landmarks Preservation Commission, "Madison Belmont Building" (181 Madison Avenue, New York City), 20 September 2011, at J.F. McCandless, buyer, "Reminiscent of Early Silk Buying Days," *The American Silk Journal* (33: 2), 31-32; Clifford, "When the Silk Journal Was Started," 69.
10. "Pinking Shears Corp., 102 Prince St., New York, 1986"; John Evans's pinking shears in G. Evans Papers.
11. "500 Hear Pastor at Joy Dinner of Sibley Employees," *Democrat and Chronicle*, 11 February 1925; "Sibley Employees to Conduct Spring Dance," *Democrat and Chronicle*, 14 May 1930; "Employees of Store Dance and Play Cards," *Democrat and Chronicle*, 15 May 1930; "Sibley Employees to Take Over Park," *Democrat and Chronicle*, 11 July 1930; "Employees of Sibley's Have $24,680 Fund," *Democrat and Chronicle*, 11 February 1931; all at www.DemocratandChronicle.com. "228 New Citizens to Attend Supper," *Democrat and Chronicle*, 15 February 1925; "Store Chorus Conducts Sixth Annual Dinner," *Democrat and Chronicle*, 9 June 1929; "Sibley Chorus Folk Dine at Brockport, *Democrat and Chronicle*, 3 June 1930; www.Democrat and Chronicle.com. The *Democrat and Chronicle* article reporting this gala event included a picture of eight of the committee members responsible for organizing the picnic, including John Evans. "Store Family of Sibley, Lindsay & Curr Enjoy Big Day of Merrymaking Down at Sea

Breeze Park," *Democrat and Chronicle,* 13 July 1930, www.Democratandchronicle.com.

12. "The Department Store, Museum, Sibley, Lindsay & Curr Co., Rochester New York."

13. "Society Gathers for Dinner Talks," *Democrat and Chronicle,* 2 March 1937; "The Cambrian Society of Rochester . . .,"*Democrat and Chronicle,* 24 September 1922, and "Canners' Picnic to Be Held at Manitour Beach," *Democrat and Chronicle,* 20 August 1922.

14. "Welsh to Honor St. David To-day," *Democrat and Chronicle,* 2 March 1925; "Farnum Heads Cambrians," *Democrat and Chronicle,* 2 February 1933; "Welsh Say It with Songs, In Honor of Patron Saint," *Democrat and Chronicle,* 1 March 1942; "Cambrian Society to Meet Tomorrow," *Democrat and Chronicle,* 28 March 1926; "History Obscure, Declares Cambrian Minister, but He Was Great Teacher," *Democrat and Chronicle,* 2 March 1927; "Welshmen to Hear Talk on Australia," *Democrat and Chronicle,* 26 January 1928; "Cambrian Welsh Society to Meet," *Democrat and Chronicle,* 25 January 1930; "Welsh Society Elects," *Democrat and Chronicle,* 3 February 1933; "Welsh Society to Have Dinner," *Democrat and Chron icle,* 24 January 1926; "Welsh Plan Banquet," *Democrat and Chronicle,* 3 February 1926; all at www.Democratandchronicle.com.

15. "Upstate New York Welsh: Rochester Welsh Organize," Ancestry.com. Elmer Davies was associated with the Tire Merchants Association; Edward Lloyd headed the Rochester Cold Storage Packing Company; Arthur L. Griffiths led the Egbert F. Ashley Insurance Company; Llewelyn C. Watkins was a sugar broker; and David Hughes was a grocer; *Democrat and Chronicle,* 10 February 1929, 7; 26 March 1943, 17; 14 January 1968, 52; 9 May 1962, 26; 20 December 1941, 17. "Joins New York Firm of Patent Attorneys," 28 November 1924, and "Rochesterian Admitted to Bar in Patent Court," 14 November 1931, both in *Democrat and Chronicle.*

16. "Sings Praise of Welshmen to Cambrians," *Democrat and Chronicle,* 2 March 1930, p. 9.

17. *Rochester Directory, 1921,* Rochester Public Library. Noyes Bartholomew left Rochester in late 1921 or early 1922. The January 7, 1923 South Congregational Church Sunday calendar, indicating the arrival of a new pastor, Reverend Joseph B. Kettle, after the recent departure of Noyes Bartholomew, noted John Evans's service as a deacon and usher and involvement in the Church Committee. The names of family friends, such as Egbert Cain, deacon, and Mrs. R.C. Harris, president of the Ladies Missionary Society and the mother of J. Harvey Evans's childhood friend Charlie Harris, were also noted in this calendar. "Harvey Evans" scrapbook, G. Evans Papers.

18. "South Congregational Church, cor. Alexander & Pearl Streets, Rochester, NY, Rev. Henry Mosley, Minister," March 2, 1930, in

John Harvey Evans Scrapbook, G. Evans Papers.

19. "South Congregational Church," *Democrat and Chronicle*, 10 April 1925; "Women Alliance to Have Supper," *Democrat and Chronicle*, 3 December 1936, 13; "Sponsors Sale," *Democrat and Chronicle*, 21 October 1938, 19. Charles Harris, who was born and lived in Rochester, later moved to Berea, KY; phone interview by G. Evans, 8 January 2011.

20. Richard Klin, "The Women's Suffrage Movement: Made in New York," *Hudson Valley Magazine*, November 2017.

21. Along with Auley Cain, other South Congregational Church friends of Mabel's included: Mary Howell, Julia Bailey, Mabel Hatch, Alice Denny, Ada Nobles Leaty, Gladys Clapp, Bess Greene, Bertha Will, Helen Curtis Smith, Eunice Daniels, and Martha Philip, G. Evans Papers.

22. "Frank H. Evans," U.S. Veterans Gravesites Transcription. John Evans in Pittsford, NY, letter to John Harvey Evans in Liverpool, 10 March 1937, G. Evans Papers. ("she gets depressed, but nothing like what she used to be.")

23. Image of the house at 516 Meigs Street is at Google maps. See *Rochester Directory* for the years ending 1923, 1924, 1926, 1928, 1929, and 1931, City Directory Collection, Central Library of Rochester and Monroe County.

24. Photo of Clara, Lloyd, and Opal Bartholomew, with identification on the back, in leather scrapbook created by J. Harvey Evans, now in G. Evans Papers.

25. Thomas X. Grasso, *Rochester History*, "The Erie Canal and Rochester: Past, Present, and Future" 72: 1 (Spring 2010), 14-18.

26. Charles R. Harris, letter to Gail and Michael Evans-Hatch, October 10, 1999.

27. Stephanie Harris, Charles and Justin Harris's daughter, remarks given at the "Service of Celebration and Thanksgiving for the Life of Dr. Charles Richard Harris," Union Church, Berea, Kentucky, June 12, 2011, G. Evans Papers.

28. *A History of the Public Schools of Rochester, New York, 1813-1935* (Rochester, NY: Rochester Bd. of Educ., 1935), Charles Harris, interview by G. Evans, 9 January 2011.

29. *A History of the Public Schools of Rochester, New York, 1813-1935* (Rochester, NY: Rochester Board of Education, 1935), Chapter III, "New Days and Ways, 1900-1934."

30. "Mummers" were seasonal folk plays performed by troupes of actors known as "mummers" or "guisers." These plays were popular in England in the eighteenth and nineteenth centuries; "South Congregational Church," Rev. Joseph B. Kettle, pastor, January 27, 1923; and "South Congregational Church," Rev. Robert E. Brown, January 14, 1945; all three in J. Harvey Evans "Scrapbook," G. Evans Papers.

31. "South Congregational Church," *Democrat and Chronicle*, 19 December 1924, p. 10 April 1925, 31; Current Weddings in Rochester Area; Ludwig-Gouger," *Democrat and Chronicle*, 20 July 1936, 9.

32. "Church Club Plans Play," *Democrat and Chronicle*, 21 May 1932.

33. Harvey Evans "Scrapbook," pp. 17, 21, 23, in G. Evans Papers.

34. *A History of the Public Schools of Rochester, New York, 1813-1935,* Chapter III, "New Days and Ways, 1900-1934." J. Harvey Evans, "Scrapbook," G. Evans Family Papers.

35. J. Harvey Evans, "Scrapbook," 4; "A Brief History of the Washington Birthday Exercises, the Washington Convention and the Transfer of Flags, 1889-1939" The Public Schools, Rochester, NY.

36. Harvey Evans "Scrapbook," see "Proposed Course of Study" 1929; "Report Card," Feb. 1932, in G. Evans Papers.

37. J. Harvey Evans Scrapbook, see pp. 14, 15, 16, and 17 (photos, tickets, announcements, etc.), in G. Evans Papers.

38. "743 Boys and Girls Enroll in Airplane Model League," *Democrat and Chronicle*, 1 April 1928, www.DemocratandChronicle.com. Later in his life, J. Harvey Evans listed all twelve ship models he made from plans of Captain E. Armitage McCann in *Popular Mechanics* magazine between the age of twelve and his early twenties. Those models he was most proud of he later donated in the 1960s to the Hart Nautical Collections, at the MIT Museum. Harvey Evans "Scrapbook," photos on pages 17, 19, and 22 and also family/professional papers, G. Evans Papers.

39. A. Isabella Cook, *Pioneer History of Sodus Point, NY,* March 1915, reprinted by the Sodus Bay Historical Society, 1994; Rosa Fox, *Great Sodus Bay (Postcard History Series),* (Charleston, South Caroline, Arcadia Publishing , 1916). Mrs. D. F. McNett, "Great Sodus Bay; A Booklet from 1912," Sodus Point, NY: Sodus Bay Improvement Association, 1912; "History of the Village," in. Harvey Evans "Scrapbook," photos by Doris Cain with IDs on the back, G. Evans Papers.

40. Karl Jacoby, *Crimes against Nature: Squatters, Poachers, Thieves, and the Hidden History of American Conservation* (Berkeley: University of California Press, 2014), 9-28; "The Adirondack Park" website.

41. Ted Rafuse, "Cobourg's Rail Car Ferry History—Part 1, Part 2, and Part 3,"; "Car Ferry 'Ontario No. 1' plying between Charlotte, N.Y. and Coburg, Ont."

42. Photo includes: Hank Robson (?), Etta Cook and Lois Heisler, both South Congregational Church parishioners and participants in church plays: Wayne Baker, Mary Greene, Harvey Evans, Gordon Harris, and Charles Harris, all South Congregational Church members and participants in church plays; in photo album, G. Evans Papers.

43. Rafuse, "Cobourg's Rail Car Ferry History—Part 2. "

44. George Chauncey, "A Gay World, Vibrant and Forgotten," *New York Times;* Darryl W. Bullock, "Pansy Craze: The Wild 1930s Drag Parties that Kickstarted Gay Nightlife;" *The Guardian*; Lucinda Fleeson, "The Gay '30s, *Chicago Magazine*; "How Gay Culture Blossomed During the Roaring Twenties."

45. "Mabel left the dishes to be washed by Harvey and Evan, after many arguments," according to Charles Harris, letter and questionnaire responses to G. Evans, 10 October 1999, in G. Evans Papers. Charles Harris, notes from telephone interview with G. Evans, 8 January 2011, G. Evans Papers.

46. Charles Harris phone interview by G. Evans, 9 January 2011.

47. J. Harvey Evans, "Family Folklore," 1982 or 1985, G. Evans Papers.

48. Charles Harris, letter and questionnaire responses, to G. Evans, 10 October 1999, G. Evans Papers.

49. Harvey Evans, "Family Folklore," 2 January 1985, G. Evans Archives.

50. Rochester History, https://roccitylibrary.org/digital-collections/rochester-history/

51. "Ready-to-Wear," *Encyclopedia of Clothing and Fashion* (The Gale Group, 2005).

52. "Lamont Gives Out Plan after Worst Crash in History," *Democrat and Chronicle,* 30 October 1929, 1.

53. Bennett Lowenthal, "The Jumpers of '29," *The Washington Post*, October 25, 1987.

54. "Market Break Reverberates across Ocean," *Democrat and Chronicle*, 30 October 1929, 16.

55. "Depression in the UK, 1929-30s," online.

56. "A Short History of U.S. White Women's Measurements Used for Patternmaking," online. Madelyn Shaw, "American Silk from a Marketing Magician: H.R. Mallinson & Co.," Digital Commons@University of Nebraska—Lincoln, 2002), 247. Jacqueline Field, Marjorie Senechal, Madelyn Shaw, *American Silk, 1830-1930:Entrepreneurs and Artifacts* (Lubbock, Texas: Texas Tech Univ. Press, 2007), 253-57.

57. Andrew D. Wolfe, *1868-1968, 100 Adventurous and Happy Years of Merchandising/The Story of Sibley, Lindsay & Curr Company of Rochester, Monroe, County, New York* (Rochester, NY: 1968), 37-30.

8. Realizing a Dream

1. "A Short History of Pittsford," online.

2. Robert Corby, "A Brief History of the Village of Pittsford," ca. 2000. "History of the Rochester & Eastern Rapid Railway," online.

3. Trulia Company website for off market details of 179 East Brook Road, Pittsford. "Town Map of Pittsford, 1934," *Pittsford General*

Directory (Boston, Mass: Sampson & Murdock Co., 1934), inside front cover.

4. "Indenture," [sale of 179 East Brook Road to Evanses], original in County Clerk's Office, Monroe County Courthouse, Rochester, copy in G. Evans Papers.

5. "This Indenture, Made the 22 day of September, Nineteen Hundred and thirty between Rhoda A. Renshaw and John Evans and Mabel I. Evans, his wife," County Clerk's Office, Monroe County Courthouse, Rochester, NY; Rochester city directions, 1924, 1925, 1929, 1931, 1932, Central Library of Rochester and Monroe County.

6. "State of New York—Department of Taxation and Finance—Bureau of Motor Vehicles, Operator's License, Harvey Evans "Scrapbook," p. 25; JHE, "Diary Notes" (between January and June 1933). Mabel at some time had an accident and wrecked the Model A, according to family friend Charles Harris. Charles Harris, notes from telephone interview with G. Evans, 8 January 2011, all in G. Evans Papers.

7. "Annual Picnic of Sibley, Lindsay & Curr Group:" *Democrat and Chronicle*, 5 July 1931, 11; "Washington Party Held at Sibley's, *Democrat and Chronicle*, 10 February 1932, 13; DemocratandChronicle.com. "St. David's Day to Be Marked by City Welsh," *Democrat and Chronicle*, 27 February 1932, 15, DemocratandChronicle.com. "Farnum Heads Cambrian," *Democrat and Chronicle*, 2 February 1933, 7; 3 February 1933, *Democrat and Chronicle*, 3 February 1933, 14; Welsh of Rochester Mark St. David's Day, 3 March 1933, DemocratandChronicle.com .

8. Stephen Harvey, "Deaths in the Sub-District of Southend on Sea," and Martha Harvey, "Deaths in the Sub-District of Raleigh," both in Registration District Rochford, General Record Office, Death Certificate, PDF file sent to G. Evans, 15 February 2019. Stephen Harvey, memorial service bulletin, St. Paul's and St. Peter's Church, Hockley, 1931; Newspaper clipping, death notice of Martha Harvey in J. Harvey Evans leather scrapbook, p. 17, G. Evans Papers.

9. Harvey noted in his 1933 diary that he drove Evan to Monroe High School. JHE, "Diary Notes" (between January and June 1933), G. Evans Papers. "Commencement Exercises, Monroe High School, Class of January 1935."

10. "32 Honor Diplomas Are Won at Monroe," *Democrat and Chronicle*, 11 December 1932, 37, DemocratandChronicle.com. "Notes from the Schools—Monroe High," *Democrat and Chronicle*, 8 November 1931, 36, DemocratandChronicle.com.

11. Programs for various plays, Harvey Evans "Scrapbook," 17, 21, 23, and "Report of Entrance Credit," Massachusetts Institute of Technology, July 1932, J. Harvey Evans "Scrapbook," 21, G. Evans Papers.

12. Charles Harris, phone interview by G. Evans, 9 January 2011. "Allen dale Gridders Score Verdict over Pittsford Outfit," 11 October 1932,

newspaper unknown, and "Long Meadow Wins," no date, newspaper unknown, J. Harvey Evans "Scrapbook," in G. Evans Papers, 20, 22. "Pittsford High School—Academic Department," Quarter Report Card, School Year 1932-1933, J. Harvey Evans; J. Harvey Evans "Scrapbook," G. Evans Papers, 22. Decades later, Gail Evans recalled J. Harvey Evans's story of just barely missing the score needed in French for him to be accepted at MIT, and, even then, expressing great disappointment about barely missing it.

13. W. E Hawley, "Certificate of Recommendation," September 14, 1933, for (John) Harvey Evans, G. Evans Papers.

14. JHE, "Diary Notes," between January and June 1933; and John Harvey Evans "Scrapbook," newspaper photos and JHE notes, both in G. Evans Papers.

15. JHE, "Diary Notes," between January June 1933, G. Evans Papers.

16. JHE, "Diary Notes," between January June 1933, G. Evans Papers. Several photos showing Rena Dumas, her mother, plus Mabel, John, J. Harvey, Evan, and Frank taken in Old Forge, New York, August 1933, at Topp's at Old Forge, from Blue Mountain House on Blue Mountain, in Harvey Evans Scrapbook, 23-24, G. Evans Papers.

17. "Weather Underground," Rochester, NY, 22 September 1933, "Chelsea Piers History 101," https://www.chelseapiers.com/company/history/

18. J. Harvey Evans, "Travel Diary," written on pages inside H. A. Frank, *All about Going Abroad* (Brentano's, 1927), G. Evans Papers; hereafter cited as: JHE, "Travel Diary," *Going Abroad,* 1933.

19. JHE, "Travel Diary," 1933. Also see: "New York City—Ambrose Channel," at YODELOUT, New York City History; "Upper New York Bay."

20. All fourteen letters, predominantly bon voyage cards from friends at the South Congregational Church, were saved by Harvey, in G. Evans Papers.

21. JHE, "Travel Diary," *Going Abroad,* 1933, 115, Sept. 23.

9. Britain Becomes Home

1. Sykes, et al., "A City Profile of Liverpool." *J. Cities,* 2013.

2. Museum of Liverpool, *Liverpool: The Story of a City* (Liverpool: Liverpool University Press, 2012), 14; Kelly, *For Advancement of Learning,* 16.

3. Sykes et al., "A City Profile of Liverpool," *J. Cities,* 2013, 1.

4. Museum of Liverpool, *Liverpool: The Story of a City* (Liverpool: Liverpool University Press, 2012), 35; Sykes, et al, "A City Profile of Liverpool," *J. Cities,* 2013, 8.

5. Harvey Evans, handwritten on the back of a map of the docks entitled, "Mersey Dock Estate, Plan of Liverpool Docks, 1930," *Transac-*

tions Institute Naval Architects, LXXII (1930), Plate XXXI, G. Evans Papers.

6. JHE, "Travel Diary," in Harry A. Franck, *All About Going Abroad* (New York: Brentano's Publishers, 1927), 115.

7. *Ibid.*, 115-18.

8. "Uncle Reg," Post Office Telegraphs, sent from Newport, Essex, JHE Papers, G. Evans Papers.

9. JHE, "Travel Diary," in Harry A. Franck, *All About Going Abroad*, 118-19.

10. "The Story of Wales"at BBC – History – Wales, Ward, and Depression.

11. Sykes et al., "A City Profile of Liverpool." *J. Cities*, 2013, 9.

12. N. V. Scarfe, edited by L. Dudley Stamp, *The Land of Britain: The Report of The Land Utilisation Survey of Britain* (London: Geographical Publications Ltd., 1942), 462.

13. "Kingsmans Farmhouse, a Grade II Listed Building in Hullbridge, Essex," online at "British Listed Buildings."

14. JHE, "Family Folklore," 31 January 1985,. 22, G. Evans Papers; "JHE, Family Folklore,"G. Evans Papers.

15. "The Freehold Farm Known as "Kingsmans," 1935, D/DTo E233, Essex Record Office, Chelmsford, Essex. Also quoted in JHE, "Family Folklore," 31 January 1985, 22.

16. JHE, "Family Folklore," 31 January 1985, 22.

17. JHE, "Family Folklore," 31 January 1985; "Agriculture of the County of Essex, 1794—part 1," History House. Mangales are also known as mangel wurzel, or mangold wurzel, and mangold, mangel beet, field beet, and fodder beet; JHE, very small black Charles Pell's Diary"; Travel Diary," in Harry A. Franck, *A" About Going Abroad* (New York: Brentano's Publishers, 1927), 119.

18. JHE, "Travel Diary," in Harry A. Franck, *All About Going Abroad*, 119.

19. Thomas Kelly, *For Advancement of Learning: The University of Liverpool, 1991-1981* (Liverpool, England: University of Liverpool Press, 1981), 196, 266-67.

20. "Basic Biographical Details: George Ashdown Audsley," Dictionary of Scottish Architects (DSA); Archive of the University of Liverpool: Records of Halls of Residence; "44 Ullet Road, A Grade I Listed Building in Liverpool.

21. Louis Rosenhead, *When I Look Back, 1873-1933* (Liverpool: University of Liverpool Press, 1974), 12, 16.

22. Museum of Liverpool, *Liverpool: The Story of a City* (Liverpool: Liverpool University Press, 2012), 14-27; Kelly, *For Advancement of Learning*, 14-15.

23. Kelly, *For Advancement of Learning*, 17; "Liverpool: The University," in *A History of the County of Lancaster, Volume 4*, ed. William Farrer and J. Brownbill (London, 1911), 53-54; *British History*, 53-54; "Liverpool:

The University," ed. Farrer and Brownhill, 53-54, *British History;* "Red Brick University," online; Barni Homden, "What Is a Red Brick University?, online.

24. Kelly, *For Advancement of Learning;* Thomas Bertrand Abell, "Grace's Guide, British Industrial History"; Kelly, *For Advancement of Learning,* 520. In 1940, three years after Harvey completed his studies at the university, Abell became emeritus professor, and the Naval Architecture Department closed. "Thomas Bertrand Abell, "Grace's Guide, British Industrial History"; Kelly, *For Advancement of Learning,* 520, 528; Louis Rosenhead, *When I Look Back, 1873-1933* (Liverpool: University of Liverpool Press, 1974), 12.

25. "A Legacy of the Great Depression," online; —based on the PhD thesis, Charlie Wildman, "Spec tacular Urban Culture in the Age of Decline: Liverpool and Manchester, 1918-1939.

26. Museum of Liverpool, *Liverpool: The Story of a City,* 21, 27-29. Liverpudlians greatly missed the Overhead Railway which was closed in 1956. *Liverpool: The Story of a City,* 35-41; "A Legacy of the Great Depression,"—based on the PhD thesis, Charlie Wildman, "Spectacular Urban Culture in the Age of Decline: Liverpool and Manchester, 1918-1939.

27. JHE, "Charles Pells's Diary," JHE's small black diary, 5 October 1933, G. Evans Papers.

28. JHE, "Charles Pell's Diary, 25 January 1934.

29. Kelly, *For Advancement of Learning,* 139; "Victoria Building, University of Liverpool"; Alan's History Spot, "School of Engineering, Brownlow Hill, Liverpool"; Liverpool, Capital of Culture, Features: "Liverpool's Last Tram."

30. JHE, "Charles Pells's Diary", October 5-December 6, 1933.

31. *Ibid.,* 8-9 December 1933.

32. JHE, "Travel Diary," in Franck, *All About Going Abroad,* 121; Elizabeth Grice, "The Mystery of the Queen's Missing Bouquet," *Daily Telegraph,* 28 August 2007.

33. JHE, "Charles Pells's Dairy," 22 December 1933-3 January 1934.

34. Hetty Evans Rowland (daughter of Tom and Eliza Evans), "Interview with Hetty Rowland," by G. Evans, 2 April 2005; Beryl Rowland Graham, notes from phone interview by G. Evans, 12 March 2017; Beryl Rowland Graham (granddaughter of Hetty Rowland), emails on 5 January 2019 and 15 February 2019 to G. Evans, all items in G. Evans Papers.

35. JHE, "Family Folklore," 31 January 1985; Beryl Elizabeth Cooke (granddaughter of Tom and Eliza Evans), email to Gail Evans, 21 April 2019.

36. Banker Griffith, letter and "Statement of Account with Lloyds Bank Limited," Ferndale, Wales, to J. Harvey Evans, 6 June 1940, G. Evans Family Papers.

37. JHE, "Family Folklore," 31 January 1985, G. Evans Papers.

38. JHE, "Diary," 10 January 1934, G. Evans Papers.
39. *Ibid.*, 4-14 January 1934, G. Evans Papers.

10. Cycling Across England

1. *Ibid.*, 19 February 1934.
2. *Ibid.*, 16 February 1934.
3. *Ibid.*, 24 March–30 April, 7, 14 and 28 May, 1934.
4. *Ibid.*, 19 May and 4 June 1934.
5. Harvey borrowed the motorbike from R. T. Simpson. JHE, "Diary," 30 May 1934.
6. JHE, "Diary," 13 June 1934.
7. JHE, "Diary, 1 July 1934.
8. JHE, "Diary, 5 July 1934.
9. JHE, "Diary," 9 July 1934; *Philips' Road Atlas of Great Britain* (1933-1937), cycle routes marked by Harvey Evans in the 1930s.
10. JHE, "Travel Diary," in Harry A. Franck, *All About Going Abroad,* 127-29.
11. JHE, "Family Folklore," 31 January 1985.
12. Around 1938, Reginald and his family moved to "The Parsonage" near Godalming, Surrey, 40 miles southwest of London. Presumably after leaving Paynes Farm, Reginald Harvey became an estate manager during World War II at Witley Park, near Godalming, Surrey (40 miles southwest of London). Reginald managed the estate of Sir John Leigh, Baronet (3 August 1884-28 July 1959), a British mill-owner, who used his fortune to buy a newspaper and launch his career as a Conservative Member of Parliament. By December 1946, the family had moved to Heydon House south of Cambridge, where Reginald managed two farms—Heydon House farm and Hill Farm. During this period, Reginald worked as an agent for Charles Butler (brother of politician, Richard Austen Butler, known as "RAB" Butler, Member of Parliament for Saffron Walden from 1929 to 1965, Chancellor of the Exchequer under Prime Ministers Winston Churchill and Anthony Eden in the 1950s). Sometime after World War II, Reginald and Winnie moved to Shortgrove, and lived at Sparrow Hill, near Saffron Walden. Nick Hards (grandson of Reginald and Winnie Harvey), email to Gail Evans, 5 April 2019. Also: telegram from Vernon Harvey at Kingston, Jamaica, to his sister Betty at Parsonage House, Witley, Surrey, dated September 1, 1942; J Harvey Evans, list of Reginald and Winnie Harvey family addresses in 1930s and 1940s taken from letters from Betty Harvey, G. Evans Papers.
13. JHE, "Travel Diary," in Harry A. Franck, *All About Going Abroad,* 129.

14. JHE, "Diary," 15-18 August 1934; *Philips' Road Atlas of Great Britain* (1933-1937), cycle routes marked by Harvey Evans in the 1930s.

15. *Ibid.,* 20 August 1934.

16. *Ibid.,* 22 August 1934; 26-29 August 1934; John Evans, letter to JHE, August 1934, G. Evans Papers.

17. Mabel Evans, letter to JHE, 17 August 1934, from Old Forge, NY, G. Evans Papers.

18. JHE, "Family Folklore," 31 January 1985.

19. Hugh Crammer-Byng, *Dialect and Songs of Essex* (Colchester: Benham & Co., 1934), 19-20.

20. JHE, "Diary," 31 August-16 September 1934; *Philips' Road Atlas of Great Britain* (1933-1937), cycle routes marked by Harvey Evans in the 1930s.

21. *Ibid.,* 17-25 September 1934.

22. *Ibid.,* 25-28 September 1934.

23. Sir Walter Scott, "Lochinvar," (1808), https://allpoetry.com/Lochinvar

24. *Ibid.,* 29 August, 1934-1938. Also see JHE's handwritten summary of diary notes, in which he added that his wet clothing had "soaked the paper on the wall where they had hung."

25. JHE, "Diary," 9-14 October 1934.

26. "The University of Liverpool, Faculty of Engineering, Sessional Examination, June, 1935," (students names, courses taken, and grades are listed), Special Collections & Archives, University of Liverpool; JHE, "Diary," 9-31 October 1934, G. Evans Papers.

27. JHE, "Diary," 1 December 1934.

28. *Ibid.,* 14-20 December 1934.

29. *Ibid.,* 25-31 December 1934.

30. "University of Liverpool: A Brief History of Panto Day," Special Collections & Archives, University of Liverpool, online, December 22, 2015.

31. JHE, "Diary," 1, 7, 12, 15, 16, 23 February 1935.

32. *Ibid.,* 18, 19, 20, 21, 26 March 1935.

33. *Ibid.,* 20-26 March, 6-24 April 1935.

34. *Ibid.,* 25-26, 28 January 1935," 28 February, 4 March 1935; "Commencement Exercises, Monroe High School, Class of January 1935," all in G. Evans Papers.

35. *Ibid.,* 3, 7, 13 June.

36. *Ibid.,* 21-22 June.

37. *Ibid.,* 23 June-2 July.

11. At Home in the U.S. and Britain

1. *Rochester Suburban Directory For the Year 1935 Including Towns of Brighton, Gates, Greece, Irondequoit, and Pittsford,* 1935; JHE Diary,

intermittently throughout July, August, and first half of September 1935, G. Evans Papers; JHE Diary, 26-27 September 1935, G. Evans Papers.

2. S.S. *Europa* (1928).

3. JHE, "Diary," 28 September—3 October 1935.

4. *Ibid.*, 4 October 1935; "Particulars, Plan and Condition of Sale of The Freehold Farm Known as Kingsmans," offered for sale by auction by Messrs. H. V. & G. Sorrell, on Saturday 17 April 1935, D/DTo E233, Essex Record Office, Chelmsford, Essex, England.

5. *Ibid.*, 27 October, 3 and 4 November, 9 and 15 December, 1935.

6. *Ibid.*, 9-20 October 1935; "Commencement Exercises, Monroe High School, Class of January 1935," G. Evans Papers; "History of Eastman—History of Eastman School."

7. Vincent A. Lenti, *The Preparatory Department; Historical Origins of Eastman School of Music,* Chapter 2, "Planning and Construction," "History of Eastman—History of Eastman School"; Vincent A. Lenti, "The Prepara tory Department; Historical Origins of Eastman School of Music," Chapter 2, 6-22, typescript, April 1978; "Preparatory Department," *Eastman School of Music: Catalogue, 1935-1937,* 35-39; "Raymond Wilson—Eastman School of Music, Eastman School of Music, University of Rochester, Directory; "Raymond Wilson, Pianist of Note, Latest to Join Instruction Staff of New Eastman School of Music," *Democrat and Chronicle,* 8 March 1921, 1.

8. Evan Evans, letter to JHE, 5 November 1935, G. Evans Papers.

9. "Brother-Sister Club Concert on Wednesday," *Democrat and Chronicle,* 29 February 1932; 17 August 2019; "Tribute: Gladys Leventon," *Yumpu Notes,* June 2005 (Rochester: Eastman School of Music); "Harmony Climaxes Musical Romance," *Democrat and Chronicle,* 26 May 1934, 12; *Democrat and Chronicle,* 19 August 2019.

10. Mabel Evans, letter to JHE, 12 January 1936; Evan Evans, letter to JHE, 13 January 1936; 30 January 1936, and 10 February 1936.

11. Mabel, letter to JHE, 25 October, 1935; Evan, letter to JHE, 5 November 1935; Mabel, letters to JHE, 14 November 1935, and 31 December 1935, and 15 May 1936.

12. Evan Evans, letter to JHE, 5 November 1935; Mabel Evans, letter to JHE, 12 January.

13. "Today and Tomorrow, Fiftieth Anniversary Services Today," South Congregational Church, 18 October 1936, Harvey Evans scrapbook; Mabel, letter to JHE, 14 November 1935, and 12 January 1936, and 15 May 1937.

14. Mabel, letter to JHE, 25 October 1935, and 31 December 1935; JHE Diary, 8 October 1935, G. Evans Papers.

15. JHE "Diary," 5, 7 and 27 November 1935.

16. Blotting papers were made out of an extra-absorbent material that generally includes ingredients such as rice, cotton, and even flax seed, and that readily absorbed moisture.

17. JHE "Diary," 20 December 1935 to 8 January 1936.

18. *Ibid.,* 7 January 1936.

19. *Ibid.,* 3 and 25 February 1936.

20. Evan, letter to Harvey, 10 February 1936.

21. Mabel, letter to JHE, 13 February 1936; Mabel, letter to JHE, 19 February 1936; JHE Diary, 5 and 9 March 1935.

22. JHE "Diary," March 20, 21, 23, 25, 26, 27, 30, and 31; April 3, 6, 7, 9, 10, 13, 16, 17, 20, 21 1936.

23. Mabel, letter to JHE, 3 April and 15 May 1936; JHE Diary, 24 April 1936.

24. "RMS Queen Mary Ship–History, Specifications, Facts," online; "RMS Queen Mary," online; "Queen Mary Brings Back to Britain the Blue Riband of the Atlantic," online.

25. Mabel, letters to JHE, 14, 15 May, 1 June 1936; JHE Diary 5 May, 8 May, 13 May 1936.

26. Mabel, letter to JHE, 15 May 1936.

27. Evan, letter to JHE, 5 November and 5 December 1935; John, letter to JHE, 1 July 1936.

28. Frank, letter to JHE, 5 December 1935.

29. Mabel, letter to JHE, 14 May, 1 June, and 16 October 1936.

30. JHE "Diary," 29 May; 18, 20, 21 June 1936.

31. Evan, letter to JHE, 2 July 1936.

32. Evan, letter to JHE, 31 August 1936.

33. *Ibid.*

34. Mabel Evans, letter to JHE, 26 April 1937.

35. George Chauncey, "A Gay World, Vibrant and Forgotten,"*New York Times*, 26 June 1994, online; "LGBT History in the United States," online; Erin Blakemore, "This Short-Lived 1930s Speakeasy Was a Sanctuary for Gay Londoners," online; Tania Branigan, "Pride and Prejudice in the Gay 1920s," online; Lucinda Fleeson, "The Gay '30s," *Chicago Magazine*, November 2005, online.

36. Evan, letter to JHE, 2 July 1936.

12. Travel Adventures

1. M.V. *Abosso*; "Official Log-Book," M.V. *Abosso*, Official No. 164265, voyage to west coast of Africa, The National Archives, Kew, London, England; Crew List Index Project ("CLIP"), Part I: Alpha betical List of British Registered Steam Vessels"; JHE, diary of five weeks on the M.V. *Abosso*, July 15-August 20, 1936, handwritten and typescript.

2. JHE "Diary," 29, 30 June and 2, 6, 8-10, 13-15 July.

3. JHE "Diary," *Abosso* Log, 15 July 1936, p. 1, typescript.

4. *Ibid.*, 1.

5. *Ibid.*, 1.

6. *Ibid.,*" Diary" *Abosso* Log, 18 July 1936, 2-3, typescript.
7. *Ibid.*
8. *Ibid., Abosso* Log, 18 July 1936, 4, typescript, and 20-21 July 1936, 6, typescript.
9. *Ibid., Abosso* Log, 23 July 1936, pp. 7-9, typescript.
10. *Ibid., Abosso* Log, 25, 28-30 July 1936, 12-14, typescript; and JHE Diary, 25-28, 30 July 1936.
11. *Ibid.,* 4 August 1936; JHE "Diary" *Abosso* Log, 4, 5 August 1936, 20-21, typescript.
12. *Ibid., Abosso* Log, 15-16 August 1936, 21-24, typescript.
13. *Ibid., Abosso* Log, 19-20 August 1936, 25-27, typescript; JHE Diary, 12-22, August 1936.
14. *Ibid.,* 25-28 August 1936.
15. "Cairngorms National Park," online; JHE Diary, 29 August-2 September 1936.
16. JHE "Diary," 29 August-2 September 1936.
17. George Philip & Son, Ltd., "Philips' Main Road Map of Great Britain" (London, no date; presumed in the 1930s), G. Evans Papers.
18. JHE "Diary," 5-7 September 1936.
19. *Ibid.,* 8 September-5 October 1936.
20. *Ibid.,* 10 September 1936 and 5 October 1936.
21. *Ibid.,* 6-8 October 1936.
22. *Ibid.,* 23 November 1936.
23. *Ibid.,* 25-26 November and 1 December 1936.
24. *Ibid.,* 18 December 1936.
25. *Ibid.,* 12 December 1936.
26. Nansi Pugh, *The Liverpool Welsh Choral Union: The First 100 Years* (Liverpool: Countyvise Ltd, 2007).
27. JHE Diary, 14 October, 4, 11, 13 and 14 November 1936; E. Edward, secretary of the Liverpool Welsh Choral Union, letter to Mr. Evans, 15 October 1936; "Central Hall, Renshaw Street, Liverpool, 37th Season, 1936-1937" brochure; "Welsh Choral Union's "Elijah" newspaper article; all in Harvey Evans scrapbook, G. Evans Papers.
28. JHE "Diary," 14-18 December 1936.
29. *Ibid.,* 26 November, 2-31 December 1936.
30. *Ibid.,* 7, 15, and 18 January 1937 and 2, 4, 6, 9 and 23 February 1937, and 2, 6, and 18 March 1937.
31. *Ibid.,* 10 February 1937.
32. *Ibid.,* 12 February 1937.
33. Frank Evans, letter to JHE, 22 February 1937; JHE Diary, 5 March 1937.
34. JHE "Diary," 20, 21, 22, 23, 26 February 1937.
35. *Ibid.,* 19 February 1937.
36. *Ibid.,* 20 and 22 February 1937; Tom Evans, letters to JHE, 22 February and 3 March 1937.
37. *Ibid.,* 9 and 10 March 1937.

38. John Evans, letter to JHE, 10 March 1937.
39. JHE "Diary," 20 March 1937.
40. Harvey reconstructed his cycling adventure through the South Downs coastal area. According to him, he became lulled into oblivion by the lovely spring air, singing birds, the fresh scent of cut grass, the sight of a tiny, quaint Norman church, and two wooden windmills atop a hill he cycled by. Additionally, he took two wrong turns. When the sun dropped behind the western hills, it became painfully cold. After Harvey arrived in Brighten in total darkness, he managed to call his Uncle Tom and explain his predica ment, who relayed the message to Rollo not far away, who came to rescue him and pay for the two of them and the bicycle to ride the train to Worthing. The story of Harvey's misadventures on Rollo's bicycle was told many times years later by Rollo and Hetty with a great smirk on their faces. JHE, "45 miles of pre-April Foolishness," 31 March 1937; JHE Diary, 29 March–3 April 1937.
41. JHE, "Diary," 23 March–17 and 22 April 1937.
42. *Ibid.*, 26, 29-30 April, 4 May 1937, G. Evans Papers; Ethel Langridge, letter to JHE, 2 July 1937.
43. *Ibid.*, 10 May 1937; "Ede & Ravenscroft; the Company."
44. John Evans, letter to JHE, 4 May 1937.
45. *Ibid.*
46. John Evans, letter to JHE, 18 May 1937.
47. JHE, "Diary," 19 May 1937 and JHE Diary, 7-9, 14-18, etc., 20 May 1937.

13. Falling in Love

1. JHE, handwritten recollections, May 12, 1937.
2. JHE, handwritten recollections of May 12, 1937; JHE Diary, 11-13 May 1937; "Edward Stanley, 17th Earl of Derby"; "Knowsley Hall, Prescot, Merseyside, Historic Houses," "A Sense of Place," From Pitt Street to Granby," online.
3. JHE, "Diary," 13, 14, 17, 20, 21, 23, 25, and 27 May and 1, 14, 15, 17, 22, 24, 25, and 30, June, and 1-2 July 1937.
4. *Ibid.*, 19 June 1937.
5. *Ibid.*
6. *Ibid.*, 29 June 1937.
7. T. B. Abell, Alexander Elder Professor of Naval Architecture, letter of recommendation for Mr. J. Harvey Evans, ca. June 1937, envelope in JHE scrapbook, unnumbered pages, G. Evans Papers.
8. JHE, "Diary," 6-12, 15-20 July 1937.
9. Harvey's letter to Bethlehem Shipbuilding Company was written at the Reginald and Winnie Harvey , Sparrows Hill Farm, G. Evans Papers.

10. "Today and Tomorrow, Fiftieth Anniversary Services Today," South Congregational Church, October 18, 1936, Harvey Evans scrapbook, G. Evans Papers.

11. Letter, Mabel and also John Evans to JHE, June (postmarked June 22); "Arthur Burton Kettle,"Ancestry," Arthur Kettle, "manager, steel mill," 1930, U.S. Census; Arthur Kettle, "department manager," 1938. Ancestry, City Directories, 1822-1995; Austin-Hast ings Co., Inc., *A Century of Progress in New England* (Cambridge, Mass: Austin-Hastings, 1949, unnumbered page featuring Arthur B. Kettle.)

12. JHE, thoughts written on United States Lines stationery, 23 July 1937, G. Evans Papers.

13. Evan Evans, letter to J. Harvey Evans, 23 February 1937.

14. JHE, "Diary," 23 and 24 July 1937.

15. JHE, thoughts written on United States Lines stationery, 23 July 1937, G. Evans Papers.

16. *Ibid.*, G. Evans Papers.

17. JHE, "Diary," 23-30 July 1937.

18. JHE, "Debts," 1938, "Total English Debts, 1944," G. Evans Papers.

19. JHE, "Diary," 31 July to 3 August 1937.

14. Approaching War

1. "One Looks at Germany," *The Sphinx,"* October 1933, 13.

2. "Obstacles to World Peace and Their Removal," *The Sphinx,* February 1934, 26.

3. J. Harvey Evans Diary, 28 September-3 October 1935, G. Evans Papers. Hereafter cited as: JHE, "Diary," [with date.]; "The Jew," *The Sphinx,* June 1935, 24.

4. "Air Raid on Liverpool," *The Sphinx,* July 1938, 18-19.

5. Thermite is a combination of metal powder and metal oxide. When ignited, thermite undergoes a reduction-oxidation reaction. Most thermites are not explosive, but can create bursts of heat and high temperature in a small area; "Rearmament and the Student," *The Sphinx,* November 1937, 14-15.

6. JHE, "Diary," 4-21 August 1937.

7. JHE, "Diary," 29 August 1937, 23 October 1937, and 30 August-6 September 1937.

8. "Charles W. Allen," U.S. Census 1930 and 1940.

9. "Kings County, Nova Scotia"; "Grand-Pré, Nova Scotia"; "Township of Horton, Acadia University Library," Malinda Barton Burton, "Canada Births and Baptisms, 1661-1959"; "Canada Census, 1881"; "Canada Census, 1891"; "Charles Wesley Allen; Massachusetts Marriages, 1841- 1915" for "Malinda" Burton and Charles Wesley Allen give their marriage location as Newton, Massachusetts. " United States Census, 1900."

10. Thomas Weston, *History of the Town of Middleboro, Massachusetts* (Boston and New York: Houghton, Mifflin and Company, 1906), 477-80.

11. Steve Annear, "Newton's Second Baptist Church Celebrates 175th Anniversary," *Wicked Local Newton*. All four of the Allen's' children were born in Middleboro. Eugene Edward Allen, born 14 February 1901, married Doris Leola Thompson in 1931 and became a doctor who practiced in New York City. Gladys Burton Allen, born 21 June 1902, married Judson Stewart MacGre gor. Herman Loring Allen and twin Fred Wesley Allen were born 28 January 1906. Herman received four years of college and became a business manager, following World War II, when he was in the Signal Corps Reserves. Later, he worked in a bank in downtown Boston for many years. Twin brother, Fred, may have died at a young age. "C.W. Allen Accepts Call to Milford Church," *Middleborough Gazette*, 18 March 1910; Thomas Weston, *History of the Town of Middleboro, Massachusetts* (Boston and New York Houghton, Mifflin & Company, 1906), 477- 80; *The Boston Transcript*, "Dedham"; Frank Smith, *A History of Dedham, Massachusetts* (Dedham, Massachusetts: Transcript Press, 1936), 98-98; "Dedham's History"; "Original Settlers of Dedham, Massachusetts"; Rev. Charles W. Allen," obituary, *Quincy Patriot Ledger*, 8 December 1948.

12. Eugene Allen married Doris, and Gladys, the Allen's second child, married Judson MacGregor; "Destroyer History Founda tion"; "History: A Brief Survey of Weymouth's Past"; "Wessagusset Colony"; "Town of Weymouth: Open Space and Recreation Plan."

13. Nathan Eusebius Wood (1849-1937) and Nathan Robinson Wood (1874-1961), grandfather and father, respectively; both wrote well-respected theological books, some still being republished in the early twenty-first century (including *The History of the First Baptist Church in Boston (1665-1899)*, Philadelphia: American Baptist Publication Society, 1899). Nathan R. Wood, after studying at Harvard, Newton Theological Institute, and in Germany, went to Gordon College to teach in 1908, but soon became an administrator. He then became the dean of the school in 1910. In 1919 he became president of Gordon College. See "Nathan E. Wood, The Online Books Page," online; "Nathan R. Wood–Gordon College," online.

14. Doris Fernald Cotton, *Letters to My Grandchildren* (Jackson, NH: Jackson Historical Society, 2004), 22, 24.

15. Cotton, *Letters to My Grandchildren, Memories of Jackson*, 22, 24, 26; Alice Warwick Pepper (daughter of Nathan & Doris Wood), phone interview by G. Evans, 23 October 2020.

16. *Ibid.*, 38-43, 63; Margaret B. Garland, *Yesterdays: Lodging Places of Jackson and Their Recipes* (Jackson, NH, Jackson Historical Society).

17. John Harvey Evans (JHE), "Mt. Adams (5,808 feet)," October 1938, "Mountain Climbing Logs." Trails taken were marked on a U.S.

Department of Agriculture, Forest Service map, "White Mountain National Forest, New Hampshire and Maine," 1939, G. Evans Papers.

18. JHE, "Diary," 7-9 September 1937; 9 September 1937.

19. JHE, "Diary," 30 September, 3; 17 October 1937, 21; 28 December 1937; Betty Harvey, letter to J. Harvey Evans, 18 July 1942. This letter mentions that Betty saw Desmond when home on leave from the Orkneys in early June 1942; JHE, "Diary," 9 and 16 December 1937 and 12 September 1937 and 23 & 26 February 1938.

20. JHE, "Diary," 1 and 8 December 1937; 16, 22 November 1937; 12 December 1937; 8 October 1937; 6 November 1937; 16 November 1937.

21. JHE, "Diary," 3 April 1938.

22. JHE, "Diary," 25 October 1938.

23. Phyllis Hargreaves, letter to JHE, 9 July 1937, G. Evans Family Papers.

24. Phyllis Hargreaves, letter to JHE, 26 August 1937.

25. Phyllis Hargreaves, letter to JHE, 19 December 1937, 25 March 1938, and 3 May 1938.

26. JHE, "Diary," 24-27 December 1937; 9 October, 24-28; November, 24-27 December 1937; 31 December 1937.

27. JHE, Calendar ("Mass Gears"), 12 August 1938; 13, 15, 16, 18, 19, 23, 26 September 1938; 1, 3 October 1938; JHE, "Diary," mid-late July 1938; J. Harvey Evans, interview by Robbie Mason, February 1989, in Lexington, Massachusetts; JHE, Calendar ("Mass Gears"), 8 July 1938; JHE, Diary, 6, 16, 23, and 28 August 1941; all in G. Evans Papers.

28. "USS *Salem* CA-139; the Only Preserved U.S. Naval Heavy Cruiser," online.

29. JHE, "Diary," 13 and 17 September, 1937; 23 September 1937; 17 and 30 September; 4, 14, 19 October 1937; 5 and 8 November 1937; 15 January; 2, 8, and 9 February; 13, 19, 23 May 1938; 24 September 1928; Photo of S.S. *Panama* with JHE notation on back: "worked on at Bethlehem Steel Co."; "S.S. *Panama*, a Proud Ship of the Panama Line,"; Wayne G. Miller, *Quincy Massachusetts: A Shipbuilding Tradition* (Quincy, MA: Quincy Historical Society, 2017), 164; William Churchill Edwards, *Historic Quincy, Massachusetts* (Quincy, Mass: City of Quincy, 1957), 220-21, 223; Anthony F. Sarcone and Lawrence S. Rines, *A History of Shipbuilding at Fore River* (Quincy, MA: Department of History, Quincy Junior College, 1975), 23, 24, 25; Miller, *Quincy Massachusetts: A Shipbuilding Tradition*, 165.

30. 28. Finance Officer, The University of Liverpool, to J. Harvey Evans, 6 July 1938, 29 September 1938, 24 February 1939, 4 October 1939, 15 July 1940, 6 September 1940; "Institution of Naval Architects," London, 3 April 1941, to J.H. Evans, Esq., B.Eng.

31. Mr. Griffith, Lloyds Bank Limited, Ferndale, Glam. to "Mr. J. Harvey Evans," 15 Arcadia Road, Weymouth, Mass, 14 June 1940, G. Evans Papers.

32. Ravenscroft & Willis, Academical Robe Makers, September 1940 to J. H. Evans, Esq., B. Eng., September 1940, G. Evans Papers.

33. "United States Maritime Commission," Frederic C. Lane, *Ships for Victory: A History of Shipbuilding under the U.S. Maritime Commission in World War II* (Johns Hopkins University Press, 1950).

34. Miller, *Quincy Massachusetts*, 165.

35. JHE, "Diary," 27 September 1938.

36. "Hitler Granted the Sudentenland by Britain, France, and Italy," *The New York Times*, 30 September 1938.

37. Susan Dunn, "The Debate behind U.S. Intervention in World War II," *The Atlantic,* July 8, 2013.

38. "Naval Act of 1938,"J. David Rogers, "Development of the World's Fastest Battleships," The Second Vinson Act (1938).

39. "Fore River Shipyard Production Record," htps://everything.explained.today/List_of_ships_built_at_the_Fore_River_Shipyard/

40. "Sept. 27, 1941: First Liberty Ship Launched, More to Follow," at https://www.wired.com/2011/09/0927first-liberty-ship-launched/

41. Local Board #159, Town Hall, Weymouth, Norfolk County, Massachusetts, "Notice of Classification," John Harvey Evans, Class II-B, Sept. 30, 1941, 2-B; October 23, 1942; 2-B, Nov. 24, 1942-May 23, 1943; 2-B November 23, 1943; 2-B, May 1, 1944; 2-B October 1, 1945; 2-B May 1, 1945; then 4-A, Dec. 27, 1945; G. Evans Papers.

42. Phyllis Hargreaves, letter to J. Harvey Evans, 18 May 1943.

43. "The Harrison Hughes Engineering Building after being struck by a land mine on 13 March 1941," at University of Liverpool Library.

44. Phyllis Hargreaves, letter to J. Harvey Evans and Edith Evans, 16 December 1943.

45. J. Harvey Evans, letter to Phyllis Crossley, 24 March 1943.

15. Harvey and Evans Families Together at War

1. Vernon S. Harvey, letter to his sister, Betty Harvey, no date, Geraldine Harvey Newmark (Betty's daughter) Papers.

2. Hilda Ellen Harber, WAAF (Women's Auxiliary Air Force). Angus Calder, *The People's War: Britain, 1939-1945* (London: Jonathan Cape, 1969); https://www.nationalarchives.gov.uk/education/resources/home-front/

3. Angus Calder, *The People's War: Britain, 1939-1945,* (London: Jonathan Cape, 1969); "United Kingdom Home Front during World War II," "Women in World War II."

4. "Wrecksite – Boulderpool Cargo Ship, 1928-1941," https://www.wrecksite.eu/wreck.aspx?70275; Radio Society of Great Britain, "Radio Officers' Association, https://rsgb.org/main/clubs/special-interest-groups/radio-officers-association-roa/; Vernon S. Harvey, letter to Betty Harvey (his sister), Turkish flood noted, no date; Vernon S. Harvey, letter to Betty Harvey, from Quebec, October 1939; both in Geraldine Hards Newmark (Betty's daughter) Family Papers; J. Harvey Evans, letter to Phyllis Crossley, 24 March 1943, G. Evans Papers.

5. Betty Harvey, letter to Harvey Evans, 15 July 1942, G. Evans Papers.

6. JHE mentioned in a letter to Phyllis Crossley that Vernon's freighter was torpedoed in August 1942, JHE letter to Phyllis Cross ley, 24 March 1943, G. Evans Papers.

7. "Torpedoed Yes, Terrified No" Jamaican newspaper and "Post Office Telegram", 1 September 1942; both in Nick Hards' Family Papers. The newspaper was presumably published in August 1942 (based on a reference to this date in a letter from J. Harvey Evans to Phyllis Crossley in England, written on 24 March 1943).

8. Nick Hards, email to Gail Evans, Jenny Bibby, David Langridge, Tim Harvey, and Wayne Gardner, 1 December 2019, G. Evans Papers.

9. Sheil Ouzerdine, email to Gail Evans, 14 May 2020, G. Evans Papers.

10. Desmond Henry Langridge, account of his World War II military service and a second account by Desmond Harvey entitled, "Desmond Henry Langridge," in David Langridge Family Papers; The Miniature Armoured Fighting Vehicle Association, "Weybourne Camp, 1944," online.

11. JHE, letter to Phyllis Crossley, 24 March 1943.

12. Betty Harvey, letter to J. Harvey Evans, 15 July 1942, G. Evans Papers; Desmond Langridge, account entitled, "Desmond Henry Langridge," in David Langridge Papers; Betty Harvey, letter to Harvey Evans, 15 July 1942, G. Evans Papers. Desmond may have just missed being on a boat to the Orkneys. His boat just missed being bombed.

13. Desmond Henry Langridge, account of his World War II military service, David Langridge Papers.

14. Clare Jocelyne Harvey, email to Gail Evans, 16 May 2020; Arthur Jocelyne, "One Fine May Morning" (account of evacuation), unknown date written, Clare Jocelyne Harvey Papers.

15. Beryl Cooke (granddaughter of Tom Evans), email to Gail Evans, 27 December 2018.

16. Keith Archibald Forbes, "Bermuda's History from 1939 World War 2 to 1951"; Evan Evans, letter to "Mom, Dad, and Frank," 24 April 1941, 5 May 1941, in G. Evans Papers.

17. Evan Evans, letter to Gail Evans, 27 October 1973. "I had a great letter from Phil, my alter ego and old Army sidekick. (I used to mention his daughter, Claudia, who had a ballet scholarship at Bennington a few years ago.) Among other things, he invited me in his letter to come down to Florida to vacation; he momentary lost his head and forgot that nothing, including my affection for him, could possibly budge me out of New England now that Fall and Winter are upon us . . . "; Evan Evans, card to Edith and Harvey Evans, 19 April 1966, in which Evan mentioned Phil calling him from New Jersey and reporting that his daughter, Claudia had a scholarship at Sarah Lawrence; G. Evans Papers. Over five million men served in the British armed forces during World War Of these, it is likely that at least 250,000 were gay or bisexual (based on projections from the 1990-91 National Survey of Sexual Attitudes and Lifestyles The National Survey of Sexual Attitudes and Lifestyles (NATSAL) is the name given to a series of face-to- face surveys of people in the United Kingdom regarding their sexual behavior and patterns. The results are widely used in research and policymaking. NATSAL's principal investigator is Anne Johnson, a professor at University College, London, and co-leader Kaye Wellings, a professor at the London School of Hygiene & Tropical Medicine "The Conversation," "Belles in Battle: How Queer US Soldiers Found a Place to Express Themselves in WWII, 18 December 2017.

18. Evan Evans, letters to "Dear Mom, Dad, and Frank," 7 June 1941, 5 May 1941, letter to "Dear Mom, Dad, and Frank," 15 July 1941; "My dearest Mom, Dad, and Frank," 1 November 1941; and "My darlin kids," 24 December 1941; G. Evans Papers.

19. JHE, letter to Phyllis Hargreaves Crossley, 24 March 1943.

20. "Evan R. Evans," untitled single-lined page, no date, filed as "Momentos of Evan," "Enlisted Record and Report of Separation, Honorable Discharge," Evans, Evan R., Army Serial No. 32031 644, Grade Tech. 5; JHE, letter to Phyllis Hargreaves, 27 October 1943; Evans, Evan R., "Enlisted Record and Report of Separation, Honorable Discharge"; both in G. Evans Papers.

21. "Bermuda during the Second World War," *The Bermudian,* April 27, 2019.

22. Memo, "From the Desk of J. Harvey Evans," April 29, 1945 (Major Eugene E. Allen); "Notice of Change of Address" for Prt. Herman L. Allen, March 10, 1944, to Mr. and Mrs. J. Harvey Evans in Weymouth, Massachusetts; Memo "From the Desk of J. Harvey Evans," both in J. Harvey Evans's "Address" book dating from the 1940s and 1950s, G. Evans Papers.

23. Miller, *Quincy Massachusetts: A Shipbuilding Tradition,* 165; J. Harvey Evans, interview by Robbie Mason, February 1989.

24. "Bethlehem Steel Company, Quincy, MA, (most recently updated April 2, 2019).

25. "'Winnie the Welder': Former Female Shipbuilder Recalls War Days," *The Patriot Ledger*; "Emergency Shipbuilding Program."

26. J. Harvey Evans, interview by Robbie Mason, February 1989.

27. JHE, letter to Phyllis Hargreaves Crossley, 24 March 1943.

28. J. Harvey Evans, long hours worked at Fore River recorded on April 26, 1944; May 15, 17, 19, 22, 24, 26, 29, 31, June 2, 12, 14, 16; July 2, 4, 7, 9, 16, 21, 23, 25, 28, 30, Sep 1, 7; Birth of David in Milton Hospital, October 7-20, 1944; G. Evans Papers.

29. William Churchill Edwards, *Historic Quincy, Massachusetts* (City of Quincy, Massachusetts, 1957), 231; "USS *Quincy* History.

30. The wedding took place at 4:30 on July 3. Frank Evans was the best man, Marguerite Goodrich was maid of honor, and Helen Bryant played the organ. The bride and groom stayed the evening of July 3 at Longfellow's Wayside Inn, in South Sudbury, Massachusetts. "Edith Price Bride Today of J.H. Evans," unidentified newspaper clipping in "The Bridal Book" of Edith and Harvey Evans; all G. Evans Papers. The couple honeymooned in Jackson, New Hampshire; Evans family folklore. "J. Harvey Evans, Edith Price Married," *Democrat and Chronicle*, July 1943.

    Harvey and Edith Evans were extraordinarily busy in October and November 1944. David's birth on October 7 proved difficult; his voice afterwards was "husky." "A little surgery" was performed on David on October 14. Edith and David stayed in the hospital for thirteen days before coming home. Mrs. Doris Wood, Edith Erickson, and Price family members came to 555 North Street to help Edith with David. Evan arrived on furlough from Bermuda on November 20, probably on his way to see Mabel and John in Pittsford. Harvey came down with the grippe in the second week of November, and stayed in bed for several days. Then, in the third week in November, Harvey, Edith, and friends helped them pack up their belongings and move to 31 Totnes Road in Braintree. After December 17, 1944 there were no more entries in Harvey's diary for the rest of the year, suggesting that news of his father's failing health and his death on December 28 fully occupied Harvey's time and all his thoughts. Harvey Evans's "Toledo" "Daily Reminder of Important Matters," 1944, G. Evans Papers.

31. Miller, *Quincy Massachusetts: A Shipbuilding Tradition*, 167-67.

32. "USS *Salem* CA-139 (a Des Moines-class heavy cruiser); the "Only Preserved U.S. Naval Heavy Cruiser."

33. "U.S., School Yearbooks, 1880-2012," 1943; "Altobell Group Starts Season Tomorrow," *Democrat and Chronicle*, 8 June 1939; "Summer Group Offers Play Tonight," *Democrat and Chronicle*, 16 June 1939; "Churchville, Pittsford Bag County Titles," *Democrat and Chronicle*, 25 May 1944; "Episcopal Diocese of Rochester," "My dear Mr. Frank

Harold Evans, satisfied that you have met the requirements of Canon 1, & 1., I have admitted you as a Postulant in this Diocese," 29 May 1944, Bartel H. Reinheimer; Bartel H. Rein- heimer, letter to Frank H. Evans, 13 Brook Road, Pittsford, 9 June 1944, which said in part:

"What you have written in your letter of June sixth confirms the impression which I formed at the time of our recent interview. I am therefore with confidence accepting you as a Postulant for Holy Orders in the Episcopal Church and am inclosing a Certificate."

While you are in military service I shall remember you in my prayers, and I hope that the war will end soon so that you can enter college. When that time comes you will want to consult with your rector and with me as to the choice of courses for your pre-theological work."

"Army of the United States: Certificate of Service," Frank H. Evans, 2 November 1945; "Enlisted Record and Report of Separation, Certificate of Service," Evans, Frank H., A.A. Anderson, Captain Air Corps, 12-5-46; copies of all documents in G. Evans Papers; Louis Dansami, Sergeant, card sent to "Mr. J. Harvey Evans at 555 North Street, Weymouth, 18 October 1943"; "Christ Church, Pittsford, N.Y.," 30 January 1944 bulletin, G. Evans Papers; Episcopal Diocese of Rochester, "My dear Mr. Frank Harold Evans, Satisfied that have met the requirements of Canon 1, § 1., I have admitted you as a Postulant in this Diocese. The date of record thereof is May 26, 1944. Faithfully yours, Bartel H. Reinheimer, Rochester, June 2, 1944;" David Hefling, email communica tion with Gail Evans-Hatch, January 29, 2018.

34. "Army of the United States, Certificate of Service, "Frank H. Evans, 12 239 671, Private First Class, 2140th AAF Base Unit"; Mabel Evans, letter to Harvey and Edith Evans, December 1944; both in G. Evans Papers (Frank Harold Evans file); J. Harvey Evans, 5 July 1944, calendar noted Frank's departure to Fort Dix; J. Harvey Evans, "Addresses," Frank H. Evans, scrap of paper inserted in "Addresses"; both in G. Evans Papers; Mabel Evans, letter to Harvey and Edith Evans, 555 North Street, Weymouth, Mass., 23 October 1944, Pittsford, J. Harvey Evans "Addresses" book; G. Evans Papers; Mabel Evans, postcard to Harvey and Edith Evans at 555 North Street, Weymouth, Mass., 18 July 1944; paper scrap with Frank's typed address at Greenwood A.A.F., no date; in G. Evans Papers.

35. "India Command," https://www.britishmilitaryhistory.co.uk/documents-india-1930-1947/

36. Maggie Farley, "Gurkha Soldiers Losing Battle against Extinction," *Los Angeles Times*, 11 January 1994; Jessica Brain, "The Gurkha Rifles," https://www.gurkhabde.com/the-second-world-war/

37. Tim Harvey, email to Gail Evans, 2 and 10 January 2020; Tim Lambert, "A Brief History of Burma," http://www.localhistories.

org/burma/html; Tim Lambert, "A Brief History of Sri Lanka," http://www.localhistories.org/srilanka.html; "The Forgotten Force: the Gurkhas and the Partition of India, Super vised by Dr. Talat Ahmed, online; Maggie Farley, "Culture: Gurkha Soldiers Losing Battle Against Extinction: Famed for Their Curved knives and Do-or-Die Spirit, They Are Bowing to Budge Cuts and New Technology, *Los Angeles Times,* January 11, 1994; Stephen's "War Department Driving Permit" expired on 17 April 1948, suggesting that he didn't remain in the army after that date. Tim Harvey and Penny Harvey Papers, England.

38. Stephen Geoffrey Harvey, ID card, serial 157907, 19 July 1946, Tim and Penny Harvey Family Papers, England; "Indian Army Service Corps."

39. Bruce Hoffman, "The Palestine Police Force and the Challenges of Gathering Counterterrorism Intelligence, 1939-1947"; Learning Network, "Nov. 29, 1947; U.N. Partitions Palestine, Allowing for Creation of Israel."

40. Betty Harvey, letter to JHE, 15 July 1942, G. Evans Papers.

41. Typed extracts from letters from Mabel and John to Harvey, 1934-1937; "John Evans, 1940 United States Federal Census."

42. John Evans, letter to Harvey Evans in Liverpool, 10 March 1937 and Mabel Evans, letter to Harvey Evans, 28 March 1937, in which she wrote: "This is certainly one big trial and I am afraid if it were not so near the end [of your education at Univ. of Liverpool], we would have to change our plans somehow, but I guess we can struggle on for a few more weeks." G. Evans Papers.

43. "State of New York, Supreme Court, County of Monroe, The East Side Savings Bank of Rochester against John Evans, Mabel I. Evans his wife, Rhoda A. Renshaw and Edward H. Rhine," November 3, 1919, recorded and dated June 27, 1940, Monroe County Courthouse, Rochester, NY.

44. "This Indenture," between John Evans and Mabel I. Evans and David Renshaw and Rhoda A Renshaw, September 13, 1941, Monroe County Courthouse, Rochester; Pittsford, New York city directory, 1940, at https://www.libraryweb.org/rochsubdir/1940/1940names-pittsford.pdf; "13 Brook Rd., Pittsford, NY," online at https://www.zillow.com/homedetails/13-Brook-Rd-Pittsford-NY-14534/31026239_zpid/

45. JHE, "Family Folklore," 31 January 1985.

46. Mass Gears, 1941 Calendar, March 20 and August 6, 1941, G. Evans Papers.

16. An End and a Beginning

1. Dr. Roland C. Harris, letter to Harvey Evans, 31 Totnes Road, Braintree, Mass., 20 December 1944, G. Evans Papers.
2. J. Harvey Evans, "Family Folklore . . . More Notes," 1 December 1982, "Family Folklore"; references are all in G. Evans Papers.
3. "John Evans, Certificate of Death New York State Department of Health," December 28, 1944.
4. *Ibid.*
5. "Today at South Church," "In Memoriam," 14 January 1945, G. Evans Papers.
6. "Dear Members of South Church . . ., From the Desk of Mr H. Evans," penciled thoughts, c. early January 1944, G. Evans Papers.
7. H. N. Gilbert, Army Service Forces, Office of Dependency Benefits, 30 January 1945, letter to Mrs. Mabel Evans, 31 Totnes Road, Braintree, Mass., re. Evans, Evan R.; also hand-written note by Mabel Evans on "Mr. H. Evans" note paper. It appears that Evan applied first to the War Department of the Army Service Forces for Dependency Benefits in January and February 1945, but for some unknown reason the application was not processed or it was decided that no benefits could be awarded. "Evans, Evan R.," application to Army Service Forces, Office of Dependency Benefits, for Mrs. Mabel Evans, 30 January 1945 and 8 February 1945. Also see Evans, Frank Harold, War Department, Office of Dependency Benefits, "Certificate to Be Completed by All Adult Individuals Living in One Household Claiming Dependency on Enlisted Man in Army," no date. "Application for Dependency Benefits," U.S. War Department, G. Evans Papers. It is unclear whether John Evans ever enrolled in the Social Security Administration, created in 1935 by President Franklin Roosevelt, and deposited any of his pay into it; "Social Security Administration – Date Founded – August 14, 1935, United States."
8. Evans, Frank Harold, "War Department, Application for Dependency Benefits," effective February 1945. (Mabel's residence is listed as 31 Totnes Road, Braintree, Mass. on this application.); S.S. Pierce wooden box addressed to Mrs John Evans at 50 Mulberry Street, Rochester, from J.H. Evans, 31 Totnes Road, Braintree, Mass, no date; Chris Gehret, email to Gail Evans, 1 November 1916, "Hobart College," all in G. Evans Papers; *Persons Listed by the Board of Registrars in the Town of Weymouth* (Weymouth: Alden Press, 1950, 1951, 1952, 1953, 1954, and 1955).
9. The Reverend David Hefling, ObJN, Archivist, Diocese of Rochester, emails to Gail Evans, 29 and 30 January 1918; "Army of the United States, Certificate of Service, 5 July 1944 to 2 November 1945" and "Enlisted Record and Report of Separation, Certificate of

Service;" "Headquarters, Maxwell Field, Alabama," 28 August 1945, copies in G. Evans Papers.

10. Rev. David R. Covell, L.H.D., "A Program for Religion," *The Living Church*, 1 May 1949; Warren Bruner, Director, Admissions and Placement, Hobart College, letter to J. Harvey Evans, re. Frank H. Evans, 4 October 1945; "Scott-Craig, Potter Will Speak at Vespers,"*The Herald of Hobart and William Smith Colleges*, 24 September 1942; "Rt. Rev. Bartel H. Reinheimer, Native of Sandusky, Dies," *The Sandusky Register*, 12 November 1949, 1; "Added Facilities Need Cited by Hobart-Smith President," *Democrat and Chronicle*, 14 December 1948, p. 33; "For Tomorrow, The Educational Opportunity," Hobart & William Smith Colleges, Geneva, New York, G. Evans Family Papers; J. Harvey Evans, "Addresses" book, 1930s-late 1940s; G. Evans Papers.

11. Frank shown in photo (top row) of the "Trinity Choir – Trinity Sunday. 1946," G. Evans Family Papers.

12. "Announce Daughter's Engagement at Party," Society page (news-paper unknown), December 1948, G. Evans Family Papers. "Barbara J. Turck," born to Morton J. and Josephine Turck, lived on Potomac Avenue, Buffalo, 1940 Census.

13. Evans, Frank Harold, "Grade Report, 1st semester, 1948-49," sent to "Mrs. John Evans, 31 Totnes Road, Weymouth, in G. Evans Papers; Evans, Frank Harold, "Hobart College Record," Registrar's Office, emails between Rebecca Frank, Hobart College and Gail Evans, November 2016; Karen Ilacqua Reuscher, Director of Advance ment Services, Hobart College, email to Gail Evans, July 2019; Hobart and William Smith Colleges, Theta Delta Chi Xi Charge Chapter; Rev. David R. Covell, "A Program for Religion," *The Living Church*, Vol. 118: 18 (May 1, 1949), p. 12, November 2016, G. Evans Papers. "Berkeley Divinity School, The Episcopal Seminary at Yale," https://berkeleydivinity.yale.edu.

14. Evans, Frank Harold, "Hobart College Record," Registrar's Office, Hobart and Smith Colleges; The Reverend David Hefling, ObJN+, Archivist, Diocese of Rochester, email to Gail Evans, 30 January 2018.

15. The Reverend David Hefling, ObJN+, Archivist, Diocese of Rochester, email to Gail Evans, 30 January 1918; "Consider Resigna-tion," *Press and Sun-Bulletin*, Binghamton, 6 August 1949; "Rt. Rev. Bartel H. Reinheimer, Native of Sandusky, Dies," *Sandusky Register*, 12 November 1949; "Former Bishop of Rochester Is Dead," *Evening Independent*, 12 November 1949; "Bishop Reinheimer Is Dead: Until 1931 Was Secretary of Episcopal Diocese Here," *Cincinnati Enquirer*, 13 November 1949; "Bishop Reinheimer Funeral to Be Held Tomorrow Morning," *Democrat and Chronicle*, 14 November 1949; "Bishop Reinheimer is Dead," *The Living Church*, Vol. 119, 20 November 1949, p. 5.

16. Chris Evans Gehret, email to Gail Evans, 24 September 2020.

17. *Persons Listed by the Board of Registrars in the Town of Weymouth* (Weymouth: Alden Press, 1950 and 1951); Evans, Frank Harold, "Unofficial Transcript," Boston University College of Liberal Arts, Office of the University Registrar, email from Adam French, Enrollment Services Advisor to Gail Evans, 16 November 1916; Chris Gehret, email to Gail Evans, 16 November 2016 and 6 January 2018; Chris Gehret, email to Gail Evans, 31 March 2020 and 2 April 2020. Photo of Frank Evans on his wedding day, 28 July 1951, album of Gail Evans, papers in G. Evans Family Papers; *Polk's Weymouth Directory, Vol. 13, 1953* (Boston: R.L. Polk & Co., Publishers, 1953), 88.

18. Arthur B. Kettle, *Orient 1923*, East High School Yearbook, Rochester, 58, at U.S. School Yearbooks, East High School, 1923; Arthur B. Kettle, "manage of, steel mill," 1930 U.S. Census; Arthur B. Kettle, 1940 US Census; *A Century of Progress in New England* (Cambridge, MA: Austin-Hastings Co., Inc.), five pages on the "History" of the company and of "Arthur B. Kettle," located in Baker Library, Harvard Business School, Cambridge, MA; "Building Permits," *Cambridge Tribune*, vol. L, No. 25, 20 August 1927, and "Real Estate and Building News," *Cambridge Tribune*, vol. 23, 9 August 1935, copied and sent by Eric Hill, Survey Director, Cambridge Historical Commission, Cambridge, MA, to Gail Evans, 10 September 2019.

19. John J. Devine, Jr., Reference Librarian II, Research Specialist, Boston Public Library, List of Weymouth residents, 1959-1969, email to Gail Evans, 8 October 2019; "Austin & Hastings Are Cleaning Up," *Cambridge Sentinel*, XXII, No. 29, 24 July 1926, Cambridge Public Library.

20. Chris Evans Gehret email to Gail Evans, 16 November 1916, 26 June 2019, 4 September 2019, and 8 October 2019, in G. Evans Papers; John Joseph Devine, Jr., Reference Librarian II, Research Specialist, Boston Public Library, 8 October 2019, emails to Gail Evans; "Weymouth Polling List, 1961-1967, 150; "Austin Strongly Objects to NASA at Kendall Sq.," *Cambridge Chronicle*, 13 May 1965; "Relocation Costs Bill Unopposed at Public Hearing," *Cambridge Chronicle*, 2 September 1965. Chris Evans Gehret, email to Gail Evans, 30 March 2020; Jeff Shmase, "Rotary Names Kennedy, Evans as Its 'Outstanding Citizens'," *Daily Evening Item* (Lynn, Massachusetts), 19 April 1995; "Temporary Treasurer Appointed," unknown local newspaper ca. 1989, both articles in Chris Evans Gehret Papers.

21. Evans, Evan R., "Enlisted Record and Report of Separation, Honorable Discharge," copy in G. Evans Papers; "Final Payment Roll," Evans, Evan R., U.S. Army, National Personnel Records Center, St. Louis.

22. American Red Cross, "World War II and the American Red Cross," online; "Red Cross Timeline," online; "The American Red Cross

Field Directors: At His Side Mini-Q Teach Guide," online; "Red Cross Adds New Record to Rochester's List of Worth While Achievements," *Democrat and Chronicle,* 5 November 1922, 59; "Quickly Organized," *Democrat and Chronicle,* 3 April 1927, 53; "Half Century of Red Cross is Celebrated," *Democrat and Chronicle,* 22 May 1931.

23. The Red Cross opened emergency hospitals including: Infants Summer Hospital, the local YMCA, the Baden Street Emergency Hospital, the Housekeeping Center on Lewis Street, and for only nine days the Gannett House, the First Unitarian Church parish house. "Rochester, New York and the 1918-1919 Influenza Epidemic," *The American Influenza Epidemic of 1918: A Digital Encyclopedia;* "Financial Statement of the South Congregational Church," January 1 1917 to January 1 1918; "Work Finished and Sent Away," *Democrat and Chronicle,* 30 September 1917, 23; "Red Cross Adds New Record to Rochester's List of Worth While Achievements," *Democrat and Chronicle,* 5 November 1922, 59; "Half Century of Red Cross is Celebrated," *Democrat and Chronicle,* 22 May 1931, 24; American Red Cross, "World War II and the American Red Cross, 3-4, 7-8, no date; American Red Cross, "Global Red Cross Network,"; "Red Cross Timeline."

24. American Red Cross, "World War II and the American Red Cross, 3-4, 7-8, no date, online; 28 March 2020; "Red Cross – Supporting Our Nation's Military," online; "British Red Cross," 1 April 2020; Bermuda's History from 1939 World War 2 to 1951," online; Evans, Evan Reginald, Application card for employment, completed ca. 1965-66, online.

25. American National Red Cross, *The American Red Cross with Armed Forces* (1945), World War II Regimental Histories, 169; American Red Cross Field Directors: At His Side Mini-Q Teacher Guide; American Red Cross, "Global Red Cross Network." Western Union telegram to John Harvey Evans, 31 Totnes Road, Braintree, 29 November 1945; "Evans with Red Cross in European Theatre," Braintree and Weymouth, *Observer,* 11 January 1946; "Employment Record" card, Evan R. Evans; "Evan with Red Cross in European Theatre," *Observer* (Braintree and Weymouth), 11 January 1946; Evans, Evan Reginald, Application card for employment, completed c. 1965-66; all in G. Evans Papers.

26. Evan R. Evans, postcard to Mr. and Mrs. J.H. Evans, 31 Totnes Road, Braintree, Massachusetts, 30 November ca. 1947, G. Evans Papers.

27. Evan R. Evans, "New York Passenger Lists, 1820-1957," *Blanche F. Sigman,* departing Bremerhaven, arriving New York, New York, on 12 February 1948, 1897-1957; Evan R. Evans, "New York Passenger Lists, 1820-1957," Pan American Airways, departing London, arriving New York, New York, 23 September 1948, New York, New

York; Evan R. Evans, "New York Passenger Lists, 1820-1957," *General R. E. Callan,* departing Bremerhaven via Southampton, arriving New York, New York, on 3 December 1949.

28. "Devens Red Cross Assistant Dir. Departs," newspaper clipping from unknown source, G. Evans Papers.

29. Truman Solverud, director of operations, HQ, Far Eastern Area, San Francisco, letter to Evan R. Evans, American Red Cross, Tachikawa for Air Bases, APO 704, U.S. Forces, 6 September 1955; "Evans Works Closely with Buccaneer Men," no date; "Evans New Buccaneer Red Cross Director," no date; "Red Cross, We Thank You," no date; "Devens Red Cross Assistant Dir. Departs,: no date; Evan R. Evans, Identification Card, American Red Cross, Limestone AFB; John F. Albert, Chaplain (Major) USAF, Base Chaplain to Director of Personnel Services, American National Red Cross, Alexandria, VA, letter of recommendation; all in G. Evans Papers.

30. "Employment Record" card, Evan R. Evans; Evan Reginald Evans, Passport, United States of America, (stamps showing entry into Japan, 30 June 1954, and departure on 7 July 1956; both in G. Evans Papers; Black and white photos of major European cities, saved by JHE for their interesting stamps, both in G. Evans Papers.

31. Evan R. Evans, letter to Christine Evans, 5 February 1973, copy in G. Evans Papers.

32. At the beginning of his employment, Evan was offered housing at a nearby YMCA nearby on North Main Street. "Employment Record" card, Evan R. Evans; Joseph Thornton, The Deaconess Home, letter to Mr. Evans, 31 December 1958, both in G. Evans Papers.

33. "Employment Record" card, Evan R. Evans; Postcard, "The Fall River Deaconess Home and Community Center, 825 Second Street, Fall River, Mass; Evan R. Evans, "Application for Employment," Massachusetts Eye and Ear Infirmary, ca. 1965; "Employment Record" card, Evan R. Evans, all in G. Evans Papers.

34. Evan R. Evans, letter to Christine Evans, 5 February 1973, copy in G. Evans Papers.

35. Miller, *"Quincy Massachusetts: A Shipbuilding Tradition*, 168; "Fore River Shipyard"; Anthony F. Sarcone and Lawrence S. Rines, *A History of Shipbuilding at Fore River.*

36. Davis, D., editor, *The Journal of the Engineering Society,* Vol. XVIII (Liverpool, University Press of Liverpool, Liverpool, England), May 1947.

37. Jerome C. Hunsaker, "Edward Lull Cochrane, 1892-1959, A Biographical Memoir" (Washington, DC: National Academy of Sciences, 1961); "Admiral Cochrane Dies: Headed Industrial Liaison,"*The Tech,* Massachusetts Institute of Technology, November 20, 1959.

38. J. E. Burkhardt, "John Harvey Evans," qualifications presented to Admiral Cochrane, 8 September 1947, handwritten notes by J. Harvey Evans, G. Evans Papers.

39. Admiral E.L. Cochrane, part of a memo to Dean Sherwood, 22 September 1947, G. Evans Papers.

40. "Braintree Man Named to Post at MIT, Ends Shipyard Duty," *Quincy Patriot Ledger,* 31 October 1947; "Monroe High Grand Named to MIT Post," *Rochester Democrat and Chronicle,* 9 November 1947; Edward L. Cochrane, "Naval Architecture and Marine Engineering," *Massachusetts Institute of Technology Bulletin, President's Report Issue,* 84: 1 (October 1948), 130-32.

41. Avery A. Ashdown, secretary, SIGMA XI, MIT, letter to John Harvey Evans, 6 May 1949, G. Evans Papers; "Coming Up Higher: The History of Sigma Xi"; "Joel Primack, "From the President: Developing Scientific Intuition, 12 December 2018.

42. J.R. Killian, Jr., invitation to Professor and Mrs. Evans for black-tie dinner in honor of Winston Churchill and President Harry S. Truman, 10 March 1949; "Mid-Century Convocation, Second General Assembly, March 31, Boston Garden," and "Events for Friday, April 1"; "The MIT Convocation on the Social Implications of Scientific Progress at the Mid-Century Point," The Massachusetts Institute of Technology, March 31 and April 1 and 2, 1949; all in G. Evans Papers.

43. Harvey Evans, letter to Robert G. Mende, 29 October, 1976; G. Evans Papers.

44. Evans, John Harvey, "School of Engineering Faculty Personnel Record," 25 September 1959, G. Evans Papers.

45. Harvey Evans, compiler and editor, *Ship Structural Design Concepts* (Cambridge, MD: Cornell Maritime Press, Inc., 1974). When published this book was reportedly the only study of the design process relating to the formation of a ship's structure. See also: J. Harvey Evans, senior author, *Ocean Engineering Structures* (Cambridge, MA: MIT Press, 1969).

46. "Notes on the Career of Assistant Professor J. Harvey Evans," December 1951, "1952 Career Data," "1953 Career Data," 1954 Career Data," and "Notes on the Career of Associate Professor J. Harvey Evans," 27 September 1956; "Weymouth Man Named Associate Professor of MIT Department," *Quincy Patriot Ledger,* May 3, 1952; "Additional Information on J.H.E. Supplementing the 'Notes' Dated September 12, 1957 and Bringing Them Up to Date; "Notes on the Career of J.[ohn] Harvey Evans, Technical Contributions, 11 October 1957; Robert G. Mende, Secretary, Society of Naval Architects and Marine Engineers, letters to J. Harvey Evans on 14 August 1976 and 29 October 1976; all in G. Evans Papers.

47. Harvey's work as a visiting professor materialized as part of provision of the Cooperative Project established between the Seoul

National University and the University of Minnesota. Yung Mo Hwang, Dean, College of Engineering, Letter of Thanks to Prof. J. Harvey Evans, 24 June 1957; American Automobile Association, "United States" map, 1956, marked by Harvey Evans with the route and dates of travel between Boston and California; in G. Evans Papers.

48. J. Harvey Evans, penciled draft letter to Guy Stever, ca. 1961, J.H. Evans Papers, "Biographical" folder, G. Evans Family Papers; Harvey Evans, letter to Harry Benford, National Academy of Sciences (faculty at University of Michigan), 26 March, 1960; Harry Benford, letter to Harvey Evans, 4 April 1960; both in G. Evans Papers.

49. Harvey himself may have hesitated to move. He and his family had strong ties to New England, the White Mountains, an aging mother, and two rambunctious children, ages fifteen and thirteen, who required attention. "J. Harvey Evans," *Patriot-Ledger,* Quincy, 17 June 1952 and also: "Professor J. Harvey Evans Dies at 78," *MIT News,* G. Evans Papers.

50. Edith Evans and Harvey Evans, letters to Gail Evans, 20 October and 6 and 17 November 1966; in G. Evans Papers.

51. Mabel Ida Harvey Evans, The Commonwealth of Massachusetts, "Standard Certificate of Death," 31 October 1967; Christine Evans Gehret, interview by Gail Evans, February 2020.

17. Epilogue

1. Terri DiFiore, Administrative Support Services Manager, White Haven Memorial Park, email sent to Gail Evans, 8 July 2020, G. Evans Papers; *Democrat and Chronicle,* "Evans, Mabel I." and "Weather Watch," *Democrat and Chronicle,* 2B and 14C, 1 November 1967; *Democrat and Chronicle,* Edgar Cain, March 20, 1952, 26 and Auley Cain, July 24 and 25, 1973, 20 and 34; Chris Evans Gehret, email to Gail Evans, 8 July 2020.

2. Metropolitan State Hospital.

3. Edith Evans, letter to Gail Evans, 6 August 1968, 16 October 1966, 6 November 1966, 17 November 1966, 27 January 1967, and 27 July 1973; J. Harvey Evans, letter to Gail Evans, 7 November 1966, 15 January 1970, 10 March 1970, all in G. Evans Papers.

4. Elizabeth D. Hay, MD, Professor and Chairman [*sic*], Harvard Medical School, letter to J. Harvey Evans, 12 April 1978, G. Evans Papers.

5. The ISSC began meeting in 1961, and meets every third year in different countries around the world. "History of ISSC,"at http://www.issc2018.org/content/Overview_history; J. Harvey Evans, letter to Chesley and Nancy Dunlap, 23 June 1982, G. Evans Papers;

Joe Gavaghan, "Harvey Evans: The Fascinating Life of a Naval Architect," *Lexington Minute Man,* 30 December 1976.

6. David and other subsistence residents on the Yukon at that time are described briefly in John McPhee's national bestselling book, *Coming into the Country* (New York: Farrar, Straus & Giroux, 1977), 275.

7. Wolfgang Saxon, "J. Harvey Evans, 78, Shipbuilding Expert with M.I.T. Is Dead," *New York Times;* "Obituaries: J. Harvey Evans, Naval Architect, MIT Emeritus Professor, at 78," *Boston Globe,* 24 November 1992; "J. Harvey Evans, Was MIT Prof of Naval Architecture," *Boston Herald,* 25 November, 1992; "Professor J. Harvey Evans Dies at 78," *MIT Tech Talk,* 2 December 1992; "Obituaries, J. Harvey Evans," *Times Record* (Brunswick, ME), 24 November 1992; "J. Harvey Evans," *Lexington Minuteman,* 26 November 1992; "Memorial Resolutions: J. Harvey Evans," *Society of Naval Architects and Marine Engineers, Transactions, 1992;* "J. Harvey Evans, *Portland Press Herald,* 24 November 1992.

8. Article about the demise of Austin-Hastings and the purchase of their building in Woburn by Admiral Metals in the mid-1970s, *Woburn Daily Times,* 10 May 1977; Chris Evans Gehret, email to Gail Evans, 27 August 2019 and 4 September 2019; Chris Evans Gehret, email to Gail Evans, 18 March 2015 and 27 August 2019 and 30 March 2020; Jeff Shmase, "Rotary Names Kennedy, [Frank] Evans as Its 'Outstanding Citizens," *Daily Evening Item,* Lynn, Massachusetts, 19 April 1995; "Temporary Treasurer Appoint," ca. 1981-82 (newspaper unknown).

9. "Epictetus, Quotes, Quotable Quotes," Neel Burton, "Man's Search for Meaning," *Psychology Today,* posted 24 May 2012; "Notable Quotes, Mahatma Gandhi Quotes," *Open Your Mind, Open Your Life: A Book of Eastern Wisdom.*

10. J. Harvey Evans, letter to Gail Evans, 29 May 1969, G. Evans Papers.